STORMING
VICKSBURG

CIVIL WAR AMERICA

Peter S. Carmichael, Caroline E. Janney,
and Aaron Sheehan-Dean, editors

This landmark series interprets broadly the history and culture
of the Civil War era through the long nineteenth century and
beyond. Drawing on diverse approaches and methods, the
series publishes historical works that explore all aspects of
the war, biographies of leading commanders, and tactical and
campaign studies, along with select editions of primary sources.
Together, these books shed new light on an era that remains
central to our understanding of American and world history.

EARL J. HESS

STORMING VICKSBURG

GRANT, PEMBERTON, and the BATTLES of MAY 19-22, 1863

THE UNIVERSITY OF NORTH CAROLINA PRESS

Chapel Hill

This book was published with the assistance of the
Fred W. Morrison Fund of the University of North Carolina Press.

Designed by Jamison Cockerham
Set in Arno, Scala Sans, Calt, Dear Sarah, Isherwood, and Rudyard
by Tseng Information Systems, Inc.

Cover art: (front) *Siege of Vicksburg,* Kurz & Allison lithograph, ca. 1888;
(back) *Admiral Porter's Fleet Running the Rebel Blockade of the Mississippi at Vicksburg,
April 16th 1863,* Currier & Ives lithograph. Both courtesy Library of Congress.

LIBRARY OF CONGRESS CATALOGING-IN-PUBLICATION DATA
Names: Hess, Earl J., author.
Title: Storming Vicksburg : Grant, Pemberton, and
the Battles of May 19–22, 1863 / Earl J. Hess.
Other titles: Civil War America (Series)
Description: Chapel Hill : The University of North Carolina Press, [2020] |
Series: Civil War America | Includes bibliographical references and index.
Identifiers: LCCN 2020013193 | ISBN 9781469660172 (cloth : alk. paper) |
ISBN 9781469684109 (pbk. : alk. paper) | ISBN 9781469660189 (ebook)
Subjects: LCSH: Vicksburg (Miss.) — History — Siege, 1863. |
Mississippi — History — Civil War, 1861–1865 — Campaigns. |
United States — History — Civil War, 1861–1865 — Campaigns.
Classification: LCC E475.27 .H47 2020 | DDC 973.7/344 — dc23
LC record available at https://lccn.loc.gov/2020013193

For

PRATIBHA & JULIE

always with love

CONTENTS

ILLUSTRATIONS

MAPS

PREFACE

This book is an in-depth study of a short but important phase of the long Federal campaign to capture Vicksburg, Mississippi, in the Civil War. Its focus is the period from May 18 through May 23, 1863, which serves as the end of Maj. Gen. Ulysses S. Grant's overland march to the rear of the city in the first three weeks of May and the beginning of his siege. These five days were a watershed in the development of Grant's eight-month-long campaign to capture the Gibraltar of the Confederacy. His hope of ending the campaign quickly by assaulting the place on May 19 and 22 was crushed by the failure of those attacks. The only recourse was a siege that extended Federal operations against Vicksburg another six weeks.

The campaign for Vicksburg, one of the longest and most important of the Civil War, falls into six distinct phases. The first Federal effort to capture the city occurred in the summer of 1862 when a combined army and navy force steamed up the Mississippi River from New Orleans only to fail due to lack of resources. The rest of the campaign for Vicksburg was directed by Grant. His first effort, the second phase of the Vicksburg campaign, involved his advance down the Mississippi Central Railroad from November 1862 until January 1863, and Maj. Gen. William T. Sherman's river-borne expedition to Chickasaw Bayou in late December and early January. The Bottomlands phase of the campaign, the third in the series of efforts, occurred from late January to late April 1863 as Grant's army struggled to access the high ground east of the Mississippi. Once Grant found a way — by marching along the Louisiana side and crossing the Mississippi many miles south of the Vicksburg defenses — he was able to initiate the fourth phase of Federal efforts against the city. Often called the overland march or the inland movement, Grant defeated the Confederates in five separate engagements and approached Vicksburg from the east.

Most historians consider the siege of Vicksburg to be the fifth and final phase of Union efforts against the city, but I believe it is helpful to consider the time period from May 18 to May 23 as the fifth phase, with the siege of May 23 to July 4 constituting the sixth and final period. The attacks on May 19 and 22 had the potential to end the campaign. If circumstances had been different, those days could have given Grant what he wanted: a quick victory to avoid a siege, along with several additional weeks of campaigning to clear the Confederates out of middle Mississippi. Grant thought the attacks of May 19 and 22 were promising; he intended to end the struggle for Vicksburg in one stroke by storming the town. The fact that he failed is no excuse for passing over the May 19 and 22 battles as merely a prelude to the siege.

"There were several engagements yesterday which really deserve the name of battles," wrote a correspondent of the *Chicago Daily Tribune* on May 23.[1] He was right. The Army of the Tennessee launched its largest tactical offensive of the war on May 22. Its officers spent more time and effort preparing for it than for any other set-piece battle they fought during the conflict. How the army conducted the attacks, and why they failed, illuminates a good deal about the history of that storied field army.

Most previous historians of the Vicksburg campaign do not delve as deeply into the details or analysis of the May 19 and 22 battles as I do in this book. Edwin C. Bearss wrote a three-volume study of the entire effort against the city entitled *The Campaign for Vicksburg*. In it Bearss focuses on the grand tactical perspective. He devotes five chapters out of twenty-six in the third volume to this time period, mostly using reports in the *Official Records*, supplemented now and then with a few other published primary sources. Michael B. Ballard has written the standard one-volume overview of the campaign, entitled *Vicksburg: The Campaign that Opened the Mississippi*, which does not dig as deeply into the grand tactics as Bearss's book because of space limitations. Both of these historians have contributed greatly to our understanding of the subject. A good, shorter overview can be read in William L. Shea and Terrence J. Winschel's *Vicksburg Is the Key*. A short book on Grant's handling of the operations against Vicksburg by Timothy B. Smith has a brief chapter on this phase, and an anthology of essays about this time period, edited by Steven Woodworth and Charles D. Grear, contains articles on selected aspects of the story.

Timothy B. Smith has recently written a study of the May 19–22 phase of the Vicksburg campaign, *The Union Assaults at Vicksburg*, which appeared when

Storming Vicksburg was in the copyediting phase. His objective was different from mine. Smith based his work on wide and deep research but aimed to produce a descriptive rather than an analytical text. It is consonant with an old tradition in Civil War studies, a narrative storytelling aimed at a general audience. In contrast, *Storming Vicksburg* aims at an analytical text that mixes narrative storytelling with probing questions and answers. It treats the battles of May 19 and 22 as case studies in the tactical and operational history of the Civil War, asking questions that a military historian would want to know the answers to. These include an intense look at the impact of terrain on the course of events, locating the exact starting points of units (which Smith sometimes gets wrong), and questioning the level of command and control among the Federal units conducting the attacks. Moreover, *Storming Vicksburg* looks at many other aspects of these battles that Smith ignores, such as the huge burial truce of May 25, battlefield preservation, commemoration, and memory.

It is important for historians to go beyond a narrow research base to study the Vicksburg campaign. The footnotes of Bearss's three-volume work refer to relatively few archival and published personal accounts. Ballard used more unpublished personal accounts than Bearss, but he could not do an exhaustive job of it given his task of examining many months of campaigning. Shea and Winschel also based their accounts on a narrow range of published primary sources. While Smith conducted extensive research in archival sources, he did not use them in the way I use these same sources in my book. For example, a key document exists in the Vicksburg National Military Park, a postwar letter written by a survivor of the assault on May 22 with a hand-drawn map showing the exact starting point of Benton's Brigade when it began to approach the 2nd Texas Lunette. Finding this letter was crucial to my understanding of the brigade's location. The ravine where the brigade started is still there on the battlefield, although not marked by the park service. It is located just north of the Baldwin's Ferry Road (which also is intact and not marked). In fact the park service does not accurately locate the 2nd Texas Lunette. This hand-drawn map was the key to understanding the story of Benton's brigade in the attack of May 22, but no other historians of the Vicksburg operations have used it.

Because my research agenda involved digging deeply into one phase of this campaign, it was possible for me to fully consult essentially all the unpublished letters, diaries, and memoirs by participants that exist for that phase. In fact, I was surprised to find so much unpublished material on the Vicksburg operations that has never been used by previous historians.

Repositories from California to New England have material relevant to the May 19 and 22 phase of the campaign, but none are more unique or important than the thousands of documents held by the Vicksburg National Military Park. When the park was created in 1899 former lieutenant William Rigby was named its first resident commissioner. Having served as an officer of the 24th Iowa during the campaign, Rigby was keen on enlisting the aid of surviving veterans to locate unit positions and illuminate military operations, mostly during the siege. Literally hundreds of aged veterans of both armies responded over the next few years. The collection, more than 10,000 pages of documents filling some 1,400 folders stored in seven large archival boxes, is a gold mine of detailed information about the May 19 and 22 attacks. In half a dozen important instances, these letters provide the only answer to tactical puzzles associated with those assaults, puzzles that cannot be solved using any other sources.

Moreover, Rigby encouraged the veterans to let him make typed copies of their wartime letters and diaries. These transcripts are equally important sources of information on a wide variety of topics and often span more than just the siege period of the campaign. While previous historians have used a handful of these postwar letters and transcripts of wartime personal sources, so far no one had looked through all of them.

This Rigby material is a vital but underused source. The fact that most of it was written nearly forty years after the event should not dissuade scholars from utilizing the information. As with any source, no matter when it was written, historians need to evaluate the reliability of each document based on their knowledge of the writer and on the internal clues contained in the text. A letter written half a century after the event has the potential to be just as valuable or just as irrelevant as one written days afterward.

Most of the new interpretations to be found in this study of the May 19 and 22 attacks came from a thorough look at the unpublished archival material at Vicksburg and at other repositories listed in the bibliography. For example, previous accounts indicate that Grant justified his decision to launch the assault of May 22 largely on the fact that his troops were in high spirits and would not have wanted to construct siege approaches before they had an opportunity to storm Vicksburg and capture it quickly. However, there are many unpublished letters and diaries of Grant's soldiers that clearly indicate the opposite. These men were stunned by the order to attack and would much rather have dug siege approaches than risk their lives in open assault.

In fact, a careful analysis of events during May 18–22 raises several questions about Grant's handling of affairs. I do not intend to bash Grant's generalship, but a balanced view of any general is needed for a true appreciation of his role in history. Most writers have tended to take Grant's version of affairs for granted and overlook events that do not support a glowing portrayal. But there is ample reason to question some aspects of Grant's judgment in this phase of the Vicksburg campaign, and that is done in this book when appropriate. The reader should keep in mind, however, that every general makes mistakes. The ultimate test of his leadership lies in the end result of his operations rather than a myopically focused indictment of every misstep along the way.

Conversely, there is every reason to conclude that Lt. Gen. John C. Pemberton outgeneraled Grant during the period of May 18–23. He returned to his stronghold after the terrible defeats at Champion Hill and the Big Black River, astutely placed his men where they could perform the best duty, and held out against the hammering of May 19 and 22 even though he was outnumbered by the Federals. Southerners tended to remember their defeats on May 16 and 17 but gave less attention to their defensive success on May 19 and 22. Pemberton was vilified by his men even before the fall of the city on July 4. He therefore received scant credit for handling his troubled command effectively before Grant committed himself to siege operations on May 23. This is not to say that Pemberton bested Grant consistently during the Vicksburg campaign. He did not. But even men who often fail deserve credit when they now and then do things right.

Grant worked against many pressures during this phase of the campaign. He felt compelled to capitalize on the momentum created by his overland march and was desperate to take advantage of his success before that advantage dissipated. He also worried about Gen. Joseph E. Johnston's shadowy force near Jackson, which had the potential to cause trouble to the Federal rear. He also had precious little information about the Confederate position, the earthworks that shielded Vicksburg, and the placement of Rebel troops within those works. The attack of May 19 was an exploratory effort, similar to a large reconnaissance in force. But the operations on May 22 were planned as a major assault all along the line.

May 22 bears many characteristics similar to the assault Grant ordered at Cold Harbor on June 3, 1864. Both failed and Grant regretted, with hindsight, that both were conducted.[2] But one must evaluate decision-making based on what the commander knew at the time, and Grant can be accorded leeway by the historian for his decision to attack on May 22. It was a rational decision, based on what he knew. But the fact is there was a lot he did not know about the Confederate position.

Another contribution of this study is a critical appraisal of Grant's Army of the Tennessee. It failed on May 19 and 22 not only because of stout Confederate defenders but because of poor preparation, lax command and control at the point of assault, and uneven combat morale. While we have several histories of field armies in the Civil War, they tend to be little more than narratives of the campaigns and battles these field armies fought. We need to analyze how armies worked on the battlefield, during a campaign, and while resting in camp. Battle books are wonderful opportunities for looking at how field armies organized and conducted attacks; May 22 is one of the best case studies for a hard look at this subject.

It also is important to understand the attacks of May 19 and 22 within the context of Civil War operational history. I do not agree with the old interpretation that the rifle musket doomed frontal attacks to failure, nor do I support the notion that this weapon gave a preponderant advantage to any military force acting on the tactical defensive.[3] There were many factors that contributed to the outcome of any given Civil War engagement, and we need to avoid making assumptions about them. Instead, it is vital that scholars take every battle on its own merits and understand the contingencies that came into play in determining its outcome.

In other words, I do not assume that the Union attacks on May 19 and 22 were doomed to fail. The Federals faced a very tough job, but if they had planned better, maintained better command and control, and applied more consistent effort at key locations at key times, the assaults might have worked.

The rugged terrain east of Vicksburg posed an especially difficult problem for the attackers. While historians note the high river bluffs that the town of Vicksburg occupied, and they acknowledge that the ground east of the city was heavily cut up into steep-sided ravines, they rarely delve into how that unusually rough landscape affected military operations after Grant reached the outskirts of the city. The Federals had a good deal of difficulty fitting their army into that landscape and negotiating it to conduct the attacks on May 19 and 22. In a very real sense, the terrain shaped their operations as well as the nature of the fighting on those two days. The Federals tried to find solutions to the problems posed by the landscape. They experimented with column formations and sought ways to use the torturous ravines to hide their approach to the target. But in the end, terrain proved to be an impediment to their success and an advantage for the Confederates. Scholars interested in the environmental impact on military history would be well advised to pay close attention to the attacks of May 19 and 22.

An intensive study of one phase of the Vicksburg campaign allows us to pay a lot of attention to many topics associated with Civil War military history in general and with battles and campaigns in particular. For example, soldier morale, the experience of battle, the care of the wounded, the burial of the dead, logistical support of the armies, how operations affected civilians, and memory and commemoration are all relevant to the study of battle and to the study of Civil War military history as a whole. Every well-rounded battle book should do more than merely chronicle grand tactics. It should attempt to tie its information in with the larger trends to be seen in the study of the Civil War. Military historians of the conflict have for too long isolated themselves from those larger trends, and it shows in the scholarly work they produce. I have in this study, as with all my other campaign and battle books, tried to construct well-rounded approaches to studying battles that go beyond basic narratives of the grand tactics as far as possible.

There is much to be gained by plotting a course that digs deeply into all phases of the Vicksburg campaign, and I plan to do more such work in the future. Hopefully this study will encourage other historians to do the same. Much needs to be done in terms of questioning the standard narrative of this important operation, which involved more time and resources than all other campaigns to control the Mississippi River. The struggle for Vicksburg dominated the struggle for the valley, and historians still have much to do in their effort to understand it.

My thanks to all the staff members at the archives listed in the bibliography, who have been so helpful in making their wonderful material available to me. Anton Vershay, museum technician, was especially helpful in making available the rich holdings of the Vicksburg National Military Park. I also wish to thank several researchers who helped me access material at archival institutions that I was unable to visit. I also thank the reviewers of the manuscript for their suggestions for its improvement.

Most of all, I am eternally grateful to my wife, Pratibha, for everything.

STORMING
VICKSBURG

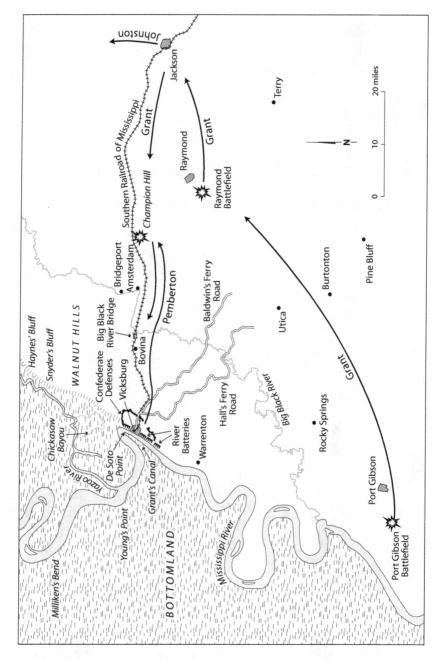

They Are upon Us

MAY 17

A new phase of the Union effort to conquer Vicksburg, a town that had become an important symbol of victory or defeat for both sides in the Civil War, began on May 17, 1863. On that day, the citizens of Vicksburg were confronted with the first clear sign that the troops of Lt. Gen. John C. Pemberton's Army of Mississippi and Eastern Louisiana were in trouble. Having operated for several days in the countryside east of Vicksburg, Pemberton's men now began streaming back to town in disorganized masses. They spread alarming tales of utter defeat in two battles.

BACKGROUND

Maj. Gen. Ulysses S. Grant's Army of the Tennessee could not be kept at arm's length any longer. Grant had been operating against the Confederate Gibraltar since the previous November but had so often been stymied that a sense of stalemate had settled into the long Vicksburg campaign. But Grant had quietly masterminded a turning point when he bypassed the heavy artillery placed along the east bluff of the Mississippi River at Vicksburg, running gunboats and transports downstream under cover of darkness. He also marched his army along the Louisiana bottomlands, using the transports to cross the river near Bruinsburg by the end of April.[1]

When Grant started his inland, or overland, march east of the river, he seized control of the strategic context around Vicksburg and conducted one of the most brilliant campaigns of the war. Moving three corps in different directions, portions of his command fought several battles along the way. Maj. Gen. John A. McClernand's Thirteenth Corps defeated a detached

Rebel force at Port Gibson on May 1, while Maj. Gen. James B. McPherson's Seventeenth Corps defeated another detached force at Raymond on May 12. Maj. Gen. William T. Sherman's Fifteenth Corps troops captured the state capital of Jackson, forty-five miles east of Vicksburg, on May 14. Sherman's men destroyed much public property and buildings in the city before evacuating it.[2]

The capture of Jackson separated the main Confederate army defending Vicksburg from a small force accumulating near the capital under the direction of Gen. Joseph E. Johnston, who supervised all Rebel forces in the western theater. Having divided his opponents, Grant now had the option of heading directly toward Vicksburg to deal with Pemberton alone.[3]

Twenty years later, Grant correctly pointed out in his memoirs that the key to his success was "in meeting them in detail" and beating the enemy "upon their own ground." Of course there were other factors to consider, including Johnston's reluctance to dictate operational decisions to Pemberton, who in turn was very reluctant to take chances in protecting Vicksburg. The lack of coordination between these two Confederate generals played directly into Grant's hand. Pemberton thought that protecting Vicksburg "was of paramount importance" and was uneasy about moving his 28,000 men any distance from the city. He felt safe holding the countryside east from Vicksburg to the Big Black River, which flowed generally toward the southwest about twelve miles east of Vicksburg. The crossing of the Southern Railroad of Mississippi, which linked Vicksburg with Jackson, marked a key point of his defensive posture.[4]

Operating out of this small pocket was dangerous in Pemberton's view. Yet when Grant moved northeast from the Port Gibson area he threatened to cut off Pemberton from the rest of the Confederacy. Johnston, with only 5,000 troops, could not hope to stop Grant's 30,000 men. This is why Johnston urged and then ordered Pemberton to move the bulk of his army east of the Big Black River. Leaving 1,500 men to protect the railroad crossing, Pemberton reluctantly marched 18,500 troops east of the river and toward Jackson with the intention of forming a union with Johnston.[5]

This scenario set up the climax of the overland march at Champion Hill on May 16. It was a classic pitched battle, each commander feeding troops into the fight as it evolved, both sides winning and losing local actions. A slashing attack by two Missouri brigades of Maj. Gen. John S. Bowen's Division pushed back part of Brig. Gen. Alvin P. Hovey's Federal division, but Bowen's men stalled due to lack of support. When Union commanders urged their units forward all along the line, the Rebel position crumbled. An entire division, under Maj. Gen. William W. Loring, became separated from the rest of the Confederate force, marching north and east to join Johnston. Pemberton lost 3,840 men, more than 60 percent of them classed as missing or captured. Grant lost 2,441 troops in the swirling combat.[6]

Champion Hill was the largest and most important engagement of the Vicksburg campaign. Grant was now in position to dominate the strategic and operational environment in Mississippi. Having separated the two opposing commanders and severely defeated the force under Pemberton, he could cross the Big Black River and advance on Vicksburg.

Worried that Loring would need a crossing of the stream to rejoin him, Pemberton detached 5,000 men to hold a bridgehead on the east side of the river on May 17. What possessed him to do this is difficult to fathom. He could expect Grant to close in on the railroad crossing with overwhelming force to crush this small detachment while the rest of Pemberton's army could not help the small force defend the bridgehead. Moreover, even if Loring could have reached the vicinity, he had no hope of fighting his way through Grant's army to use the crossing.[7]

Bowen, who was placed in charge of the bridgehead, had a nearly hopeless task. Careful reconnaissance and aggressive handling by Brig. Gen. Michael K. Lawler led to a piercing assault by Thirteenth Corps troops early in the morning of May 17. Targeting the sector held by the 61st Tennessee, the attack met with stunning success. The Tennesseeans folded and a chaotic retreat ensued as the fortified line collapsed. The Confederates set fire to the railroad bridge, leaving the floating bridge intact for the retreating Confederates. Still 1,751 Rebels fell into Union hands along with eighteen pieces of artillery. Further Confederate losses in killed and wounded were never reported, but Grant's army lost only 279 men in this brilliant affair.[8]

The twin defeats of Champion Hill and the Big Black River were the key to understanding the course of events during the following week. The tide of the entire campaign had turned in a way that inflated the morale and optimism of all Federal officers and men. Conversely, those twin events deflated the morale of all Confederates who took part in the double disasters. For the Federals, the next week brought with it expectations of walking into Vicksburg almost unopposed. For their enemy, the next week brought desperate efforts to salvage something from the course of events.

The fact that many Rebel soldiers fled the bridgehead in panic was obvious. John Cowdry Taylor, Pemberton's aide-de-camp, noted in his diary that "our troops shamefully abandon[ed] the trenches" at 9:00 A.M. An hour later, Pemberton issued an order to return to Vicksburg. He assigned division commander Maj. Gen. Carter L. Stevenson to take charge of the retreat as he rode to town ahead of the troops.[9]

Pemberton's ride that morning was the most distressing of his life. He was a Northerner fighting in gray. Born in Philadelphia in 1814, he had graduated from the U.S. Military Academy in 1837. Conspicuous service in the Mexican War was followed by his marriage to Martha Thompson of Norfolk, Virginia. That union swayed Pemberton to join the Confederacy on the outbreak of war even though his mother and siblings disapproved. The decision proved to be "a sore ordeal," in the words of R. H. Chilton, Pemberton's friend and classmate. The Confederate public never knew whether to trust him. But that lack of faith did not keep Pemberton from rapid promotion to lieutenant general by October 1862, even though he had performed modestly as department commander in inactive areas of the South. In fact, he lost the confidence of Charleston residents in South Carolina because of his decision to give up many of the outer defenses of the city to conserve manpower.[10]

Partly to get him away from Charleston, but mostly because Confederate president Jefferson Davis believed in Pemberton's abilities, the general was shifted to the Department of Mississippi and Eastern Louisiana in October 1862. It was one of the most important departments in the Confederacy.[11]

Pemberton addressed a host of difficult problems but was hampered by a lack of resources, even though the Confederate government gave him the largest army it ever created for the direct defense of the Mississippi River. That army was initially referred to as the Army of Mississippi and Eastern Louisiana, but after the siege began in late May 1863, it was more often called the Army of Vicksburg. Pemberton's field command was largely a stationary force. It had stayed in one place for many months and had lost much of its fighting edge and many of its campaigning skills. While Pemberton was a relatively good administrator, his own campaign and fighting skills had never been developed. Johnston's tentative relationship with Pemberton (Davis had not given explicit authority for him to command Pemberton but rather to advise him, at least in Johnston's view of the matter) did not help the situation.[12]

Pemberton's hopes dissipated with the defeats at Champion Hill and the Big Black River. He was "very much depressed" while riding with his staff toward Vicksburg during the late morning of May 17. His mind was filled with the black irony of the situation. "Just thirty years ago," he confided to chief engineer Maj. Samuel H. Lockett, "I began my military career by receiving my appointment to a cadetship at the U.S. Military Academy, and to-day—the same date—that career is ended in disaster and disgrace." Lockett tried to console him by noting that he still had two fresh divisions holding the town and associated positions north and south of Vicksburg. The dejected survivors of Champion Hill and the Big Black River could be put in less dangerous positions until they regained their morale. Pemberton was barely touched by these thoughts. He admitted to Lockett that he did not believe the troops could "stand the first shock of an attack" on the city.[13]

By the time Pemberton reached Bovina, ten miles east of Vicksburg, Lockett wanted to rush to Vicksburg with authority to compel all officers in and around the city to obey his request "for men, materials, and labor, and to render all possible aid" in readying the defenses. The general complied.[14]

PREPARATIONS

When he reached Vicksburg about midday, Pemberton relied on the two fresh divisions that had missed the fights at Champion Hill and the Big Black River. Maj. Gen. John H. Forney's Division consisted of two brigades, both of which were widely separated from each other. Brig. Gen. Louis Hébert's Brigade held the bluffs north of Vicksburg, mostly posted at Snyder's Bluff (eleven miles north of the city) and Haynes' Bluff (four miles north of Snyder's Bluff). Hébert also covered the approaches to Vicksburg by way of Chickasaw Bayou, about six miles north of the city. Brig. Gen. John C. Moore's Brigade, reinforced by 600 Mississippi State Troops under Brig. Gen. Jeptha V. Harris, held the area around Warrenton nine miles south of Vicksburg.[15]

Maj. Gen. Martin L. Smith's Division also held positions at and near Vicksburg. Brig. Gen. Francis A. Shoup's Brigade covered the riverfront while Brig. Gen. William E. Baldwin's Brigade, plus Col. Thomas N. Waul's Texas Legion, screened the east side of town from the Hall's Ferry Road to the Big Black River Railroad bridge. Baldwin guarded the southeastern approaches to Vicksburg because reports indicated that Grant was in that direction during the early part of his inland march. The heavy artillery batteries lining the east bluff of the Mississippi were under the control of Col. Edward Higgins.[16]

Pemberton ordered Forney to evacuate Snyder's Bluff, Haynes' Bluff, and Warrenton and protect the eastern approaches to Vicksburg. Forney instructed Hébert at Snyder's Bluff to move all the subsistence and ordnance stores he could pile onto wagons. He also told Hébert to send all the river-boats at Haynes' Bluff up the Yazoo River to keep them out of enemy hands. Those boats were loaded with up to 30,000 bushels of corn that now were denied Pemberton's army.[17]

Hébert had held his brigade at Snyder's Bluff since December 2, 1862, so his evacuation became a complicated leave-taking. Beginning at 11:00 A.M., he loaded what he could and destroyed the rest so as to be nearly ready to leave by 5:30 P.M. Hébert left behind Lt. Col. J. T. Plattsmier and two companies of the 21st Louisiana to spike the heavy guns that could not be moved. Then he set out at 7:30 P.M. for Vicksburg.[18]

The brigade reached town by 2:30 A.M. on May 18. A total of twenty pieces of artillery and on average 200 rounds per piece had accumulated at Snyder's Bluff since last December. Hébert could take only half the powder and cartridges and half the fixed ammunition to Vicksburg. He transported six artillery pieces but left behind fourteen more, ranging from a twenty-four-pounder rifle to a ten-inch columbiad. Plattsmier's men spiked the fourteen pieces and destroyed what they could of the ordnance stores before obeying Pemberton's order to leave Snyder's Bluff early on the morning of May 18.[19]

John Moore's Brigade of Forney's Division had occupied the area around Warrenton for a couple of weeks before the crisis of May 17. Its component regiments had been dispersed to several fortifications in and near the village. Members of the 35th Mississippi, posted just north of Warrenton, heard the firing of field artillery at the Big Black River on the morning of May 17. They also saw the column of black smoke produced by the burning of the railroad bridge. Not long after that ominous smoke signal, the brigade received an order to retire to Vicksburg.[20]

Before leaving Bovina, Pemberton had telegraphed Forney to gather food and move it to Vicksburg. He listed cattle, sheep, hogs, corn, and usable wagons. "A large amount of fresh meat was secured in this way," reported Pemberton after the siege, but it was done at the expense of citizens living near Vicksburg.[21]

Pemberton positioned his two fresh divisions to hold the town while waiting for Carter Stevenson to bring his defeated army into the city. Elements of Baldwin's Brigade, which already were stationed at the railroad bridge, helped to cover the retreat. These troops had not been involved in the fight at Champion Hill or for the bridgehead.[22]

Stevenson conducted the march to Vicksburg "in a leisurely and orderly manner." Along the way he encountered Col. Alexander W. Reynolds' Brigade of his own division. Reynolds had been detached to protect Pemberton's wagon trains to the north of the battle area and now rejoined the column. Baldwin waited a couple of hours and then retreated from the railroad bridge about noon, trailing the body of defeated troops. A mix-up in conveying orders resulted in Col. Franklin K. Beck's 23rd Alabama of Brig. Gen. Stephen D. Lee's Brigade, Stevenson's Division, being left behind. Beck's men were harassing McClernand's Thirteenth Corps troops, who were trying to cross near the railroad bridge. Unaware that Beck had been left behind, Baldwin met Col. Hylan B. Lyon's 8th Kentucky Mounted Infantry at Bovina and utilized the regiment as his rear guard.[23]

Members of Beck's 23rd Alabama continued to fire at the Federals while the regiment held a line that straddled the railroad on the west bank of the Big Black River. McClernand's crossing was located about 150 yards north of the bridge piers, now blackened and empty of trestle. Finally, at 1:00 A.M. of May 18, the Alabamians retired in the night, reaching Vicksburg late in the morning. Along the way Beck was severely kicked by a horse and suffered a broken leg.[24]

VICKSBURG

Long before the arrival of Pemberton's last regiment, Vicksburg suffered the worst shock of its experience. Fear, excitement, and exhilaration had been building since May 16 when news that the enemy had captured Jackson two days before reached town. On the morning of May 17 citizens could hear guns firing at the Big Black River, and alarming reports about Champion Hill began to filter in.[25]

Just after breakfast on May 17, Dora Richards greeted a visitor to her house, an acquaintance of the family. The visitor told her that Pemberton had been severely defeated in two battles and was in retreat. "They are upon us," he frankly told her. "The Yankees will be here by this evening." Grant's men were "in such numbers nothing can stop them. Hasn't Pemberton acted like a fool?" Accurate reports spread rapidly through town. A soldier named Lt. Gabriel M. Killgore, on detached service from the 17th Louisiana, heard many bits of news throughout the late morning. The worst report indicated that the Rebel army was utterly demoralized and retreating like a rabble. Killgore heard his comrades had thrown away their weapons "and all is confusion and dismay."[26]

As far as Pemberton's men were concerned, the town was the only place to go. "Everything now pointed to Vicksburg," wrote Maj. Raleigh S.

Camp of the 40th Georgia. The arrival of the Confederate army in the city was a moment long remembered by observers. Col. Winchester Hall of the 26th Louisiana was staying with his wife and children in Vicksburg. His wife noticed "scattered bodies of troops coming in, on the Jackson road, which ran near my quarters" on the morning of the 17th. Hall knew it meant trouble, for the men were acting "with no more order than travelers on a highway, seeking Vicksburg as a shelter."[27]

What Hall noticed was only the beginning. By midafternoon a flood of beaten men poured into town. They represented "humanity in the last throes of endurance," thought Dora Richards. She was shocked at their appearance: "Wan, hollow-eyed, ragged, footsore, bloody, the men limped along unarmed." Many residents complained of Pemberton's incompetence and feared that Vicksburg was doomed.[28]

The mood of these retreating men was indeed bad. "Oh, how discouraging this was to us," admitted William A. Ruyle of the 5th Missouri. John Cowdry Taylor noted that the troops were "shockingly demoralized" as they trudged into town. Demoralization was strongest among the Missourians who had experienced battle that morning and the Georgians who had been worsted at Champion Hill. Many soldiers blamed Pemberton, and some declared they would desert rather than risk their lives under his command. Vocal denunciations that he had sold out their cause and was prepared to hand Vicksburg to the enemy began to circulate.[29]

Francis A. Shoup saw the men as they marched into town. "All I need say," he told an interviewer thirty years later, "is that through heat and dust the troops came tumbling back into Vicksburg in utter confusion."[30]

For the rest of the afternoon these fugitives jammed together with wagons and artillery pieces on the streets. Many civilians offered food and water as the officers tried to bring order out of chaos. They established rallying places, spreading the word for members of a particular unit to assemble at a particular place. Missouri batteries, which had lost all their guns at the Big Black River, now had to act as infantry until replacement guns could be found. Nerves steadied with the return of order. To encourage the disheartened, two or three regimental bands assembled on the hill close to the Warren County Courthouse and played as loud as they could.[31]

Along with Pemberton's troops came a stream of civilian refugees from the countryside around Vicksburg. Frightened by the prospect of living within enemy lines, they chose to share the fate of the army. Lida Lord Reed's family had spent the previous winter on a plantation near the Big Black River. They were shocked by news of Pemberton's defeat at Champion Hill, packed all night of May 16, and moved toward Vicksburg the next day, spurred on by "an awful bugaboo" of rumors about the Yankees. A wagon loaded with their belongings accompanied the carriage filled with family members, both of which entered Vicksburg on the evening of May 17. The Reeds were astonished to see the chaos and the atmosphere of dread and anxiety, but there was no turning back.[32]

THE DEFENSES

The thin line of earthworks screening Vicksburg's eastern approaches now became the primary hope of the city. Its origins dated to near the beginning of Vicksburg's war experience. Just before New Orleans fell in late April 1862, Gen. Pierre G. T. Beauregard initiated plans to fortify Vicksburg, because it was the first spot along the Mississippi River south of Memphis that was suitable for artillery emplacements. He sent engineer Capt. David B. Harris to plan the works so that forty pieces of heavy and field artillery could defend the city, supported by a garrison of 3,000 infantrymen. With the fall of New Orleans, Harris concentrated on placing batteries on the high bluffs east of the river and just south of town, using hired black laborers. Martin L. Smith, then a brigadier general, arrived to take command of the place on May 12, 1862. He brought Samuel H. Lockett as chief engineer in late June. Lockett found the river batteries south of Vicksburg to be nearly finished, so he concentrated on laying out the heavy artillery emplacements north of town and began work on a map of the area.[33]

Smith led the garrison until Earl Van Dorn arrived later that summer to take charge. Meanwhile, during both Smith's and Van Dorn's tenures, the Yankee fleet arrived and instituted a sporadic bombardment of Vicksburg. Federal troops landed on De Soto Point opposite town and began to dig a canal in an attempt to bypass the batteries. Both sides in this confrontation could call on only minimal resources of artillery and manpower, but the Federal force was severely hampered by disease. In the end the Confederates outlasted their opponents. The Federals gave up their first strike against Vicksburg and sailed downriver on July 27, 1862.[34]

Soon after the end of this "siege," the Confederates began to construct a system of defense for the land approaches to Vicksburg. Lockett spent a full month "reconnoitering, surveying, and studying" the terrain east of town. "No greater topographical puzzle was ever presented to an engineer," he asserted. The countryside consisted of twisting ravines and narrow ridges running in few consistent patterns. A thick growth of trees, including large magnolias, combined with thick underbrush and dense canebrakes to make it difficult to see the lay of the land. "At first it seemed impossible to find anything like a general line of commanding ground surrounding the city; but careful study gradually worked out the problem."[35]

After four weeks of scouting, Lockett submitted a plan and Smith approved it, having reassumed command of Vicksburg when Van Dorn left for other duties. Beginning about September 1, 1862, the work of building these defenses fell mostly on the shoulders of slave laborers hired from nearby plantations. Lockett now turned his attention to planning the batteries at Haynes' Bluff and Warrenton.[36]

When Pemberton assumed command of the Department of Mississippi and Eastern Louisiana in late October he approved Lockett's plan. Because Pemberton also assigned him as chief engineer of the department, Lockett traveled widely across the state. Capt. David Wintter, who commanded a company of sappers and miners in the Confederate army, assumed responsibility for building the land defenses of Vicksburg.[37]

Work on the line continued during the winter and spring months of 1863. Sgt. Edmund Trent Eggleston of Company G, 1st Mississippi Light Artillery, saw Vicksburg in early March after having left the place only two months before. Eggleston was astonished at how the town and its surroundings had changed in that short time. Many trees had been cut down, fences had been removed, and fortifications scarred the landscape.[38]

Lockett's line of works now faced the supreme test: Grant's victorious and confident army would soon arrive within striking distance. After he left Pemberton and rode toward town, Lockett set Wintter's company to work improving the fortifications because erosion had worn down the parapets. Wintter, however, could muster no more than twenty-six men in his company. Moreover, by May 17 there were no more than seventy-two black laborers available (twenty of whom were ill) and four white overseers to manage them. Lockett also had twenty-five oxen, a dozen mules, and 500 picks and shovels. Altogether, his resources were inadequate for a line of defense eight miles long. Knowing the odds facing him, Lockett smuggled "all my most important maps and papers" out of Vicksburg, trusting Col. D. H. Huyett, his assistant engineer, to take them around Grant's army on the night of May 17 and on to Jackson.[39]

When the Confederates took post in the earthworks on May 17 they were not impressed. "The fortifications were found to be very poorly constructed and afforded very little protection to the men behind them," recalled Cpl. Charles I. Evans of the 2nd Texas. At four feet wide and four feet deep, the trench was "too narrow and shallow," reported brigade leader John Moore. Parts of the line needed covered approaches—trenches stretching back from the line to allow troops to move to the works in safety. No traverses had been constructed to protect the troops from flank fire, a necessity in a line that curved on top of a snaking ridge.[40]

Newspaper reports had spread the erroneous idea that Vicksburg was girdled by immense fortifications. But when Bowen's Division marched through the line, William L. Truman of Wade's Missouri Battery thought it was only "about half finished." He assumed this was an outer line for a small advanced guard. But later Truman was "astounded to learn" that the incomplete work was the main line of defense. "I have not gotten over it until this day," he admitted long after the war. Another Missourian, Henry Martyn Cheavens, agreed with Truman. "The defenses were not such as we had expected to find, in fact almost nothing. Our men had to go to work to complete what laziness and 2 years had failed to do."[41]

Lockett's line certainly was incomplete, but soldier reaction to it speaks more to the men's emotional state on May 17 than it reflects on Lockett's skill as an engineer. All Lockett could be expected to do was to stake out the line and complete the first stage of construction, which was to erect a parapet at the enclosed works and a basic trench for the connecting line. He could not be expected to do more with so few workers. Moreover, infantrymen and artillerymen always had their own ideas about how to finish earthworks to suit their needs, which they knew how to do better than Wintter's sappers and miners or the slave laborers. With the enemy only hours away, the Confederates wanted full protection immediately. They were disgusted when it was not provided and had no time to understand the limitations under which Lockett had worked.

These critical Confederates also ignored a vitally important fact: incomplete as it was, Lockett's line saved the Army of Mississippi and Eastern Louisiana. Grant might well have been able to fight his way into the city on May 18 if there had been no earthworks, overwhelming Forney's and Smith's fresh divisions.

The thin line of earthworks now became the center of Confederate attention, shifting the defense of Vicksburg from the heavy batteries along the Mississippi to the tangled terrain east of town. Pemberton moved field artillery from the riverfront to Lockett's line and found small arms for infantrymen who had lost or abandoned their guns. By dawn of May 18, 102 artillery pieces lined the defenses east of town. At various places along the earthworks, wherever scattered houses lay close to the parapet, Confederate parties sallied forth to burn them during the night of May 17. They also burned any houses that lay near the rear of the trench, clearing an open space front and back of the line. Pemberton issued a circular prohibiting unnecessary firing of small arms. His chief aim was to conserve ammunition "for use solely against the enemy."[42]

JOHNSTON

As Pemberton readied for Grant's approach Johnston found himself in a precarious situation. His authority embraced Gen. Braxton Bragg's Department of Tennessee and Pemberton's Department of Mississippi and Eastern Louisiana. Special Orders No. 275, issued by the Adjutant and Inspector General's Office in Richmond on November 24, 1862, defined the boundaries of his command but, in Johnston's view, did not explicitly give him authority to command his chief subordinates.[43]

This proved to be a bone of contention between Johnston and Davis, and it colored their already troubled relationship. Johnston saw his role primarily as a military advisor to Pemberton, while Davis insisted he had the authority to give orders to the department commander. Perhaps the real problem was that Johnston was uncomfortable issuing orders to anyone. Johnston sought ways to support the harried defender of Vicksburg rather than seizing control of Confederate strategy in Mississippi.

The Richmond authorities had ordered Johnston to rush to Mississippi on May 9. He left Tullahoma, Tennessee, early the next morning and reached Jackson on May 13 to find that only 5,000 troops under Brig. Gen. John Gregg held the capital. Johnston tried to defend west central Mississippi but he had too little control over events.[44]

GRANT

The true shaper of affairs at this stage of the campaign was Grant. He faced delay for the time while creating usable crossing points of the stream to follow up his victory at the Big Black River, giving Pemberton time to retreat, but the momentum was all on his side. Thirteenth Corps engineers constructed a bridge made of rafts 150 yards upstream from the burned railroad bridge, harassed by fire from the 23rd Alabama, well into the night. McClernand deployed skirmishers and a battery to protect his bridge builders. At Amsterdam, five miles upstream from the railroad crossing, McPherson's men created a pontoon bridge consisting of cotton bales they found in the vicinity. Seventeenth Corps troops began a second crossing by chopping down large trees growing near the bank and managed to get some men over the river to cut down corresponding trees on the west bank, lacing their branches in the middle. Then, with lumber taken from nearby buildings, they constructed a bridge floor on this structure.[45]

Sherman began to lay the Army of the Tennessee's pontoon bridge at Bridgeport, six miles upstream from the railroad bridge. A Confederate pontoon bridge located there had just been destroyed by troops of Alexander Reynolds' brigade before he left the Bridgeport area. A small rear guard of Rebel troops remained dug in on the west bank at Bridgeport and began firing when Maj. Gen. Frank P. Blair's division arrived about noon. Capt. Peter P. Wood set up two guns of his Battery A, 1st Illinois Light Artillery, and bombarded them until the Confederates decided to give up. A Rebel officer crossed the river in a dugout canoe, flying a white flag, and offered to surrender to Wood.[46]

With the arrival of Maj. Gen. Frederick Steele's division at Bridgeport, Sherman sent a regiment across the river to hold the opposite bank while his pontoniers worked on the bridge. He sent a message to Grant at 2:00 P.M., promising to cross in three hours. Grant remained near the burned railroad bridge and knew that McClernand and McPherson could not cross until next morning. But he urged Sherman to place troops on the west bank of the Big Black as soon as possible. "If the information you gain after crossing warrants you in believing you can go immediately into the city, do so," he told him. Grant planned to move to Vicksburg in three parallel columns and hoped to be in the city or at least gain possession of Haynes' Bluff by dusk on May 18.[47]

Sherman issued orders for the crossing of his corps even before the bridge was ready. He planned to lead with Blair's division, then Steele's command, and finally Brig. Gen. James M. Tuttle's division. Tuttle was to leave one brigade to protect the pontoon bridge. Blair began moving over the river on the evening of May 17, and Steele began to cross by 10:00 P.M. Tuttle remained on the east side of the Big Black for the night. Blair bivouacked his leading division two miles west of the river.[48]

Grant was brimming with confidence. "The enemy have been so terribly beaten yesterday and to-day that I cannot believe that a stand will be made," he told Sherman. Grant was convinced that Johnston had too few men to dare a move toward Vicksburg if the true condition of Pemberton's shattered army was known to him.[49]

During the past seventeen days Grant had marched 30,000 men about

200 miles through enemy territory, defeated his opponents in four battles, inflicted 7,000 casualties on the Confederates, and captured sixty-five pieces of artillery and 7,000 stand of small arms. Counting the detachment of Loring's Division, Pemberton had lost a total of 14,000 troops while Grant had lost only 3,500 men. Most important, Grant had seized control of the strategic initiative.[50]

Grant's men shared his sense of confidence. "We expect to take Vicksburg tomorrow if we get there soon enough," exulted Curtis P. Lacey of the 55th Illinois. Capt. L. B. Martin of the 4th Minnesota reasoned that "Grant has shown himself the ablest strategist of them all, and there is but one voice here now: 'We are all Grant men.'"[51]

In stark contrast to the mood among Union soldiers, widespread despair characterized the thoughts of many Confederates on the night of May 17. Quartermaster Samuel A. R. Swan in Lee's Brigade thought that "the feeling was general that they would run over our entrenchments at the first outset. Gloomy forebodings were marked in every countenance."[52]

On the War-Path for Vicksburg

MAY 18

As the morning of May 18 dawned beautifully, with temperatures soon to reach eighty degrees, it was still uncertain what course the campaign for Vicksburg might take. The Federals consumed nearly the entire day in finishing their crossing of the Big Black River and moving to the city. The Confederates were busy completing the placement of their forces in Maj. Samuel H. Lockett's works. Only time would tell whether the opposing forces would engage in an attack countered by a defense or settle in for a siege.[1]

LOCKETT'S LINE

Whatever might happen on May 18, one thing was certain: Lockett's line of defense was the most important barrier separating the Confederates from their enemy. "Remember . . . the trenches were *everything*," wrote Francis G. Obenchain of the Botetourt Virginia Artillery after the war. If not for them, "Grant would have marched his Army into Vicksburg on 18th of May." Lockett had planned and built nine major works to cover the land approaches to Vicksburg, which included six roads and one railroad. The defenses stretched for eight miles in a semicircle from the river north of Vicksburg to the river south of the city. They lay one to one and a half miles from town along a "much broken and irregular" ridge that had many spurs thrusting forward.[2]

Lockett's nine major works varied in shape and size according to the ground. He also adapted them so the occupants could see into the ravines immediately in front. Most of the works were open at the rear (the gorge),

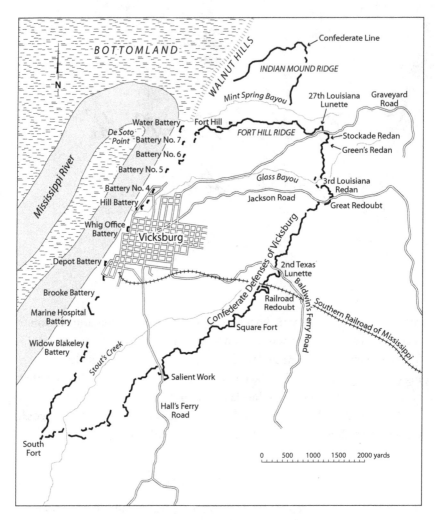

May 18

except Square Fort, the largest of the nine, which was enclosed. According to Federal engineers, none of the works had a strong profile (the height, shape, and angle of the parapet). But Lockett provided for a ditch six to ten feet deep in front of all but one (the 3rd Louisiana Redan). He also constructed a firing step (banquette) inside the works and embrasures and platforms for artillery.[3]

To connect the nine major works Lockett constructed a line of infantry trench along the top of the ridge. The parapet was up to six feet thick but no ditch was dug in front, while the trench was little more than two feet deep and three feet wide. Lockett sprinkled a total of forty-six small artillery emplacements along the length of his line, placing them between the major works.[4]

Lockett's line started at the highest point north of Vicksburg, the location of a Spanish fort built in 1791 and a Confederate work later called Fort Hill, which was constructed in 1862. It was on the end of Fort Hill Ridge, which extended inland for some distance and carried Lockett's line with it. Two small streams flowed into the Mississippi, one north of the ridge and one south. One and half miles from the river, a spur jutted south from Fort Hill Ridge—here the line turned sharply to the south.[5]

Lockett built three works near this angle to block Graveyard Road, which approached from the northeast. He planted Stockade Redan at the angle and a bit south of the road. North of the road and seventy-five yards west of Stockade Redan lay the 27th Louisiana Lunette. Seventy-five yards south of the main work at the angle lay Green's Redan. Graveyard Road directly approached Stockade Redan but ran just outside its north face before crossing the Confederate line between the redan and the 27th Louisiana Lunette. A stockade consisting of logs eight feet tall ran about 100 yards to either side of the point where Graveyard Road passed through the line.[6]

The north wing of Lt. Gen. John C. Pemberton's defense line—stretching from Fort Hill to Stockade Redan—was shadowed on the north by a corresponding feature called Indian Mound Ridge. Mint Spring Bayou drained toward the Mississippi between Indian Mound Ridge and Fort Hill Ridge. Lockett recognized the possibilities inherent in using Indian Mound Ridge and began the construction of an infantry trench along its crest. It was not completed by May 18 and contained only one artillery emplacement. As Indian Mound Ridge approached the area of Stockade Redan, a large spur protruded from it toward the southeast and nearly connected with Fort Hill Ridge. A deep ravine some 400 yards wide separated the end of this spur from Fort Hill Ridge, and Mint Spring Bayou flowed through the ravine to head for the Mississippi River.[7]

The east face of Pemberton's line headed south from Stockade Redan. It crossed a deep and narrow gorge through which Glass Bayou drained west about 900 yards south of the redan. Two hundred yards south of Glass Bayou a ridge also ran west, carrying Jackson Road toward Vicksburg. Lockett planted the 3rd Louisiana Redan just on the north side of the road and the Great Redoubt south of the roadway.[8]

One mile south of the Great Redoubt, Baldwin's Ferry Road approached Vicksburg from the southeast. Lockett placed the 2nd Texas Lunette on the south side of the road, but a gap of 100 yards existed north of the lunette before the connecting infantry line resumed its course. Only 500 yards south of the 2nd Texas Lunette, the Southern Railroad of Mississippi sliced through Lockett's line with a twenty-foot-deep cut. The engineer placed Railroad Redoubt just south of the tracks. A mile south of this large work lay Square Fort, later renamed Fort Garrott.[9]

The north and east faces of Lockett's line — from Fort Hill to the vicinity of Square Fort — were the only portion of the defenses directly threatened by the Federals during the next few days. Grant had enough troops to cover only this part of Vicksburg's perimeter, but Lockett had provided for all-around defense. One mile south of Square Fort, the Hall's Ferry Road crossed the ridge that carried his line southwest toward the Mississippi. He planted the Salient Work just east of the road. West of the road, the connecting line crossed Stout's Creek and ended at South Fort, located on top of a high river bluff next to the bottomland.[10]

Not only the earthworks but the soil they resided on played a role in coming events. The area for ten to fifteen miles east of Vicksburg consisted of loess soil deposited over thousands of years by the wind. Loess is brown silt, light and porous. Water drains rapidly through it contributing to flash flooding, but it stands together very well. It is possible to dig trenches or tunnels into it without having to shore up the sides. Loess does erode, making for a crazy kind of topography. Near the Mississippi River the loess stratum is up to 200 feet thick, but it becomes much thinner toward the east.[11]

The crazy-quilt pattern of ground formed by erosion posed a difficult problem when Lockett laid out the defense line. His works snaked along the only discernible ridge in the terrain, leaving the opposing Yankees to make do with "the spurs and the hollows." The line was located on ground about 200 feet above the river level. Ravines tended to have very steep sides ending in V-shaped bottoms that flattened out into bottomlands only when time allowed for continual erosion. The tops of the ridges and spurs tended to be quite narrow. Even Confederate soldiers who complained that Lockett's line was poorly constructed admitted that he had selected the best ground available.[12]

When they arrived in front of this line, the Federals were astonished by the jumble of ravines, short ridges, and spurs. "There is not enough level land within 10 miles of here to lay down on without rolling away somewhere," reported Edwin A. Loosley of the 81st Illinois. But the terrain also offered cover for the Federals to approach the enemy.[13]

The topography supported irregular tree and plant growth, altered by human activity. The area just east of Vicksburg had an original tree cover of hardwoods, especially black walnut. With the beginning of white settlement, the trees covering the tops of ridges were cut to make way for farming. By 1863 that cutting had promoted even more erosion. This led to more accumulation of silt in the ravine bottoms, which in turn promoted the growth of canebrakes in the silt. Cane liked the boggy conditions and grew to fifteen feet tall in places. Vines thrived in this environment as well, and a second growth of trees had begun to emerge on many ridgetops.[14]

Lockett had detailed crews to cut trees to create a field of fire. At Stockade Redan, the clear-cutting of timber extended 200 yards in front of the works, but at most other places it was not so extensive. The trees were felled toward the enemy, forming obstructions to an assault. As a result, the ridgetops were generally clear of timber but the ravines close to the line were littered with cut timber and brush.[15]

MANNING THE WORKS

Pemberton deserves credit for placing his available manpower in thoughtful ways. He wanted Maj. Gen. Martin L. Smith's Division to cover the north face up to Stockade Redan, a sector one and a quarter miles long. Maj. Gen. John H. Forney's Division would cover the east face of the perimeter from the Stockade south to the railroad, a sector two miles long. The rest of the perimeter was less likely to be threatened, so Maj. Gen. Carter L. Stevenson's Division held five miles of line from the railroad to Warrenton on the Mississippi. Brig. Gen. Stephen D. Lee's Brigade, on Stevenson's left, would be hit in the fierce battles to come, as would most of Forney's men and much of Smith's Division. Pemberton decided to use Maj. Gen. John S. Bowen's Division and Col. Thomas N. Waul's Texas Legion of 500 men as his mobile reserve rather than assign them to a sector. He could put 15,500 men into the works while holding a total of 2,900 in reserve.[16]

These troops finished taking their position in the works on May 18. A potentially dangerous misunderstanding of orders occurred when Smith thought his division was to hold the south face of the perimeter, perhaps because Brig. Gen. William E. Baldwin's Brigade already was there. Smith started Brig. Gen. John C. Vaughn's Brigade toward that sector on the morning of May 18, as Brig. Gen. Francis A. Shoup's Brigade lolled about during the course of the morning with no instructions.[17]

Smith's position was not clarified until the enemy approached. Pemberton, Lockett, and a handful of officers were inspecting the defenses when word arrived that the Federals were coming along Jackson Road. Soon after,

Capt. Thomas Henderson rode in with a dispatch from Gen. Joseph E. Johnston. Henderson had ridden around the Federals to bring a message urging Pemberton to give up Vicksburg and save his army.[18]

"The evacuation of Vicksburg!" Pemberton wrote three months later. "It meant the loss of valuable stores and munitions of war collected for its defense; the fall of Port Hudson; the surrender of the Mississippi River, and the severance of the Confederacy. These were mighty interests." Pemberton doubted it was possible to make his way around Grant's army and was strongly inclined to remain at Vicksburg anyway.[19]

Pemberton called a council of war and asked his subordinates one question: Did they believe it was possible to give up the city and make their way to Johnston? All agreed "that it was impossible to withdraw the army from this position with such *morale* and material as to be of further service to the Confederacy." As if to confirm their opinion, the sound of skirmishing could be heard.[20]

"I have decided to hold Vicksburg as long as possible," Pemberton told Johnston, "with the firm hope that the Government may yet be able to assist me in keeping the obstruction to the enemy's free navigation of the Mississippi River. I still conceive it to be the most important point in the Confederacy." Three months later, he further expressed his feelings on this point. "I believed it to be in my power to hold Vicksburg. . . . I knew, perhaps better than any other individual, under all the circumstances, its capacity for defense." He felt that by economizing ammunition and food he could wait until the Richmond authorities assembled enough power to save his army.[21] The immediate course of events had been sealed. There would be no flight from Vicksburg, only the prospect of a grinding siege with the hope of relief in the near future.

Pemberton had called the council of war on news that Federal skirmishers were approaching along Jackson Road. The council broke up as another report indicated the Federals were advancing along Graveyard Road. Francis Shoup played a large role in alerting the generals to this danger. In the late morning he received instructions to move one regiment along the road to support Confederates who were driving in cattle. Shoup accompanied the 27th Louisiana, but when the head of the regiment reached Stockade Redan, it was met by an excited citizen riding toward Vicksburg with the news that the Yankees were close behind him. Shoup could see no evidence that Rebel skirmishers were in place, so he stopped the 27th, placing eight companies in the works and sending two companies to skirmish along Graveyard Road. Those two companies met Federal skirmishers only 300 yards from the redan. Shoup sent the civilian to his division commander and dispatched a courier with a note to Pemberton. Both messengers reached the council of war at about the same time, 1:00 P.M.[22]

This was a close call. If not for Shoup, the Federals might have breached Lockett's line before the Confederates were ready for them. The cause of this near catastrophe was the mix-up in orders between Pemberton and Smith concerning where Smith was to place his division. Smith allowed Shoup's Brigade to remain idle all morning even though he sent Vaughn toward the south, his assumed sector.

When Shoup's message reached the council of war, Pemberton said to Smith, "Well that is your position of the line." Surprised, Smith replied, "No sir, you have directed me to take charge of the extreme right." Pemberton denied ever having said such a thing and reiterated that he was to hold the extreme left. Smith quickly sent a staff officer, Lt. George H. Frost, to retrieve Vaughn's Brigade. Frost caught up with Vaughn and urged him to move his men quickly to Indian Mound Ridge.[23]

THE FEDERALS ARRIVE

As Smith placed his division along the north face of the perimeter, Grant's army arrived at the defenses of Vicksburg. Maj. Gen. James B. McPherson's men were the first to cross the Big Black River that morning, using two bridges they had constructed north and south of Amsterdam. Regimental bands positioned on the west bank played national airs to celebrate the crossing of Grant's Rubicon. McPherson left one brigade to protect the bridges and pushed the rest four miles to Flowers' Plantation. Here he found a crossroad already filled with troops of Maj. Gen. William T. Sherman's Fifteenth Corps, which had crossed the river the evening before. Brig. Gen. James M. Tuttle's division, the only Fifteenth Corps formation still on the east side of the river, crossed the Big Black on the morning of the 18th and moved forward to catch up with Maj. Gen. Frank P. Blair and Maj. Gen. Frederick Steele. Maj. Gen. John A. McClernand's Thirteenth Corps also crossed on the morning of the 18th, using its bridge located north of the burned railroad trestle.[24]

Grant and his staff crossed the Big Black with Tuttle's division. The general could count on anywhere from 35,000 to 40,000 men in this last stage of his drive toward Vicksburg. Sherman took the lead with Blair's division followed by Steele and Tuttle. Lt. Col. James H. Wilson, Grant's assistant inspector general, gathered information about what lay ahead. He encountered a black man named John Wesley Jackson, a "hack driver from Vicksburg," who assured him that the roads were in "pretty good" shape and alerted him to an important crossroads near Mount Alban on Jackson Road. One and a half miles west of this junction a side road veered off toward Snyder's Bluff and another veered south toward Baldwin's Ferry Road. Jackson also told Wilson he could expect little resistance from Pemberton's men. "Thinks they will surrender after a show of fight," as Wilson put it.[25]

Sherman led the way with Blair moving along Bridgeport Road, but he stopped near the junction of Benton Road about five miles short of Vicksburg at 10:00 A.M. Sherman's column waited nearly two hours before Tuttle caught up; then Blair resumed the cautious approach, detouring onto Benton Road for a mile until reaching its junction with Jackson Road. One thousand yards farther on lay the intersection with Graveyard Road, and Sherman veered onto it at Grant's order.[26]

The fine loess soil dried easily in the sun to create dusty road conditions, but Sherman's men pushed on. "We expect a fight or foot race this afternoon" noted Lt. Noble Walter Wood of the 26th Iowa, while another Iowa man proclaimed that Grant's army was "on the war-path for Vicksburg." Blair's column intercepted a party of thirty ladies, mostly wives of Confederate officers, who had been on a picnic and were trying to return to Vicksburg. To prevent them from divulging information, officers selected an abandoned house for them and placed guards to make sure they remained there.[27]

After marching about 1,000 yards along Graveyard Road, Blair encountered the 27th Louisiana skirmishers that Shoup had sent forward. He deployed his own skirmishers, commanded by Capt. Charles Ewing of the 1st Battalion, 13th U.S. Infantry. Ewing was Sherman's adopted brother as well as his brother-in-law. The regulars pushed the Louisiana men until they neared the Confederate works.[28]

Blair deployed his division with Col. Thomas Kilby Smith's brigade straddling Graveyard Road about 800 yards from Stockade Redan. Kilby Smith sent out a skirmish line to front his brigade, which lodged 200 yards from the works. He also deployed the 54th Ohio in an effort to cover a gap of one and half miles that existed between Blair's division and McPherson's corps to the south. Battery B, 1st Illinois Artillery, fired the first shots at Vicksburg from the east. Observing the works from Kilby Smith's skirmish line, Capt. Thomas Sewell of Company G, 127th Illinois, believed they were weakly held and thought Sherman could have broken the line that afternoon.[29]

Col. Giles A. Smith deployed his brigade to Kilby Smith's right. Blair's other brigade, commanded by Brig. Gen. Hugh Ewing (another of Sherman's adopted brothers and brothers-in-law), had been late in joining Grant's movement from the Mississippi River but was fast catching up. Blair's two available brigades were in place by 5:00 P.M.[30]

As soon as Sherman learned that a byway called Countryman Road branched off from Graveyard Road toward the Yazoo River north of Vicksburg, he instructed Steele to move west along it. Col. Charles R. Woods's brigade led the way at about 1:00 P.M., followed by the brigades of Brig. Gen. John M. Thayer and Col. Francis H. Manter. Members of the 30th Iowa noticed a group of officers standing at the junction of Graveyard Road and Countryman Road as they passed by. The group included Grant and Sherman, the former calmly smoking his cigar as the column streamed past.[31]

Steele moved cautiously, not knowing if the enemy lay in strength. The Federals caught glimpses of gray-clad troops in the incomplete works on Indian Mound Ridge. By the time Woods neared Walnut Hills, the bluffs along the Yazoo River, he reported that five or six Confederate regiments and some artillery were "strongly posted" in the area. Unwilling to lose connection with the rest of the division, Woods halted his slow advance and established a defensive position fronting the north face of Lockett's perimeter. He had not yet occupied Walnut Hills or made contact with the U.S. Navy or the transports that supplied Grant's army. Woods established a skirmish line 200 yards from the Rebel works and reported that his brigade lost no one to enemy action on May 18.[32]

Woods, Steele, and Sherman remained ignorant of how close they came to breaking into Vicksburg that day. They knew nothing of the misunderstandings between Pemberton and Smith that prevented the latter from filling the north face of Lockett's perimeter until late in the day. As Woods cautiously led Steele's division toward the river, Smith was shoving troops into the works. For most of the day the northern door to Vicksburg was wide open.

After rushing Vaughn to Indian Mound Ridge, Smith hurried his two remaining brigades into the works. Brig. Gen. Seth M. Barton's Brigade of Stevenson's Division relieved Baldwin's Brigade in the area near South Fort, allowing Baldwin to put his men on Indian Mound Ridge between 4:00 and 5:00 P.M. The brigade extended the Confederate line from Shoup's left flank. Shoup placed the 27th Louisiana on Indian Mound Ridge and the 26th Louisiana to hold the gorge connecting that ridge with Fort Hill Ridge. Two six-pounder guns of the 14th Mississippi Artillery Battalion crossed Mint Spring Bayou and took post on the left of Baldwin's line. Two others tried to cross but were stopped by Union skirmish fire that opened at 5:00 P.M. This fire also mortally wounded Baldwin's chief of artillery. The Confederates suffered because the works on Indian Mound Ridge were incomplete. According to Col. Claudius Wistar Sears, commander of the 46th Mississippi, the works consisted of unconnected sections with parapets only three feet high. Moreover, Sears was compelled to stretch his line thinly to cover the space assigned his regiment.[33]

Pemberton ordered Bowen to fill out the Confederate line on Indian Mound Ridge. Col. Francis M. Cockrell marched his men across Mint Spring Bayou and extended Baldwin's line toward the river by 5:00 P.M. Cockrell's Missourians received a good deal of skirmish fire and artillery punishment. Cockrell himself was slightly injured by a shell fragment and lost one man killed and eight wounded that evening.[34]

Smith's aide, George H. Frost, barely got Vaughn's Brigade to the vicinity of Fort Hill before the Federals neared the area. "Fifteen minutes later," Frost asserted, and the Yankees would have entered the works. Vaughn placed his troops in Fort Hill and along Fort Hill Ridge, 600 yards south of Indian Mound Ridge. He put all of the 31st Tennessee and 53rd Tennessee plus part of the 3rd Tennessee in the trenches while holding the rest of the 3rd Tennessee and the 43rd Tennessee in reserve. Vaughn also had the services of men belonging to the 54th Alabama and the 6th Mississippi who had been cut off from Maj. Gen. William W. Loring's Division, plus Brig. Gen. Jeptha V. Harris's Mississippi State Troops.[35]

The door to Vicksburg closed with a thump on the evening of May 18. If Grant had known that the northern sector of Pemberton's defense line was unfilled, he surely would have pushed his troops faster and sought a quick entry into the city.

Most Union soldiers were feeling the shortage of food and the exhausting nature of Grant's inland march by May 18. They had foraged enough provisions from the countryside to get by, and the weather was particularly hot on May 18, producing dusty roads and scarce water along the route. "I have seen the boys offer a dollar for a hard tack," commented Pvt. Calvin Ainsworth, "but no one had any to sell."[36]

Grant was anxious to restore his supply line and rode with Sherman to the van of Woods' brigade. It was obvious the Federals could not reopen communications that evening, but being so near Walnut Hills made Sherman realize what Grant had accomplished to this point in the campaign. The two stood close to the spot Sherman had assaulted in his bloody repulse of December 29 during the battle of Chickasaw Bayou. As Grant remembered it, Sherman told him "that up to this minute he felt no positive assurance of success. This, however, he said was the end of one of the greatest campaigns in history and I ought to make a report of it at once. Vicksburg was not yet captured, and there was no telling what might happen before it was taken; but whether captured or not, this was a complete and successful campaign."[37]

Sherman's assessment was absolutely right. The Federal deployment near Vicksburg that evening marked the end of the inland campaign and the beginning of a new phase in the struggle for Vicksburg, and the result thus far assured Grant's place among the best field commanders in American history.

The rest of the Federal army lagged behind Sherman in approaching Vicksburg. The bulk of McPherson's corps reached the junction of Jackson Road and Bridgeport Road four miles from town that evening. Then McPherson advanced his forward unit, Brig. Gen. Thomas E. G. Ransom's brigade, until it took position 1,200 yards from the Confederate line north of Jackson Road. Ransom deployed skirmishers and ordered his battery to open fire at 5:00 P.M.[38]

After beginning to cross the Big Black River at 7:30 A.M., McClernand's Thirteenth Corps also marched along Jackson Road until it reached Mount Alban. Here Grant's message instructed him to move south to Baldwin's Ferry Road and approach Vicksburg from the southeast. Brig. Gen. Andrew J. Smith led McClernand's advance and forwarded skirmishers who encountered Rebel pickets one and half miles from Lockett's line by about 1:00 P.M. An hour later, Smith formed line in the shelter of a ravine and ordered his division to advance into the works if possible. The division moved onto the top of a cleared ridge, where it was hit by heavy artillery fire. The troops hurried into the next ravine for shelter but came into full view of the Confederate works on top of the next ridge. Here Smith found that his formation was already broken by the rugged terrain. The Federals backed into the nearest ravine for shelter and reorganized. "The idea of an immediate assault was abandoned," as Lt. Col. Lysander R. Webb of the 77th Illinois put it.[39]

Smith bivouacked 600 yards from the Rebel entrenchments while his skirmishers maintained a position 400 yards from the enemy that evening. The rest of McClernand's corps remained much farther behind, two and a half miles from the Rebel line.[40]

THE CONFEDERATES PREPARE

As their enemy closed in, Confederate soldiers looked to the future with both dread and courage. Wesley O. Connor of Capt. M. Van Den Corput's Cherokee Georgia Artillery feared that his comrades would fail the test of courage that lay ahead. Others, such as cavalry officer Sidney S. Champion (who found himself trapped in the city), expressed defiance. "We are all determined to fight at Vicksburg—so that our foes will [know] we are at least not destitute of *pluck*."[41]

"It is now a foregone conclusion that we are to be besieged," noted Lt. Jared Young Sanders of the 26th Louisiana in his diary. There was still time to get messages out of the city. William H. Brotherton of the 39th Georgia had wanted to write his father, a minister living in Dalton, Georgia, about the death of his brother James at the battle of Raymond. No opportunity presented itself until officers authorized an outgoing mail just before the siege began. All Brotherton could find was a scrap of paper to scribble on. It was barely large enough for him to convey the sad news to his father and include a final message about his own situation. We "are now surrounded by the Enemy, don't Know wether we will be surrendered or cut our way out."[42]

Rumors of surrender, including a wild story that Grant and Pemberton had secretly arranged for the delivery of Vicksburg into Union hands within two days, ran like a contagious disease through the ranks. Hearing these rumors all day, Bowen informed Pemberton of their dire effect on morale. He urged him to issue an order that Pemberton's intention was "to hold the place to the bitter end."[43]

There is no convincing evidence that Pemberton acted on Bowen's suggestion. Instead, the general tended to other matters, such as the dim prospect of feeding his army and supplying it with ammunition during what could evolve into a long siege. He issued orders for the horses and mules inside Confederate lines to be grazed rather than fed corn, saving the grain for human consumption. He also began to caution the men to save their ammunition.[44]

Pemberton also sent word to a small cavalry force near Vicksburg to harass the enemy. Col. William Wirt Adams commanded an ad hoc brigade consisting of the 1st Mississippi Cavalry, 8th Kentucky Mounted Infantry, and 20th Mississippi Mounted Infantry to the northeast of town. Pemberton urged Adams to strike the enemy's flank and rear, especially his supply arrangements, but Adams failed to make an impression. Pemberton admitted that the cavalry force was "very inadequate to this purpose."[45]

The small infantry force that Joseph E. Johnston controlled near Jackson also was inadequate. Early on May 18, Johnston expected Pemberton to evacuate the town and join his force. Then he heard from two civilians that the army had fallen back to the city. Soon after, a courier brought Pemberton's announcement that he would stand a siege in Vicksburg. "I shall endeavor, after collecting all available troops, to hold as much of the country as possible," Johnston told the authorities in Richmond.[46]

Johnston could count only 11,000 men in the Department of Mississippi and Eastern Louisiana, excluding the garrisons of Vicksburg and Port Hudson. Only about half of those men were under his direct command. He expected up to 7,000 more within the next few days, the result of previous efforts to shift regiments from less threatened parts of the Confederacy. Johnston estimated Grant's strength at up to 80,000 men (nearly three times his actual number) and Pemberton's at 28,000 (a few thousand more than his actual number). Reports indicated that the storehouses in Vicksburg contained enough food to last sixty days (also more than the reality). "Very large reinforcements will be necessary" to break up Grant's arrangements, Johnston wrote Adj. Gen. Samuel Cooper. "I hope that the Government will send without delay all that can possibly be spared from other points." Loring's Division was still on the loose, so Pemberton sent a note on May 18 advising him to seek a union with Johnston.[47]

Toward the evening of May 18, Pemberton became aware that yet another misunderstanding between his wishes and Smith's actions had occurred. He meant for the division to occupy Fort Hill Ridge, but an engineer officer, Capt. James T. Hogane, told him Smith held Indian Mound Ridge instead. Hogane had inspected the outer line held by Smith that evening and did not like what he saw. If forced to give up the line under pressure, the troops would have to cross Mint Spring Bayou with the enemy hot on their heels. A lieutenant accompanied Hogane on his inspection, and when the engineer asked him if there was a better position, the lieutenant pointed to Fort Hill Ridge. Hogane sent his recommendation that the outer line be abandoned directly to Pemberton's headquarters.[48]

Pemberton had already concluded that the outer line should not be held and immediately ordered Smith to evacuate under cover of darkness. Part of Shoup's Brigade, all of Baldwin's Brigade, and part of Cockrell's Brigade began to move.[49]

Smith issued orders for Baldwin's Brigade to pull off the ridge between 3:00 and 3:30 A.M., leaving two twenty-four-pounder siege guns for Lockett to evacuate. The 17th Louisiana had started to dig a trench along an unprotected segment of Indian Mound Ridge at midnight; Company H managed to complete it for thirty yards when the time for pullout arrived. Baldwin established his new line on Fort Hill Ridge with his rightmost regiment, the 17th Louisiana, joining Shoup's left near the Riddle House. He found several incomplete segments of trench and began to finish them.[50]

Shoup pulled his 26th Louisiana from the outer line as soon as Baldwin evacuated the ridge. To make his position more compact, he closed the 27th Louisiana to the right and pulled the 26th Louisiana back in the early morning hours to take place to its left, connecting with Baldwin's right flank near the Riddle House. Like Baldwin's men, Col. Winchester Hall's 26th Louisianans found many segments of their new line unprotected by a trench. Cockrell also pulled back after Baldwin retired to Fort Hill Ridge, assuming a reserve position behind Baldwin. Hogane marked out the incomplete segments of trench along Fort Hill Ridge so Baldwin and Hall would know where to dig.[51]

While some Confederates thought there was an advantage to holding the outer line, most agreed that Fort Hill Ridge constituted a stronger position. The valley floor of Mint Spring Bayou, 200 to 300 yards wide, had been cleared and cultivated; it made a perfect moat protecting Fort Hill Ridge from sudden assault.[52]

Grant failed to discover the hole in Pemberton's line caused by Smith's idea that his division was to hold the south wing. Until about fifteen minutes before they arrived, Sherman's men would have faced empty earthworks along Indian Mound Ridge and Fort Hill Ridge and even straddling Graveyard Road. If Sherman could have moved faster, and the Confederates had not received word of his approach, the Fifteenth Corps might have broken into Lockett's perimeter on the afternoon of May 18. Whether it could have held its advantage long enough for the other two corps to arrive is another question.

As Fifteenth Corps troops settled in, skirmishing continued after dusk. Muzzle flashes punctuated the darkness and created "a beautiful sight." Another startling effect was produced as the Confederates burned houses near their fortifications along the perimeter. Emma Balfour noticed this from her home in Vicksburg and was awed by the spectacle.[53]

PORTER AND THE NAVY

The first Union artillery fire on Vicksburg from the east alerted the large fleet of gunboats supporting Grant's army on the Mississippi River. It was confirmation that the infantry had marched to the rear of Vicksburg. Acting Rear Admiral David D. Porter was exhilarated by the sound of those guns. Positioned with the boats that lay north of Vicksburg, Porter could see the artillery in action and observed Steele's careful extension toward Walnut Hills.[54]

The navy had always been an important element in Grant's operations against Vicksburg. By early May 1863, Porter commanded eighty vessels in the Mississippi Squadron, a combination of heavy ironclad boats with large-caliber guns, smaller light-draft wooden gunboats, and an intermediate class of lightly armored and light-draft vessels. Moreover, some new model ironclads with turrets had become available.[55]

Porter helped Grant move down the Louisiana side of the river by running several gunboats and transports past Vicksburg's batteries in mid-April. Then, as Grant began his inland march, Porter steamed down to the fleet commanded by David G. Farragut, which was supporting Maj. Gen. Nathaniel P. Banks's operations in Louisiana. Farragut's seaborne vessels could not steam up the Red River to support Banks's move to Alexandria, so Porter took some of his riverboats to secure the city. When Banks turned back to cross the Mississippi and strike at Port Hudson, Porter personally returned to Grant's command. He reached the vessels stationed at the mouth of the Yazoo River by May 15. Word circulated among the crew members that he thought "the downfall of Vicksburg a sure thing, and is looking for its evacuation or surrender every day."[56]

Porter wanted to help the army but his fleet was scattered. Two ironclad gunboats were stationed at the mouth of the Red River 200 river miles south of Vicksburg, while one guarded the strong artillery position at Grand Gulf, forty river miles south of town. Another ironclad guarded Federal assets at Carthage, Louisiana, twenty-four river miles downstream from Vicksburg. Porter had three ironclads positioned near Warrenton and two more north of the city.[57]

When he realized that Grant had arrived east of Vicksburg, Porter ordered USS *Baron DeKalb* and USS *Choctaw* to prepare for a push up the Yazoo River. Four small wooden gunboats, USS *Linden*, USS *Romeo*, USS *Petrel*, and USS *Forest Rose*, readied to accompany the ironclads. Porter put Lt. Cdr. K. Randolph Breese in charge of the expedition, with orders to reach Snyder's Bluff.[58]

Porter also contacted Maj. Gen. Stephen A. Hurlbut, commander of the Sixteenth Corps at Memphis, who was responsible for protecting posts in West Tennessee and North Mississippi. "I am not in any way authorized to say so, but my opinion is that General Grant should be re-enforced with all dispatch, and with every man that can be sent him from all directions. He will have the hardest fight ever seen during the war. The attention of the nation should now be devoted to Vicksburg."[59]

Toward evening of May 18, Porter ordered the three ironclads stationed near Warrenton to steam upriver and harass the city with naval gunnery.

While Porter reported that they fired on the city that evening, Col. Edward Higgins, who was in charge of the Confederate river batteries, indicated that they remained just beyond range of his heavy guns. Their appearance nevertheless had its effect. Combined with the sight of Union gunboats showing themselves in the Mississippi River north of Vicksburg, Higgins correctly concluded that the investment of the city, at least by water, was complete.[60]

But Grant's investment of Vicksburg by land was far from complete and he was not thinking of siege operations. Instead, Grant contemplated an attack the next day. Many of his men seem to have taken the prospect of an assault for granted. "Went to sleep early every expectation of entering Vicksburg to-morrow," wrote Charles F. Smith of the 83rd Ohio. In fact, Lt. William Titus Rigby of the 24th Iowa expected to mail a letter to his brother from inside the town.[61]

Sixty miles up the Yazoo River from Haynes' Bluff, James Oliver Hazard Perry Sessions of Rokeby Plantation was isolated from the immediate effects of Grant's campaign but dreadfully worried about the news. "Our army at Big Black has been badly whipped and driven into Vicksburg," Sessions admitted in his diary. "Our troops are scattered in every direction." He concluded that "thousands, have deserted, straggled or run away from the army, and the main body shut up in Vicksburg. We expect to see Yankees here in a very short time. If our army has to evacuate Vicksburg, they have no other way of retreating except this way. I'm afraid we are lost."[62]

{3}

A Long Dreadful Day

FIFTEENTH CORPS, MAY 19

As day dawned on the morning of May 19, Grant realized that more time was needed before he could issue orders to conduct an assault. Most of his army was not close enough to the enemy to mount an attack. Pressured by the knowledge that Johnston might be operating against him from the east, and worried about waiting so long that the emotional advantages gained in the overland march might dissipate, Grant had to make a decision on the morning of May 19 as to his immediate course of action. But he could not take too much time to decide.

After spending the night at Cook's plantation, Grant rode to McPherson's corps by 8:40 A.M. There he established a command post at Mount Ararat, 1,000 yards southwest of the intersection of Graveyard Road and Jackson Road. The place was on an elevated bit of ground that enabled him to see the Confederate line from Stockade Redan to Square Fort. "I was not without hope of carrying the enemy's works," he later reported. "I believed he would not make much effort to hold Vicksburg."[1]

By late morning Grant decided to move up the rest of his army and attack at the same time. Written at 11:16 A.M., Special Orders No. 134 instructed corps commanders to "push forward carefully, and gain as close position as possible to the enemy's works until 2:00 P.M. At that hour they will fire three volleys of artillery from all the pieces in position. This will be the signal for a general charge of all the corps along the whole line." Grant was in a hurry and barely allowed his men the chance to move forward into better positions for the assault.[2]

Grant's decision to attack so soon was justified. He had to strike quickly to take advantage of his enemy's low morale. But the "rush to charge," as Michael Ballard has put it, meant there would be little time for preparation. No scaling ladders were constructed to enable troops to cross or climb out of the ditch in front of Rebel works. McPherson and McClernand would barely have enough time to move forward, examine the terrain, and place assault troops before 2:00 P.M. Only Sherman was in place, but he faced the strongest part of Pemberton's line, the sector from Stockade Redan to Fort Hill. Grant reasoned that even a poorly prepared rush could take his men over the works and into Vicksburg before the opportunity to consummate the campaign ended.[3]

PREPARATION

Blair pushed his division skirmish line farther out and evaluated reports of the terrain. Col. Thomas Kilby Smith personally examined the ground along Graveyard Road but did not like what he saw: the "hills and knobs being exceedingly precipitous, intersected by ravines in three directions, the bottom treacherous, filled with sink holes, concealed by dried grass and cane; the whole covered by abatis of fallen timber from a dense forest cut six months or more ago, affording spikes . . . most difficult to surmount." He noted that Graveyard Road snaked along the top of a narrow ridge and had a cut that could restrict troop movement along the roadway.[4]

Stockade Redan stood out as a heavy bastion of the opposing line, anchoring the angle where Lockett's position turned south. From Blair's post, the parapet seemed ten feet high and the ditch five feet deep and ten feet wide. The nature of the topography, combined with many felled trees, presented a tactical problem never equaled in the experience of the Army of the Tennessee.[5]

Since Blair's was the only division well placed to assault, his was the first artillery to open fire. Some batteries began at 8:00 A.M. while others started three hours later. Steele's artillery opened at 10:00 A.M. By 12:45 the pounding worried Confederate officers. Forney warned Lockett that Union guns enfiladed parts of his line near Graveyard Road. He asked the engineer to send an officer familiar with the work to investigate.[6]

Along the Confederate line, Rebel troops crouched in their trenches to escape the worst of the artillery fire. Some men of the 26th Louisiana, finding the trenches too hot, fell back twenty yards into the shade of a few trees.

Stockade Redan, 1899. Taken when the Vicksburg National Military Park was created, and after most of the small trees and undergrowth were removed, this image portrays the rugged terrain along Graveyard Road and around Stockade Redan. Thomas Kilby Smith's brigade advanced in line, straddling the road, and Giles A. Smith's brigade advanced in line across the deep ravine well off to the right of this picture on May 19. (Vol. 111, 5720, Massachusetts Commandery, Military Order of the Loyal Legion and the U.S. Army Military History Institute)

Shells overshooting the line tore through the woods, knocking down limbs that proved as dangerous as shell fragments.[7]

Col. Winchester Hall stayed with his 26th Louisiana in the works. He disciplined an eager lieutenant named Richard West of Company K, who became overly excited. "He stood up fully exposed" and challenged the Federals "to come on." Hall yelled for West to get down, but the lieutenant turned and said, "Colonel do you order me to get down?" Hall said yes. "Well, if you order me to get down, I will get down."[8]

Hall felt it was important to reinforce the mood of his men as they endured their first fire. He paced calmly fifteen steps behind the works so the parapet and the lay of the land would offer him some protection. In early afternoon he felt something "strike the calf of my right leg, as though a clod had been thrown against it; in a moment I became dizzy." He sat on the ground and felt as if he would faint. An orderly provided whiskey, which

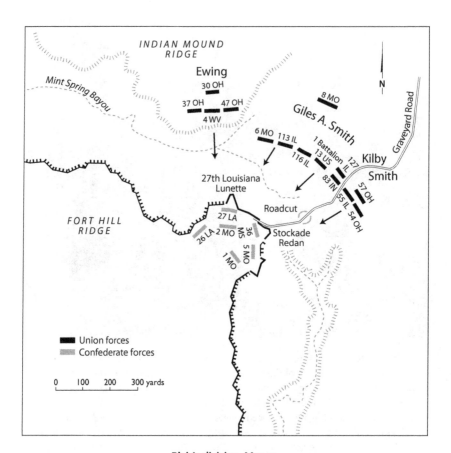

INDIAN MOUND RIDGE

Mint Spring Bayou

Ewing

30 OH

37 OH   47 OH

4 WV

8 MO

Giles A. Smith

6 MO   113 IL

116 IL

1 Battalion   127
13 US

Kilby

Smith

83 IN   55 IL   57 OH   54 OH

Graveyard Road

N

27th Louisiana Lunette

Roadcut

27 LA

26 LA 2 MO   36
MS

5 MO

1 MO

Stockade
Redan

FORT HILL
RIDGE

■■■ Union forces
▬▬▬ Confederate forces

0   100   200   300 yards

Blair's division, May 19

revived the colonel until a stretcher party could carry him to a sheltered place in a wagon roadcut—the Federal artillery fire was too heavy to risk going back to town. Lt. Col. William C. Crow took command of the 26th Louisiana. As Hall lay in the roadcut, a stray bullet from the skirmishing that was taking place a few hundred yards away struck him and inflicted a flesh wound. "I was exceedingly nervous," Hall recalled. "I knew the regiment was hotly engaged, and my anxiety was strung to its highest pitch." He must have been anxious about his own safety as well, for there seemed to be no safe place. Hall waited until dark before stretcher-bearers carried him to his quarters, where his wife took charge of him about midnight.[9]

With an open landscape, it became obvious by early afternoon that the Yankees were preparing for an assault. Pemberton authorized the deployment of his reserve on the north face, mainly to bolster the key angle at Graveyard Road. Four regiments of Cockrell's Brigade moved into the works, leaving one regiment as a reserve. Cockrell shifted the 1st Missouri and 5th Missouri into Stockade Redan to help Hébert's 36th Mississippi. The 2nd Missouri moved to a point behind the 27th Louisiana, and the 6th Missouri shifted to support Vaughn's Brigade on the extreme left. The 3rd Missouri remained in reserve. Cockrell's men received new Enfield rifles early on May 19 and now had a chance to try them.[10]

Blair readied his division for action. Kilby Smith formed his brigade in line across Graveyard Road, placing the 83rd Indiana right of the roadway and the 127th Illinois to its rear. The 55th Illinois took position to the left of the road. Kilby Smith received the attack order by 11:30 A.M. with more than two hours for final preparation. At 1:00 P.M. he called in his skirmishers, including the 54th Ohio, which had been strung out to make contact with McPherson's skirmishers to the south. While his other skirmishers rejoined their parent units in the brigade, Kilby Smith placed the 54th Ohio to the left of the 55th Illinois. He passed on word of the pending attack to all regimental leaders and placed Col. Benjamin J. Spooner of the 83rd Indiana in charge of his right wing (the 83rd Indiana and 127th Illinois). Kilby Smith personally supervised the left wing. He also positioned the 57th Ohio to the rear of his left wing, behind the 55th Illinois and 54th Ohio, to follow up the other units as a support.[11]

KILBY SMITH

At precisely 2:00 P.M. Capt. Levi W. Hart's Battery H, 1st Illinois Light Artillery, fired three rounds in quick succession from four pieces as the signal for the assault. Blair proudly reported that his entire division stepped off at the same moment that the guns sounded. His left wing, Kilby's Smith's brigade, was the first to draw attention from Confederate artillery. To the right of the road, the 83rd Indiana and 127th Illinois advanced across brush and felled timber that broke their lines "and scattered to a considerable extent the men," reported Col. Hamilton N. Eldridge of the 127th Illinois. "The Order was given forward boys forward," Andrew McCormack told his family, "and away we went over the hills [and] over logs helter skelter the balls coming thick and fast men falling wounded and killed on every side, but we pressed on loading and firing as fast as we could."[12]

Kilby Smith's left wing was forced to cross two narrow ravines that jutted south from Graveyard Road. These features were "very steep and difficult to pass over under the most auspicious circumstances," wrote Lt. Col. Cyrus W. Fisher of the 54th Ohio. Kilby Smith instructed Fisher to guide his regiment on the movements of the 55th Illinois to the right. Fisher passed on that instruction to his color-bearer, but the men became disorganized due to the rough terrain. Kilby Smith ordered the brigade to stop three times during its advance in order to dress the ranks before moving on.[13]

The brigade struggled on until it reached a terrain feature that jutted south from Fort Hill Ridge about 150 yards from Stockade Redan. Kilby Smith's left wing stopped behind the welcome shelter of its crest. The men seemed "thoroughly exhausted." On the right wing there were no well-defined terrain features to tempt the men, so they continued struggling forward, making it nearly to the foot of the parapet of Stockade Redan. Here most members of the 83rd Indiana and 127th Illinois took some degree of cover behind undulations of the slope fifty yards from the enemy. There are reports that the flags of both regiments were planted on the parapet by enterprising color-bearers.[14]

By this time Kilby Smith had lost sight of his right wing, its position shielded from view by the terrain. He walked up the embankment of the cut and saw the colors of his two regiments near the base of the enemy works. He also saw that his command was unsupported to the right. Col. Giles A. Smith's brigade had difficulty crossing the deep ravine north of Stockade Redan. Only a portion of the 13th U.S. Infantry had been able to come up to the right of the 83rd Indiana and 127th Illinois. To the left, McPherson's men were nowhere to be seen. Kilby Smith decided to stay where he was, the crest offering some degree of shelter.[15]

Kilby Smith sent one of his aides to report the situation to Blair and received an answer that Sherman wanted all units to close on the works and then "to jump in when they began to yield." Sherman also reported that McPherson was working forward to the south, that Grant was observing the Fifteenth Corps attack, and that Federal artillery would silence the opposing guns. None of this impressed Kilby Smith, but he ordered his left wing to fix bayonets and prepare to advance on the entrenchments. Then, "upon closer view, I discovered the works too steep and high to scale without proper appliances; a few men could have gotten over by the aide of a ladder of bayonets or digging holes in the embankment, but these would have gone to destruction." Kilby Smith disobeyed orders and stayed put. He ordered up ample supplies of ammunition and ordered his regimental leaders to detail sharpshooters and snipe at the Confederates. The heavy fire his left wing lay down helped support the right wing in its close position to the works.[16]

Fisher's 54th Ohio had already used up most of its ammunition while on the skirmish line. It obtained a resupply just before the advance started, but someone had made a mistake. The ammunition boxes were marked on the outside with the right caliber, but when the men opened them, they found they contained a different caliber. Soon after taking up the stationary position, Kilby Smith replaced the 54th Ohio with the 57th Ohio. Fisher moved his men seventy-five paces to the rear and arranged for proper cartridges.[17]

Kilby Smith's brigade received fire not only from the 5th Missouri and 36th Mississippi in Stockade Redan but from other Confederate units. The right wing received some fire from the 27th Louisiana Lunette before the rest of Blair's division approached that work. The left wing received fire from Confederate units located south of Stockade Redan, the 37th Mississippi and 7th Mississippi Battalion aiming left oblique at the brigade. Two guns located in works at Jackson Road could reach Kilby Smith as well. They included a twenty-pounder Parrott and a three-inch Ordnance rifle.[18]

GILES A. SMITH

To the right, Giles A. Smith's brigade started advancing at 2:00 P.M. Word had circulated through the ranks that an assault was pending, so many men gave their valuables to comrades who were to stay behind. Smith arrayed his units with the 1st Battalion, 13th U.S. Infantry, on the left, connecting with Kilby Smith's right flank. Then he placed the 116th Illinois, the 113th Illinois, and the 6th Missouri on the right, connecting with Ewing's brigade. Smith positioned the 8th Missouri on the crest of a spur to act as a reserve and fire over the heads of the other regiments as they attacked.[19]

The impediments to Smith's advance were daunting. A deep ravine with steep sides intervened between his starting point and the objective, a distance of 300 yards, and a great deal of cut timber lay in the bottom. When the brigade advanced, its alignment wavered and broke apart. Henry C. Bear of the 116th Illinois tripped and fell five times going down the ravine slope because one of his legs was lame. The troops lost touch of elbow and broke into small groups and individuals.[20]

Then the Confederates opened fire. It was "absolutely blinding," recalled J. J. Kellogg of the 113th Illinois. "The very sticks and chips scattered over the ground were jumping under the hot shower of rebel bullets." Kellogg was marching on the far right of his regiment only a few steps from a lieutenant of the 6th Missouri. Because of the heat that afternoon, the lieutenant was dressed in a white shirt with his sleeves rolled up. Soon the Missouri officer "lunged forward upon the ground." Kellogg kept moving but glanced back and remembered the sight of "a circle of red forming on his shirt back."[21]

On the far left of Giles Smith's brigade the regulars gained an enduring fame that afternoon. The 13th U.S. Infantry was a new unit; seven companies had been organized at St. Louis in May 1861, with William T. Sherman as the unit's colonel. Many Iowans joined the regiment. The seven companies were provisionally designated the 1st Battalion, with a second battalion authorized but never created before the war ended. Capt. Edward C. Washington, a grandnephew of George Washington, led the 1st Battalion, and Sherman's adopted brother, Capt. Charles Ewing, led Company A. Capt. L. E. Yorke brought 120 recruits to the battalion on the forenoon of May 18, just in time for the assault the next day. Sgt. Robert M. Nelson of Company B drew the 250 men in the battalion forward by carrying the regimental colors, while Sgt. James E. Brown of Company C carried the national colors. Just before Smith ordered the advance, Brown asked Capt. Theodore Yates if the flags were to be a few steps ahead of the battalion or even with its front. "Sergeant, you can see a little of what is before us," replied Yates. "We shall not be able to preserve much of a line, but the flag must be the first up."[22]

Brown and Nelson led the way down the slope and into the felled timber lining the ravine's bottom. Brush, cane, and fallen logs disrupted the formation and scattered the troops. "Each man got along as best he could," recalled Joseph C. Helm. According to the most convincing evidence, Washington was shot while crossing a fence that lay along the bottom of this ravine, although some members of the battalion insisted he was hit closer to the enemy line. Wherever it occurred, Robert M. Nelson saw the captain "quiver" and tried to help him. Washington unfastened his sword belt, took out his pocketbook and watch, and gave command to Charles Ewing. Sherman's foster brother led the battalion over the fence, through the remaining timber, and up the opposite slope of the ravine.[23]

Near the top of the slope, color-bearer Brown fell. Cpl. Daniel Payne picked up the flag and then fell, to be followed by Cpl. Edward Maher, who also was killed. Ewing grabbed the flag and continued to push uphill. He approached the north side of Stockade Redan, facing close-range fire by the 36th Mississippi. Twenty-five yards short of the work, Ewing sat on a stump to catch his breath but waved the flag to inspire the men. Color-bearer Nelson continued with the regimental colors until he gained the ditch at the foot of the parapet, where he planted the flag. Nelson would later be credited with placing the first U.S. banner on the land defenses of Vicksburg. Perhaps inspired by Nelson's accomplishment, Ewing stood on the stump and continued waving the national colors. A single Minié ball tore into his right thumb and nearly severed the staff. Soon another bullet passed through his

Charles Ewing. Brother-in-law and foster brother of William T. Sherman, Capt. Charles Ewing of Company A, 1st Battalion, 13th U.S. Infantry, became conspicuous for taking up the battalion's national colors and advancing them close to Stockade Redan on May 19. He also led the battalion after its commander fell partway through the advance. Ewing later served on Sherman's staff for most of the rest of the war and ended it as a brigadier general of volunteers. He briefly served as a captain in the regular army after Appomattox and then practiced law in Washington, D.C. (Library of Congress, LC-DIG-cwpb-06582)

hat. Col. Benjamin J. Spooner of the 83rd Indiana also stood on a stump near Ewing, waving his sword to encourage the troops. At least ten men of the battalion made it into the ditch of the redan but found it to be "our almost living grave," as Washington W. Gardner put it.[24]

Hugh Ewing, moving forward with his own brigade to the right, later estimated that seventy members of the 1st Battalion managed to get into the ditch of Stockade Redan. They could do little more than protect the two flags. Fire sailing in on both flanks "nearly annihilated us." Gardner dug small holes in the scarp to serve as footholds for an attempt to scale the parapet, but the men in the ditch received no support from those outside and never tried to crawl up. Some members of the 116th Illinois reached the ditch to the right of the battalion's position. After a while the 8th Missouri, delivering cover fire for the brigade, began to endanger its comrades by firing too short. Federals lodged outside the ditch began to be hit, and Ewing ordered the regulars to fall back a few yards for their own safety. John A. Phelan of Company C became so angry at the Missourians that he was ready to fire back at them.[25]

Most of Giles Smith's men failed to get that far. J. J. Kellogg of the 113th Illinois found a tree trunk two-thirds of the way from the starting point toward the Rebel line, somewhere near the crest of the Confederate slope. He and a corporal took cover behind it and waited for their comrades to catch up. Meanwhile, a canister ball tore into the corporal's ankle, and Kellogg helped him cut off what was left of his shoe just as the remnant of their company passed by. Kellogg stood and quickly surveyed the situation; he saw his colonel and the regimental colors off to the left, still heading forward, but an artillery shell exploded so near them that he decided to head toward the right. There were some men of his company lying in a shallow gully in that direction.[26]

Kellogg counted seventeen men in that gully besides himself; most of them tried to lay down a covering fire for their comrades. They had to lie on their backs to reload and roll over to fire. The enemy targeted their little group, and bullets lopped off short cane stalks surrounding the gully. Here the group lay for the rest of the afternoon. One man among them was killed and five were wounded by dusk. "Such a long dreadful day it was," recalled Kellogg, "without food or water, under the excessive heat of the sun, lying flat in that old gully, but hardly daring to move a limb or change our position for fear of attracting a rebel volley."[27]

From the Confederates' viewpoint, Giles Smith's brigade seemed to emerge from the depths of the ground at 2:00 P.M. and swarmed in unorganized masses toward their position. Most of the Federals who got close to the works stopped twenty to thirty feet away, but a handful managed to plant two flags at the redan. Of course the Confederates could not capture those banners, but they could keep the Federals pinned down, creating a tactical stalemate that benefited the Confederates. Rebel troops held their weapons over the parapet and pulled the triggers at Federals who were lodged close to the bank.[28]

To the right of Giles Smith, Hugh Ewing's brigade had only recently caught up with Blair's division. After pushing eighty-five miles from Grand Gulf in three days, Ewing's men had reached the battlefield about midnight of May 18–19. Along the way they gathered up 203 stragglers from Maj. Gen. William W. Loring's Division. Ewing placed his men to the right of Giles Smith, the 47th Ohio on his left, the 4th West Virginia in the center, and the 37th Ohio on the right, with the 30th Ohio in reserve. The three regiments in line fixed bayonets and contemplated the deep ravine that separated them from the 27th Louisiana Lunette. Ewing firmed up his men's spirits by telling them that "it would be a short job, and that we would be inside of the works, in less than ten minutes after receiving the order to move."[29]

When Ewing started at 2:00 P.M. his men descended the slope with difficulty. The left wing of the 47th Ohio found the going relatively easy near the foot of the slope. These five companies passed through an open field on the bottom of the ravine and moved to the base of Fort Hill Ridge. But the right wing of the 47th Ohio, plus the 4th West Virginia, crossed the end of Indian Mound Ridge and then traversed Mint Spring Bayou to reach the same position. The 37th Ohio, on the far right, found the going too difficult and did not make it to the base of Fort Hill Ridge. In fact, three companies of the 37th Ohio had been detached as skirmishers to make contact with Steele's division. By the time they returned, the brigade had already advanced, so the three companies took position on top of the ridge Ewing started from and fired long-distance.[30]

Only the 47th Ohio and 4th West Virginia lodged "very near" to the 27th Louisiana Lunette. Ewing's other two regiments failed to close in on the base of the slope. This sector of the Confederate line was held by the 26th and 27th Louisiana, with the 1st Missouri in reserve. The 27th Louisiana Lunette was a half-circle parapet just to the left of the stockade's end. It was crowded with the 556 members of the 27th Louisiana. For the time, the two Federal regiments were mostly sheltered from enemy fire as long as they rested at the foot of the ravine slope.[31]

But regimental commanders urged their men on, and the 47th Ohio and 4th West Virginia began to climb. They mostly fronted the 27th Louisiana, enabling the 26th Louisiana on the left to deliver "a galling flank fire" on the two regiments as they crawled uphill. "Our fire staggered him," reported Shoup, "but the fragments of several regiments succeeded in gaining the cover of" an undulation in the ground just short of the earthwork. A color-bearer took shelter in a clump of bushes and waved his flag "as though he would stay there."[32]

The two Louisiana regiments seemed to need help, so Cockrell sent Lt. Col. Pembroke S. Senteny's 2nd Missouri to the lunette at 2:30 P.M. The Missourians moved for a mile along the inside of the Confederate line from left to right, exposed to Steele's skirmish fire wherever the works were low and losing several men along the way. When they arrived Col. L. D. Marks refused to let Senteny's men relieve his 27th Louisiana, so the Missourians lay down to the rear of the lunette. Cockrell also rushed the 6th Missouri behind Senteny's regiment. It lost 20 men moving across open ground. By this time the Federals settled into protected places 40 to 100 yards away, with a group of them occupying a house twenty paces in front of the line. Both sides kept up a sniping fire for the rest of the afternoon. A section of guns in the lunette worked by Landis's Missouri Battery suffered a great deal because the parapet was too low. They "were compelled to load and handle them in a kneeling posture," recalled Ephraim McDowell Anderson. Even so the battery lost six men to Union fire.[33]

By about 4:00 P.M. Ewing arranged for a renewed push, which he hoped to coordinate with a renewal of Giles Smith's attack. Ewing shifted the 37th Ohio, which had failed to close on Fort Hill Ridge, over to his left. He also moved the 30th Ohio from its reserve position to join the 37th Ohio. His plan was to advance both regiments along the same path taken by the 47th Ohio and the 4th West Virginia, since that line of approach was less obstructed by natural impediments. The two regiments would advance at a prearranged signal, and immediately after that the division artillery would open fire.[34]

The carefully laid plan fell apart before it started. The artillery officers became confused and opened fire before the attack signal was given. Moreover, officers in the 47th Ohio and 4th West Virginia assumed this barrage was to cover their retreat. As a result, both regiments fell back down the ravine slope. There was no point in going on, so Ewing canceled the attack by the 37th Ohio and 30th Ohio.[35]

This ended the first Federal effort to break into Vicksburg. Blair's division mounted a serious attack and it was bluntly repulsed. Two of Kilby Smith's regiments lodged fifty yards from the Rebel works with their colors planted on the edge of the fortifications. Three of Kilby Smith's other regiments got stuck 150 yards from the target. In Giles Smith's brigade, some members of two regiments managed to gain the ditch of the Confederate fortifications and plant two flags in the dirt. Only two of Ewing's regiments got close to the Confederate earthworks, but they failed to cross them.

Thomas Kilby Smith. Born in Massachusetts and moving with his family to Ohio at an early age, Kilby Smith graduated from Cincinnati College and entered the law profession. Most of his prewar life, however, was spent in holding government positions, including that of U.S. marshal in southern Ohio. Kilby Smith commanded the 54th Ohio early in the war and as a colonel ably led a brigade during the summer of 1863. A sensitive man, he emotionally felt the loss of his men during their advance along Graveyard Road on May 19. Kilby Smith was later promoted to brigadier general and took part in the Red River campaign of 1864. (Library of Congress, LC-USZ62–90937)

"The assault of the 19th was the most murderous affair I was ever in," Kilby Smith told his mother. He had witnessed "no such slaughter in so brief a space of time. . . . God! What a charge it was! Talk of Balaklava—it sinks into insignificance." He remained distraught over the loss of his men for a long while. They were shot down unsupported on either flank, a claim that was to some degree true. The 127th Illinois lost eight killed and thirty wounded, amounting to 17.5 percent of the men taken into action. The 54th Ohio lost one killed and thirteen wounded, the 57th Ohio five killed and twelve wounded, and the 55th Illinois suffered the loss of 9.6 percent of its manpower.[36]

Kilby Smith's attack produced a great deal of suffering. For example, Capt. Thomas Sewell of Company G, 127th Illinois, was shot early in the advance when he turned briefly to call out an order to his men. A newspaper man by trade, he had worked as a printer for the *Utica Herald* in New York before moving to Chicago to work for the *Tribune*. The ball cut into Sewell's side and he was forced to wait for assistance after the regiment had moved forward. Two stretcher-bearers finally arrived and carried him to the rear "amidst a perfect [storm] of shot and shell."[37]

The most famous personal story to emerge from the Kilby Smith attack involved a drummer boy named Orion P. Howe. His father was principal musician of the 55th Illinois and took Orion and older brother Lyston Howe to war with him. Orion volunteered to carry fresh cartridges from the ordnance wagon to the regiment while it was lodged 150 yards from Stockade Redan. When he started back, Col. Oscar Malmborg called out for him to remember to bring only .54-caliber cartridges. Howe was slightly wounded in the leg during his walk to the rear, but he made his way to Sherman's command post and told him of Malmborg's need. Then Sherman told the boy to find a surgeon. He made a few steps and turned to yell at the general "Calibre 54!" as he continued to head toward the rear. Sherman was astonished that such a young boy would have the presence of mind to make sure his mission was complete. "I'll warrant the boy has in him the elements of a man," Sherman supposedly said at the time.[38]

Howe became a minicelebrity because of what happened on May 19. Sherman recommended him as a midshipman in the U.S. Navy because he was too young to be admitted to the U.S. Military Academy. That appointment never took place and Howe continued to serve with the 55th Illinois, but his exploit produced great interest in the North. George Boker wrote a maudlin and patriotic poem titled "Before Vicksburg, May 19, 1863," which was published in the *Atlantic Monthly* in September 1864. Howe was wounded a second time on May 28, 1864, near Dallas during the Atlanta campaign while serving as an orderly at Giles Smith's headquarters. After his recovery Abraham Lincoln appointed Howe as a cadet at the U.S. Naval Academy. He was examined on June 25, 1864, and found to be deficient in academic studies. Allowed one year to catch up, he finally became a cadet in July 1865, but it was no use. Howe's grades were not up to standard and he left the academy after two years of effort. The young man served in the merchant service, during which he survived the wreck of the *Thornton* off the Irish coast in November 1867. He later became a Texas cowboy. According to Henry S. Nourse, a veteran of the 55th Illinois, a "slangy plagiarism" of the Boker poem appeared along "with a full-page illustration" of the incident in *Harper's Weekly* on August 22, 1885. Two years later Howe returned to Illinois where he and brother Lyston ran a harness business. Orion later became a dentist in Buffalo, New York, and died after he moved to Denver.[39]

Howe's fame paled in comparison to that accorded the regulars in Giles Smith's brigade. "On the 19th the Battalion made its name," proudly reported Charles Ewing to his father. According to the unit's adjutant, seven men carried the colors during the attack; two were killed and five were wounded. The flags were saved but torn to rags. Battalion members counted eighteen holes in the cloth of the national flag and recalled that two canister pieces and one bullet hit the staff. The regimental flag sported fifty-six holes. Out of 250 men involved in the charge, seventy-one fell that day, for a loss ratio of 28.4 percent. Some reckonings of casualties in the battalion ran as high as 43 percent.[40]

The blunt repulse registered with the survivors of Giles Smith's brigade. "Thare was a sat mistack mate in timing to tack the rebel strong hold by storm," Ebenezer Werkheiser of the 116th Illinois told his siblings. "Our hol line was repulst." As surgeons worked through the night of May 19, clerks tallied the cost in life and limb. Out of 240 men participating in the 116th Illinois, between sixty and seventy (or 25 to 29 percent) were lost that day. Like Sewell, Henry Bear of the 116th Illinois was shot in the side. "The ball went in through where the ribs join and I suppose lodged there," he reported to his wife. "I can go around, give water to the boys and am quite lively and am very thankful it is no worse. It may prove worse than I think as the Ball is still in there yet but I hope not." A month later Bear was doing well in the hospital at Milliken's Bend, although he did not indicate whether surgeons had yet removed the ball. "I will soon be able to go at them again. May be I will help to take Vicksburg yet."[41]

Ewing's brigade lost heavily as well—246 men. Lt. James W. Dale of the

4th West Virginia was wounded in the foot and fell into Confederate hands. He was paroled and sent into Union lines across the Mississippi where he recuperated in the convalescent camp near Milliken's Bend.[42]

STEELE

While Blair fought his division with energy if not success, Steele positioned his men with little effort to fulfill Grant's order for a general attack. He spent the morning following up the Confederate withdrawal from Indian Mound Ridge. When his troops occupied the ridge, they realized the new Confederate line was 500 to 600 yards away on the other side of Mint Spring Bayou. A few Yankees also found some food carelessly left by their opponents. "Plenty of corn meal mollassus honey meat & c and you believe we had a good breakfast," reported James Thomas of the 25th Iowa.[43]

Both sides settled into new positions as the morning progressed. The Confederates had plenty of artillery arrayed along Fort Hill Ridge. On Baldwin's sector alone there were a dozen pieces including five different calibers. The Federals deployed field batteries, which at the time were hardly more numerous and not as heavy as the largest calibers on Baldwin's line. Capt. Clemens Landgraeber's Battery F, 2nd Missouri Light Artillery, was compelled to race over rugged terrain for half a mile "under a tremendous fire" of both artillery and small arms to obtain a position.[44]

Col. Charles R. Woods's brigade held the right near the river, while Col. Francis H. Manter's brigade held the center and Brig. Gen. John M. Thayer's brigade secured the left. Then Steele shifted right to connect with Walnut Hills by 8:30 A.M. Most of his men understood the significance of gaining control of the Yazoo River bluff. "We hav traveled to get here 175 miles," wrote Robert Bruce Hoadley of the 26th Iowa, "and it is about 12 miles to whare we started from."[45]

A house owned by Martha Edwards, 300 yards southwest of Woods, protected Confederate sharpshooters who harassed Landgraeber's battery. Woods sent Capt. Leo Rassieur and some men of the 30th Missouri to drive them out. From there, the Federals advanced an additional 300 yards southwest to occupy Indian Mound. Taking scope of their position, these Federals realized they were now only 150 yards from the bank of the Mississippi River and could overlook the northernmost water battery of four heavy guns that bore on the stream. They immediately opened fire on the battery and soon forced the Confederates to abandon it. To advance and occupy the water battery would have extended Rassieur's detachment too dangerously, so

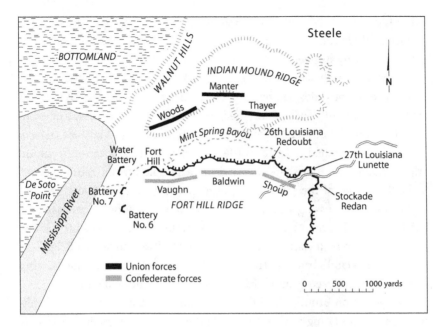

Steele's division, May 19

the Federals did not do so. After nightfall, the Confederates returned, constructed traverses to screen the exposed work, and put the guns back into action.[46]

At 9:30 A.M. Steele received the order to launch an attack at midafternoon. It is unknown how he planned to execute the order. What is known is that his division failed to conduct a coordinated effort. Woods's brigade on the right merely skirmished with the entrenched enemy on Fort Hill Ridge. The entire 25th Iowa participated in this skirmishing, each man firing about twenty rounds. The regiment lost seven men.[47]

In the center, Manter's brigade received instructions to attack at 2:00 P.M. The men were apprehensive but ready. "Here are the steepest hills and bluffs in confederate states," commented Maj. Abraham Jefferson Seay of the 32nd Missouri. His men prepared to "scale them with bayonets fixed ready to meet the foe." But just before the expected time, Manter issued an order canceling the attack. "A fortunate occurence for us," Seay admitted.[48]

On the left, Thayer advanced at 2:00 P.M., crossed Mint Spring Bayou, and received Confederate fire at the bottom of the ravine. It was "a perfect shower of Canister & Grape," according to Robert Bruce Hoadley of the 26th Iowa. He was convinced that half of Thayer's men would have fallen if the brigade had not taken shelter. They moved forward to the foot of Fort

Hill Ridge, where the profile of the slope protected them opposite the 26th Louisiana Redoubt. Thayer lost only a couple of dozen men in his advance, which was easily stopped by the 17th Louisiana.[49]

Sherman barely used Brig. Gen. James M. Tuttle's reserve division. He sent one of its brigades, led by Brig. Gen. Charles L. Matthies, on a march toward Walnut Hills well behind the Union line to support Steele's effort to secure the bluffs, but Steele accomplished that goal before Matthies arrived. The brigade marched back to Tuttle's division, making a ten-mile round trip by noon. Two hours later the division assembled for "a grand charge," as Harkness Lay of the 72nd Ohio put it. His regiment lost two killed and eight wounded crossing a couple of exposed bits of ground to reach the assembly point. The men were keyed up, expecting an order to attack at any moment. When Blair called for help at 3:00 P.M., Tuttle advanced Brig. Gen. Ralph P. Buckland's brigade. The 72nd Ohio lost twenty men while moving forward over exposed ground, but the brigade was not called into action. Lt. Col. Jefferson Brumbach of the 95th Ohio saw Blair "swearing & drinking from a whisky jug now & then." He did not know if Blair was intoxicated but wished all officers would swear off liquor during a battle. In contrast, Lucien B. Crooker saw Tuttle stand boldly in the open, arms folded and "sucking an old pipe," waiting for orders that never came.[50]

SHERMAN

The uneven nature of effort on Sherman's sector is striking. Blair commanded the only serious assault. Steele busied his men with too much positioning and failed to fulfill Grant's attack order. There was no place for Tuttle's division to attack except to duplicate the line of advance already charted by Blair.

Shoup repulsed Blair's attack, while Baldwin and Vaughn had a relatively easy time holding the line against Steele. Part of Baldwin's sector was held by Brig. Gen. Jeptha V. Harris's Mississippi State Troops. Consisting of Col. H. C. Robinson's regiment, Lt. Col. Thomas A. Burgin's battalion, and a battalion composed of stragglers from Loring's Division, Harris's troops were of questionable quality. Col. Claudius Wistar Sears of the 46th Mississippi referred to them as "wild Militia."[51]

At Pemberton's headquarters, the news of Sherman's repulse was received with gratification. "Feds press upon left," recorded a chaplain of Cockrell's command in his diary, "repulsed 6 times." But Shoup recalled the loss of Capt. Louis Florence of New Orleans, serving as an aide on his staff. "We were standing together in a battery of six-pounders and howitzers, when he turned to me in great excitement and said: 'See, General, they are running!' He fell, and never uttered another word." In addition, Shoup's adjutant "was shot ... while looking over my shoulder. Poor fellow! a minie ball struck him in the neck, and he died at once."[52]

While many Confederates recognized Blair's attack as "a Severe Battle," Shoup disagreed. In 1897 he told an interviewer that Sherman "moved out far enough to get a great many of his men killed, but he did not get near enough to make it seem anything more than a gratuitous slaughter."[53]

Sherman ignored the uneven efforts of his corps on May 19, reporting that the enemy works were "very strong." Charles Ewing told his father that Sherman exposed himself a great deal, "as he always will, and then at night wanted to persuade me that he took good care of himself." The mood of the Fifteenth Corps troops turned sour in the wake of their failed attacks. "We have received a very severe check," commented John Merrilles of Battery E, 1st Illinois Light Artillery, in his diary, "and everybody is badly discouraged." Merrilles spoke only for those Fifteenth Corps troops actively engaged in heavy action. McPherson's Seventeenth Corps and McClernand's Thirteenth Corps were still to be heard from.[54]

{ 4 }

I Hope Every Man Will Follow Me

SEVENTEENTH and THIRTEENTH CORPS, MAY 19

McPherson's Seventeenth Corps and McClernand's Thirteenth Corps failed to launch general attacks on May 19. The men were not in assaulting distance that morning, requiring more moving and positioning than Sherman's command was compelled to do. Grant's expectation of a general attack proved illusory, but that expectation could have been met if McPherson had been more active and McClernand had been able to reposition his corps more quickly. Circumstances prevented the latter from contributing more to the general effort, while native caution hamstrung the actions of the former. Grant's mode of command—to issue general instructions for the army and allow corps leaders to implement them by deciding the details on their own—failed to work in this case. McPherson and McClernand were not able to overcome the obstacles to a concerted, serious attack that they found in their corps sectors.

RANSOM

The only active effort along the Seventeenth Corps sector was contributed by Brig. Gen. Thomas E. Ransom's brigade. It had served as the van of McPherson's advance the day before. Ransom moved forward on the morning of May 19 along a ridge that separated the northern and southern forks of Glass Bayou. He aimed directly at the position of the 36th Mississippi of Brig. Gen Louis Hébert's Brigade, located halfway between Stockade Redan and Jackson Road, with the 37th Mississippi to its left and the 7th Mississippi Battalion to its right. After skirmishing forward, Ransom's troops reached good defensive ground 700 yards from the entrenchments by 11:00 A.M.[1]

Ransom laid plans after receiving an order from corps headquarters to attack at 2:00 P.M. His brigade was temporarily detached from Brig. Gen. John McArthur's division, which was operating along the Mississippi below Vicksburg, so he reported directly to McPherson. Ransom instructed Col. Thomas W. Humphrey to move his 95th Illinois closer to the enemy without exposing the regiment too much. Humphrey scouted the terrain and then advanced his men to shelter behind the second ridge from the Confederates. The rest of Ransom's brigade moved forward to align with the 95th Illinois about 500 yards from the enemy. The 17th Wisconsin arrived first, taking place to Humphrey's right as brigade skirmishers drove Rebel skirmishers back into their own works.[2]

While the two regiments waited for the rest of the brigade to close up, one of those mistakes that characterize military operations took place. The signal for attack was to be an artillery salvo, which was expected at 2:00 P.M. But Lt. Col. Thomas McMahon of the 17th Wisconsin became confused. Half a dozen batteries were in action against the Confederates, and this made it difficult to tell the regular firing from the anticipated signal. At seventeen minutes before 2:00 P.M., McMahon ordered his men forward. Humphrey, whose 95th Illinois lay immediately to McMahon's left, glanced at his watch to verify that it was not yet time to attack. But then he assumed that McMahon thought it was time — no one had synchronized their watches. Moreover, it would be useless for a lone regiment to attack the works, so Humphrey ordered his men forward. The rest of the brigade — 14th Wisconsin, 11th Illinois, and 72nd Illinois — were not yet up.[3]

This miscue doomed any possibility of success. McMahon's regiment moved downslope into the first of two ravines separating his starting point from the enemy and found a tangled cover of felled timber at its bottom. The 17th Wisconsin got hung up in this tangle, and its forward progress came to an abrupt halt.[4]

But Humphrey's 95th Illinois, to McMahon's left, managed to deal with the tangle, which was "an almost impenetrable abatis of felled timber, exposed to a direct and concentrated fire of musketry and a murderous enfilading fire," according to Humphrey. These rounds came from Confederate artillery located in Green's Redan to the north and the 3rd Louisiana Redan

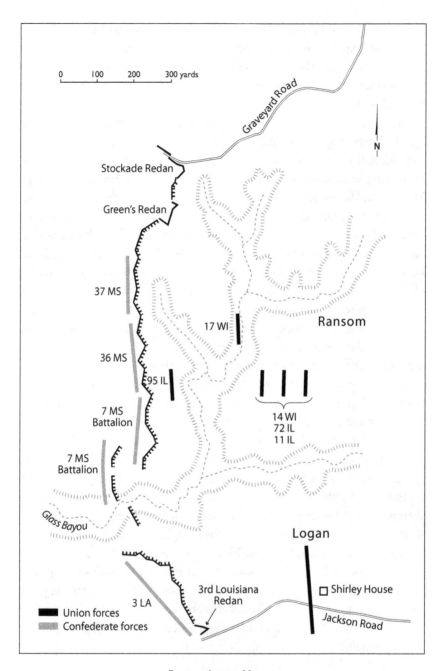

0   100   200   300 yards

Graveyard Road

N

Stockade Redan

Green's Redan

37 MS

17 WI

Ransom

36 MS

95 IL

7 MS
Battalion

14 WI
72 IL
11 IL

7 MS
Battalion

Glass Bayou

Logan

3rd Louisiana
Redan

Shirley House

3 LA

Jackson Road

■ Union forces
▨ Confederate forces

Ransom-Logan, May 19

to the south. Humphrey received a slight injury in the foot but maintained his post for the duration of the assault.[5]

When Ransom saw the 17th Wisconsin and 95th Illinois move forward, he had no choice but to urge the other three regiments on as well. It took some time for them to gain the ridge from which McMahon and Humphrey had started and then to continue forward into the tangled bottomland that lay ahead. Mostly following Humphrey's route, the three regiments managed to get through the tangle and up the next slope until they landed about 300 yards from the Confederate line with another, unknown ravine yet to cross. Ransom felt uncomfortable going any farther, as no Federal troops appeared to support his men.[6]

But Humphrey refused to stop until the 95th Illinois crossed the next ravine and ascended the opposite slope. His men got to the crest of the last ridge before the Rebel line, when prudence gained the upper hand and Humphrey ordered the regiment to halt. He was only 100 yards from the fortifications and utterly alone. It would be foolish to continue advancing and unnecessary at this point to fall back, so Humphrey stayed where he was for the rest of the day. Meanwhile his men sheltered themselves behind the crest of the ridge and fired at the enemy for hours.[7]

Humphrey wrote a note to Ransom explaining his situation. After some time, a reply arrived with encouraging news. "You have done well, nobly," wrote Ransom. "I desire that you hold your position. Do not expose your men or waste ammunition. I occupy the rear of the ridge back of you. Will move forward as soon as we can be supported on the right and left. I expect to hear from General McPherson."[8]

But the expected support never arrived. Sherman could not close the gap to Ransom's right and McPherson had no troops to close on Ransom's left. The brigade's contribution to Grant's attack had ended. Ransom waited until after dark before instructing Humphrey to fall back, and Humphrey waited until 4:00 A.M. of May 20 to do so. He lost seven killed and fifty-four wounded, or 15 percent of his manpower.[9]

The Confederates opposite Ransom's brigade were ready for an assault. Lt. Gen. John C. Pemberton had issued an order that day encouraging his men to be calm, to take aim deliberately, and to wait until the enemy came close. The order had its desired effect. James West Smith of the 37th Mississippi sought consolation in the Bible. He read from the ninety-first psalm "with peculiar interest" and "felt that I could claim the promise therein contained. Indeed I was both spiritually and physically strengthened, and believed I could go into battle without a dread as to the consequences."[10]

Thomas W. Humphrey. Born in Illinois, Humphrey became colonel of the 95th Illinois in Ransom's brigade. He survived both attacks against Vicksburg on May 19 and 22 only to be killed at the battle of Brice's Crossroads on June 10, 1864. (Vol. 130, 6654L, Massachusetts Commandery, Military Order of the Loyal Legion and the U.S. Army Military History Institute)

Smith estimated that the Federals appeared 200 yards away before his officers gave the order to fire. After that, everyone in the regiment peppered Humphrey's 95th Illinois. When the rest of Ransom's brigade made its appearance farther away, they turned their muskets on these other units. Smith fired a total of twenty-one rounds from his Enfield rifle during the course of the engagement on May 19.[11]

Despite his meager advance, Ransom turned in the most aggressive Seventeenth Corps effort on May 19. Humphrey's errant assault placed him in the closest position to the enemy on McPherson's sector. Two divisions operated south of Ransom's position but they did not coordinate their action with his isolated brigade. Nor did they do anything more than move closer to the Rebel line on May 19, firing their weapons. Grant's general attack became a general fizzle on the Seventeenth Corps sector.

LOGAN

Along Jackson Road, Maj. Gen. John A. Logan's division straddled the road-bed and began a cautious advance by 9:00 A.M. Logan's skirmishers preceding the line, the division endured artillery fire as it crept forward. Skirmishers of Brig. Gen. John E. Smith's brigade drove Rebel skirmishers out of a large white house owned by the Shirley family about 1,200 yards east of the 3rd Louisiana Redan. By 2:00 P.M., Logan's line advanced a bit more until it lay roughly 1,000 yards from the Confederate works, still too far from which to mount an assault over rugged terrain.[12]

The creeping advance served notice on Confederates north and south of Jackson Road to be ready. Surgeons prepared field hospitals in hollows that lay behind the line and detailed stretcher-bearers to handle the few litters available. Many of the bearers improvised more litters by using poles they found at various homesteads.[13]

But the time set by Grant for a general assault came and went. Logan rode his horse along the division line calling on his men to be brave. Col. Manning F. Force told his 20th Ohio the same thing. He "made his way in front of the different companies and spoke familiarly to his men words of encouragement," recalled Osborn Oldroyd. "Said he, 'boys, I expect we will be ordered to charge the fort. I shall run right at it, and I hope every man will follow me.'" But no attack took place.[14]

Logan's artillery chief positioned three batteries 2,500 yards from the Rebel works. The Confederates had only two pieces in the 3rd Louisiana Redan, a twenty-pounder Parrott worked by men of Capt. J. F. Waddell's Alabama Battery and a three-inch rifle operated by gunners of Lt. R. N. Cotten's Appeal (Arkansas) Battery. Other Rebel guns placed in works north and south of the 3rd Louisiana Redan scored some hits. In addition, accidents took a toll among Union artillerists. A gunner of Capt. Henry Dillon's 6th Wisconsin Battery suffered from the effects of a premature discharge. It tore off his left hand and forearm and his right hand. In addition, the blast "burned the side of his face and set his shirt on fire which he cried to have cut off," wrote Cpl. Gould D. Molineaux of the 8th Illinois.[15]

By day's end, the Seventeenth Corps merely closed in on the Rebel position rather than attacked in force. McPherson tended to be overcautious, and it rubbed off on his division leaders. Only Ransom, alone and detached as he was, made a sincere effort to fulfill Grant's directive. Without support on either flank, it is unlikely Ransom would have accomplished much even if McMahon had not botched the brigade attack.

MCCLERNAND

The Thirteenth Corps had farther to move but acted with more vigor than its neighbor to the north. McClernand infused a higher degree of energy into his command than McPherson and made sure his work was documented with reports. He had the added worry of holding down Grant's left flank, which fell far short of extending to a defensible feature such as the bank of the Mississippi. The ground his Thirteenth Corps troops contended with was even harder to negotiate than that which confronted McPherson.

The corps rested the previous night near Beechwood, about 3,000 yards from the Confederate line. By dawn McClernand and his staff were riding forward to high ground that offered a view of Two Mile Creek. From there they caught sight of the Rebel earthworks and gained some idea of the intervening ground. McClernand described it as "a series of deep hollows separated by narrow ridges, both rising near the enemy's works, and running at angles from them until they are terminated by the narrow valley of Two-Mile Creek. The heads of the hollows were entirely open. Nearer the termination they were covered with a thicket of trees and underbrush." Confederate skirmishers hidden in the thickets opened fire on McClernand's party.[16]

By 6:30 A.M. the troops moved in column along Baldwin's Ferry Road to McClernand's vantage point and deployed. The lead division, commanded by Brig. Gen. Andrew J. Smith, formed to the right of the road, its left flank resting at the roadbed, while Brig. Gen. Peter J. Osterhaus's division formed to the left of the road. Osterhaus had recovered enough from the slight wound inflicted by a shell fragment at the Big Black River to resume command of his division on May 18. Smith deployed Brig. Gen. Stephen G. Burbridge's brigade on his left and Col. William J. Landram's brigade on his right with two batteries to support the division. Because he had to protect Grant's left flank, Osterhaus placed Brig. Gen. Albert L. Lee's brigade in line south of the road. He then positioned Col. Daniel W. Lindsey's brigade behind Lee in a column of battalions. Both divisions occupied a feature called Durden's Ridge, just east of Two Mile Creek. McClernand placed Brig. Gen. Eugene A. Carr's division to the rear as a reserve for the corps. The Federals were still 2,000 yards, more than a mile, from the enemy.[17]

It took some time for the Thirteenth Corps to assemble on Durden's

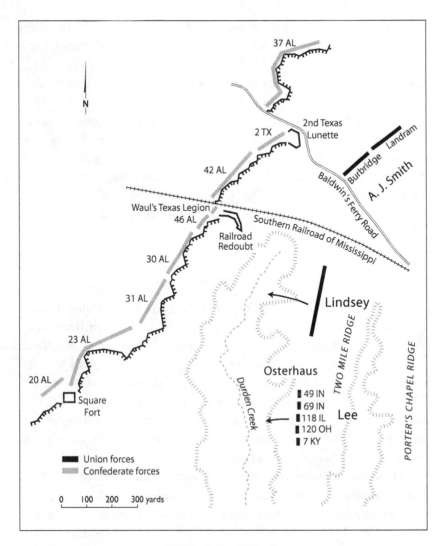

Thirteenth Corps, May 19

Ridge. When the deployment was nearly complete, McClernand received Grant's attack order at 10:30 A.M. Word filtered down the chain of command that everyone was to move as close as possible to the enemy works and participate in "a general charge" at 2:00 P.M. When A. J. Smith called his regimental commanders for a consultation, the officers received "in a quiet and serious manner" the news that they were to attack.[18]

When it began to advance, the Thirteenth Corps made a grand appearance descending Durden's Ridge into a wide valley filled with thickets that hid Confederate skirmishers. Federal skirmishers easily drove those Rebels out of the woods as the main formation followed behind them. The corps ascended the next rise of ground and stopped on top of Porter's Chapel Ridge 1,000 yards from the Confederate line. As Rebel artillery opened, McClernand's officers saw one more ridge between them and the entrenchments, a feature called Two Mile Ridge.[19]

"I was ordered to advance over rough and unexplored ground and attack the enemy's works," McClernand explained to Abraham Lincoln. He began his final push at 2:00 P.M. as scheduled but quickly encountered difficulties. Descending Porter's Chapel Ridge was easy enough, but ascending the irregular slope of Two Mile Ridge broke up formations. On reaching the top, Thirteenth Corps units were exposed to artillery fire at a range of 500 to 800 yards.[20]

OSTERHAUS

The left flank of the Thirteenth Corps, indeed of Grant's entire line at Vicksburg, faced Square Fort and found the going particularly tough. Even before starting the attack at 2:00 P.M., Lee's brigade of Osterhaus's division suffered from accurate artillery fire. Lee therefore instructed Col. Marcus M. Spiegel to place the 120th Ohio in a ravine a short distance west of the Porter's Chapel Ridge crest, where it was more sheltered. Later Lee moved the 7th Kentucky forward to Spiegel's left and the 118th Illinois to his right, also for better protection. The 69th Indiana lay to the right of the 118th, and the 49th Indiana held the brigade's right flank.[21]

On the signal to continue from Porter's Chapel Ridge at 2:00 P.M., Lee's men "advanced in splendid order" but were pummeled with what the brigade leader called "a most murderous and raking fire" of artillery from the front and left. The terrain consisted of "deep gorges and almost impassable ravines." "The poor fellows could hardly go at all," recorded Jeptha S. Dillon of the 118th Illinois in his diary. "Many of them did give out Climbing over so many steep hills." The brigade line began to break up and Lee tried to move each regiment forward by sheltering them with the "irregularities of ground." But his advance slowed to a crawl as regiments bunched together in a large ravine. Lee then tried to disperse the mass by shifting units to the right.[22]

Then Lee, with Col. James Keigwin of the 49th Indiana, went forward to the top of the ridge, where he saw yet another deep ravine between them and the enemy. Square Fort appeared a bit to the right. "We can't make it Col.," Lee told Keigwin. A smaller, narrow ridge extended toward the right, and

Albert L. Lee. Born in Fulton, New York, Lee graduated from Union College in Schenectady before moving to Kansas Territory, where he practiced law and served as a justice of the state supreme court after the territory was admitted to the Union in 1861. He entered military service as major of the 7th Kansas Cavalry before he was elevated to the command of an infantry brigade in McClernand's Thirteenth Corps at the rank of brigadier general. He survived his wound on May 19 and spent most of the rest of the war in command of cavalry in the Department of the Gulf. (Library of Congress, LC-DIG-cwpb-05805)

Lee ordered Keigwin to move the 49th Indiana along it by the flank until he was directly opposite Square Fort. Then he was to form line and charge. Lee promised to bring the rest of the brigade up as support. Keigwin started for his regiment, and Lee went back to the other units.[23]

When Lee reached the 120th Ohio he complimented the regiment to Colonel Spiegel. "By G——d Spiegel, you are a man after my own heart and your Regiment stands like a Rock; Aye the line is as straight as on Dress parade; take a drink with me." Soon after expressing that vigorous sentiment, Lee was wounded in the face. Many reports indicated the wound was caused by a shell fragment, but Lee reported that a bullet entered his right cheek and came out through the back of his neck. It was not a mortal wound but serious enough for him to give up command of the brigade to Keigwin. "Stick up to them boys," Lee called out as he made his way to the rear.[24]

The brigade reached Two Mile Ridge by the time Lee was hit and lodged 400 yards short of the Confederate line. The 49th Indiana moved forward as Lee had instructed and advanced close to Square Fort, but the rest of the brigade failed to advance farther because of Lee's wound — Keigwin remained with his regiment and did not exert control over the other units. "It was a fearful charge," commented Spiegel, "and never in my life did I see shell, [g]rape and so forth fly thicker."[25]

Lee's brigade had veered too far left during this advance because of the need to find protected lines of approach. By the time it reached Two Mile Ridge, a gap had developed between Lee's right and the left of Smith's division. Osterhaus noticed this in time to move Lindsey's reserve brigade forward to fill the gap. When Lindsey's men reached the ridge, they too settled behind its crest and opened fire on the enemy. Osterhaus also saw that his artillery advanced to the ridge, but his division had reached its high tide for the day.[26]

SMITH

A. J. Smith's division fared little better than Osterhaus's men. Upon setting out at 2:00 P.M. to the right of Baldwin's Ferry Road, the men cheered but soon the terrain got the better of them. The cheering stopped and the panting, pushing, and sweating started on this warm afternoon. Patches of brush and felled timber stood in the way and alignment broke up as regiments struggled to catch up with their neighbors. And the troops received quite a bit of artillery fire. As the 77th Illinois crossed "a high hill right in fair view of all their batteries," Rebel rounds knocked down twenty men "in a few minutes."[27]

But Smith stopped when he reached Two Mile Ridge. McClernand explained this halt by noting that "exhaustion and the lateness of the evening interrupted" the advance. His men had now reached the true staging point of an attack on the works. They needed to re-form, scout the ground ahead, and gauge the strength of the target. McClernand's comment that the day was too far advanced for all this to be done rings true.[28]

Seventeenth and Thirteenth Corps, May 19

For the Confederates who opposed Thirteenth Corps moves that day, the battle of May 19 was relatively easy. Only those sent out to skirmish had to brave enemy fire, while sheltering behind felled trees and terrain features. The Rebel skirmishers put up some resistance as they fell back. Col. Ashbel Smith lost only two men out of the two companies he sent forward to skirmish, even though they met the enemy half a mile from the 2nd Texas Lunette and fell back firing until they returned at 3:00 P.M.[29]

"I am on the line, looking to our general interests," Pemberton informed Maj. Gen. John S. Bowen. He authorized him to use discretion about sending reserve troops to threatened parts of the line while he was away from headquarters. Bowen maintained his division headquarters in a ravine located between the railroad and Jackson Road. When Martin L. Smith requested authority to order Bowen's men into his line if he thought it necessary, Pemberton refused. Bowen had to be "consulted as to the necessity of the movement, and, he concurring, the movement will be made, provided the general commanding cannot be consulted."[30]

In short, Pemberton wanted to maintain tight control over his reserves. When John H. Forney detected signs of McClernand's advance early that morning, he reported the news to army headquarters. Staff members relayed the information to Carter L. Stevenson and to Bowen, alerting both to be prepared to send reinforcements if called on. As Seventeenth and Thirteenth Corps advances petered out that evening, Pemberton worried that the Federals might assault Fort Hill the next day. He told Stevenson to be ready to move the handful of reserve regiments the division leader had pulled out of his line in case they were needed at Fort Hill. The Confederates had few reserve troops to spare, and most of Pemberton's energy was spent in trying to manage them on May 19.[31]

As evening descended, the Confederates continued girding for a prolonged siege at Vicksburg. Pemberton had issued a circular that morning asserting that the ammunition supply was limited and irreplaceable. He thought skirmishing was fruitless and should stop. "Soldiers; withhold your fire wait for the near approach of your enemy and then when each man is sure of his mark and each round counts . . . then fire one more round for Vicksburg." Another circular urged division leaders to clean up the offal resulting from slaughtering beef cattle and dump it in the Mississippi as a sanitary measure.[32]

Forty miles northeast of Vicksburg, Joseph E. Johnston spent May 19 in ignorance of the drama unfolding before its defenses. He was with Brig. Gen. John Gregg's Brigade near Vernon when Pemberton's letter of the previous day arrived. It informed him there would be no evacuation of Vicksburg, and Johnston was compelled to accept that decision. He ordered Gregg to Canton, fifteen miles east of Vernon and twenty miles north of Jackson. Johnston also moved Brig. Gen. States Rights Gist's Brigade from Jackson to Canton.[33]

"I am trying to gather a force which may attempt to relieve you. Hold out," Johnston wrote to Pemberton on May 19. Johnston also wrote to Franklin Gardner, commander of Port Hudson, and urged him to evacuate the place as it was now of little importance. William W. Loring finally joined Johnston on May 19 after wandering with his division for three days since he had been cut off from Pemberton at Champion Hill.[34]

MORALE

As far as everyone was concerned there was a real possibility that Johnston would descend on Grant. For the Federals, it produced an aching worry and for the Confederates a desperate dream. As Lt. Maurice Kavanaugh Simons of the 2nd Texas noted, everyone on the Rebel line believed it was possible to hold out for at least a few days until Johnston rescued them. But Simons did not necessarily believe Johnston was on the way, knowing "that these reports are often gotten up to encourage the men."[35]

The realization that they were trapped in Vicksburg sank into the minds of soldiers and civilians alike. Brig. Gen. Stephen D. Lee was friendly with Emma Balfour's family and advised her to take shelter in caves. One day the general asked "if we were provided with a rat-hole," according to Balfour. "I told him it seems to me that we were all caught in a rat-hole."[36]

But the Confederate mood began to change on May 19. Early that day Pemberton informed Jefferson Davis of the fights at Champion Hill and the Big Black River. "The army was much demoralized; many regiments behaved badly," he admitted. They now were waiting for an assault and had "considerably recovered their *morale*, but unless a large force is sent at once to relieve it, Vicksburg must before long fall."[37]

It is possible that the defeated soldiers of Stevenson's and Bowen's Divisions had regained much of their composure by May 19, but Vicksburg dentist Rowland Chambers saw Confederates "hiding in the hollows and behind trees" during the battle of May 19. In fact, seven or eight of them "crawled into our old cave and lay there all day just like so many scared dogs."[38]

When word circulated that the Federal attack had started at 2:00 P.M., Chaplain William Lovelace Foster of the 35th Mississippi became worried. He knew how demoralized some Confederates had become, and "a strange uneasiness and dread came over my mind." By evening word circulated that all attacks had been repulsed. "All my fears in reference to taking the place by storm now vanished," he wrote a few days later.[39]

"This inspired our troops," declared John Miller Leach of the 6th Missouri, "and they thought that if our enemy continued to charge our works, we would surely whip them." Another Missouri Rebel named Henry Martyn Cheavens argued that Confederate spirits "rose from the Slough of Despond and seemed to stand on firm ground once more. The feeling was, 'We can save half the war by keeping Vicksburg.'" The results of May 19 improved everyone's morale within the isolated city. "My men are in excellent spirits," Forney told Pemberton, "and will behave as they should." Lieutenant Simons of the 2nd Texas often heard his men "say that they will never disert the trenches that they would rather die than give up this place."[40]

Pemberton deserves some credit for bucking up his men's spirits. James West Smith noted that Pemberton's circular urging them to be cool and fire deliberately was helpful when he prepared for his first battle on May 19. "I never saw boys so cool in my life," Smith heard his lieutenant say of the troops.[41]

No one in Vicksburg was more relieved by the results of May 19 than Pemberton. That day was the acid test of his men's morale, of his decision to stand a siege, and of the prospects for salvaging victory from the disasters of May 16–17. Most Confederate soldiers who were tested on May 19 proved they were willing to fight.

Pemberton was aware that the troops tested on May 19 had not participated in the prior defeats. That is why he penned a letter to Stevenson, whose division had been at the epicenter of disaster on May 16. "It is with pride I refer to the admirable conduct of the men in the trenches," he wrote. "I trust and believe that your command will emulate the glorious example of their comrades."[42]

But what of Federal troops outside Vicksburg? They seem to have retained a positive mood and continued to assume that Grant would take the town pretty soon. Confederate sharpshooters seemed to cow behind their works, while Federal sharpshooters exposed themselves recklessly—so thought Lt. William Titus Rigby of the 24th Iowa, who took this as a sign of confidence among his comrades and despair among the enemy. Most Federals were still riding high on the effects of Champion Hill and the Big Black River. But that does not mean they were eager to attack earthworks or thought that storming Vicksburg was necessarily the right course of action.[43]

PORTER AND THE NAVY

Grant made contact with the navy on May 19. Porter's flagship, the *Black Hawk*, was tied up at Young's Point and fired rockets as a signal, which Steele's men acknowledged that morning. But it took a bit longer to establish a means of exchanging dispatches with the fleet. Capt. James M. McClintock, Sherman's signal officer, could not get the navy to acknowledge his flag waving, so he sent a signal officer by boat to the *Black Hawk*. That officer probably took along Grant's dispatch to Porter informing the admiral of his success in the overland march. "If you can run down and throw shell in just back of the city, it will aid us, and demoralize an already badly beaten enemy," Grant wrote.[44]

Porter became a popular correspondent as both Sherman and Steele sent him messages that morning. Sherman informed him that the right flank of his corps was on Walnut Hills and could use the aid of a couple of gunboats to bombard the water batteries and enfilade Martin L. Smith's position. Steele informed him that the line of bluffs extending northward from Vicksburg was in Federal hands and Grant's men needed rations as soon as possible.[45]

Porter had anticipated the generals. Lt. Cdr. James A. Greer had led a group of boats up the Mississippi from the south on the evening of May 18 to be in position to fire on the city the next day. Porter instructed Greer to bombard the enemy if he detected signs of a Federal land attack on the east side of Vicksburg. "The object is to disconcert the enemy and by firing shell at your longest range, you can do so."[46]

Greer made an effort but accomplished little. With ironclads uss *Benton*, uss *Tuscumbia*, uss *Carondelet*, and uss *Mound City*, plus ram uss *General Price*, he engaged the lower water batteries by 12:20 P.M. The *Benton* fired seven rounds at long range while the other vessels also fired, but Greer judged it would be too dangerous to go beyond the southern end of Grant's Canal, fearing the enemy could concentrate too many guns on his squadron if he ventured farther. Although the rounds fell around the main water battery, which contained a ten-inch columbiad, no serious damage was done, according to Confederate reports.[47]

When Porter learned of Greer's action, he instructed him to try again. In a directive dated 4:10 P.M., the admiral told Greer to proceed farther upstream but scatter the boats to present a less vulnerable target. Greer should move each vessel to further lessen their vulnerability, never staying in the same spot. "Fire heaviest charges and long ranges, and scatter your shot around the forts and town." Greer set out at 4:30 P.M. when three of the ironclads (*Benton, Tuscumbia,* and *Carondelet*) steamed upriver and engaged South Fort. The *Benton* fired fifty-five rounds with the others contributing to the bombardment until dusk put an end to it. The three vessels received no hits in return.[48]

Porter was still not satisfied. At 9:40 P.M. he complained to Greer that his earlier message urging him to arrange for night firing on the city had gone astray. Now he reiterated his instructions with clear details. Porter wanted the squadron to use ten-second fuses at 2,100 yards, which would necessitate steaming upstream from the mouth of the canal. After a short bombardment, each vessel should take turns shelling throughout the night. "The object is to throw shell about the courthouse, if possible." There would be little danger, as Confederate return fire "won't amount to much in the dark." Porter was desperate to help Grant. "The Army will likely go in to-morrow," he told Greer, "and we must do our share, even if the vessels suffer."[49]

Greer advanced the *Benton* and *Carondelet* above the mouth of Grant's Canal and opened fire as directed. The Confederates returned fire but, as Porter anticipated, without damage to the boats. The *Benton* expended a total of forty-three rounds, "then dropped down out of range." Greer did not mention whether he fulfilled Porter's instructions to have each vessel maintain an intermittent fire the rest of the night.[50]

As demonstrated by the naval action of May 19, there was little Porter could do to help Grant break into Vicksburg. His boats could deliver harassing fire on the city generally but could not pinpoint the sectors of Rebel lines targeted by Grant's attacks. But the navy played a vital role in reconnecting Grant with his river-based supply line.

SUPPLIES

The reestablishment of a supply line came none too soon. "Most of the boys entirely out of rations," commented Charles F. Smith of the 83rd Ohio, "and suffering much from lack of food." Grant ordered not only rations for his men but forage for his horses and mules to be sent to Lake's Landing at Chickasaw Bayou and instructed his corps commanders to empty all their wagons and send them to Lake's for the material. He asked Porter to convoy the supply vessels to the landing. The troops of Steele's division experienced the effects of this effort before any others because they were much closer to the new supply depots. "We have now plenty of rations," commented Pvt. Calvin Ainsworth of the 25th Iowa. "Never did hard tack and salt pork taste as well as it did tonight, washed down with a cup of good black coffee."[51]

EVENING OF MAY 19

Ainsworth enjoyed the fare because his regiment had not advanced close under Confederate guns that day. But for the men of Blair's division, the evening of May 19 was anything but pleasant. They held at the high tide of their attacks for half the afternoon under a hot sun.[52]

Thomas Kilby Smith thought his left wing, south of Graveyard Road, held a viable position behind the crest of a ridge within 150 yards of Stockade Redan. He believed he could stay there and dig in during the night. But Blair sent verbal instructions to fall back to his starting point under cover of darkness. Kilby Smith made his way back to division headquarters to talk it over with Blair. Even though Kilby Smith declared his spot to be "the best position to fortify in our whole front," Blair reiterated his instructions. The brigade commander insisted on written orders and Blair provided them.[53]

Then, just as he was returning to his brigade, the night sky erupted in light. The Confederates sent out details to burn houses near the earthworks because these buildings had sheltered Federal snipers during the day. Lt. Henry Gillespie led a detail from the 2nd Missouri to torch the Adam Lynd house located near the 27th Louisiana Lunette. His men captured eleven Federals at the house and removed two wounded officers and seventeen injured men who were sheltering behind the building. Then they burned the structure and returned to the works.[54]

Kilby Smith's right wing, under Col. Benjamin J. Spooner, had started to fall back just as Gillespie began to fire the house, which lay a couple of hundred yards away. Spooner's 83rd Indiana and 127th Illinois made it back to the Union line without incident. Kilby Smith pulled the left wing back in stages, beginning with the 55th Illinois at about midnight. The 57th Ohio retired from the ridge at 2:00 A.M. and was followed by the 54th Ohio, which retired one company at a time until the brigade was in its old position by 3:00 A.M.[55]

On Col. Giles A. Smith's sector, units fell back under cover of darkness and retraced their steps across the deep ravine to the starting point of their advance. J. J. Kellogg of the 113th Illinois found that confusion reigned as stragglers looked for their regiments and stretcher-bearers collected the wounded. No one could tell him where the 113th Illinois was gathering. "I was heartsick and tired," he recalled. Kellogg could hardly sleep because of all the activity and the chilly night.[56]

The Confederates were well aware of their success as evening descended. Kilby Smith's 83rd Indiana and 127th Illinois had planted flags quite near Stockade Redan within ten feet of the parapet, but the Confederates could not reach them. They "were either destroyed or taken away after dark," Forney told Pemberton. Martin L. Smith sent a flag recovered near the 27th Louisiana Lunette, along with fifty-two small arms and ten prisoners, to army headquarters. The color had been left by one of Ewing's regiments, and the prisoners came from Gillespie's house-burning sally.[57]

Pemberton made the most of the recovered Union flags. He wrote to Stevenson announcing "the complete failure of the enemy in his various assaults on our works to-day," estimated their losses as "very large," and claimed the Yankees lost three colors.[58]

But the Federals made the most of every flag they were able to save from their failed assault. Both colors of the 1st Battalion, 13th U.S. Infantry, were brought back that evening. Sgt. Robert M. Nelson saved the regimental flag and found that it contained eighteen bullet holes and the staff had been hit by two canister balls and one bullet. He also found four spent balls lodged in his clothing. Pvt. Patrick Maher brought in the national flag with fifty-six bullet holes and the staff broken into three parts. Sherman insisted that the regimental colors be placed in front of his tent because it was the flag his foster brother had carried. Capt. Charles Ewing was lucky: the bullet that cut into the staff while he held it merely took "the flesh out between the first and second joint" of his forefinger but did not injure the bone.[59]

The grisly task of collecting the dead and injured from the battlefield continued under cover of darkness. The Confederates called out to warn the Federals not to come too close to their works, promising to care for the wounded within that zone. Some Confederates not only came out to secure enemy wounded but robbed the dead of personal belongings. Members of the 13th U.S. Infantry tried to find their injured commander, Capt. Edward C. Washington, but failed. When they neared the works, some Rebels called out to them not to come closer, as they had already taken him in. Washington was dying. His men would never again see him, and they remained confused about whether he had been hit in the bottom of the ravine or closer to the Rebel line, a confusion that still has not been cleared up.[60]

The Federals improvised suitable places for the caring of their wounded. A. J. Smith's medical officers established a hospital four miles from the battlefield at Swett's Farm, which consisted of a log house situated on top of a hill with lots of shade trees around. Surgeons set up three operating tables as ambulances began to cart in the wounded, and attendants placed injured men side by side under the trees. When room ran out, they were laid down in the sun as men cut brush and tree branches to make arbors for them. Charles Beneulyn Johnson of the 130th Illinois, an attendant, recalled many pitiful cases. One in particular stood out. A bullet had penetrated a man's skull, but he lived for several days, "walked about and waited largely upon himself. He seemed dazed, however, from the first, and after awhile became stupid, helpless and died."[61]

Capt. Thomas Sewell of Company G, 127th Illinois, maintained a detailed record of his medical care after being hit in the side with a bullet early in the attack of May 19. Stretcher-bearers took him toward the rear, where a surgeon offered a drink and put him in an ambulance. Sewell remained at the nearest field hospital until May 22, when he was transported to a hospital boat at Chickasaw Bayou. The vessel seemed like heaven compared to the squalid field hospital. After several days he was transferred to another boat for transport upriver to Memphis and Cairo, and then to Chicago by June 4. Sewell spent several weeks recuperating in his home city but yearned to rejoin the regiment. When friends asked him when he would return, Sewell took it badly and became sensitive on that point. Because of that sensitivity, he left before the wound was fully healed, returning in mid-August 1863. His comrades were greatly surprised because they had assumed he died. Sewell still carried the ball, which was lodged in too dangerous a spot to be cut out, as late as 1889 when he penned his memoirs.[62]

Grant's army lost 942 men on May 19. Of that number only eight were listed as missing, while 777 were wounded and 157 were killed. Fully 75 percent of Grant's losses (or 712 men) fell on the Fifteenth Corps sector, the great majority of them in Blair's division, which counted 613 losses. Blair, in short, accounted for 86 percent of Sherman's total casualties. McPherson's Seventeenth Corps lost 16 killed and 113 wounded in its tentative advance, with the majority lost by Ransom's brigade. McClernand's Thirteenth Corps suffered a total of 100 casualties in its movements that day. A Confederate officer reported that 166 Union prisoners were released by Pemberton and sent across the Mississippi River because he did not want to feed them. These prisoners probably had been collected for some time past.[63]

Pemberton never reported his losses, but they have been estimated at about 200. Forney believed the Confederates lost fifty men in the Graveyard Road sector and thirty-seven men between that locale and Jackson Road. Col. Francis M. Cockrell reported seventy casualties in his Missouri brigade, which was heavily involved in repelling assaults on and near Graveyard Road.[64]

Grant fairly evaluated the results of May 19 in his official report. Sherman had "a good position" and was able "to make a vigorous assault." In contrast, McPherson and McClernand "succeeded no further than to gain advanced positions covered from the fire of the enemy." Of course, he had hoped for more. Grant anticipated breaking through and seizing Vicksburg in one stroke. Unfortunately, most of the army was not in a position from which to launch a campaign-winning attack. Other than Blair's division, every other unit in the Army of the Tennessee simply maneuvered in order to snuggle up closer to the objective.[65]

"The enemy still holds out obstinately," commented Lt. Col. James H. Wilson of Grant's staff. Lt. Col. Henry Clay Warmoth of McClernand's staff admitted that "it is hard work to take this position by storm. I don't think it can be done by such weak lines, only a more concentrated movement and with great loss of life, we may be able to take them by charge." Sherman felt bitter over the slaughter of Blair's division but bypassed McPherson when doling out criticism. Instead, he blamed McClernand, "who *did not* press his attack as he should."[66]

Federal generals failed to understand that the tactical advantage had begun to shift to their enemy because of Lockett's earthworks and Pemberton's use of two fresh divisions at the most likely places to be attacked. The Federals assaulted with inadequate preparation, counting on Rebel demoralization to replace careful reconnoitering, troop placement, and artillery support. The only serious assault was aimed at the strongest part of Lockett's line and ended in a blunt repulse, which greatly increased morale among the Confederates. It was just enough of a battle to give the Rebels courage but not enough of a fight for the Federals to test all parts of the opposing position.

{ 5 }

This Will Be a Hard Place to Take

MAY 20-21

The poor results of May 19 posed a quandary for Grant. He still knew relatively little of the Confederate position, and Fifteenth Corps operations had demonstrated the strength of the Stockade Redan sector, in terms of both the landscape and the nature of the Confederate earthworks. On the other hand, neither McPherson nor McClernand made a serious effort that day. The results of their operations could not be taken as proof that the enemy works were impregnable elsewhere.

As a result, Grant refused to give up hope of storming Vicksburg, but if another try was to be made it had to be conducted after more careful thought and preparation. The two-day delay offered Grant more time to plan and prepare, but it also offered the Confederates more time to get ready for him. It also allowed Johnston more time to gather troops and position them in potentially threatening places. Grant had to consider all of these factors, and it is to his credit that he dared to take two days to think about them. In the end, he probably lost more than he gained by postponing a major attack for two days.

Because of this delay in the decision-making process, May 20 and 21 proved to be days of waiting by the rank and file as their commander pondered his next course of action. The Federals worked to strengthen their position, skirmish, plant artillery, and establish supply lines. For the time being, the army had to act as if it were destined to hold its position indefinitely.

Troops of Steele's division finished their extension toward the river on May 20. The 12th Missouri moved onto the bottomland next to the Mississippi at the mouth of Mint Spring Bayou and north of Fort Hill, driving away Brig. Gen. John C. Vaughn's pickets. The right flank of the Union line finally touched the muddy waters. Some regiments, such as the 32nd Missouri of Col. Francis H. Manter's brigade, intensively skirmished, but other men were not impressed. "It was the laziest fighting I ever seen," commented Harkness Lay of the 72nd Ohio. "We would go to the top of the ridge and shoot as long as we wanted to & then fall back and read the news, play euchre, or any thing else to pass away the time."[1]

The intensity of skirmishing varied widely in other corps sectors too. In places, regimental commanders rotated their men in and out of forward positions to maintain constant fire, and members of the 4th Minnesota received 100 rounds of ammunition, which they expended from noon until dusk. "Skirmishing was unceasing during the day," wrote Col. Marcus M. Spiegel of the 120th Ohio. Owen J. Hopkins of the 42nd Ohio fired ninety-five rounds.[2]

Because of the need to place artillery behind the infantry line, friendly troops became unintended casualties. Sgt. John Kuykendall led sixty men of the 33rd Illinois to a point 200 yards from the Confederate line to skirmish. A Union battery located 600 yards to the rear began firing, and shells exploded among Kuykendall's men. He raced back to inform the battery commander, who changed the position of his guns. "Such, of course are the accidents of war," mused Cpl. Charles E. Wilcox.[3]

MCCLERNAND

McClernand adopted a bellicose attitude on the morning of May 20, boldly telling Grant, "I propose to assault the enemy's works." But a few hours later he changed his mind. The Confederates held "a formidable line of earthworks, chiefly square redoubts or lunettes, connected together by a line of rifle-pits, and the whole line in a very commanding position." Moreover, McClernand heard reports that one or two additional lines of earthworks existed behind the one that was visible. "I do not think the position can be carried with our present extended lines," he told Grant. The army should concentrate its strength "on some particular point or points. Otherwise, perhaps, a siege becomes the only alternative."[4]

Grant visited McClernand early in the afternoon of May 20 to consult. An officer of the 16th Indiana, who signed himself JRSC, was serving as an aide on the staff of Brig. Gen. Andrew J. Smith. He witnessed the meeting and described it for an Indiana newspaper. Grant was "smoking as usual," wrote JRSC. "I had formed an idea from the description that he was a whisky barrel on legs, but found myself greatly in error. Paying little attention to dress, he usually wears a stand up collar, with cap and coat much the worse for wear. He seemed a plain unassuming man, whether studying his maps, or, as is his custom, smoking, walking up and down with his hands behind him, grave and thoughtful."[5]

JRSC overheard the end of Grant's conference with McClernand. "We will throw in a few shells, and then try it," the commander said. "Try it is then," McClernand responded. The corps commander asked McPherson to support his right flank, which was exposed by a gap of 1,000 yards between the two corps. A. J. Smith relied on Brig. Gen. Eugene A. Carr's division for immediate support.[6]

At 2:00 P.M. on May 20, Smith's division started from a point 600 yards from the 2nd Texas Lunette in two lines. Brig. Gen. Stephen G. Burbridge's brigade occupied the first line, with its leftmost regiment south of Baldwin's Ferry Road and the next, the 67th Indiana, straddling the roadbed. Col. William J. Landram's brigade constituted the second line, fifty yards behind Burbridge with one regiment south of the road and the next, the 19th Kentucky, straddling it. The troops marched across the rugged terrain exposed on the higher ground to intense artillery fire. They reached a point halfway between their start and the objective, stopping 250 to 350 yards from the Rebel line. All desire to close on the works evaporated as Landram moved his brigade to the left to extend Burbridge's line nearly to the railroad. No one charged "and I was glad of it," confessed Merrick J. Wald.[7]

Exactly what McClernand had in mind for Smith is uncertain. Lt. Col. Henry Clay Warmoth, his assistant adjutant general, asserted that a real assault was intended. "A. J. Smith ordered to attack the Enemy in his works," Warmoth noted in his diary, but "he fooled away all day and finally" did nothing. "I have suffered considerable loss, but am pressing for a sharp engagement up to the enemy's works," McClernand told Grant sometime that afternoon. He apparently was looking for an opportunity to launch the charge he had been contemplating since morning. Grant supported McClernand's effort and told McPherson, "If you intend assaulting the fort in front of your position send word to Sherman as long before the hour as possible. He will engage the enemy on the right so as to keep them from concentrating on you."[8]

Sherman ordered his men to demonstrate that afternoon to divert attention from operations on the left. At 3:00 P.M. the 30th Ohio and several other regiments took position 300 to 400 yards from the works and fired until 7:00 P.M. The Ohioans expended 30,000 rounds during those hours, and the regiment lost three men wounded in the process.[9]

McClernand did not have his fourth division, commanded by Brig. Gen. Alvin P. Hovey, on the line. It had been heavily engaged at Champion Hill and was left behind to clean up the field and care for wounded comrades and prisoners. Hovey received McClernand's note to hurry forward on May 19 but could not comply. "My command is too much fatigued to move tonight," he wrote. With about 4,000 prisoners to guard and 3,400 small arms and several pieces of artillery to move, Hovey told McClernand his men would start early on the morning of May 20.[10]

But Grant had different plans for Hovey. His chief of staff wrote to the division commander on May 19, which did not reach Hovey until early the next morning, that he should guard the crossings of the Big Black River in case Johnston advanced. Prisoners and captured ordnance should go to Young's Point under escort. Hovey was confused. He informed Grant that he was heading for McClernand and assumed it was consonant with Grant's intentions. Grant had failed to inform McClernand of his order to Hovey, and McClernand had failed to inform Grant of his instructions to the division leader.[11]

Grant sent a staff officer to McClernand's headquarters to see what was going on. There the officer met not only McClernand but Hovey, who had ridden ahead of his troops because he sensed something was wrong. Hovey was quick to inform the staff officer that there were no signs of Johnston near the Big Black River and that he had left two companies to guard the crossings of the stream. When Grant learned this news, he allowed McClernand to use one of Hovey's brigades, but the other had to return to the Big Black. Hovey detached Brig. Gen. George F. McGinnis's brigade to McClernand while Col. James R. Slack's brigade tended to the prisoners and captured ordnance. McGinnis reached the Union lines outside Vicksburg late on May 20.[12]

Grant could not yet commit to another assault, but Sherman believed something had to be done soon. Estimates placed Pemberton's strength at 15,000 to 20,000 men, "and Johnston is hovering about with reinforcements," Sherman told his wife on May 20. Even though the Rebels were strongly fortified, "we must attack, quicker the better." Sherman tried to push Grant toward this conclusion but his superior hesitated.[13]

Meanwhile, Federal soldiers could see that the fortifications were well placed and getting stronger. Brig. Gen. Peter J. Osterhaus passed on information gained by his skirmishers who managed to get close to them. "This will be a hard place to take," commented Job H. Yaggy of the 124th Illinois. "The timber is cut down and lay so thick that on level ground it would be hard enough to get over, and here are hills yet that a man can hardly climb with nothing to keep him back." Yet some Federals, such as Thomas Gordon of the 1st Minnesota Battery, thought they should attack immediately while the enemy was demoralized. Although Maj. Abraham Jefferson Seay of the 32nd Missouri thought Grant was taking too much time to decide what to do, he also knew the army had never faced more formidable earthworks.[14]

THE CONFEDERATES

Along the Confederate line outside Vicksburg, May 20 dawned with an expectation that Grant would launch another assault. Artillery fire and skirmishing resumed that morning, but Maj. Gen. John H. Forney could detect no "appearance as yet of an advance." Brig. Gen. Stephen D. Lee saw the preparation for A. J. Smith's move forward as the prelude for an assault, but that was not the case.[15]

The Confederate rank and file assumed the repulse of May 19 had taken the steam out of Grant. "The result of the engagement on yesterday has caused a general glow of satisfaction to pervade our entire army," wrote Samuel Fowler of the 2nd Missouri. In fact, the Confederates now were eager for the Yankees to try it again. "We all feel pretty confident that if they attack us we will defeat them," wrote Lt. Maurice Kavanaugh Simons of the 2nd Texas. According to a newspaper correspondent of the *Memphis Daily Appeal*, the repulse of May 19 also restored confidence among the civilians of Vicksburg.[16]

Pemberton moved his headquarters from the Garland House on Grove Street to a location closer to the lines on May 21, placing himself and staff at 1018 Crawford Street. Here the general digested reports about Federal signal corps flags wagging from the top of Ferguson's House on McClernand's sector and dust rising from marching men as the Yankees moved troops.[17]

The Federals maintained an intense skirmish fire on the Confederate works during May 20–21. "I'll tell you a gnat cant live for em," complained William Lewis Roberts of the 31st Alabama. "They shoot at ever hat they see stick above the ditch." The Confederates were at a disadvantage. Their works in many places were not thick enough to withstand short-range artillery fire, and without head logs it was too dangerous to fire properly over the parapet. Moreover, Pemberton had already issued orders to conserve ammunition.[18]

In the 37th Mississippi, only ten rounds were expended all day of May

20. The next day, a few men continued to fire when they saw a Federal exposing himself. James West Smith shot three times that day. In turn the Confederates suffered casualties. The 3rd Louisiana lost nine killed and wounded on May 20, and the 2nd Texas suffered ten losses the next day.[19]

Federal artillery dominated the firing on May 20–21. Brig. Gen. John C. Moore lost twelve wounded and six killed in his brigade on May 21, and four artillery pieces were disabled. "In some instances their shots passed entirely through the parapets, killing and wounding men on the inside," Moore reported. Brig. Gen. Louis Hébert's brigade lost six killed and thirteen wounded on May 21. The Confederates were winning when it came to assaults on their line, but they were losing when it came to the attrition of siege operations. "Our artillery is almost useless," complained Brig. Gen. Francis A. Shoup to Maj. Gen. Martin L. Smith, "since we have no properly constructed protection. Being almost without intrenching tools, we can do little to repair the evil."[20]

Maj. Samuel H. Lockett did try to improve the works. He had too few engineer troops for the task, so he relied heavily on men detailed by brigade leaders. The 500 entrenching tools were always in use, scattered up and down the trench line, and Lockett did not even try to keep records of which command currently held them. Improvements focused on constructing traverses to protect from enfilading fire and digging covered ways toward the rear. Behavior was a problem too. "It took several days for our men to learn the caution necessary to protect themselves," Lockett admitted.[21]

Forney sent forty-five bales of cotton from Vicksburg to Moore's sector as a way to quickly strengthen the parapet and ordered forty additional bales to the Graveyard Road area. When installed, the white bales became readily apparent to the Federals. Forney ordered skins of slaughtered cattle, horses, and mules to be wrapped around the bales to reduce the possibility of catching fire.[22]

Pemberton devoted a good deal of his attention to managing reserve troops. He divided Maj. Gen. John S. Bowen's Division, consisting of 3,600 men, into detachments at several segments of the line. He also held Col. Thomas N. Waul's Texas Legion as a general reserve. Several brigade commanders held back a regiment or two as their private reserve force, such as Vaughn did with the 43rd Tennessee and Brig. Gen. William E. Baldwin with the 17th Louisiana.[23]

Pemberton tended to respond to signs of an attack by shifting units about nervously. Bowen was annoyed and suggested he assign his division permanently to one sector and require each division commander to provide his own reserve. He was right, but Pemberton wanted to be in charge of these troops so as to plug holes when they developed, so he continued his policy.[24]

Pemberton became almost obsessed with conserving supplies of all kinds. He told Maj. Gen. Carter L. Stevenson, who doubled as commander of the post of Vicksburg, to drive horses and mules south beyond the lines because there was only limited forage available for them. Pemberton felt small-arms ammunition was not sufficient "for an unlimited daily expenditure for a protracted period." He also told Stevenson to arm reliable civilians from Vicksburg and post them as guards at ordnance magazines to prevent sabotage.[25]

Confederate morale was rapidly improving. Stephen D. Lee had confided to Emma Balfour soon after the army reached Vicksburg that he was afraid his Alabama troops would not stand another battle but now thought "they would fight next time." Surgeon Joseph Dill Alison also expressed optimism. "We . . . are in fine spirits and satisfied that we can hold out a month."[26]

Hoping the "siege" would be short, Rebel soldiers settled into life in the trenches. Their food was carried up to the works under cover of night, and many took advantage of the dark to sleep just behind the works. In fact, Forney instructed his brigade leaders to scour the rear areas and round up stragglers. "Suffered much in pits from sun & dust," complained Lt. Jared Young Sanders, which may well explain why so many troops straggled from the works. "Our boys remain cool and cheerful; when not sleeping, reading, or shooting, employ their time in jesting, telling anecdotes." But near the scene of Blair's repulse on May 19, the stench of rotting corpses permeated the air.[27]

FEDERAL SUPPLIES AND COMMUNICATIONS

As the Federals settled down opposite Pemberton's line, Grant and his subordinates reestablished a flow of material to the army. Ever since beginning the overland march, quartermasters had relied on a wagon road from Milliken's Bend to Hard Times Landing, a distance of sixty-three miles over Mississippi River bottomland that was subject to flooding, sticky mud, and swampy ground. On May 10, engineer Capt. William L. B. Jenney plotted a new road from Milliken's Bend across De Soto Point to a spot on the west bank of the river a bit downstream from Warrenton. The idea was to create Bowers' Landing (named for one of Grant's staff officers), and then transfer goods onto steamers for a faster trip downstream to Hard Times. The new road would be only eight miles long. But a casemated artillery battery at

Warrenton had to be eliminated first. USS *Mound City* damaged the Confederate position from May 10 to 13 but could not silence the guns. Only when Pemberton ordered the evacuation of Warrenton on May 17 did the battery fall silent.[28]

Work on the road from Milliken's Bend to Bowers' Landing proceeded smoothly. Jenney was able to get wagons through as early as May 12 because the falling river lowered water levels in a swamp along the route. His details built a bridge and a corduroy roadbed for nearly one and a half miles through the swamp.[29]

But the new road was used only a short time because Grant brought his troops to a place where better supply lines could be developed north of Vicksburg. Jenney left on May 14 to join Brig. Gen. Hugh Ewing's brigade in its roundabout march to Vicksburg, reaching the Fifteenth Corps by May 19. Acting as Sherman's chief engineer, he scouted the location for a road linking Sherman with the Yazoo River at Chickasaw Bluffs. Capt. W. A. Johnson's plantation on the Yazoo had a good steamboat landing that became the chief unloading point. From here Jenney plotted a route ten miles to Sherman's line.[30]

It was necessary to bridge 300 feet of water near the head of Chickasaw Bayou, so Jenney moved Grant's pontoon train to the spot on the night of May 19. The next day he found that McClernand had sent one of his staff officers and some troops to begin work on the bridge. Jenney helped them to finish it as three companies of Col. Josiah W. Bissell's Engineer Regiment of the West worked on the road, clearing places blockaded by the Confederates during the Chickasaw Bayou campaign of December 1862.[31]

As work proceeded on the road, Capt. Herman Klosterman scouted an alternate route that would be shorter and less obstructed. It utilized a levee that ran along the east side of Thompson Lake and connected Johnson's plantation with Mrs. Anne E. Lake's farm. Jenney approved and committed Klosterman's pioneers to the work. He also prevailed on Blair to send the 83rd Indiana to help. Klosterman's route was finished by 11:00 A.M. on May 20. In contrast, the first (or main) road that Jenney started on May 19 was not ready until May 22.[32]

By the time these roads opened the Federals were nearing the end of their patience with supply shortages. Grant estimated his troops had received only five days' rations from their commissaries during the overland march, but they stretched that out to last twenty days by feeding from the countryside. It was difficult to continue foraging now that the army was stationary outside Vicksburg.[33]

Grant got the message from his troops quite clearly. When he visited the 83rd Ohio of McClernand's corps on May 20, he and some staff members entered the works to observe the Rebel position. Most Federals quietly watched their general but a few of them yelled, "Crackers! Crackers!! Crackers!!!" Their officers tried to hush them up, but Grant took no apparent notice as he continued his observations. When finished, the commander took post where he could be readily seen and told the men that Sherman had possession of Walnut Hills and the engineers were making wagon roads to connect the army with river steamers on the Yazoo. "You will soon have all you want," he concluded and received thunderous cheers in return.[34]

The first supply train arrived from Chickasaw Bayou by 6:00 P.M. on May 20. A man on USS *Baron DeKalb* counted fifteen transport steamers at and near Johnson's plantation. Sherman's troops were the first to benefit; troops stationed farther south had to wait a while longer.[35]

While food for men and forage for animals were in short supply, the Army of the Tennessee never suffered from want of ammunition. Lt. Stephen Carr Lyford provided 500 rounds per artillery piece, 300 rounds per infantryman, and 150 rounds per cavalryman by April 30. He considered this "a liberal supply," which was adequate for the needs of the overland march.[36]

Capt. Ocran H. Howard, Grant's chief signal officer, created stations at Grant's, McPherson's, and McClernand's headquarters and at Chickasaw Bluffs and Young's Point. This enabled Grant to communicate with David D. Porter and in a larger sense with points up the Mississippi River.[37]

PRISONERS OF WAR

Reconnecting with the outside world enabled Grant to dispose of prisoners accumulated during the march from Port Gibson. By May 19, McGinnis's brigade of Hovey's division, Col. Samuel A. Holmes's brigade of Brig. Gen. Isaac F. Quinby's division, and the 108th Illinois of Landram's brigade had moved 2,500 prisoners taken at the battles of Raymond, Jackson, and Champion Hill to Edwards Station. Meanwhile the 23rd Iowa of Brig. Gen. Michael K. Lawler's brigade and the 6th Missouri Cavalry added 1,500 Confederates captured at the battle of the Big Black River to the other group. Hovey pared down the escort to the 23rd Iowa, 80th Ohio (of Holmes's brigade, Quinby's division), 54th Indiana (of Col. Daniel W. Lindsey's brigade, Osterhaus's division), and 108th Illinois. The combined group of 4,000 prisoners crossed the Big Black River on the evening of May 19 and bivouacked on the west side.[38]

Grant wanted these prisoners moved to Young's Point. They started early on May 20 and made it to Walnut Hills by that evening. When they reached Johnson's plantation, the Confederates embarked on steamboats and moved down the Yazoo to Young's Point on May 21. Once deposited there, Federal quartermasters set up tents to shelter the prisoners and commissaries issued rations. The Confederates stayed at the point four days while transportation north was arranged.[39]

More prisoners, captured after May 17, were added to the 4,000 at Young's Point. Col. George Robbins of the 8th Wisconsin used 150 of his men to escort prisoners caught by the Fifteenth Corps. He reported to Sherman that landings along the Yazoo River seemed to be a haven for "Several Hundred *well* [Union] Soldiers" who were shirking duty in addition to a number of troops properly detailed to work on the supply line. Lt. William Titus Rigby of the 24th Iowa in Slack's brigade escorted a number of prisoners captured by the Thirteenth Corps to Lake's Landing on the Yazoo. In addition, Company B, 33rd Illinois, escorted several artillery pieces captured in the overland march to the river. Eight wagons detailed from the 113th Illinois transported abandoned rifles from the Big Black battlefield to Chickasaw Landing, where the weapons were stacked up like cordwood.[40]

By the time the gathering was complete, 4,535 prisoners crowded at Young's Point. "Some is always wanting something they cannot get," complained Lt. Aquilla Standifird of the 23rd Iowa. "They sometimes quarlel among themselves. Some claim to be good union men but I think their loyalty is not very good." In the eyes of Henry Walbridge Dudley, these prisoners had little reason to complain. Detached from Battery B, 1st Illinois, to ordnance duty, Dudley observed them as he took charge of captured Rebel ordnance. They appeared "well clothed and their appearance indicated that they had not suffered for lack of food."[41]

"What shall I do with the prisoners I have?" Grant asked General-in-chief Maj. Gen. Henry W. Halleck on May 22. The answer was to ship them north to prison camps. But Halleck wanted Grant to separate the officers from the men because of an ongoing feud that concerned treatment of officers by both sides. Rebel officers would be sent to Johnson's Island in Lake Erie, while the enlisted men would go to Camp Douglas near Chicago. Grant sent his aide-de-camp, Col. Clark B. Lagow, to take charge of the prisoners on five steamboats headed for Memphis, where Maj. Gen. Stephen A. Hurlbut would arrange the rest of their journey. Lagow made a list of the prisoners and assumed command of the guards. Porter provided an escort of warships for the transports.[42]

Lagow took along the 23rd Iowa, 54th Indiana, 108th Illinois, and 80th Ohio to guard the prisoners. The five steamers left Young's Point on May 25 and reached Memphis by the early morning of May 29. Hurlbut was less than pleased with Lagow. The staff officer delivered 4,408 prisoners without explaining what became of the other 127 Rebels held at Young's Point. The prisoners appeared to "have suffered for want of Provisions." In Hurlbut's view, Grant's aide did "not appear to have paid any attention to this duty or to have taken any care of the officers and men under his charge nor even to have known how many men constituted the Guard." Hurlbut's men replaced Lagow's, and after resting for a couple of days, three of the four Union regiments returned to Young's Point by June 2. Hurlbut shifted the captured officers to Johnson's Island but sent the enlisted men to Camp Morton at Indianapolis rather than Camp Douglas.[43]

REINFORCEMENTS

In addition to moving prisoners north, Federal quartermasters shifted reinforcements to the Army of the Tennessee. The first contingent was Brig. Gen. Jacob G. Lauman's division, sent in response to Grant's message to Hurlbut on May 5. Col. George Bryant's brigade left Memphis on May 12 and arrived at Young's Point two days later. By that time Bowers' Landing was operational, so Bryant marched across De Soto Point and took steamers down to Grand Gulf by May 16. Col. Cyrus Hall's brigade was the next to leave Memphis, on May 14, and arrived at Young's Point two days later. It left for Bowers' Landing on May 18 and took steamers down to reinforce Bryant at Grand Gulf. On May 16, Col. Isaac C. Pugh's brigade left Memphis with Lauman's headquarters. One of the boats carrying Pugh's command fought a small battle with 500 mounted Confederates and three artillery pieces above Greenville, Mississippi, on May 18. The Rebels fired on the *Crescent City*, taking the Federals by surprise. Two guns on board fired back, but the boat was riddled as it passed the most dangerous spot. None of its machinery was damaged, although the 3rd Iowa lost fourteen men wounded. Pugh's command arrived at Young's Point on May 19.[44]

By the time Pugh reached the theater of operations, Grant changed his mind about where to place him. Before learning of this change of plan, Pugh and Lauman marched across De Soto Point to Bowers' Landing. There they received an order to go to the Yazoo River. By the time the brigade returned to Young's Point, it was too late in the day to proceed farther. The next day,

May 20, Pugh loaded his command on transports and steamed up the Yazoo to Snyder's Bluff. From there he marched toward Grant's line, but when he was halfway to that destination word arrived to retrace his route to Snyder's. Grant was worried that Johnston might advance from the north. As a result, Pugh's brigade remained at Snyder's Bluff from May 20 to 24. The men camped on high bluffs from which they could see artillery shells explode over Vicksburg ten miles away.[45]

Grant wanted Brig. Gen. John McArthur's division to move up from Grand Gulf and occupy Warrenton. McArthur had protected Grant's supply line along the Louisiana side of the Mississippi down to Hard Times Landing. Once the shorter route was opened to Bowers' Landing, McArthur moved Brig. Gen. Thomas E. G. Ransom's brigade over the river at Hard Times on May 12. Soon after, Ransom escorted a wagon train toward Grant's rapidly moving army. Ransom now became detached from McArthur and took orders from McPherson's Seventeenth Corps headquarters.[46]

Col. William Hall's brigade of McArthur's division also crossed to the east side of the river at Hard Times Landing on May 12 and occupied Grand Gulf. On May 19, Hall received orders to move north and occupy Warrenton. The men were eager to go, but a mix-up occurred that sent Hall's brigade to Bowers' Landing on May 20. Hall thought he was to proceed to the Yazoo and thus marched across De Soto Point to Young's Point. From there the troops boarded boats and left at dawn of May 21, steaming up to Haynes' Bluff. This was not according to Grant's directive. After receiving counterorders, the troops reembarked and left Haynes' Bluff at 3:00 P.M., reaching Young's Point two hours later. They marched across the point to Bowers' Landing, where other steamers took them across the Mississippi to Warrenton by the night of May 21. McArthur accompanied Hall's brigade; in fact, it was the only part of his dispersed command that he had left.[47]

The confusion about Lauman and McArthur shows how fluid the situation was around Vicksburg. Equally fluid was the possibility that Grant could receive help from Maj. Gen. Nathaniel P. Banks, whose troops in the Department of the Gulf were on the move through central Louisiana. There had been little cooperation between Grant and Banks before the arrival of one of Banks's brigader commanders, Brig. Gen. William Dwight. He consulted with Grant before starting back to Banks on May 20 with a request that his commander bring all his men to Warrenton to help capture Vicksburg. It would prove to be a vain hope, for Banks had no intention of giving up his planned strike against Port Hudson.[48]

Porter's fleet constituted the communications link between Grant and Banks, and it also provided much needed support of other kinds to the Army of the Tennessee. Porter had already sent supply boats to Chickasaw Bluffs on May 19 and planned to use mortar boats when Grant asked him for fire support on the water batteries north of Vicksburg. "I congratulate you with all my heart, on your splendid success," he wrote Grant on May 20. "I suppose with Haynes' Bluff in our possession, and Warrenton, the city must fall in a day or two." In fact, without waiting for Grant's reply, Porter told Secretary of the Navy Gideon Welles that "in a very short time a general assault will take place, when I hope to announce that Vicksburg has fallen." Porter's confidence was shared by many of his sailors. "The place is *virtually ours,*" wrote acting ensign Symmes E. Browne of the gunboat *Signal*.[49]

If the city had not yet fallen by the night of May 20, Porter wanted Lt. Cdr. K. Randolph Breese, who commanded the boats stationed downstream from Vicksburg, to move upriver after dark and bombard the center of town. Breese moved USS *Carondelet*, USS *Mound City*, and USS *Benton* beginning at 9:10 P.M. on May 20 and opened fire at 11:28 P.M. He kept it up for thirty-three minutes before dropping downstream. Then the *Mound City* steamed back to continue firing, replaced by the *Carondelet*. When Lt. Cdr. James A. Greer's USS *Benton* had its turn, it fired forty-two rounds. Return fire from the Marine Hospital Battery hit the *Benton* twice in the upper works but no crewmembers were lost. Greer finished his attack by 12:30 A.M., returning to fire forty-one rounds at 2:00 A.M. of May 21. The *Carondelet* replaced the *Benton* at 2:30 A.M. as the intermittent shelling lit up the sky over Vicksburg.[50]

Breese continued to harass the Rebels on May 21. The *Mound City* opened on the lower river batteries from 8:00 A.M. until noon. Then the *Carondelet* took its turn from 1:00 P.M. to 5:00 P.M. Greer's *Benton* opened at 5:28 P.M. All three boats trained their sights on South Fort and its ten-inch columbiad. The gun returned fire all day at the vessels. When the gunboats continued to fire at intervals during the night, the Confederate gun crews soon realized it was only meant to harass them, so they retired for sleep.[51]

While ironclad gunboats located downriver from Vicksburg concentrated on shelling water batteries, the Union mortar fleet upriver concentrated on shelling the town itself. Tugboats brought six scows armed with one thirteen-inch mortar apiece and anchored them near De Soto Point in a protected spot. The mortars opened fire at first light on May 20. Porter had taken his flagship, uss *Black Hawk*, up to Haynes' Bluff that day, but he wanted the mortar boats to fire "night and day, with nothing less than 20 pounds of powder" to propel their 200-pound shells.[52]

Many citizens took refuge in their caves, but Emma Balfour felt crowded and suffocated in her subterranean refuge and vowed to stick it out in her house. Confederate surgeon Joseph Dill Alison noted that the mortar boats "shell us incessantly" but the projectiles did "not go far into the town yet." With the ironclads bombarding the batteries from below, the mortar boats pounding the city from above, and Grant's field artillery overshooting Lockett's line from the east, the men, women, and children of Vicksburg felt surrounded. "Porter's fleet kept rolling the shell into the City all night," reported George W. Hale of the 33rd Wisconsin. The noise of the bombardment disturbed sleep for Federals and Confederates alike.[53]

The first really intense, all-around bombardment of Vicksburg began on May 20 and continued the next day. "Fire scattered all over town," reported John Cowdry Taylor, "women & children pretty generally 'caved in.'" Lida Lord Reed's family was about to move from the study to the dining room for a meal, when a shell smacked into their house, taking out the entire side and roof and creating a gigantic hole in the floor. Their meal and best china were destroyed along with part of the structure. "We certainly are in a critical situation," commented Alison on May 21. "No safe place to be found. Escape fire from one side exposes us on the other."[54]

Civilian homes were vulnerable, but the water batteries were well constructed. Only by direct hits could they be damaged, and the ironclads and mortar boats were almost incapable of such precision. Even inside Vicksburg random firing meant that most shells would not hit a building. But the naval fire stressed the citizens and wrecked their peace of mind, and even if few shells hit a structure, the destruction added up over time.

Securing the Yazoo River was something the navy could do, and Porter set into motion an expedition up that stream on May 19. uss *Baron DeKalb* led the way and reached a point two miles short of Snyder's Bluff late that day. Through semaphore signals Breese learned that Capt. John H. Peters and twenty-five men of the 4th Iowa Cavalry had already reached Snyder's. Peters found a hospital with fifty sick Confederates, nine dismounted guns, and lots of fixed ammunition. He made contact with the *Baron DeKalb* as Breese waited for the rest of his vessels to catch up.[55]

Confederate naval commander Isaac N. Brown observed some of this Federal activity on May 19. He was on his way to see if Snyder's Bluff was in enemy hands, when he received word at Liverpool (twenty-five miles south of Yazoo City) that the Yankees were steaming upriver. He also learned of the 4th Iowa Cavalry presence. Brown estimated the fleet would reach Yazoo City by noon of May 20 and began to clear the river of Confederate boats so they would not fall into Porter's hands.[56]

The Federals planned to steam as far as Yazoo City, but first they took care of business at Snyder's Bluff, spiking guns in the works and clearing passage through a large chain that stretched across the river. Porter joined Breese's expedition with the *Black Hawk* early on the morning of May 20. He toured the Confederate works and planned a further push to Yazoo City, placing Lt. Cdr. John G. Walker in charge of ironclads *Baron DeKalb* and *Choctaw*, plus tinclads *Forest Rose, Linden,* and *Petrel.* He sent Breese back to Young's Point on the tinclad *Romeo* to superintend operations around Vicksburg and joined Walker's expedition with the *Black Hawk.*[57]

After engineers broke the chain at Snyder's Bluff, Walker steamed up the Yazoo and to Haynes' Bluff on May 20. There a shore party spiked an eight-inch columbiad and burned its carriage. The Federals also destroyed forty tents and a sawmill. Porter ordered the destruction of fourteen gun carriages because he feared the enemy may return to Haynes' Bluff and reuse them. Naval crews also tore down as much of the defenses as possible and burned what was left of military camps. Henry Walbridge Dudley counted at least twelve heavy guns that the Confederates had spiked at Haynes' Bluff, and other men reported that some of them had been deliberately burst by the retreating enemy, flipping end over end and landing on the ground near their burned carriages. Washington authorities were alarmed at reports that the navy had needlessly destroyed ammunition and carriages at the bluff. Porter justified his action by stating that he was uncertain the army would hold Haynes' and Snyder's, and he had no intention of leaving usable material behind for the Confederates to use.[58]

Porter wanted to clear the river as far as Yazoo City, forty miles as the crow flies from its junction with the Mississippi. He sent Walker toward the town on May 21 while taking the *Black Hawk* downstream to the fleet anchorage near Young's Point. Walker left Haynes' Bluff at 4:00 A.M. and arrived near Yazoo City without incident by 1:00 P.M. The mayor and city council assured him that the place was undefended. They requested that "no indignity" should befall its citizens. Walker assured them of fair treatment but told the town authorities they were responsible for law and order.[59]

The Federals surveyed the Confederate navy yard, which had already been mostly destroyed by retreating Rebels. Details completed the destruction, including six sawmills and a number of machine shops, carpenter shops, and blacksmith shops. The Federals found several boilers designed to power steamboats and put the finishing touches on the destruction of three powerful rams the Confederates were building at Yazoo City. css *Mobile* was ready for its four-inch iron plates. Another boat, css *Republic*, was ready for its ram. Yet a third vessel, "a monster" boat in Walker's words, measured 310 feet long and 70 feet in the beam. Walker also paroled 115 Confederates found in a hospital. Porter estimated that his men destroyed more than $2 million worth of Confederate property at Yazoo City.[60]

After two days of destruction, Walker's expedition steamed downriver on the morning of May 23 but had to fight its way back to the Mississippi. Alerted by Isaac N. Brown, Johnston sent Col. William Wirt Adams's 1st Mississippi Cavalry and three pieces of the Brookhaven Mississippi Battery from the Big Black River to the Yazoo. Adams bivouacked four miles from Liverpool on the night of May 22 and reached the bluffs there early the next morning, just before Walker's boats approached Liverpool from the north. He could see the smoke belching from the gunboat stacks but waited until they came very close before opening fire at 8:00 A.M.[61]

Walker noted that Adams had chosen his position well, on high ground at a "sharp bend of the river." Liverpool was located ten miles in a straight line southwest of Yazoo City, the only good place for an ambush between that town and Haynes' Bluff. Three field guns roared into action and 200 cavalrymen fired their carbines, all of which were concealed in bushes near the waterline. Tinclad uss *Petrel* was in the lead and steamed close in to grapple with Adams, followed by the rest. The battle lasted at least an hour before Adams evacuated his position. Walker's boats suffered some damage and lost men in the exchange. uss *Linden*, which followed the *Petrel* in the firing line, expended thirty-nine rounds and was hit four times; its cabin and wardroom were "riddled" with bullets. The *Petrel* suffered light damage from two Confederate projectiles while firing twenty-two rounds in return. The ironclad *Choctaw* also was hit but no serious damage resulted. Walker lost one man killed on the *Baron DeKalb* and eight men wounded on the other three boats that were damaged.[62]

Adams estimated that he delayed the Federal boats at least one hour and claimed to have gotten away with no losses. Despite the fact that he got the drop on Walker's fleet, the Federal gunboats handily dealt with Adams's guns and cavalrymen. The boats proceeded downriver after their small battle and reached Snyder's Bluff by 2:00 P.M. Walker's command reached the mouth of the Yazoo by four thirty.[63]

The naval expedition up the Yazoo River on May 19–23 confirmed that the Confederates had hastily evacuated the east bank all the way up to Yazoo City. It also opened the way for permanent army occupation of the bluff line in the near future. Moreover, the expedition indicated that Confederate cavalry lurked in the area and was ready to take on boats in hit-and-run attacks.

JOHNSTON

Johnston was keen to hamper Grant's logistical support even while he struggled with the task of accumulating manpower in the Jackson area. "An army will be necessary to relieve Vicksburg," Pemberton warned Johnston on May 20. "Will it not be sent?" By May 21 Johnston had three brigades (led by Brig. Gen. States Rights Gist, Brig. Gen. Matthew D. Ector, and Brig. Gen. Evander McNair) in addition to Maj. Gen. William W. Loring's Division. More would arrive soon—Brig. Gen. Samuel Bell Maxey's Brigade by May 23 and Brig. Gen. Nathan Evans's Brigade, Maj. Gen. John C. Breckinridge's Division, and Brig. Gen. William H. Jackson's cavalry division by June 4. Johnston eventually accumulated 24,000 men, a formidable concentration by Confederate standards.[64]

But that sizeable field army was a thing of the future; as of May 21, Johnston only had the equivalent of two divisions and was heavily outnumbered by Grant. His army was top-heavy with infantry, so Johnston pleaded for more cavalry and artillery. He also needed more small arms and ammunition, but the Confederate arsenal at Selma could not fully supply them.[65]

It would take some time for Johnston to prepare a force capable of challenging Grant. In the meanwhile, Pemberton relied on Johnston as his only hope of relief. He warned him that Grant had at least 60,000 men (an estimate that doubled actual Union strength). Pemberton also requested percussion caps for his small arms.[66]

DECIDING TO ATTACK

The most important work Grant engaged in during May 20–21 was to decide his immediate course of action. He met with his corps leaders on the twentieth—Sherman was careful in his memoirs to point out this was not a council of war but a conference to compare notes about why the assault of May 19 had failed. In Sherman's words, the four men agreed that "the nature of the ground" had compelled them "to limit our attacks to the strongest parts of the enemy's lines." The group agreed that a better-planned and more general effort should be made to break through Lockett's line.[67]

Grant offered a number of cogent reasons for trying another assault when he wrote his report of the campaign in July and in his memoirs twenty years later. Johnston continued to pose a threat that would increase in potency with the passage of time. A long siege would require the transfer of reinforcements to Grant, siphoning off troops from other areas. Moreover, if Vicksburg fell soon, Grant could turn east and "drive Johnston from the State." There was yet another reason for trying a bigger assault. In fact, Grant called it "the first consideration of all." It was that his men "believed they could carry the works in their front, and would not have worked so patiently in the trenches if they had not been allowed to try."[68]

According to McClernand, Grant did not announce his intention to attack until May 21. When McClernand learned of that decision, he voiced an opinion that made sense. "Concentration of our forces against one or two points, and not the dispersion of them into a multitude of columns, was my volunteered suggestion," he wrote a few months later. Grant never explained why he rejected this suggestion but geographer-historian Warren Grabau has assumed it was because the terrain offered no good ground for concentrating large masses of men. To a large degree that was true, except along the axis of Graveyard Road where Sherman massed Blair's division for another try at Stockade Redan. Michael Ballard believes that Grant interpreted the results of May 19 in a positive way, viewing them as a limited assault that gained ground from which to try a larger attack.[69]

Another angle on this question lies in the paucity of information about the Confederate works. The Federals knew little about the size and extent of Lockett's fortifications. They could not identify weak segments, a necessity if they wanted to mass troops opposite points where they had a chance of breaking through. Theoretically McClernand was right to urge concentration, but practical difficulties such as where to concentrate and how to concentrate were the real problems. As an alternative, Grant allowed his corps commanders latitude in preparing their assaults as they saw fit in what should be defined as a general assault dispersed across a wide front.

Why did Grant not make an effort to attack the southern sector of the Confederate perimeter? The weakest Confederate troops held that line. The answer is that Grant did not have enough men to cover that sector. He was compelled to plant his right flank on Walnut Hills north of Vicksburg to secure a flow of supplies, and his available manpower was not large enough to stretch the line to the river south of Vicksburg. Fortunately for the Federals, Pemberton had no interest in escaping the city by moving south.[70]

A Confederate officer named W. H. Johnson talked to Grant after the fall of Vicksburg and asked him if he ever encouraged Pemberton to evacuate civilians from the city. Grant defended himself in this regard by pointing out that he did not have the troops to close the ring around Vicksburg. If non-combatants had wanted to leave, they could have done so. It therefore would have been "presumption in me to offer to permit Genl Pemberton to do that which I could not prevent him from doing."[71]

On May 21, Grant issued an order that set 10:00 A.M. of May 22 as the start time of the assault. He suggested his subordinates form their troops "in columns of platoons, or by a flank if the ground over which they may have to pass will not admit of a greater front." It was uncommon for an army commander to offer detailed instructions about the type of formation to be used. This bit of advice indicates how seriously Grant thought about the terrain outside Vicksburg and how he believed those terrain problems could be solved by using narrow columns. No one literally employed Grant's suggestion, for a column of platoons would have created a very long and narrow formation.[72]

Grant also urged a sense of battle spirit in his attack order. He wanted the men to go in light, carrying nothing more than ammunition, a filled canteen, and one day's ration. Grant further instructed the troops to fix bayonets and advance at quick time. They should "march immediately upon the enemy without firing a gun until the outer works are carried." Grant pinpointed the reason he wanted an attack on May 22: "If prosecuted with vigor, it is confidently believed this course will carry Vicksburg in a very short time, and with much less loss than would be sustained by delay. Every day's delay enables the enemy to strengthen his defenses and increases his chance for receiving aid from outside."[73]

To better chances of success, Grant ordered that Sherman, McPherson, and McClernand set their watches according to his so "there should be no difference between them in movement of assault." It has long been thought that May 22 was the first time that a military operation was coordinated by the use of synchronized watches, but there is evidence that Sherman had already done this at the battle of Chickasaw Bayou five months before. It is possible that Sherman suggested this method of coordinating the start of an assault to Grant.[74]

Having made his decision, Grant arranged support for the attack. He asked Porter to annoy the enemy with gunboat and mortar fire during the night of May 21. In addition, the gunboats should shell the city all morning until at least 10:30 A.M. Grant issued tentative orders to McArthur to move

Hall's brigade north from Warrenton toward Vicksburg and be prepared to take advantage of any opportunity to enter the city.[75]

Sherman spent quite a bit of time on May 21 examining the Fifteenth Corps sector and decided that the best opportunity lay in a massed assault along Graveyard Road. This was the only line of attack that did not involve climbing up and down steep slopes. Blair's division once again would conduct the assault, while Steele's division would stage "a strong demonstration" to the right.[76]

"Each column will attack by the watch, and not depend on signals," Sherman explained. Blair would select a small party of 150 men to lead his assault, and Brig. Gen. James M. Tuttle's division would be in supporting distance to the rear. All of Blair's officers were to go in on foot. Sherman allowed Steele to choose his own target but suggested the area encompassed by Brig. Gen. John M. Thayer's near approach to the enemy works on May 19. While urging his troops to their utmost, Sherman expressed hope that May 22 would be the end of the long campaign for Vicksburg. "As soon as the enemy gives way, he must be pushed to the very heart of the city, where he must surrender."[77]

Word of the pending assault filtered along Sherman's line during the afternoon and evening of May 21. Col. Thomas Kilby Smith wrote a circular explaining the plans for his regimental leaders. In Blair's and Steele's artillery, Sherman's order was read out loud to the gunners that night. At least in the 8th Wisconsin, official notification of the planned attack was met with stern resolve by the soldiers. "Boys all ready for the arduous task," noted Edwin Farley.[78]

McPherson ordered Maj. Gen. John A. Logan's chief engineer, Capt. Stewart R. Tresilian, to make scaling ladders for the infantry to mount the Rebel parapet. Tresilian found lumber at a cotton gin behind Union lines and palings from the garden fence of a nearby house. From this material he fashioned forty ladders. Tresilian made sure they were from fifteen to twenty-two feet long and light enough for one man to carry. Yet the ladders were strong enough to support the weight of two men even when laid in a horizontal position over a hole ten feet wide. The engineer cleverly tied a rope to one end of the ladders so they could be pulled along on the ground. "Thus the enemy could not perceive them until the assault was made."[79]

McClernand received Grant's order on the evening of May 21 and relayed the information to his subordinates. Carr's division relieved Smith's division on the front line; McClernand told Smith he would support Carr's men as they made the main effort on the right wing of the corps. Osterhaus would conduct the main effort on the left wing. McClernand's 10,000 troops held a sector of one and a quarter miles with a four-mile gap between his left and the river and a gap of 1,000 yards between his right and McPherson's left. Both gaps worried McClernand. In order to deceive the enemy that they were invested, he sent troops of Maj. Daniel B. Bush's 2nd Illinois Cavalry under cover of darkness to build fires and deploy pickets across the wide gap to his left.[80]

Osterhaus received word of the attack at 6:00 P.M. and wondered how to select a mode of assault. It was a "very puzzling choice." After studying the terrain, he decided to take advantage of the cover offered by the irregular ground. In addition to his two brigades, Osterhaus could use McGinnis's brigade of Hovey's division.[81]

Carr filtered the attack order to his brigade leaders and they told their regimental commanders about it. Lawler received word during the late afternoon of May 21 and called a conference at brigade headquarters. He and the regimental commanders gazed across 400 yards of rugged landscape toward Railroad Redoubt. "The whole appearance of the works was forbidding and formidable," recalled Bluford Wilson, Lawler's assistant adjutant general. Then Lawler suggested a ploy that would pay dividends the next day. He proposed that all four regiments move forward under cover of darkness and take position as close as possible to the enemy. They could avoid a good deal of exposure this way. It was done, placing Lawler's brigade some seventy-five yards from the objective by dawn.[82]

According to Col. William M. Stone, Lawler appointed his 22nd Iowa to lead the brigade and gave Stone carte blanche to choose the point of attack. This declaration is not supported by any other evidence. Stone claimed that during a personal reconnaissance at dusk he decided the brigade should attack Railroad Redoubt and soon after moved his regiment forward to snuggle closer to it, not mentioning that the entire brigade did the same thing. Stone also failed to mention that several of his men had already scouted this terrain on the night of May 20–21. John Smiley of Company G led a group that crawled past Confederate pickets until it lodged so close to Railroad Redoubt the Federals could distinguish the outline of the parapet against the night sky. Samuel C. Jones of the 22nd Iowa believed Stone used Smiley's information when he advanced the regiment on the night of May 21, the men crawling through felled timber to negotiate a deep ravine.[83]

Stone was trying to embellish his role in the attack, but McClernand also was guilty of embellishment. He claimed that when Grant's attack order reached his headquarters, he and several subordinates harbored doubts.

It seemed "unfortunate and likely to bring disaster upon us," McClernand wrote Halleck. He told his subordinates they had to obey it, and received the reply from them, "If we fail it shall not be our fault."[84]

This statement by McClernand grew out of the bitter fight he had with Grant after the May 22 attack. But before that controversy heated to its brightest flame, McClernand also wrote to a correspondent that he "thought and privately characterized the order as 'absurd.' No man, I believe in my Corps entertained a different opinion."[85]

The problem with both of these McClernand statements is that they are not supported by other evidence. There is no reliable indication that Thirteenth Corps officers felt the attack was doomed before it started. The mood among McClernand's rank and file, however, was uncertain. I. L. Fussell, in his regimental history of the 34th Indiana, reported that Grant's attack order "was not received with the enthusiasm that had characterized our former and late actions." This lack of confidence stemmed from an awareness that the Confederates had nearly a week to get over their depression concerning the disasters of May 16 and 17.[86]

Cpl. Charles Wilcox of the 33rd Illinois noted in his diary that word of the pending attack caused most regimental officers to look sad and resigned. They were opposed to assaulting "as a general thing." Even though Wilcox overheard an officer characterize the Confederate works as "a great scare-crow and that we can rush right over them," he did not believe it. "My heart is much depressed," he confessed to his diary. "The men don't want to charge and yet they say they will do it when ordered."[87]

No matter how far the will to engage spread through the ranks, one thing is certain: the Army of the Tennessee was about to launch its biggest tactical offensive of the war. For better or worse, Grant had decided on one more try at Lockett's earthworks, and it would be a bigger, better-coordinated effort than the small battle that took place on May 19. Lodged in Pugh's brigade of Lauman's division, and therefore not slated to take part in the attack, George B. Carter of the 33rd Wisconsin put it very well: "The whole Union Army is knocking at the gates of Vicksburg."[88]

Dismay and Bewilderment

BLAIR, MAY 22

The Army of the Tennessee's biggest battle to date was ready to start on the morning of May 22. It would lead off with a concentrated attack along Graveyard Road conducted by Blair's division, Sherman's old command. Formed in a column formation in contrast to the lines it had employed on May 19, the division aimed at the same target, Stockade Redan. The preparation for this attack was nearly flawless. But it would run into trouble because of the exposed line of approach along the road, the strong physical barrier posed by the bulk of Stockade Redan, and a significant breakdown of will among some leading troops when faced with the daunting challenge before them.

The day set for Grant's next storming of Vicksburg displayed typical weather for this time of season. The sun shone brightly and the temperature rose to be warm and then quite hot. Federal artillerists began preparations for a massive bombardment as early as 3:00 A.M. so they could open fire at dawn. Blair assembled a total of twenty-seven artillery pieces to support his attack on Stockade Redan, all of them no farther than 500 yards from the target. Five batteries commenced firing when the sun came up and continued without interruption until 10:00 A.M.[1]

ARTILLERY PREPARATION

The long bombardment fatigued the Federal gunners by midmorning. Nevertheless, Sherman's artillery chief, Maj. Ezra Taylor, told Lt. Joseph R. Reed that he should take two pieces of his 2nd Iowa Battery out of their protective earthworks and move them forward by hand to what Taylor thought was a better position. Reed was not enthusiastic about this, but he had to obey. To help his tired men, Reed accepted an offer by Col. James W. Judy of the 114th Illinois in Brig. Gen. James M. Tuttle's division to help him move the guns forward. Reed positioned the pieces, but as he suspected, they received too much punishment outside their works to justify the move. One shell exploded beneath a piece and wounded three gunners. He soon asked Taylor for permission to return and rolled the guns back to their earthworks.[2]

Meanwhile the bombardment continued. A correspondent of the *Chicago Daily Tribune* counted 145 rounds in just five minutes. Extrapolating that figure, he estimated that at least 2,000 projectiles sailed into the Confederate position from 8:30 to 10:00 A.M.[3]

"It was the grandest and most awe-inspiring scene I ever witnessed," thought J. H. Jones of the 38th Mississippi. The sight reminded Jones of stories he had heard of a meteor shower in 1833. Brigade leader Col. Francis M. Cockrell reported that "the air was literally burdened with hissing missiles of death." Even at Canton, fifty miles to the northeast, Rebel troops could distinctly hear the Federal guns. They characterized the sound as "very heavy and constant" and assumed it meant a major battle was under way.[4]

Despite the heavy fire, Blair's bombardment did little damage. Jones noted that even a dense fall of projectiles could be endured if one had a good trench and squatted down against the side of the ditch that faced the oncoming rounds. "A 12 pound Shell has just Struck and buried itself in the ground within 6 feet of me without exploding," wrote Lt. Gabriel M. Killgore of the 17th Louisiana in his diary. As the guns of other divisions joined Blair's, the entire Federal line from Walnut Hills to the left flank of McClernand's corps pounded the Confederates. Yet the bombardment merely put a group of Missouri Rebels to sleep. They "could plainly feel the impact of every shell or solid shot that buried deep in the yielding soil" near them. According to James E. Payne, half a dozen of his comrades dozed off because of that sensation. The effect of the shelling on Stockade Redan was a little more telling. Rounds tore apart some of the palings in the stockade, splintered them, and sent the wooden shards tearing through the ranks of men waiting behind. This shocking danger led the Missourians who manned the work to call Stockade Redan the "slaughter pen." Even so, the effect of Blair's bombardment cannot be counted as important in softening up the position. It inflicted only minimal damage to men and works.[5]

Sherman's plan constricted the main Fifteenth Corps attack to one division, supported by another, and along a narrow axis of advance. Blair's division formed a column of brigades along Graveyard Road, with Tuttle's division a bit behind, also in a column. Because Grant had settled on 10:00 A.M. as the starting time of the assault, it was possible for Blair to wait until dawn of May 22 before forming his division. The 30th Ohio in Brig. Gen. Hugh Ewing's brigade did not receive word of the attack until 6:00 A.M. when the regiment was further told it would lead the assault.[6]

Blair formed his division in a ravine to the south of Graveyard Road and about 400 yards from Stockade Redan. He planned for each brigade to debouch from the ravine and turn left to guide along the road, Ewing in the lead to be followed by Col. Giles A. Smith and then Col. Thomas Kilby Smith. Joseph A. Saunier of the 47th Ohio estimated the troops would be fully exposed to fire for 300 yards of the distance they had to travel.[7]

The regiments of Ewing's brigade formed in columns of companies. In the 30th Ohio at the head of the brigade, Company C formed in the lead to be followed by Companies A and K. Company F had been left behind to sharp shoot, but the other nine companies prepared to lead Sherman's main attack. The 37th Ohio, next behind the 30th, had also left part of its personnel behind. Companies C and G were on picket in an effort to connect with Maj. Gen. Frederick Steele's division to the right, and Company D and part of Company F were detached on fatigue duty. The men fixed bayonets, at least according to the commander of Company C, 37th Ohio, and waited for the bombardment to end.[8]

THE FORLORN HOPE

Sherman wanted a special advance unit to lead the way along Graveyard Road, and Blair put one together on the morning of May 22. It consisted of two officers and fifty men from each brigade and was led by Capt. John H. Groce of the 30th Ohio. Every brigade leader recruited a number of men in proportion to the strength of each regiment to make up his quota. In the 54th Ohio of Kilby Smith's brigade, seven volunteers were needed but eleven men offered to go. A similar scenario played out in the 57th Ohio, with fourteen volunteers stepping forward to fill nine slots in what would become known as the Forlorn Hope. Thirty-two men of the 30th Ohio stood up to volunteer.[9]

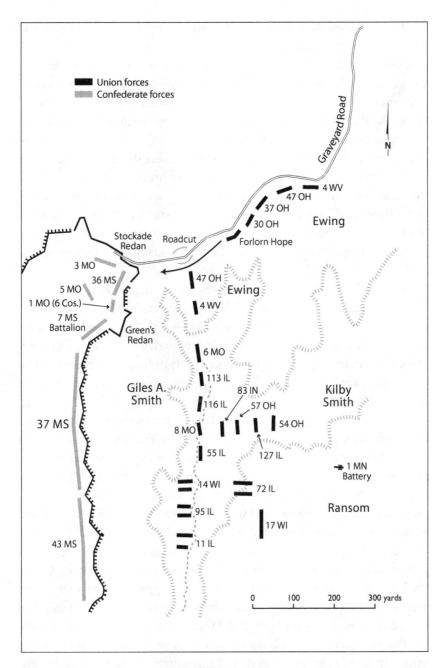

Ewing's brigade, May 22

Union forces
Confederate forces

Graveyard Road

N

4 WV
47 OH
37 OH
30 OH
Ewing
Forlorn Hope

Stockade Redan
Roadcut

47 OH
Ewing
4 WV

3 MO
36 MS
5 MO
1 MO (6 Cos.)
7 MS Battalion
Green's Redan

6 MO

113 IL

Giles A. Smith

83 IN
116 IL
57 OH
54 OH

Kilby Smith

37 MS

8 MO

55 IL
127 IL

1 MN Battery

14 WI
72 IL

Ransom

95 IL
17 WI

43 MS
11 IL

0   100   200   300 yards

Col. Hamilton N. Eldridge insisted that the troops of his 127th Illinois were so eager "to distinguish themselves and be of service to their country" that four times the number of volunteers could have been secured beyond the eleven needed for the Forlorn Hope. But Andrew McCormack told a different story. His lieutenant "called the Boys around him and wanted to know who the man was that would volunteer to go ahead and be the first on the breast works." His comrades became "all silent[,] not a word spoke for a few minutes it was a Solem thing and almost sure death but none of the Boys would go." Finally, McCormack decided to break the stalemate. "I told the Lieut that I would go as far as I could and if I was killed I knew the Lord would be with me." He was the only man of his company willing to volunteer. "As I put on my Cartridge box and shouldered my gun the Boys all wished me back safe, as I left to join the crowd there was many a wishfull eye on me. . . . I know I had their Prayers to strengthen me on."[10]

McCormack's letter to his family, written two days after the attack, reveals a different view of the will to fight than was presented in the official reports. McCormack's view was backed up by Orderly Sgt. George Theodore Hyatt, whose company commander told him to detail men to the Forlorn Hope if he could not get enough volunteers. Hyatt felt so reluctant to order men to such dangerous duty that he volunteered himself. After the war some regimental histories exaggerated the will to serve in the Forlorn Hope. The committee that put together a book on the 55th Illinois insisted the regiment produced 100 volunteers to fill only twelve slots in the organization.[11]

Soldiers in Giles Smith's brigade also hesitated upon learning that volunteers were needed for this dangerous mission. According to J. J. Kellogg of the 113th Illinois, one of Grant's staff officers broke the news to the regiment and in addition promised a sixty-day furlough to all who survived the experience. "We looked into each other's faces for some seconds," recalled Kellogg. "We were speechless and felt a dread of what might develop." After some time, Joe Smith broke the silence. He said to his bunkmate, "Come on, Lish," whereupon Smith and Elisha Johns stepped forward. Only a few seconds later, Sgt. James Henry also volunteered. He was followed by three more men, from Company B, to fill the regimental quota. "We looked upon our three comrades as already dead or wounded men," Kellogg reported. He ironically noted in his memoirs that all three survived the attack and many who had refused to volunteer died.[12]

To inspire the 150 men, Ewing provided a new headquarters flag belonging to his brigade as the banner of the Forlorn Hope. Pvt. Howell G. Trogden of the 8th Missouri in Giles Smith's brigade was selected to carry it. Trogden had a good record of service thus far in the war. He had been captured by Confederate patrols near Ripley, Mississippi, in July 1862 while delivering dispatches and was paroled and released the following October. In fact, Trogden recalled after the war that the idea of a flag for the Forlorn Hope was his own. When Sherman spoke to the group to encourage the volunteers, Trogden suggested they needed a banner. Sherman saw Ewing's brigade flag nearby and gave it to Trogden. "It's a dangerous job, my boy, to try to put that flag on that fort!" Sherman told the twenty-two-year-old volunteer.[13]

The Forlorn Hope needed scaling ladders to negotiate the ditch and parapet of Stockade Redan, and the house Grant used as his headquarters was the nearest source of lumber. The general moved into a tent and the house was quickly taken down, the boards were fastened into ladders, and the finished product was piled up for the volunteers. When they reached the house area the Forlorn Hope members found a pile of logs, a separate pile of lumber, and a collection of ready-made ladders. Groce organized the 150 men into three sections of fifty troops each. The leading section carried the logs, two men taking charge of one log, with the intention of laying them across the ditch. The second section took the lumber with the intention of laying the loose boards across the timber to assemble a bridge. The third section carried the scaling ladders and had the assignment of crossing the ditch and using the ladders to climb the steep parapet. Each man was expected to carry his gun as well as the material assigned to his section.[14]

Sherman, Giles Smith, and Ewing felt it necessary to harangue the volunteers before they set out. Smith also promised everyone a sixty-day furlough, in Sherman's presence, and according to survivors of the attack followed through with that promise. Ewing offered practical advice since his brigade would immediately follow the Forlorn Hope. If the volunteers could not cross the ditch they should "bear to the left, and cross the curtain" that connected to Stockade Redan from the south. This curtain, by definition, would have a smaller parapet than the redan and presumably would have a smaller ditch as well.[15]

THE WILL TO FIGHT

How enthusiastic were Blair's men about the prospects of success and survival in the pending assault? Some observers insisted their will to fight was strong. The 4th West Virginia in Ewing's brigade "went into this charge with great enthusiasm," reported Thomas H. Barton. But then Barton was detailed as a hospital steward and was not with the regiment when it formed for the assault. Henry S. Nourse of the 55th Illinois frankly recalled that those men who had gotten close to the Rebel works in the attack of May 19 "felt little hope of a successful issue" three days later. Perhaps sensing a lack of confidence, Col. Augustus C. Parry harangued his regiment before going in. "Every man of the 47th Regiment follow me," he began. "If you see any officer behind a tree or a stump, shoot him on the spot. If you see any privates behind trees or stumps, shoot them on the spot." Overheated rhetoric such as this could only come from a fear that the men needed some emotional stimulant to boost their will to fight.[16]

Privately, other Federals expressed their concerns about the coming battle. Brig. Gen. Ralph P. Buckland, who led a brigade in Tuttle's division, took a few minutes to tell his wife of the imminent attack only a short time before 10:00 A.M. "If I get through the assault to day safely will write you immediately. I have so many things to think of that I must close this hasty letter." Buckland planned to write another letter after the battle but only "if I get through" it. Capt. Henry Schmidt of Company C, 37th Ohio, had no time to write to his Cate before the assault. His men had stood picket duty all the previous night and, when relieved on the morning of May 22, were told to get ready to assault. "All right," he told Cate a couple of days later, "prepared for my last day on erth."[17]

The Federals had every reason to be worried about the planned attack. Stockade Redan was well manned with veteran troops, and the heated artillery bombardment was an obvious signal to be ready for an assault. The 36th Mississippi and six companies of the 1st Missouri held the southeast face of the redan and therefore would bear the brunt of Blair's attack. The 3rd Missouri held the north face of the redan and stretched out along part of the stockade, while the 5th Missouri waited in reserve near the earthwork. Cockrell had his Missouri brigade spread out in small detachments in and near Stockade Redan with some parts of it ready to go anywhere.[18]

EWING

The Forlorn Hope was formed and ready to lead Ewing's brigade before the time scheduled for the assault to begin. Ewing himself was in charge of starting it. He kept an eye on his watch, which had been synchronized with that of his superiors, and gave the word at exactly 10:04 A.M. He never offered an explanation for why he waited four minutes. The 150 volunteers emerged from the ravine and made a sharp left turn to align with Graveyard Road. In the process they saw a group of Federal officers to their left. It was Sherman

Hugh B. Ewing. Another brother-in-law and foster brother of William T. Sherman's, Ewing served as colonel of the 30th Ohio in the East before assuming command of a brigade that was transferred to the Mississippi Valley. At the rank of brigadier general, he ably led the command in the first Fifteenth Corps attack on May 22. Driving directly along Graveyard Road toward Stockade Redan, most of his men stalled at the roadcut or were diverted to the south of the road well short of the objective. Ewing later commanded a division under Sherman and practiced law after the war. (Library of Congress, LC-DIG-cwpbh-03172)

and Giles Smith, according to J. J. Kellogg, who saw the group from his position within the ranks of the 113th Illinois. The officers were "standing behind large trees, and squinted cautiously out to the right and left, exposing as little of their brass buttons as possible, and I think I saw them dodge a couple of times." Of course, Sherman did not view this as Kellogg did. "I took a position within two hundred yards of the rebel parapet," he wrote, "on the off slope of a spur of ground, where by advancing two or three steps I could see every thing."[19]

The Forlorn Hope led the van of Ewing's brigade with spirit. The 150 volunteers moved on the double-quick, "and away we went down the road for the fort as fast as our legs could carry us," reported Andrew McCormack.

Only a few shots were fired by the Confederates before the group passed through a narrow roadcut about 100 yards from Stockade Redan. The cut was four feet high on the north side and six feet high on the south side. It extended about the length of a regimental column. A lone oak tree sixteen inches in diameter stood on the north bank of the cut. Here the full force of the Rebels' first volley descended on the 150 men and brought many of them down. "For an instant I was senseless," recalled Andrew E. Goldsberg of the 127th Illinois. The survivors of the first volley turned right because the road curved in that direction, before they threw themselves into the ditch at the base of the parapet for protection.[20]

Along the way, especially when the volley hit the Forlorn Hope, many of the volunteers were so rattled by the experience that they dropped their logs, lumber, and scaling ladders. In fact, they were lucky to survive the advance. Jacob Sanford, the commissary sergeant of the 55th Illinois, escaped without a serious wound even though his ankle was sprained when a grapeshot hit the plank he carried and smashed it into his foot. In addition, two bullets made holes in his hat, carrying away a lock of his hair, and nine other bullets perforated his blouse without touching the flesh. All this happened in a very short time. An eight-inch-wide plank carried by one man was perforated with twenty-two bullet holes. It took only three minutes for the Forlorn Hope to move from the starting point of the attack to the ditch of Stockade Redan.[21]

Initially what was left of the volunteers made a show of success. Enough material had been carried to the ditch to form a crude bridge, and John H. Groce, a lieutenant named O'Neal, and color-bearer Trogden crossed it. Sgt. James W. Larabee of the 55th Illinois helped push Trogden up the steep slope of the parapet until the color-bearer planted Ewing's flag on the north front close to the northeast corner. Larabee crawled up to Trogden's right in time to hear the bearer yell, "You sons of bitches surrender this fort." Other men followed these three and began to dig into the loosely packed soil with their bayonets, forming little foxholes in the slope. To observers in Blair's division, only the flag could be seen, the men themselves disappearing into the parapet.[22]

While a few men dug holes in the slope, many more survivors of the first volley found refuge in the ditch. Andrew E. Goldsberg estimated it was twelve feet wide and four to five feet deep, with the crest of the parapet about ten feet above the bottom of the ditch. It did not provide complete protection — Confederate infantrymen could reach some parts of the ditch with their fire. But for most of the Federals — and one Missouri Rebel esti-

Stockade Redan, Federal view. A modern-day image from the Union side of the battlefield, this photograph depicts Graveyard Road, the terrain, and the objective in the distance. Ewing's brigade charged in column along the road until it came to grief at the roadcut, which is partly obscured by the limbs of the lone tree standing along the roadway. (Photograph by Earl J. Hess)

mated that fifty Yankees got into the ditch—the excavation proved to be a lifesaver.[23]

The Forlorn Hope utterly failed to break into Stockade Redan, which was its primary goal. The volunteers barely established a crossing of the deep ditch for a few of their own, much less for the bulk of Ewing's brigade, which had already started its advance. The Forlorn Hope survivors stalled on the parapet and in the ditch.

The 30th Ohio, leading Ewing's command, waited three minutes to let the Forlorn Hope get to Stockade Redan. During that short wait, Blair stood near the regiment, his head uncovered, and Ewing prepared to lead the men forward. Ewing took off his coat and rolled up his shirt sleeves. He prominently displayed a revolver in its holster and raised his sword as the time approached for the Ohio men to start. When Ewing yelled the order to advance, Lt. Col. George H. Hildt led the 30th Ohio forward into Graveyard Road and moved at the double-quick. As Blair watched, it seemed to the division commander that the regiment advanced with the same "impetuosity and gallantry" as had the Forlorn Hope.[24]

Advancing in column, the regiment received fire from the front and obliquely on both sides even before reaching the roadcut. Inside the defile

Stockade Redan, Confederate view. Taken from inside Stockade Redan, this view offers a chilling indication of what Ewing's men were up against as they charged toward Stockade Redan. The roadcut is clearly visible at the curve of the road in the midground. (Photograph by Earl J. Hess)

were the bodies of Forlorn Hope volunteers, dead and wounded, causing the regiment to slow down. But the 30th Ohio slowed even more when heavy fire from Stockade Redan directed into the roadcut brought down a number of men. Heavy casualties occurred in the first few ranks of the regiment, which littered the roadbed with bodies. "The second company forced its way over the remains of the first," Ewing reported, "and a third over those of the preceding, but their perseverance served only further to encumber the impassable way." Many members of the regiment negotiated the tangle of bodies and emerged from the roadcut to continue the advance, "bent forward about half way down" to avoid some of the flying lead, according to Robert McCrory. The rest found the cut "impassable, choked with killed and wounded men." By the time Cpl. Edward E. Schweitzer and Company I, at the tail end of the regimental column, came to the cut, bodies were so "piled up in front . . . it was impossible to get over them."[25]

From the perspective of Stockade Redan, the Federal advance inspired respect. Cpl. James Bradley of the 5th Missouri watched as the Forlorn Hope "seemed to almost melt away" at the first volley. "It halted, staggered and for the moment dismay and bewilderment seemed to seize hold upon it." But then the 30th Ohio "came rushing to the rescue." The sight of these stout men moving as if unstoppable shook the confidence of the defenders. It was difficult "to prevent a stampede," a former Confederate officer told Robert McCrory of the 30th Ohio in 1890.[26]

But the 30th Ohio men who reached Stockade Redan little more than five minutes after starting the advance could rescue no one. According to Henry R. Brinkerhoff, the survivors of the first three companies, C, A, and K, reached the Confederate fortifications and took shelter with the Forlorn Hope men in their ditch. Some of them crawled up onto the parapet to join their comrades lodged in foxholes and planted the regimental flag on the slope. But the majority of the 30th Ohio that made it past the roadcut took shelter in Graveyard Road itself only a few yards from the redan. The Confederates had dug the road down three to five feet deep near the earthwork "for the purpose of leveling the drive." This sunken section of Graveyard Road lay twenty-five yards from Stockade Redan and was long enough to shelter an entire regiment. Most men of the 30th Ohio and, as Brinkerhoff estimated, about fifty men of the Forlorn Hope sheltered in it, unwilling to brave enemy fire to reach the redan.[27]

There was little more for the 30th Ohio men to do. Those who reached the ditch soon realized that the Forlorn Hope had failed to provide crossing places over it. As Lt. William C. Porter of the 55th Illinois, one of the officers in the Forlorn Hope, put it, "Some men of Ewing's brigade came up, but not sufficient to warrant our thrusting them over the ramparts, to be either slaughtered or taken prisoners." In fact, a couple of 30th Ohio men who tried to climb the steep parapet were inadvertently shot by Federal covering fire. The rest took the lesson and gave up any effort to climb out of the ditch.[28]

Lt. Col. Louis von Blessingh's 37th Ohio immediately followed the 30th Ohio in Ewing's brigade column and encountered worse conditions than its predecessor. According to Ewing, the left files of the regimental column were so stunned by "a deadly fire" when the men approached the roadcut that they broke apart. The rest of the regiment tried to continue but found the roadcut too cluttered with the bodies of Forlorn Hope volunteers and troops of the 30th Ohio. Members of the 37th Ohio also fell inside the cut, obstructing it even more. Maj. Charles Hipp, who wrote the regimental report, portrayed the men as valiantly trying to overcome these obstacles. The men "forced their way over them, and came forward in good style." They then deployed in a line near Stockade Redan and opened fire as von Blessingh was wounded and Hipp took control of the regiment.[29]

But Blair reported far less generously about the 37th Ohio. The regiment "faltered and gave way under the fire of the enemy," he told Sherman two days later, "which was far from being severe on this regiment, and was, in fact, directed upon the head of the column. The men lay down in the road and behind every inequality of ground which afforded them shelter." Ewing, von Blessingh, and other officers tried to get them up and moving, but no one responded. A staff officer "pushed some of the men ahead by main force, but they would not go." No one associated with the 37th Ohio supported Blair's appraisal of the regiment's performance. Capt. Henry Schmidt of Company C told his wife that "the C.S. fired so hard on us . . . that we had to fall behinde a hill for we could not git up their Brest works on the above account."[30]

It is not unusual that regimental members would avoid mentioning any failure of will on the part of the 37th Ohio, but one needs to take Blair's bluntly worded report seriously. The division commander was on the ground and in a position to observe the regiment's performance. One is forced to the conclusion that his version of the story has considerable merit—at the very least, the truth lay somewhere between the extremes, and that by definition means the regiment failed to give its all in the attack.

By this time, the roadcut was so encumbered with dead and injured bodies that it proved impossible for the rest of Ewing's brigade to pass through it. According to Blair, the main fault lay with the men of the 37th Ohio, who "refused to move, and remained in the road, blocking the way." The leading ranks of the 47th Ohio "became entangled" in the human mass and stalled. Colonel Parry then extricated his troops, and Blair told him to go "by another route, to the left of the road." Parry did so, moving his regiment by the left flank off the roadway and into a convenient ravine. The 4th West Virginia, last in the brigade column, followed the 47th Ohio without becoming entangled in the gory mess around the roadcut. The two regiments formed a line extending south from near Graveyard Road and advanced forward as far as they dared, reaching a relatively sheltered bit of ground about 150 yards (Ewing thought it was closer to seventy yards) from the Confederate line. Soon many members of the 30th Ohio moved to this line and formed, willing to contribute in any way to the further progress of the fumbled assault. All these Federals could do for the time was open fire on the dirt parapets in front.[31]

Sherman's artillery tried to support Ewing's attack but failed to silence the enemy. From his station with Battery E, 1st Illinois Light Artillery, John Merrilles watched as the Forlorn Hope raced forward to be followed by the 30th Ohio. His comrades loaded and fired "just as fast as we possible could" and thought they had suppressed the Rebels. But when the Forlorn Hope appeared to be halfway to Stockade Redan, Confederate fire increased "terribly," small arms and artillery together. Merrilles watched as the formations broke up.[32]

GILES SMITH AND KILBY SMITH

Blair had enough of the attack route along Graveyard Road. It had proved to be an utter failure. He ordered Giles Smith, whose brigade was supposed to follow Ewing, to divert his regiments off the road and follow the route taken by the 47th Ohio and the 4th West Virginia. This way "was better covered" from Confederate fire, Blair admitted, but the ravine had so much felled timber in it that it prevented the massing of large formations. Blair told Smith to make his way through the ravine as best he could, take position to the left of the 47th Ohio and 4th West Virginia, and then advance in line of battle toward the Confederates. It took some time for Smith to execute these orders. Sometime early in the afternoon, nearly four hours after the start of the grand attack, he was able to form his brigade in line (100 yards from the enemy, according to Blair) and take stock of his position. Smith realized that Brig. Gen. Thomas E. G. Ransom's brigade of the Seventeenth Corps was located a short distance to his left and opened communication with its commander. The two men arranged to attack in concert.[33]

Blair's last brigade, commanded by Thomas Kilby Smith, moved behind Giles Smith's command to support it in the projected assault. Kilby Smith had prepared for the day carefully, issuing a circular to his regimental commanders that spelled out the brigade formation with the 55th Illinois in the lead, followed by the 83rd Indiana, 57th Ohio, 127th Illinois, and last the 54th Ohio. He had his men open up a place to form in the ravine south of Graveyard Road on the night of May 21 and moved through narrow passages in the felled timber the next morning when Blair's advance began.[34]

As the head of Kilby Smith's column turned left onto Graveyard Road and headed toward the target, it became apparent to him that "the programme had been changed. Instead of a dense column marching by the flank down the road, as I had expected, the ground I had passed over in the first assault on the 19th instant was covered by scattered masses." Kilby Smith could see Ewing's flag waving from the parapet of Stockade Redan. He did not know what to do; there appeared to be no possibility of going on, so he halted his brigade in the roadway.[35]

Unfortunately, that halt cost Kilby Smith some casualties. A rifled artillery projectile narrowly missed the adjutant of the 55th Illinois, who instinctively jumped even though his back was to the round's approach. The projectile sailed through the space he vacated and went on to hurt three or four men, mortally wounding a sergeant. It shattered the arm and tore off a chunk of flesh from the shoulder of Charles Dhelo. Then the round cut off both feet of Martin Popp, but both men survived their awful injuries.[36]

In the 57th Ohio, planted in the middle of the brigade column, Col. Americus V. Rice was severely wounded by a bullet. "He was in a half sitting position at the time," reported Lt. Col. Samuel R. Mott, "the ball entering below the knee and passing through the leg, entering a second time above the knee, ranging upward, lodging near the abdomen." Rice survived the injury and returned to duty many months later.[37]

As his men waited, Kilby Smith told Blair of his concerns about how to get the brigade moving forward. Blair told him of Giles Smith's route and ordered Kilby Smith to follow him. He returned to his command and redirected the 55th Illinois line of advance into the crowded ravine, annoyed by Confederate artillery fire along the way. By the time he reached Giles Smith's position it was early afternoon. Kilby Smith took in the situation and retained his formation, placing his brigade in a column of regiments behind the 8th Missouri in Giles Smith's brigade. He then moved the 55th Illinois into line to the left of the 8th Missouri, keeping the remainder of his regiments in column.[38]

EWING

As Giles Smith and Thomas Kilby Smith maneuvered along a better line of advance, Ewing tried to put the shattered pieces of his brigade together. Some of the troops were in the ditch and on the parapet, others were lodged in tenuous protection along a sunken section of Graveyard Road within a few yards of the redan, and many were scattered near the roadcut. The only intact sections of Ewing's brigade were the 47th Ohio and 4th West Virginia, positioned behind a ridge that Kilby Smith had used on May 19 and that was near Giles Smith and Kilby Smith's developing position. Gradually Ewing was able to assemble some of his men to reinforce the 47th Ohio and 4th West Virginia. Ransom's Seventeenth Corps brigade was near enough to Giles Smith to offer support, but it was detached from Ewing's improvised position. Stretching south from Graveyard Road, the 47th Ohio and 4th West Virginia held ground that could serve as the launching pad for a renewal of Blair's assault.[39]

The need to find alternatives to the line of advance along Graveyard Road accounts for the length of time, close to four hours, before Giles Smith was ready to attack. In the meanwhile, those men of Ewing's brigade who had lodged close to the enemy endured a trying ordeal. Howell Trogden stayed on the parapet although he was nearly hit many times. "My canteen was shot away, my clothes were full of holes, and the banner was hardly recognizable," he recalled. Trogden delighted in taunting the Rebels, who were literally a few feet away protected by the earthen bank. "What flag are you fighting under today, Johnny?" Trogden called out. "You'd better surrender, Yank," they replied. "Oh no, Johnny, you'll surrender first."[40]

As the only visible sign of any success on the part of Ewing's brigade, the flag became a symbol for both sides. The Confederates tried to sneak down the parapet and take it while comrades stood up to support them by firing down the slope. According to Cpl. Robert M. Cox of the 55th Illinois, a member of the Forlorn Hope, the Rebels also tried to hook the flag with the shanks of their bayonets and drag it in. Trogden asked Cox for the loan of his rifle so he could stop this. Cox was reluctant to give up his weapon. Instead, he raised himself as much as he dared from the slope of the parapet and used his rifle to parry the Rebel effort. Cox ducked just in time to avoid the bullets that sailed overhead and never played this dangerous game again.[41]

Individual stories of endurance while plastered to the dirty slope of Stockade Redan or huddled in its ditch constituted much of the story of May 22. Pvt. Ulrich H. Brown of the 30th Ohio carried one end of a log in the first section of the Forlorn Hope. He and his partner found that it was too short to span the ditch, and just then he was hit by a bullet. Brown fell into the ditch and later regained consciousness. Finding he was not too badly injured, he dragged three wounded men out of the area where the Confederates tended to roll lighted artillery shells down the slope and in this way saved their lives. An officer, however, told Brown to stop because he was exposing himself too much. Later, the restless private decided to make his way back fifty yards to a sheltered place, where he continued to collect wounded men in a spot where they could enjoy some security from Rebel fire. He also found water to slake their awful thirst.[42]

Cpl. William Archinal of the 30th Ohio also carried one end of a log in the first section. When he and his partner neared the ditch, the partner was shot and the end of the log fell to the ground. That tripped up Archinal, who fell, hit his head, and was unconscious for a time. When the corporal came to, he found that the log lay over his body and bullets from the Union line were falling like hail around him. He had the presence of mind to roll the log so it lay between him and the Federals, protecting him from the fire. Here Archinal lay that long, hot day.[43]

Federal officers suffered heavily. Capt. John H. Groce, who commanded the Forlorn Hope, was shot on the parapet. When a captain and a lieutenant of the 6th Missouri also went down, Lt. William C. Porter of the 55th Illinois reckoned he was next in line to command the Forlorn Hope, but there was nothing for him to command. The Forlorn Hope by that time had disintegrated into clusters of men who were busy trying to survive. Porter admitted that all he could do was help his men prevent the Rebels from grabbing Ewing's banner.[44]

Hours spent on the hot, dusty slope of Stockade Redan began to lull many men to sleep despite noise and danger. "The shells that swept over us blew terrific blasts of wind in our faces and the awful concussion of the guns was deafening," recalled George Theodore Hyatt of the 127th Illinois. Even so, "it took lots of pinching and thumping to keep some of the men awake." Perhaps fatigue caused James W. Larabee's injury on the slope. He was startled by a shell burst and jumped up enough to expose himself. A Rebel fired a musket at him and powder "was blown into my neck & face which was afterward picked out. In this movement I got a momentary glance into the work. It seemed to be a mass of men standing at a charge bayonet." Larabee crawled back to the rear for treatment but carried the marks of powder burn for the rest of his life.[45]

Rather than forming an organized unit, members of the Forlorn Hope now were so much flotsam stranded on the beach. Six of the seven men contributed by the 54th Ohio made it to Stockade Redan. Of those, Pvt. Henry Buhrman lost his gun when it was literally broken in two by a canister shot. Pvt. William Radtke was killed, and Pvt. Edward McGinn was badly wounded when three bullets struck his head and four more went through his hat. Andrew McCormack of the 127th Illinois survived the awful ordeal but only barely. "I got a ball through my canteen and it cut a hole through my pants on my right thigh," he told his family. "It touched the skin and that was all."[46]

One Federal soldier deliberately went forward during Blair's attack and came back unscathed. Engineer officer Julius Pitzman possessed "a good map of Vicksburg, based on triangulations made from the opposite shore." So Sherman told him "to follow the storming party." Pitzman moved forward with attacking troops and took cover for an hour where he could see something of the earthworks. When it became apparent that Blair's assault would not succeed, he made his way back to safety.[47]

That Blair's assault was over seemed evident to everyone before noon on May 22. The ghastly sight of dead and injured men in blue at and near the roadcut demonstrated that the axis of attack, in column along Graveyard Road, had not worked any better than the attack by lines of battle had along the same road and to the right of it on May 19.

Except for the controversy surrounding the actions of the 37th Ohio, no one could blame the Federals for lack of command and control in Ewing's assault on the morning of May 22. The brigade had advanced well in hand and made a serious effort to get through the roadcut. Its failure to close more heavily on the target was understandable considering the obstacles posed by terrain, enemy fire, and Stockade Redan itself.

{ 7 }

Now, Boys, You Must Do Your Duty

McPHERSON, MAY 22

Grant allowed a great deal of latitude to his corps commanders to conduct their part of the general attack as they saw fit. Sherman vigorously followed through with Ewing's brigade, and McPherson mounted a more serious effort on May 22 than on May 19. Even so, because he left behind no report of the day's action, McPherson's evaluation of the task ahead is obscure. He loyally supported Grant and was a trusted colleague of Sherman's, but like those two, he was not a friend of McClernand's. In the end, judging from performance, his Seventeenth Corps failed to press home its attacks as vigorously or as comprehensively as had Sherman's Fifteenth Corps.

Similar to Sherman's efforts, Seventeenth Corps troops advanced along one of the major roads leading to Vicksburg, targeting the two Confederate forts that flanked Jackson Road. Maj. Gen. John A. Logan's division bore the primary responsibility for this effort with Brig. Gen. John E. Smith's brigade positioned on the ridge where Mrs. James Shirley's house was located, stretching northward from the road. Brig. Gen. John D. Stevenson's brigade stretched southward from the road along another ridge. Smith would attack the 3rd Louisiana Redan while Stevenson would hit Great Redoubt. Brig. Gen. Mortimer D. Leggett's brigade acted as Logan's reserve. McPherson's men had a tendency to refer to both Confederate fortifications as Fort Hill. "A memorable day it may be," wrote John P. Davis of the 30th Illinois that morning.[1]

Brig. Gen. Louis Hébert's troops held this sector of Lockett's line. Hébert placed the 21st Louisiana just south of Jackson Road with two companies of the 22nd Louisiana attached. The 3rd Louisiana held the main redan just north of the road with the 43rd Mississippi, 38th Mississippi, 37th Mississippi, 7th Mississippi Battalion, and the 36th Mississippi stretching northward all the way to Stockade Redan.[2]

McPherson gathered a total of seventeen guns to pound the sector he targeted on May 22. They were positioned 350 to 600 yards from the Confederate line and included a few twenty-four- and thirty-pounder pieces.[3]

Some of those Federal guns were located twenty-five yards from the Shirley House, and the Unionist family agreed to evacuate the building. It seems incredible that Mrs. Shirley had refused to leave when Federals appeared from the east and skirmished past her house on May 18. Confederate skirmishers hesitated to torch the house, and when one of them tried, a Federal skirmisher shot him and saved the structure. Mrs. Shirley waved a white flag to stop the Unionists from firing on the house. Eventually she consented to her fifteen-year-old son's desire to enter the trenches and fight side by side with the Yankees, but she refused to leave the residence even though it was located within the main Union line. McPherson personally talked her into moving out on the morning of May 22. She took refuge in a cave behind Union lines that her black servants had dug. The Federals helped her move clothes and some furniture.[4]

With Mrs. Shirley out of the way, McPherson's men prepared for their risky attack. They constructed scaling ladders for easier entry into the forts. Soldiers found the ladders, made the night before, piled up behind the Union line. According to a man in the 8th Illinois of Stevenson's brigade, there were enough for each company to deploy two ladders.[5]

The mood among Seventeenth Corps men as they waited for the assault varied according to each individual. Some were confident and others pessimistic about the chances of success. In the 20th Ohio of Leggett's brigade, many men gave their personal effects to cooks and provided addresses for them to send the belongings home if they did not return. In the 45th Illinois of John E. Smith's brigade, Stephen A. Rollins found a robust spirit among his comrades. "We all felt that we could take the works" even though they knew many men would be hit, "but almost all felt that it would be some one else besides himself who would fall."[6]

JOHN E. SMITH

The line of approach taken by John E. Smith's brigade ran along Jackson Road for 500 yards from one line to the other. The road passed through a

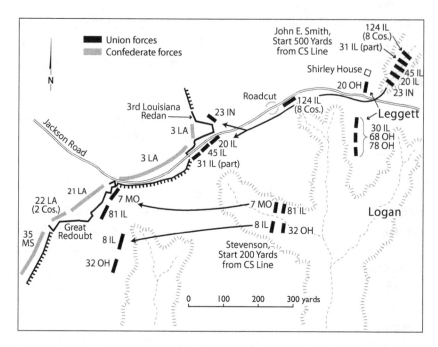

Logan's division, May 22

small cut that was, at its greatest depth, able to hide a man who was standing up. Then the road left the cut some 200 yards from the Confederate line with little to hinder the enemy from seeing and firing on the Federals. Smith formed his brigade in a column of fours inside a hollow just east of the Shirley House. He planned to pass through this cut and then deploy into line on the other side to assault the works. The 23rd Indiana was first in the column, followed by the 20th Illinois, 45th Illinois, 31st Illinois, and 124th Illinois. Smith deployed skirmishers from the latter two regiments to lay down supporting fire.[7]

After the brigade assembled at 9:00 A.M., Col. Thomas J. Sloan called for the officers of the eight companies in his 124th Illinois that were to take part in the assault. He told them of the attack to begin an hour later, instructed them to fix bayonets, and cautioned the men not to fire until ordered. Smith also instructed the men of his brigade to take only their canteens and one day's rations, leaving their knapsacks behind. The 45th Illinois listened to the regimental adjutant as he exhorted the men to their utmost: "Now, boys, you must do your duty." The regimental major gave his own short exhortation. "Let every man stand to his post," he told the troops.[8]

When Smith started his advance at 10:00 A.M., his men moved out of the hollow near the Shirley House and turned right onto Jackson Road. Then they moved at the double-quick in their column formation. Job H. Yaggy of the 124th Illinois, assigned to the skirmish line, saw his comrades move along the road. "Oh! My heart groaned within me and I wished I were there to help them," he confided to his diary. The five-regiment column moved safely through the roadcut and emerged from the western end. Although exposed to the enemy, the column was able to deploy, one regiment after another. The 23rd Indiana deployed to the right of Jackson Road into line and then advanced into fire delivered by the 38th Mississippi. The regiment managed to reach the base of the parapet stretching northward from the 3rd Louisiana Redan.[9]

While most of the 23rd Indiana lodged there, a few members braved the fire and began to climb up the slope (there was no ditch at this sector). They were led by Lt. Christian G. Zulauf. Reports indicate that this group "gained the top" of the parapet but none of them entered the works. Zulauf was killed, his body reportedly punctured by twenty-three bullets during the course of the day.[10]

The next regiment in Smith's column, the 20th Illinois, soon emerged from the roadcut and deployed to the left, south of Jackson Road. The Illinois men managed to make it to the base of the Confederate works but were unable to climb the parapet. Soon the regiment moved south a bit to seek shelter in a ravine.[11]

The 45th Illinois, third in Smith's column, encountered more difficulties in bringing its manpower to bear on the target. The troops moved through the roadcut while bending low to avoid gunfire descending on the area. Maj. Luther H. Cowan, who led the regiment that day, shouted orders to deploy into line to the left, still at the double-quick, but he was shot right after giving the order. Cowan staggered a couple of steps and fell down, mortally wounded. The ranking company captain did not know of Cowan's fall for some time, but the regiment continued to deploy far enough to the left to allow all the companies to exit the roadcut and join the battalion line. Without a leader, the troops simply lay on the ground and stayed where they were for the time being.[12]

It took a few minutes for the ranking captain to realize he had to take charge of the 45th. Then he ordered the men to advance 200 yards toward the works. There was no possibility of a quick dash across the open slope, and the regiment met what Wilbur F. Crummer described as "a sweeping volley of musketry at short range, which mowed the men down in bunches." Despite the losses, what was left of the 45th managed to lodge at the base of the parapet and stayed there for hours to come. The regimental banner was planted as the men plastered themselves on the lower slope and behind any small bit of ground that offered a hope of shelter. Stephen A. Rollins reported that many of his comrades were able to return fire at Rebels who exposed themselves at the top of the parapet. As time passed, he also realized it was possible to communicate with the enemy, in a manner of speaking. "We could pelt them with clods of dirt, on the other side of the works. They threw over an empty whiskey bottle, to show us what they had to drink; and we threw back crackers, to let them know what we had to eat."[13]

Wounded Federals made their way as best they could back to the rear for treatment. Lt. Wimer Bedford was hit in the thigh early in the assault. He wrapped his arm around the shoulders of his orderly and limped to a spot that seemed to offer some shelter. It was merely "a small indentation in the ground" but allowed Bedford to lie down. After a while one of Logan's aides offered water, "which made me feel better." When examining his thigh, Bedford found that the bone was not broken. After resting a while, he made his way farther to the rear, where surgeons probed the wound. He survived the ordeal and the war.[14]

At least one of the last two regiments in Smith's column made it to the enemy works. A portion of the 31st Illinois reached the ditch. According to survivors, Lt. Col. John D. Rees was killed there. The regimental colors were planted, but during the course of the day the staff was "shot asunder in four places" and the fabric received no fewer than 153 bullet holes. The 124th Illinois, last in the brigade column, apparently did not advance to the base of the Confederate works.[15]

Smith's attack along Jackson Road fizzled much in the way that Ewing's attack failed along Graveyard Road. Both came to grief on Lockett's earthworks manned with determined Confederates who had a clear field of fire in their front. It made little difference for the Federals to lodge at the base of those works, for they had no real chance of climbing the slope and driving the defenders away.

STEVENSON

Stevenson's brigade to the south of Jackson Road started its assault toward Great Redoubt (sometimes called Fort Beauregard or Black Fort by the Federals) at the same time that Smith attacked. The brigade prepared its formation in a ravine south of Jackson Road, forming not one but two assault columns. The right column consisted of the 7th Missouri and 81st Illinois and was led by Capt. Robert Buchanan of the former regiment. The left column consisted of the 8th Illinois and the 32nd Ohio and was commanded by Lt. Col. Robert H. Sturgess of the former battalion. The 17th Illinois deployed as skirmishers. Stevenson saw to it that his men were supplied with scaling ladders and ordered them "not to fire a gun until we were inside of the fortification," reported an officer of the 81st Illinois.[16]

Buchanan ordered his men to fix bayonets and load their muskets but passed on Stevenson's word not to fire during the advance. He then gathered the company leaders of the 7th Missouri, pointed out to them the exact point he wanted the center of the regimental line to meet "when we reached the fort," and gave instructions to the color-bearer as to where he should plant the flag.[17]

The brigade took a few casualties while forming 200 yards from the Rebel line. Lt. John Reese, who led Company E, 81st Illinois, was surprised by the number of bullets falling near his area of the assembly zone. "A Brave Boy in our co named W. P. Mcoy fell shot through the heart By my Side," he told a correspondent. "Lt. Lamer and 3 others were wounded[;] I was hit on the left arm with a glancing Ball it went through my clothes and deadened my arm[,] it is sore yet But the hide ant Broke."[18]

Stevenson began to advance, and his men immediately received what Reese called "a Murderous fire." Nevertheless, the 7th Missouri, leading Stevenson's right column, moved forward and deployed into line to the right. As the 7th Missouri neared Great Redoubt, heavy fire "cut my Regiment in two at the colors," Buchanan recalled. Both wings stalled when they reached the base of the parapet. A number of men got into the ditch but found that the scaling ladders were too short to help them up the parapet. They planted a flag on the works as a show of defiance.[19]

That banner became an icon of the attack on May 22. It was "a green flag emblazoned with a gold harp, symbolic of the men's Irish heritage." Many Confederates inside Great Redoubt noted the symbolism. The work was defended by the 21st Louisiana and Companies C and D of the 22nd Louisiana. Ironically the 21st Louisiana had been recruited largely from among Irishmen living in New Orleans, and they carried a similar green flag. A further irony lay in the fact that Capt. David Todd, one of Abraham Lincoln's brothers-in-law, fought in Confederate gray inside Great Redoubt. Another of the president's brothers-in-law, Benjamin Hardin Helm, commanded a brigade in the concentration of troops Gen. Joseph E. Johnston was assembling near Jackson.[20]

Like the troops of Smith's brigade, the 7th Missouri made it to the target but could not ascend the parapet. The 81st Illinois, which followed the Missourians, found it much more difficult to get even that far. The 81st Illinois deployed into line to the left of the 7th Missouri, but its forward march stalled halfway to Great Redoubt. For roughly ten minutes, the regiment halted in the open 100 yards from the enemy. The men were hesitant to push forward. They lay down for some protection but their officers tried to get them back on their feet.[21]

Edwin A. Loosley, a twenty-eight-year-old Englishman who worked as a baker in Du Quoin, Illinois, before the war, thought the 81st Illinois was in a "complete trap." He reported that every man "to my right for 10 yards was hit, the last one of them, leaving me solitary and alone." The troops to his left were hit almost as hard. "I would not have given A counterfeit 5 cent piece on the Southern Confederacy for my life," he told his wife. "I lay there very patiently waiting for the ball to come and do its work, but it did not come, though they were all round me. I could have picked up A hat full of balls without getting up, they hit the ground under me and hit my clothes over me, and several spent balls hit me, but did no damage."[22]

Jordon Carroll Harriss also endured a harrowing experience. The man lying within a foot of him to the right was killed. The man lying to his left, "our heads about 6 inches of each other," got a bullet through the head. The man in the rank immediately behind Harriss also was killed. Plus, "two balls after striking the ground bounced and fell on me but never hurt." Not long after that Harriss suffered slight injuries to his "left arm, right shoulder, and finger next to my little one on my left hand" plus a bullet "grazed on the neck." But "the wounds are not severe," he assured the home folks.[23]

During those ten minutes of hell, the 81st Illinois men were tested to the utmost of their endurance. Capt. Samuel Pyle of Company K lost his nerve and "strieked it for the woods and there he lay playing possum, trying to make believe he was dead." When John Reese asked Pyle after the battle if he was wounded, the captain "groaned out that he was hit no where in particular but all over." Pyle must have been paralyzed with emotional trauma by the experience. He resigned his commission on June 24, 1863, and went home.[24]

In the midst of this hellish fire, Reese heard Col. James J. Dollins urge the 81st Illinois forward. He tried to help the colonel by telling his company "to stand firm and if any person got into the fort he could." But Dollins was soon shot in the head. Edwin Loosley reported that the top of his cranium blew off when the round hit him. "We lost A leader," Loosley moaned, "he was the Soul of Bravery and honor and I felt that I lost A friend when he was gone."[25]

Right after Dollins fell, the 81st Illinois finally moved forward. Company commanders urged their men to get up and continue the advance. They did not move very much, it is true. Advancing cautiously over the open ground, the regiment stalled once again seventy yards from Great Redoubt, or forty yards if one accepts the testimony of Martin Whipkey written several decades later. There was "not a twig Between us and the fort," Reese wrote, and "no Body from our side fireing at them and they were firing at us from all Sides." Soon after the regiment stalled the second time, Burt Morris took it upon himself to do something about the uneven nature of the fighting thus far. He plopped behind "a little log" and gave "the Rebs several digs," as Edwin Loosley put it. "He loaded and shot as deliberately as if he was shoating Squirrels[;] . . . Burt Said he could hit them at the Waist every time he Shot." Loosley was mightily impressed by this show of bravado. Morris was "the most dauntless Boy I ever Saw."[26]

The terrible experience of the 81st Illinois proved once again the danger inherent in an overly cautious advance—it led to greater loss and less gain than if the regiment had moved steadily forward to the foot of the parapet. But the 81st Illinois never got that far. Its second stall compounded the casualty list until two-thirds of the men were hit.[27]

Lt. Col. Franklin Campbell, who took charge of the 81st after Dollins fell, admitted defeat and ordered the regiment to retire. "Then there was some tall running done you may be sure," Loosley told his wife. The regiment reached a shallow ravine to the rear where it could regroup in safety. Newspaper reports later praised Campbell for rallying the regiment, but Loosley was a bit miffed by all the hoopla. "He done his duty just like all the rest of us done ours," Loosley told his wife, "but performed no special wonder. There was no special wonders performed by any of us that day, but one general wonder that every one of us did not get shot instead of half of us."[28]

The 81st Illinois lost 107 men in the attack, according to Reese, but the 7th Missouri also lost 100 troops. Half of the company commanders in the Illinois unit were shot. In Loosley's company, twenty-five men were wounded, two of the three officers were hit, and four of the five sergeants and seven of the eight corporals fell.[29]

"How any of us escaped is Wonderful," mused Reese. "Oh it was a frightful Massacre[;] if we had Been allowed to fire we could of Saved ourselves a little." The loss of Dollins and the regimental adjutant, the latter of whom survived but lost a leg, was severely felt throughout the regiment. "I can truly say I lost two Warm friends," wrote Reese, "for We had been together nine Months and not one unkind Word was ever spoken by either to me."[30]

Stevenson's right column broke into two regimental battle lines that failed to support each other. While the 7th Missouri raced forward to lodge at the foot of the earthworks, the 81st Illinois failed to get that far and suffered terrible losses to boot. Stevenson admitted failure and ordered both regiments to retire.[31]

We have only sketchy information about the actions of Stevenson's left column, consisting of the 8th Illinois and 32nd Ohio. There are no regimental reports, Stevenson's report (which was not published in the *Official Records*) does not discuss these units, and Logan failed to write a report. Long after the war, Capt. Daniel Sayers of Company C stated that the 8th Illinois troops moved up to the ditch of Great Redoubt but found their ladders were too short to cross it. "Some of the men jumped into the ditch for Safety," but most retreated. That was largely confirmed by Lt. Ketchum S. Conklin of Company F, but Cpl. Gould D. Molineaux noted in his diary that the regiment never received orders to charge. All Richard Blackstone of the 32nd Ohio could remember was scrambling upslope through thick cane. Robert Buchanan thought neither regiment got close to the fort, while historian Edwin C. Bearss concludes that the 8th Illinois and 32nd Ohio stopped at a hollow 200 yards from the Confederate line and covered the retreat of the 81st Illinois and 7th Missouri with their fire.[32]

LEGGETT

Mortimer Leggett's men provided support for the other two brigades in Logan's division. Col. Manning F. Force's 20th Ohio backed up John E. Smith's brigade, while the other three regiments (30th Illinois, 68th Ohio, and 78th Ohio) supported Stevenson's brigade. After Smith's advance, Force moved his regiment until he reached a "grass-grown bank" just south of the Shirley House. There his men squatted down as the area was pelted by artillery and small-arms fire. "The balls whistled by just outside our knees," Force reported.[33]

The other three regiments of Leggett's brigade waited in reserve for orders that never came. Although at least one man of the 20th Ohio thought his comrades were "in good spirits" when contemplating the attack, Lindsay Steele recalled the mood differently. "Thank god the order was not given," he wrote.[34]

This is how John A. Logan's contribution to Grant's general attack ended on May 22. The only other Seventeenth Corps unit that made a serious effort to assault the enemy was Brig. Gen. Thomas E. G. Ransom's detached brigade. Ransom had been operating without connection to McPherson's right flank for several days. On the evening of May 21, he conferred with his regimental leaders about the planned attack. Ransom also detailed 100 infantrymen to the 1st Minnesota Battery so it could change its position that night in order to better support the charge. Beginning about 9:00 A.M. of May 22, Ransom worked his command forward "through a network of ravines filled with fallen timber and canebrakes," his men covered by the fire of a heavy skirmish line. He reached a point only sixty yards from the Confederates, but Col. Thomas W. Humphrey of the 95th Illinois thought it was actually 100 yards away. Here Ransom dressed his line "as well as the nature of the ground would admit" and prepared to assault.[35]

It was now 11:00 A.M., according to Humphrey, too late to go in at the appointed time. The 11th Illinois held the left with the 95th Illinois next to its right flank and then the 14th Wisconsin and the 72nd Illinois holding the right. Each regiment, according to Humphrey, formed in a column of companies, closed en masse, one of the tightest formations possible in Civil War tactics. The 17th Wisconsin was held to the rear in reserve.[36]

Sometime after assuming this position, Ransom saw Col. Giles A. Smith's brigade to his right. He opened communications with Smith and agreed to act in concert with him. Now he would have support to his right even though a wide gap still existed to his left. Moreover, Ransom could see that a pretty strong work, Green's Redan, lay some distance to his right. Smith's supporting brigade would draw much fire from it onto itself and strengthen his brigade's chance of success.[37]

Everyone in Ransom's command knew deadly work lay ahead. Capt. Elliot N. Bush of Company G, 95th Illinois, needed to steel his nerves and found a talisman in an inscription he had carved into the sheath of his sword. Bush repeated it often while waiting for the order to move forward. "The Lord is on my side. I will not fear; what can man do with me?"[38]

Other men in Ransom's brigade found different means of calming their nerves. Knowing their primary tactics well, they could assume, as did Lt. George Carrington of the 11th Illinois, that the intent was to move out of the assembly area in column but then deploy into line after they crossed the last rise of ground before closing with the enemy. While waiting in formation many men were able to grab cane, for much of it was literally "growing at their feet." They chewed it, Carrington wrote, "to keep our minds from what we knew was coming."[39]

But these men had to wait a long while. Ransom and Smith would not start their advance until midafternoon of May 22, after it was decided that Sherman's Fifteenth Corps should mount a renewed effort at the enemy works.

QUINBY

Meanwhile, McPherson's other available division, commanded by Brig. Gen. Isaac F. Quinby, was maneuvering but not fighting. It took position to Logan's left, south of Jackson Road. Here the terrain offered few advantages to the Federals. Ravines ran more or less perpendicular rather than parallel to the Confederate line of works, thus exposing the approaching Federals to enemy fire. As a result, when Quinby formed his division, Col. George B. Boomer's brigade on his right was placed some distance from the target. Boomer's right flank lay 500 yards southeast of the 3rd Louisiana Redan. Col. John B. Sanborn's brigade on the left placed its left flank more than 1,000 yards from the Rebel line. Col. Samuel A. Holmes's brigade lay to the rear as a division reserve. This was far from a good position from which Quinby could launch an attack; the distance was too far, and a maze of unfriendly ravines lay between the division and its target. As in Ransom's brigade, each regiment in Quinby's division formed a column and planned to deploy into line when ready to close on the Confederate works.[40]

Like the men of Ransom's brigade, Quinby's troops had no illusions about what lay ahead. Told to fill their canteens and carry only what they needed into the fight, they worried while waiting for the order to advance. "You can see many with long faces sitting down awaiting their doom," commented Richard S. Reeves of the 4th Minnesota in his diary. "Each man takes out his watch and looks[,] walks up and down. I all most fe[e]l as though my days was reckoned myself[;] the Col is putting on his sword[;] the word comes fall in[;] you can see lots with tears in their eyes[;] they can see death staring them in the face but duty calls them."[41]

At 10:00 A.M., the noise and fury of the Union assault opened to right and left of Quinby's worried troops. Off to the right many of them could see Stevenson's brigade of Logan's division advancing. Off to the left, at a distance, others could see the troops of Brig. Gen. Eugene A. Carr's division of the Thirteenth Corps moving forward and lodging on the Rebel earthworks.

Not long after, Quinby also gave the order to move forward. In Boomer's brigade, the 5th Iowa held the extreme right with the 26th Missouri immediately to its left. Lt. Col. Ezekiel S. Sampson reported that his 5th Iowa led Boomer's advance, and it may well have done so because it was closer to the target than the rest of the line.[42]

Working their way through the maze of ravines, Boomer and Sanborn made it to a ridge about 300 yards from the Confederates. Here they deployed their regimental columns and took shelter. The 18th Wisconsin went forward from Sanborn's formation to establish a skirmish line and reported that the hollow in front of the division was choked with felled timber. Moreover, the division received enfilade fire from protruding sections of the enemy works. It lost men not only to Confederate fire but to sunstroke as well, for the sun was getting hotter by the minute.[43]

Quinby conferred with his two brigade leaders and wanted Boomer to lead an assault. Boomer, however, argued that his command could not go any farther, considering the obstacles. Quinby gave him the 59th Indiana from Sanborn's brigade and told Sanborn to guide his own movements on Boomer's, but Boomer still hesitated. In the end neither brigade moved from the ridge. The division was stuck, immobilized by Boomer, who was widely respected for his personal qualities but who was out of his league as a battlefield commander.[44]

Quinby's men waited for hours on the ridge during the late morning and early afternoon. The sun was high by now and very hot, burning on them without relief. "We placed the butts of our guns and our canteens of water, in front of our head, as a shield from Minnie balls," recalled James Curtis Mahan.[45]

To be fair, reluctance to rush into the assault characterized many commanders in the Seventeenth Corps, not just Quinby. Only Logan displayed much energy that morning. Despite mounting a more serious effort than on May 19, McPherson's corps performed less vigorously than Sherman's and McClernand's commands on May 22. It contributed less than the other two corps to Grant's plan for a general assault. Because so little attention was paid to its operations in the form of official reports and other public documents, the limited Seventeenth Corps performance escaped public scrutiny or criticism.

{ 8 }

The Horror of the Thing Bore Me Down Like an Avalanche

McCLERNAND and OSTERHAUS, MAY 22

McClernand had a different tactical situation to deal with than either Sherman or McPherson on May 22. McClernand's corps held the far left of Grant's line, and his sector embraced not just one major road leading into Vicksburg but two. He intended to advance along both Baldwin's Ferry Road and the Southern Railroad of Mississippi toward two strong Confederate works. The terrain probably was more jumbled here than elsewhere, and McClernand certainly knew no more about his opponent's earthworks and troop dispositions than did his colleagues. He experimented with an unusual troop formation to bring his manpower close to the target and had good, experienced division and brigade commanders to count on.

The troops crowded up close to their targets quite early in the assault, but then the thorny question of how to get into them arose. The garrison of the 2nd Texas Lunette held firm despite heavy pressure, but Railroad Redoubt was only thinly held by a small number of Confederates. Here was the best opportunity for the attacking Federals to achieve a breakthrough, but they only dimly understood this and had difficulty finding enough troops to enter the work.

The Thirteenth Corps had lost about 3,000 men during the overland phase of the campaign and was compelled to detach the equivalent of two brigades on garrison and other duties. By May 22 the corps could muster no more than 10,000 men. It occupied a line one and a quarter miles long, but a four-mile gap existed between the left flank and the Mississippi River. The corps' right flank also was in the air with a shorter gap of a few hundred yards between it and McPherson's command.[1]

MCCLERNAND

The topography of McClernand's sector, however, offered him some advantages. He occupied two ridges within striking distance of the Confederate line. Two Mile Ridge was the first continuous feature east of the Rebel position, located 250 to 400 yards from the target. Porter's Chapel Ridge constituted the next continuous feature, 400 yards to the east of Two Mile Ridge, with a deep ravine between the two. Brig. Gen. Eugene A. Carr, whose division was assigned the task of leading the assault, developed a formation that placed his command on Two Mile Ridge. Brig. Gen. Michael K. Lawler's brigade was positioned on the left, south of the Southern Railroad of Mississippi, and aimed at Railroad Redoubt. Brig. Gen. William P. Benton's brigade lay on the right, north of the railroad, with the task of approaching the 2nd Texas Lunette. Brig. Gen. Andrew J. Smith's division supported Carr on Porter's Chapel Ridge, with Col. William J. Landram's brigade behind Lawler and Brig. Gen. Stephen G. Burbridge's brigade behind Benton.[2]

There is evidence that Thirteenth Corps troops had serious doubts about the attack. One of A. J. Smith's aides, who signed himself JRSC in his newspaper correspondence, noted that both Smith and Carr positioned their command posts near each other behind the center of their joint formation. JRSC called Smith "the oldest among the Generals in years, and one of the most fiery and impetuous in disposition." Yet he was not enthusiastic about the pending operation. After the skirmishing by Burbridge and Benton on May 20, the general impression at division headquarters was that the Confederate works could not be taken by storm. When Burbridge questioned the wisdom of Grant's order, Smith told him the directive was "plain" and had to be obeyed. "Well, we can try," Burbridge replied, "but I would like to see more artillery used to batter down their walls."[3]

To a significant degree, Burbridge got what he wanted. Thirty-nine guns roared into action, including three thirty-pounder Parrotts, a caliber normally considered to be heavy rather than field artillery. Members of the 1st U.S. Infantry worked these guns. McClernand also had six twenty-pounder Parrotts belonging to the 1st Wisconsin Battery. Because Brig. Gen. Alvin P. Hovey's division was not united (one brigade was ready to support McClernand's attack but the other was escorting prisoners), Hovey took charge of the artillery on Brig. Gen. Peter J. Osterhaus's sector. The rest of the Thirteenth Corps guns were coordinated by artillery chiefs on the division and corps levels. Tragically, some of the rounds harmed friendly troops. Three men of the 33rd Illinois in Benton's brigade were wounded when several rounds fired by a battery to the rear of the regiment burst prematurely.[4]

Confederate troops on the receiving end of this fire were impressed by its fierceness. Brig. Gen. Stephen D. Lee called it the "most terrific bombardment" he had witnessed. Lt. Maurice Kavanaugh Simons of the 2nd Texas counted ten to forty rounds per minute, creating a sound as "one continuous roar." There could be no doubt of what was to follow: "The Enemy are surley preparing to assault our works," Simons concluded.[5]

McClernand claimed that his bombardment damaged the Confederate position, "breaching the enemy's works at several points, temporarily silencing his guns and exploding four rebel caissons." Evidence from Confederate sources generally supports that claim. Maj. Gen. John H. Forney reported that a twenty-four-pounder siege gun near Baldwin's Ferry Road was disabled in the bombardment along with two twenty-pounder Parrotts elsewhere on his line.[6]

McClernand's artillery damaged the Confederate earthworks. Several Federal guns, including the thirty-pounder Parrotts, concentrated their fire on the southeast angle of Railroad Redoubt. According to Lt. Peter C. Hains, McClernand's chief engineer, the heavy projectiles "ploughed deep furrows in the parapet." The effect was to reduce the profile of the earthen mound, degrading its protective feature but not creating a true breach of the defenses.[7]

The question of whether it was possible for Thirteenth Corps artillery to pave the way for an attack is problematic. Those efforts only degraded one corner of one Rebel fort. But the impact of the heavy bombardment may have had an emotional effect on the Confederates in Railroad Redoubt, who, as we shall see, lost their nerve at a critical moment in the Union assault.

OSTERHAUS

McClernand's infantry began to move forward at 10:00 A.M., pressing toward Railroad Redoubt and the 2nd Texas Lunette at the same time. Osterhaus's division on the far left of the Thirteenth Corps sector also moved toward Square Fort. Grant had allowed his corps commanders to decide

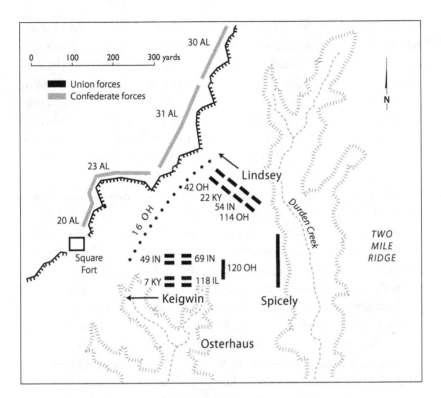

Osterhaus's division, May 22

how to form their commands, and McClernand allowed Osterhaus the same latitude. The German-born division leader adopted a column formation so as "to have the necessary pressure and connection on the point of attack" and lessen the tendency of lines to break apart while moving across rough countryside. He also sent the 16th Ohio to skirmish for the division and another regiment to cover his open left flank. Col. William T. Spicely's brigade of Hovey's division lay behind Osterhaus as a reserve.[8]

KEIGWIN

Col. James Keigwin's brigade occupied the left wing of Osterhaus's division. Keigwin formed his troops in two columns with the 49th Indiana and 69th Indiana on the right while the 7th Kentucky and 118th Illinois formed the left. The regiments formed double columns, and the 120th Ohio was held back as a brigade reserve with orders to push the other regiments forward "at the point of the bayonet" if needed.[9]

As members of the 7th Kentucky waited nervously for the bugle call that was to signal the attack, Capt. Larkin A. Byron recalled that "the moment was an awful one, silence reigned through out the ranks, all were fully sensible of the quivering lip tightly compressed and steady gaze from the eye." Jeptha S. Dillon of the 118th Illinois was told at 9:00 A.M. of the impending action. "I fear it will be an awful charge," he confided to his diary and then searched for paper so he could write his wife. At nine thirty he penned a note to her. "I may never write you any more Dearest. Oh dear Lib, should I fall do not mourn for me for it will only be a few short days till we shall meet again never more to part."[10]

At 10:00 A.M., the bugle sounded and Keigwin's two columns moved forward from Two Mile Ridge about 250 yards from Square Fort. "We found obstacles which were more in our way than the balls of the enemy," Keigwin wrote a few days later. The troops encountered felled timber in the bottom of ravines that was "almost impassable." Nevertheless, "on we went," wrote Byron, "over brush, briers, ravines and gullies." Lt. Col. John Lucas's 7th Kentucky struggled through the clutter and ascended a bare hill within short range of Square Fort. Here the Federals received "a terrible and withering fire" but continued to struggle forward. After two-thirds of the 7th Kentucky column crossed the bare crest, the rest of the battalion could not force itself forward; instead about one-third of the men simply broke ranks and fell back to seek cover. Byron, however, reported that heavy enemy fire broke up the ranks in the latter one-third of the regiment; whatever the cause, the 7th Kentucky ground to a halt.[11]

Marching behind Lucas's regiment, Col. John G. Fonda's 118th Illinois tried to continue moving forward. Fonda shifted his column to the right of the Kentucky regiment and became entangled in the timber, and the van of his column crested the bare hill. Heated fire brought the regiment to a halt, although Fonda argued that the terrain as much as enemy fire prevented his men from continuing. But there are reports that the 118th troops "faltered" and its stragglers had to be rounded up by the leading two companies of the 120th Ohio.[12]

The story remained much the same in Keigwin's other column. Maj. Arthur J. Hawhe's 49th Indiana struggled through the same area of felled timber that delayed the left formation. When Hawhe's troops approached the bare hill they made no serious effort to cross it but instead took shelter. Col. Thomas W. Bennett's 69th Indiana moved up to the left of the 49th Indiana and stopped at the bare hill too, daunted by a deep ravine in front of the regiment's position. Members of the 69th lay down just behind the crest of the ridge, and the color-bearer planted his flag. An hour later, Maj. John H.

Finley saw the flag falling over and ran to put it back in place. Just as Finley finished pushing the staff into the ground, a bullet penetrated his lungs. Oran Perry watched as Finley's face "turned deadly white." He was taken down-slope to await an ambulance and died August 27, 1863. Finley was a school friend of Perry's; the two had gone into business together and had joined the regiment as chums. "The horror of the thing bore me down like an ava-lanche," Perry wrote of Finley's death years later.[13]

In short, Keigwin's brigade came to a crashing halt. No one estimated how far they landed from the Confederate line, but Osterhaus reported they were close enough to hear shouts in the Rebel works. Col. Marcus M. Spie-gel received orders to move three companies of his 120th Ohio from its re-serve post "through a ravine to the left" until he gained a position from which he could skirmish with Confederates in Square Fort. Here he stayed, firing away, for the rest of the day. For the 7th Kentucky, the short but painful ad-vance was costly in human life. Larkin A. Byron reported the regiment lost seventy killed and wounded out of 230 men engaged.[14]

LINDSEY

Osterhaus's other brigade commander, Col. Daniel W. Lindsey, accom-plished little, even though he possessed some information about the ter-rain before his men. Early on the morning of May 22, Capt. Seth M. Barber of Company H, 42nd Ohio, pushed forward with his men and Company I under cover of McClernand's artillery fire. These seventy troops found that the ravine they advanced through curved sharply at a clump of willow trees. As the Federals emerged from the clump, they were exposed to enemy fire 300 yards from Lockett's earthworks. Barber pushed through until he lodged about fifty yards from the Confederates. He gathered all the information possible but was shot in the right leg below the knee just as he started to re-turn. The bullet broke two bones, and the leg later had to be amputated. Sgt. Joseph Ludom took charge, holding the men at their exposed position until Barber could be carried to the rear, and then they retired. The two compa-nies returned to the regiment by nine thirty, a half hour before the sched-uled attack.[15]

Barber's reconnaissance proved that a small party could get as close as fifty yards from the target, but moving an entire brigade along that line would prove more difficult. While Barber was away, Lindsey formed his regi-ments for the charge. He placed Lt. Col. Don A. Pardee's 42nd Ohio at the head of a column, constituting the third and rightmost column of Osterhaus's division. Lt. Col. George W. Monroe's 22nd Kentucky followed the 42nd and then the 54th Indiana and 114th Ohio. All regiments were in double column except the 16th Ohio, which was on the skirmish line for the division front. At least a few of Lindsey's men did not relish the order to attack. A. J. Jacobs of the 22nd Kentucky "felt dismal as I took my place in ranks. I knew, from all appearances, a terrible slaughter was to take place." M. A. Sweetman of the 114th Ohio did not believe that more than one in ten of his comrades "felt any confidence in our success."[16]

Lindsey started at 10:00 A.M. and found the ravine to be comparatively sheltered up to the clump of willows. Upon emerging from the trees, however, the 42nd Ohio received "a terrific fire" from the Confederates. "The din and confusion was something appalling," wrote Sweetman. At this point the brigade deployed. As the 42nd Ohio continued moving forward, the 22nd Kentucky shifted to the right. The 54th Indiana and 114th Ohio remained behind as support.[17]

Ahead of Lindsey's formation, Capt. Eli W. Botsford's 16th Ohio closed in on the target. Its skirmish fire triggered close-range musketry from the Confederate position. "The whole surface of the ridge up to the ditch [of the Confederate line] was raked and plowed with concentric fire of musketry and canister at pistol range," wrote Capt. Frank H. Mason and John W. Fry of the 42nd Ohio. Mason further stated that "the head of the regiment . . . was literally blown back" by the onset of this fire. The 42nd Ohio stalled at this place and took cover where the men could find it, and the 22nd Kentucky did the same.[18]

Lindsey's three regiments lodged pretty close to the Confederate works, but no one estimated the distance. Owen J. Hopkins of the 42nd Ohio exaggerated when he claimed his comrades were so close they "could aim at the buttons on the Johnnies' coats." Mason and Fry argued that the regiment was close enough to take advantage of some sheltering features so that much of the small-arms and artillery fire coming from the Confederate line sailed over their heads.[19]

Lying down for safety, the Federals stayed put for the rest of the day. At times it became almost intolerable. A. J. Jacobs grew restless and crawled forward "like an alligator" over his comrades. Officers told him to stay put, but he ignored them until he reached a hole in the ground created by an uprooted tree, where he found three other men of his regiment. Jacobs stopped and fired from the relative safety of the hole as the other three loaded muskets for him.[20]

The 54th Indiana and 114th Ohio remained lying on the ground behind the 42nd Ohio and 22nd Kentucky. Col. John Cradlebaugh of the 114th was badly wounded in the mouth by a bullet that tore out his palate. He was taken 300 yards to the rear and placed in a slave cabin, eventually recovering.[21]

Elements of Stephen D. Lee's Brigade held the line approached by Osterhaus. The 20th Alabama occupied Square Fort on Osterhaus's left, and Maj. George W. Mathieson's 31st Alabama held an unnamed redan fronting Lindsey's brigade. Mathieson's work, which had a twelve-pounder howitzer, was located to the Confederate left of Square Fort, and the 30th Alabama held the line to Mathieson's left.[22]

Soon after 10:00 A.M., Lindsey's advance became vividly evident to the waiting Confederates. In William Lewis Roberts's mind, it seemed as if the Yankees were arrayed six lines deep. Mathieson reported that "a heavy column of infantry appeared in front, and attempted to charge my position." His men "poured a heavy fire into their ranks" and stopped them well short of the ditch. Federal " killed and wounded lay thick on the field, and [they were] evidently badly crippled." In fact, Mathieson estimated that 150 to 200 Federals littered the ground in his front and reported that only one man of the 31st Alabama was hit.[23]

FAILURE ON THE LEFT FLANK

Osterhaus had the opportunity to use Spicely's brigade of Hovey's division but failed to do so in a significant way. Spicely received orders at 9:00 A.M. to support Keigwin's brigade. "On the signal, the whole line, enveloped in fire and smoke, rushed forward," wrote the historian of the 46th Indiana. Spicely followed behind Keigwin's advance and stopped when Keigwin came to a halt. After a while, Spicely ordered the 24th Indiana and 46th Indiana to the front. The former regiment closely supported the 7th Kentucky.[24]

All of Spicely's regiments took shelter within supporting distance of Keigwin where the ground provided it. Here they stayed for hours along with Keigwin's stalled units. At one point, a wounded man wandered back from the position of the 7th Kentucky. When Frank Swigart of the 46th Indiana asked him how things were going, he replied, "My regiment have all been killed or captured except myself; I am the only survivor." Swigart knew this was an exaggeration but the reality "was bad enough," he later wrote.[25]

Osterhaus could console himself with the thought that his division had tried, but the men stopped before exposing themselves to the worst fire. McClernand argued that "physical exhaustion" contributed to the muddled end of Osterhaus's advance, noting also the difficulty posed by the terrain.[26]

Nevertheless, Osterhaus's men pushed forward with less vigor than those of Carr and Smith to the right. Column formations had not helped the Federals overcome the problems of topography and enemy fire. Whether their comrades would have better luck against the 2nd Texas Lunette and Railroad Redoubt was another matter.

{ 9 }

Boys, You Have Just Fifteen Minutes to Live

2nd TEXAS LUNETTE, MAY 22

Given leeway to conduct the assault as he saw fit, McClernand focused his attention on the 2nd Texas Lunette and Railroad Redoubt, leaving Osterhaus largely on his own to approach Square Fort. McClernand concentrated the strength of two divisions, Carr's and Andrew J. Smith's, on the two Rebel earthworks. At Railroad Redoubt, Carr's and Smith's troops achieved a tantalizing hope of success, but at the 2nd Texas Lunette they met only hardship and stalemate. Here Benton's brigade broke up during a critical moment of its advance, demonstrating the difficulties of maintaining command and control on the battlefield of May 22. McClernand's rather unusual troop formation, with one division behind another rather than each one assigned to a separate sector, also complicated command and control in ways detrimental to the success of the assault. Sherman and McPherson had formed their attacking troops in smarter ways and had prepared ladders for them to use in scaling the works, but McClernand had not thought of ladders.

BENTON

Because of the unusual way McClernand formed his corps, two brigades belonging to two different divisions attacked the 2nd Texas Lunette. Benton's brigade of Carr's division waited in the first line, while Brig. Gen. Stephen G.

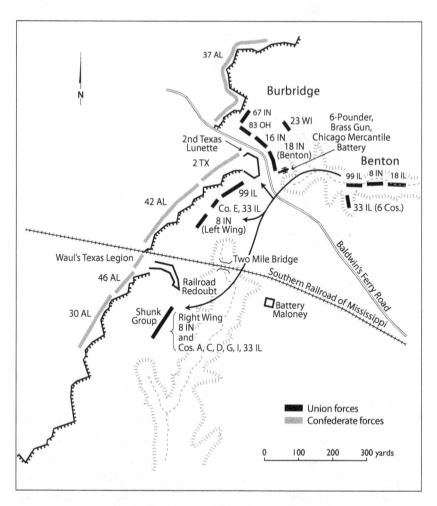

Benton-Burbridge, 2nd Texas Lunette, May 22

Burbridge's brigade of Smith's division lay in the second line, both of them to the north of Baldwin's Ferry Road. Word of the attack filtered through the ranks of Benton's troops by 9:00 A.M., only one hour before the start time. The brigade formed a column of regiments in two connected ravines, the main one ending near the left face of the lunette at a point where it gave access to the road. The 99th Illinois, 8th Indiana, and 18th Indiana were in the main ravine, while the 33rd Illinois lay in the connecting ravine that joined the main one near the head of the 99th Illinois. Because all of the regimental commanders wanted to lead the attack, Benton drew lots. Col. George W. K. Bailey won the drawing and placed his 99th Illinois in the lead. Then Col. Charles E. Lippincott's 33rd Illinois took second place, followed by Col. David Shunk's 8th Indiana, and Col. Henry D. Washburn's 18th Indiana brought up the rear. The men were told to fix bayonets but not to load their weapons.[1]

The ravine offered a covered place to assemble, but Benton's column stretched the brigade into a long and narrow block of men. The 33rd Illinois had only six of its companies in the column. Company B was on detached duty at the Big Black River, and Companies F, H, and K had been detailed to skirmish duty. Because he was the senior captain, Isaac H. Elliott's Company E led the 250 men in the six companies. Elliott later criticized the decision to assemble in this ravine. The previous day he had accompanied a scouting expedition that discovered ravines closer to the 2nd Texas Lunette, and they were wider too. In short, Benton might have been able to assemble regimental lines rather than columns in those wider ravines and improve his control of the brigade. Whether Benton knew of these ravines is unclear.[2]

At the head of the brigade Bailey cut a "colossal figure," in Elliott's words, "as he strode away in his shirt sleeves" to take place in front of the 99th Illinois. Many of his men went even further, taking off their shirts because the morning already was hot.[3]

Cpl. Charles E. Wilcox of Company A was struck with the gravity of the moment. "I cried when thinking how my comrades must soon be shot down," he confessed to his diary, "for I knew the enemy had a strong force in front of us." The crying helped and Wilcox tried to regain his composure. "At ten we were all ready for the charge," he wrote, "and though not very confident of success we put on an air of confidence."[4]

Elliott remembered the scene as he scanned the column just before the order to advance. "As I looked down the line I saw that the faces of the men were pale, but determined." Some of them arranged for messages to be sent to loved ones and asked comrades to send their few belongings home. "Others attempted jokes that were received with a good deal of solemnity." Pvt. Daniel H. Graves of Company E, at the head of the regimental column, looked at his watch and told those near him, "Boys, you have just fifteen minutes to live." His joke backfired — Graves was killed later that day.[5]

A bugler at McClernand's headquarters sounded the call and at 10:00 A.M. Bailey, without coat or vest, his shirt sleeves rolled up to his elbows, shouted, "Forward!" The head of Benton's column wound its way through the twisting contour of the ravine, which narrowed as the ground ascended and turned left toward Baldwin's Ferry Road. Finally reaching the road, Bailey found that the head of his regiment came into full view of the 2nd Texas Lunette only about 100 yards from the Confederates. Suddenly

Baldwin's Ferry Road. This modern photograph looks west along the remnant of the roadbed and about 150 yards east of the location of the 2nd Texas Lunette. Benton's brigade advanced along the ravine visible through the trees on the right and emerged from the ravine onto the roadbed about fifty yards in front of the camera, where the modern tree cover ends at an open and ascending slope. But on May 22, all the trees in this area had been cut down and the Federals were clearly seen by men of the 2nd Texas in their lunette 100 yards away. Benton's men suffered enormously because of their exposure to Confederate fire.
(Photograph by Earl J. Hess)

there burst from the fort "a withering" fire. Bailey shouted orders for the men to cross the road as quickly as possible and form line to the south of the roadway. As the regiment did so, Capt. Asa C. Matthews could see Confederate soldiers standing high above the parapet "as in astonishment" at the appearance of the Federals.[6]

Many of the 99th Illinois men were shot in the process of crossing. Others followed their colonel to the south, and still others lost their nerve and retreated back into the ravine. They accompanied other men who were hit at the roadway but were able to go to the rear for treatment. For the 33rd Illinois, next in the brigade column, this stream of walking wounded and frightened comrades was the first indication of trouble. They "came crowding back upon the 33rd that was winding up the narrow way," commented Elliott. "This spectacle, with the awful roar and turmoil just ahead, was a frightful indication of what was in store for us."[7]

Lippincott, at the head of the 33rd Illinois, quickly sized up the situation and decided his men should deploy before crossing Baldwin's Ferry Road. A "slight embankment" at the head of the ravine that was barely three feet high

2nd Texas Lunette, May 22

and just long enough for one company to form along offered an opportunity to do so. The embankment lay only about five to ten yards from the roadway. Lippincott gave instructions for each company to form line behind the embankment and then move over Baldwin's Ferry Road, believing that formation would expose the men less than a column. He left regimental adjutant E. Aaron Gove at the embankment to instruct each company commander as he arrived.[8]

Elliott formed Company E under Lippincott's guidance; then the Federals sprang across the embankment. The men rushed as fast as they could across the dusty road. Elliott expressed it powerfully when he wrote that "balls and shells were ripping along this road like storm-driven hail, and our way was straight across it."[9]

The men of Company E lay flat on the ground south of the road to wait for the rest of the regiment. But this spot was also exposed to fire, so the company started to advance, following the 99th Illinois, which had already begun to move toward the southern face of the lunette and the connecting line south of the work. The 33rd Illinois not only was separated from the 99th Illinois but was beginning to fracture. Lippincott's order that each company form and move over the road resulted in delays; by the time the next company crossed the road Company E had already moved forward and was out of sight. Succeeding companies came south of the road and grouped near the second company as Lippincott's regiment continued to dribble across Baldwin's Ferry Road. Albert O. Marshall of Company A remembered how Rebel bullets kicked up dust in the roadbed. After crossing, the five companies lay down and waited for orders.[10]

It was a hellish wait. Charles E. Wilcox recalled that a wagon road provided very slight shelter for a part of the regiment, but bullets sailed little more than a foot above his head as he pressed his face into the Mississippi dust. "What an awful eight minutes it was," he estimated. "The sweat from off my face run in a stream from the tip ends of my whiskers." To relieve the emotional stress he cried, "My God, why don't they order us to charge." The ground was becoming "covered with the dead and wounded."[11]

Lt. Col. Edward R. Roe took charge of the five companies of the 33rd Illinois because Lippincott was off with Company E, supporting the 99th Illinois. Roe ordered the troops to stand up and move south, but he was shot in the leg almost immediately afterward. The Illinoisans had no stomach to obey the order after their commander fell, so they lay down again. Soon the right wing of the 8th Indiana, the next regiment in the brigade column, finished its crossing of Baldwin's Ferry Road and formed near the five compa-

2nd Texas Lunette from the Federal perspective. This work, protecting Baldwin's Ferry Road as it sliced through Lockett's line, was situated on the high ground in this modern photograph. About 1869, the Jewish residents of Vicksburg leveled the lunette and placed a cemetery on the hill. Then in 1899, when the Vicksburg National Military Park was established, park officials constructed a tour road that sliced across the slope leading up to the former site of the lunette, bisecting the line of Union advance on May 22. This tour road is visible in the foreground of the picture. The area around the 2nd Texas Lunette has been so heavily altered as to mystify most visitors who are not told on the signs exactly where the work had been located. (Photograph by Earl J. Hess)

nies of the 33rd Illinois. Col. David Shunk took command of both formations and ordered the men to rise and move south rather than west toward the Confederates.[12]

The Shunk group came to the track of the Southern Railroad of Mississippi. Once again the Illinois and Indiana men rushed across a high, open space fully exposed to Confederate fire. Worse, no one knew that telegraph wire had been cut along the right of way and left lying in place. When the first troops crossed the tracks "nearly every man was thrown to the ground by" it. Despite the wire, Wilcox estimated he was exposed to the worst Rebel fire for only a minute as he dashed across the railroad and thought few of his comrades were shot in doing so.[13]

Benton's brigade was not only losing its cohesion but veering south toward an unintended target. Thus far only the 99th Illinois and Company E, 33rd Illinois, were heading toward the general area of the 2nd Texas Lunette. Companies A, C, D, G, and I of the 33rd Illinois and the right wing of the 8th Indiana were headed south of the railroad, eventually to contribute to Brig.

2nd Texas Lunette from the Confederate perspective. From the top of the hill where the lunette was located, this view looks toward the Federal advance. The 100-yard-long descending slope between the lunette and the place where Benton's brigade emerged from the ravine has been bisected by the 1899 park tour road. The Federals emerged about where the modern tree cover meets the open grassy area. One can see a slight break in the tree cover in the center of the picture. This is where Baldwin's Ferry Road approaches the site of the lunette. (Photograph by Earl J. Hess)

Gen. Michael K. Lawler and Col. William J. Landram's attack on Railroad Redoubt.[14]

The left wing of the 8th Indiana remained in the area between Baldwin's Ferry Road and the railroad, facing the curtain between the 2nd Texas Lunette and Railroad Redoubt. But Colonel Washburn kept tight control of the 18th Indiana north of Baldwin's Ferry Road and pushed toward the 2nd Texas Lunette. The regiment reached the ditch and Sgt. Francis M. Goss planted the colors. About forty of Washburn's men and one officer jumped into the ditch, but the rest stayed out. By this time several units were in position to deliver covering fire at the top of the parapets, so Confederate fire had decreased to the point where it was possible to line up in the open along the glacis without too much danger. Most of the 18th Indiana did so, but they could not see their comrades who were lodged in the ditch. The left of the regiment was opposite the embrasure of the 2nd Texas Lunette that looked directly onto Baldwin's Ferry Road. It had a cotton bale in it, but the Indiana men set it on fire by placing pieces of tow (which they had with them to clean out their musket barrels) on top of the cartridge.[15]

Bailey's 99th Illinois provided a colorful incident when it moved for-

Thomas J. Higgins. This corporal of Company D, 99th Illinois, gained a measure of fame for single-mindedly carrying the regimental flag into the connecting line south of the 2nd Texas Lunette, surviving the experience because the Confederates did not have the heart to shoot him. He survived the war and lived for many years among ex-Confederates in Missouri. Although the caption of this image gives his rank as private and his middle initial as H., the official roster gives the rank as corporal and the initial as J. (Beyer and Keydel, *Deeds of Valor*, 198)

ward south of Baldwin's Ferry Road. Here it aimed at the connecting line south of the 2nd Texas Lunette that was held by the two right companies of the 2nd Texas. Pvt. Thomas J. Higgins of Company D carried the regimental flag and had listened carefully as Capt. Asa C. Matthews told him "not to stop until he got into the Confederate works."[16]

The 99th Illinois halted short of the Confederate works, but not Higgins. Alone and moving steadily forward, he emerged from the smoke. Cpl. Charles I. Evans of Company G, 2nd Texas, estimated that up to 100 of his comrades aimed at Higgins but all missed; some fired two or three times because they had accumulated several muskets. Suddenly the Confederates felt Higgins did not deserve to die. "Don't shoot him! he is too brave! don't kill him; let's capture him alive!" Everyone in the area stopped firing. Higgins was true to his charge—he did not stop, and because his enemy displayed mercy he also was not shot. The young man clambered across the parapet 150 feet south of the 2nd Texas Lunette and into the arms of his admiring enemy. Evans snatched the flag from Higgins and waved it a bit in defiance of the Federals. The other regimental color-bearer was not so fortunate. Sgt. William B. Sitton was shot in the side and dropped his flag, which was never recovered by the regiment. Not until 1873 were both flags sent from Richmond to Philadelphia and then to Springfield, Illinois. As of 1886, they were still on display, with Sitton's blood staining one of the flags.[17]

The widespread interest garnered by Higgins's act (he later received a Congressional Medal of Honor for it, mostly due to testimony provided by his Confederate captors) obscured the fact that his regiment failed to make much of an impression on the enemy. The 99th Illinois came close to the southern face of the 2nd Texas Lunette but did not press closer, its left flank somewhere near where Higgins had crossed the enemy line and its right near the angle of the work. Bailey was wounded about the time the Illinois regiment reached its high tide. Other field and staff officers fell until Matthews took control of the regiment for the rest of the day.[18]

Company E, 33rd Illinois, followed the 99th Illinois and also lodged near where Higgins had crossed the enemy line. The company received so much fire that reportedly eleven of its thirty-two men were killed and everyone else was hit in some degree except Lt. Lyman M. Pratt. In fact, Pratt was the only member of the company who reached the ditch of the connecting work south of the 2nd Texas Lunette. He stayed there only a short while before running back to rejoin what was left of his company, sheltering in a "slight depression" only "a few rods" from the enemy.[19]

Benton's brigade made a shambles of its attack. The 99th Illinois and Company E, 33rd Illinois, crossed Baldwin's Ferry Road and then advanced toward the connecting line south of the 2nd Texas Lunette. Five other companies of the 33rd and half of the 8th Indiana crossed both that road and the Southern Railroad of Mississippi to participate in an attack they were not intended to support. The 18th Indiana advanced on the 2nd Texas Lunette north of Baldwin's Ferry Road and a few men lodged in its ditch but could not exploit their slim success. The brigade spun out of control and Benton was unable to stop it.

Behind Benton, Stephen Burbridge maintained better control over his brigade. He issued a circular on the morning of May 22 offering guidelines for the assault. "All loungers were ordered to their regiments," noted Thomas B. Marshall of the 83rd Ohio. The men were instructed to take only weapons, accoutrements, ammunition, one day's ration, and a canteen filled with water. Burbridge formed his brigade in a column behind Benton between 9:00 A.M. and the scheduled time for the assault. In a rare instance of confidence, Charles F. Smith of the 83rd Ohio noted in his diary that "everybody was sanguine of success." But other members of the brigade disagreed with him. "The boys thought it was pretty tough," John D. Parish wrote of the attack order. "There was not much talking done" while the 23rd Wisconsin waited, according to John W. Paul. "None of us knew which would survive."[20]

Having the example of Benton's brigade as a guide, Burbridge refused to cross Baldwin's Ferry Road once the advance started. He deployed his brigade out of the ravine to the right, or north, of the roadway as Washburn had done. Once deployed, the brigade arrayed in a line with the 67th Indiana on the right, the 83rd Ohio in the center, and the 16th Indiana on the left. The 23rd Wisconsin stayed to the rear as a reserve.[21]

Burbridge pushed his brigade forward and was very close to the 2nd Texas Lunette and its connecting line to the north by about 10:30 A.M. The troops snuggled within 30 feet of the ditch with their left flank very near the 18th Indiana. The right flank of the brigade lodged on a slight bit of high ground northeast of the 2nd Texas Lunette and was in the air. Burbridge ordered Col. Joshua J. Guppey to detach four companies of the 23rd Wisconsin to screen his right flank. On Burbridge's instructions, Guppey took the rest of his 23rd Wisconsin to the left to help Washburn and the 16th Indiana.[22]

The Federals found the ditch fronting Lockett's line to be a major impediment. Observers noted it was ten feet deep and twelve feet wide. While they could take shelter in it, they could not climb out and up the parapet. Nevertheless, Burbridge proclaimed that "the regiments had their colors flying against the walls of the fort." Capt. Ambrose A. Blount of the 17th Ohio Battery saw the colors of at least the 83rd Ohio and possibly the 16th Indiana planted at the Rebel works, while veterans of the 23rd Wisconsin recalled that their flags were placed near the outside edge of the ditch.[23]

In stark contrast to Benton, Burbridge was able to maintain control of his brigade, bringing it intact to a point close to the objective. But, like other

Federal commanders that day, he was unable to breach the earthen walls of Vicksburg.

2ND TEXAS

The 2nd Texas mustered 468 men on the morning of May 17 and probably had very close to that number five days later. Col. Ashbel Smith put two companies in the connecting line north of the work, four companies inside the lunette, and four companies in the connecting work to the south. Two guns of Capt. Thomas F. Tobin's Tennessee Battery were inside the work. Brig. Gen. John C. Moore, Smith's brigade commander, placed Col. John W. Portis's 42nd Alabama to the south of the 2nd Texas and Col. J. F. Dowdell's 37th Alabama to the north to complete defensive arrangements for this sector.[24]

The 2nd Texas Lunette was an irregular work because Lockett had placed it forward of the main line to prevent the Federals from seizing a swell of ground. Baldwin's Ferry Road ran just beyond its ditch, along the left or northern face of the lunette, before crossing the main line through a gap in the defenses about 100 yards wide. Even on the south, the connecting line was located quite a distance back from the easternmost point of the lunette in order to take advantage of the best defensive ground. According to Cpl. Charles I. Evans, a gap of twelve feet existed between the lunette and the connecting line to the south. In short, the lunette was in some ways vulnerable. Its garrison was protected only by the thickness and profile of the parapet and the depth of the ditch, which Smith cited as six feet. He also noted that, from the bottom of the ditch to the top of the parapet, one would have to climb up a slope of fourteen feet. Inside the work, his men were protected by a parapet that rose four and a half feet. The lunette had two gun emplacements with a traverse for lateral protection between them.[25]

Smith was very concerned about the uneven nature of the ground east of the 2nd Texas Lunette. Although very cut up, he detected two promising approaches for an assault on his position. One was a valley south of Baldwin's Ferry Road that could allow the Federals to advance on the right flank of the lunette. Apparently this approach was not taken by the 99th Illinois and Company E of the 33rd Illinois. The other approach lay north of Baldwin's Ferry Road. It was "a long, straight valley approaching obliquely and terminating" at the 100-yard gap in the defenses between the lunette and the connecting line to the north. "Coming up this latter valley, takes the front of the fort in enfilade and its right flank and rifle-pits in reverse," warned Smith. Between these two approaches the terrain rose as high as the ground that the lunette occupied, and Baldwin's Ferry Road ran along the high elevation. As far as Ashbel Smith was concerned, the landscape offered as many advantages to the enemy as to the defender.[26]

Federal reports are not detailed enough concerning the terrain to know for sure, but it appears that Burbridge's brigade line straddled the northern approach to the lunette. A column formation might have been able to move more advantageously along the ravine and penetrate the gap in the Rebel defensive line. Whether the Federals even knew that such a gap existed is questionable.

But Ashbel Smith certainly was aware of the terrain, and he worried during the intense artillery bombardment that morning. The Union artillery disabled one of Tobin's pieces inside the work, but the other gun continued to fire.[27]

At 10:00 A.M., the landscape east of the 2nd Texas Lunette transformed into a bloody battlefield. "Instantaneously," wrote Smith, "the enemy springing up from the hollows and valleys to our right and front—the earth was black with their close columns." In front, Benton's men crossed Baldwin's Ferry Road and then broke up into fragments farther to the right of the lunette. To the left, Smith could see Washburn's regiment and then Burbridge's four regiments move toward his left flank. "It was certainly the most superb spectacle that the eye of a soldier ever beheld," thought Charles Evans.[28]

Burbridge's approach worried Smith more than any other threat. The best field of fire here extended only about fifty yards from the Rebel earthworks, and the defenders let loose with heavy volleys when the Federals neared that zone. It did not stop the Unionists from taking refuge along Baldwin's Ferry Road as it ran close to the ditch of the lunette, for here the roadbed was sunken, or "worn into a trench."[29]

Moreover, when Smith's men glanced south, they could see that Railroad Redoubt was in trouble. Located 400 yards south of the 2nd Texas Lunette, some Federal colors already flew on its parapet. The sight was "very discouraging" to the Texans.[30]

STANDOFF AT THE 2ND TEXAS LUNETTE

As far as Smith could tell, the Federals who lodged close to the 2nd Texas Lunette also were cheered by the sight of those Union flags at Railroad Redoubt. But the Unionists achieved little more than a stalemate at the lunette. "We could keep them down in our front, but from both right and left they could murder us," commented Pvt. Charles D. Morris of Company E, 33rd Illinois. "It was a hot place," admitted James Stevenson of the 16th Indiana, "and had it not been for our incessant firing we would have all been cut to pieces." Stevenson was close enough to speak with the Rebels and amused himself by throwing a shell fragment in their direction.[31]

When any Texans rose up to shoot over the top of the parapet they risked life and limb from the heavy Federal fire that was bound to sail over. "Sometimes they get their hands shot off," commented Isaac Jackson of the 83rd Ohio, who observed the battle from the 17th Ohio Battery, to which he had been detailed several days before. There was a considerable amount of yelling across no-man's-land, most of it by the Federals who tried to taunt the Confederates into looking over the parapet. The Yankees "hooted, cussed & dared them, but they would not show themselves." Colonel Guppey of the 23rd Wisconsin reported that the Unionists also "tried to dig them down," but there was no way they could create a sap through the thick parapet without tools.[32]

Given the tactical stalemate, Carr wanted to even out his troop disposition. Benton's brigade had fractured into pieces and was unable to cover the ground between Burbridge's brigade and the Lawler-Landram formation that was then lodged outside Railroad Redoubt. Walter Scates, McClernand's adjutant general, therefore sent an order to Andrew J. Smith that two of Burbridge's regiments should move south to support Shunk's 8th Indiana and those companies of the 33rd Illinois that were stalled near Railroad Redoubt. In Scates's words, the regiments were "to fill up the space between Lawler's and Benton's brigades, and cover the space between the forts, and that the whole force move forward immediately and vigorously."[33]

When Smith read this order, a short while after it was written at 1:30 P.M., he relayed it to Burbridge. "I cannot move," the brigadier told Smith, adding that the order would take away half his line. The division leader replied that it was not his order; McClernand had placed Carr in charge of operations against the 2nd Texas Lunette. So Burbridge went back to the main Union line and consulted with McClernand. The corps leader sympathized but told him to talk to Carr.[34]

Carr put on an air of stern resolve. He and his staff deliberately exposed themselves to enemy fire as examples to the men. Carr appeared to be "the most cool and business like man on the field," according to JRSC of Smith's staff. When someone called out, "Look at the men falling," Carr rebuked him. "Who talks of dead men here? Think of the enemy, and of killing them. It is no time to speak of dead men now."[35]

When Burbridge consulted with him about the order, Carr refused to back down. He insisted that Burbridge shift the regiments. Having exhausted all avenues, Burbridge returned to his brigade and issued orders for the 83rd Ohio, 16th Indiana, and four companies of the 23rd Wisconsin to move south. They took position near Shunk's improvised command but were unable to cover all open ground between Shunk and the rest of the Union line. Moreover, they were unable to advance. When Shunk received instructions to move forward, he replied, "Half of my men are killed and wounded, but I will go with the rest." Yet there is no further report that such a move was attempted. In short, there was little the regiments Burbridge had detached could do.[36]

It seemed to Burbridge that the Texans who opposed his brigade knew he had reduced his troop strength by half and increased their fire at his position. He therefore sought ways to reclaim his regiments. Benton agreed he should recall the troops, and Burbridge did so without asking Carr's permission. Soon after this, Carr sent a note authorizing Burbridge to recall the units if necessary. The brigadier estimated that the 83rd Ohio, 16th Indiana, and the four companies of the 23rd Wisconsin lost about 100 men while moving back and forth.[37]

While the attackers could not find a way to break into the 2nd Texas Lunette, the defenders found it impossible to drive them away. Federal troops were positioned from 60 to 200 yards away, ready to take a shot at any Rebel within sight.[38]

Ashbel Smith worried that the Yankees might be able to rush over the parapet before his men could see them. He therefore organized a system, organizing one rank to continue firing over the parapet and instructing the men in a second rank to bend their knees, fix their bayonets, and keep their weapons loaded. Smith also selected a small number of men to act as a reserve, placing them four paces to the rear, lying on the ground with guns loaded and bayonets fixed. These reserve troops held the least comfortable position, for bullets and shells fell into the interior of the lunette; the only truly safe place was close to the parapet. When the guns of the first rank became too hot to handle, Smith allowed the second rank to move up and fire awhile to allow the weapons to cool.[39]

"It would be a great mistake to imagine that our men fought under cover," reported Smith. "To reach the enemy our men were compelled to expose the whole of their bodies, & the enemy's fire through the embrasures swept a large portion of the interior area of our fort."[40]

This enemy fire caused unusual trouble for the Confederates. Union artillery rounds broke open several bags of cotton that had been used to create a traverse between the two gun positions. Small-arms fire also tore into the bags, "playing on them incessantly bowed out the cotton as if from the flue of a gin-stand, and scattered it all over the area of the fort," Smith wrote. This loose cotton caught fire, probably from the muzzle flashes of the Confederate rifles, and smoke filled the air. Enough cotton was clumped together to create a fire that approached some ammunition boxes. Smith ordered a few men to crawl around and brush away loose cotton near the boxes, creating a fire break that saved the ammunition. The caissons inside the fort also were threatened, but the Texans got to them in time. Still, the smoke from the burning cotton almost blinded the defenders of the lunette.[41]

Smith was frustrated that he could not use the one remaining piece of Tobin's Tennessee Battery that remained operational. The gun crew had lost men and hardly enough were left to work it. Moreover, cotton bags used to revet the embrasures were on fire. But by 2:00 P.M. Smith managed to subdue the fires and ordered the gun crew to push the piece into one of the embrasures. "As the last remaining corporal raised himself over the trail to aim, a Minie ball . . . passed through his heart and he rolled over dead," Smith wrote.[42]

The Federals were lodged so close to this embrasure they could fire right through it. Smith called for volunteers to clear the enemy away. Four men, Sgt. William T. Spence of Company B, Pvt. T. E. Bagwell of Company C, Pvt. A. S. Kittridge of Company C, and Pvt. J. A. Steward of Company C, stood up. The small group steeled their nerves and rushed into the embrasure, firing as quickly as they could and at short range. Spence was mortally wounded and Bagwell was killed, but the rest managed to clear most Federals from their position near the embrasure.[43]

The Texans could no longer use their artillery, but they could use the shells. A few projectiles from Tobin's caissons were fused and rolled down the parapet into the ditch of the 2nd Texas Lunette. According to Maj. Gen. John H. Forney, five-second fuses did the trick.[44]

The Federals tried to make better use of their own artillery against the Confederate work. Burbridge asked A. J. Smith for close gun support, and Smith sent a message to Capt. Patrick H. White of the Chicago Mercantile Battery a bit after noon. White, a thirty-year-old Irishman, remembered that the message instructed him to take two guns forward "to the breastworks and hammer down a fort." White further recalled that Smith assured him, "We shall be inside the rebel works in half an hour."[45]

White explored a route to cross the uneven terrain and during this reconnaissance obtained a close view of the lunette. He thought it would be easier to take just one piece through the terrain features. White selected a gun and arranged a prolonge, or rope, for the crew to drag it. He also asked for help from the 83rd Ohio—Guppey, however, reported that he supplied Companies B and E of the 23rd Wisconsin to help White move the gun. It took a bit of time for the troops to negotiate the terrain, but they managed to push and pull the brass six-pounder until they placed it twenty feet from the left, or north, face of the 2nd Texas Lunette. Members of the 18th Indiana also helped move the piece during the last few yards of its advance, placing it just to the left of the regimental line.[46]

White and his gun crew pumped fourteen canister and spherical case rounds across the parapet and through the embrasure. "The gun was most skillfully handled," admitted Texan Charles Evans. White agreed. "I never saw a gun loaded and fired so fast," he recalled. "Every man was at his best." The crewmen were a bit nervous and "did not take much care in sponging, and once or twice the gun was prematurely discharged."[47]

Despite their effort, the gun crew did little damage to the enemy. White's expectation that the infantry would storm the lunette with the support of his gun was false; no such plan was communicated to the officers outside the work. "It was pretty safe to be around" the gun, Asa C. Matthews reported, because enemy return fire was already suppressed. "The whole thing amounted to very little, except to make a great noise, and keep up the spirits of the men."[48]

White probably opened fire about 2:00 P.M. Firing at a rapid rate, it would have taken but twenty to thirty minutes to let loose fourteen rounds. Then the gun crew and supporting infantrymen retired to the battery position, but they apparently left the gun in place close to the lunette. Despite the limited damage, Burbridge was delighted with White's exploit, slapping him on the back and saying, "Capt I woul[d] rather have your honor now than the Star on my Shoulder." The detailed men from the 23rd Wisconsin were employed in carrying ammunition along with the gun as it advanced. One of them was accidentally hit by a round fired by the 17th Ohio Battery, apparently the only casualty of this daring experiment in close artillery support. Six surviving members of the gun crew, plus White, received Congressional Medals of Honor many years later.[49]

The effort by this gun crew and its detailed infantry failed to break the tactical stalemate around the 2nd Texas Lunette. Burbridge's brigade and Washburn's contingent of the 18th Indiana from Benton's brigade lodged close enough to pressure the garrison, but neither side could drive the other away. Shunk's wing of the 8th Indiana, the five companies of the 33rd Illinois, the 99th Illinois, and Company E of the 33rd Illinois were all stuck some distance away from the connecting line between the 2nd Texas Lunette and Railroad Redoubt and south of the latter work. Half of the Carr-Smith plan of attack had broken down mostly due to the rugged terrain and, in Benton's case, poor tactical control of his formation. The other factors that spelled failure included an earthwork well sited and built, manned by a stout garrison. Perhaps the other half of the Carr-Smith attack, directed against Railroad Redoubt, would fare better.

{ 10 }

A Thousand Bayonets Glistened in the Sunlight

RAILROAD REDOUBT, MAY 22

The last Thirteenth Corps attack to go in on the morning of May 22 took place south of the Southern Railroad of Mississippi and was conducted by two brigades. It targeted one of the largest and most complex of Lockett's forts, Railroad Redoubt. The leading brigade, commanded by Michael K. Lawler, had mainly been responsible for the capture of the fortified bridge-head at the Big Black River five days before, with its rich haul of prisoners and guns. There at least was a possibility that Railroad Redoubt might fall as readily as the fieldworks at the river.

But the Federals knew very little about the layout of the work or the garrison that held it. They could not be expected to know that only a small number of Confederates occupied this large work and that it represented a genuinely weak link in Lockett's line. If they had realized all this it might have led to a revision of their attack plan, an arrangement to have reserve troops handy to exploit any initial success. As it was, the Union plan of attack was not geared to exploiting success but was little more than a large recon-naissance in force designed to explore whatever possibilities lay ahead.

There even was widespread confusion about the name of the earthwork to be attacked. Railroad Redoubt often was referred to by the Federals as Fort Beauregard. After the siege, Lockett called it Fort Pettus, but a corporal in the 77th Illinois heard Rebels refer to it as Fort Pemberton.[1]

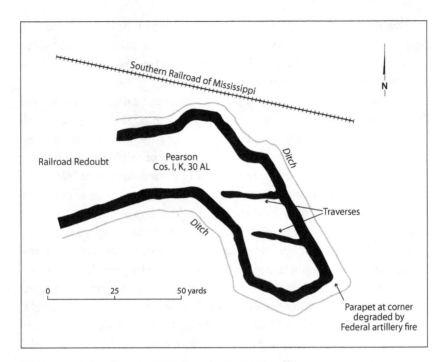

Railroad Redoubt sketch map

By whatever name it was known, the work was the only part of Lockett's line damaged by Federal guns that morning. As Lt. Peter C. Hains, McClernand's chief engineer, put it, thirty-pound projectiles "battered the salient angle" and "ploughed deep furrows in the parapet." Those furrows were three or four feet deep, "leaving but little of the original parapet standing." The rounds failed to collapse the scarp (the interior wall of the outer ditch around the redoubt). That scarp wall was not only intact but seven feet tall, according to Hains, and the parapet was an additional seven and a half feet tall. In other words, the deep furrows ploughed in the parapet might be used to enter the fort, but getting out of the ditch and into them would be a problem.[2]

Like the 2nd Texas Lunette, Railroad Redoubt was placed forward of the main line to deny advantageous ground to the Federals. It covered half an acre and was divided into three compartments separated by two parallel traverses for protection against enfilading fire. The eastern compartment was only eighteen by twenty-four feet in space. The traverses ran across almost the whole interior of the work, allowing a narrow passage between the end of the traverse and the parapet. The redoubt was open at the rear, 80 to 100 yards west of its eastern parapet.[3]

Railroad Redoubt "was thought to be a point of danger," recalled Stephen D. Lee, whose sector included the fort. "It was the most exposed to a continuous fire of artillery, and immediately in front was the heavy siege battery" that gouged the parapet.[4]

Lockett had no choice but to place the work as he did, for allowing the Federals to occupy the eastward-stretching spur of ridge that lay just south of the railroad would have jeopardized the security of his main line. The ground "sloped off in all directions" from the top of this spur, as Hains put it. About 150 feet east of the eastern salient of the redoubt, there "was a terrace, or sudden depression on the surface of the ground, such as one often sees in a garden located on the slope of a hill." The terrace was about 100 feet long and offered a handy bit of protection for infantrymen approaching the redoubt. The Confederates had placed a thick abatis forty yards from the eastern tip of the redoubt to trip up attackers before they reached the fort.[5]

Lee's Brigade held this general area with the 46th Alabama on the extreme left and just south of the railroad. The 30th Alabama lay to its right. Lt. John M. Pearson, who had left his studies at the University of Alabama to join the army, had been holding the work with Companies I and K, 30th Alabama, since the night before. A small brass gun was located in the southeast angle of the work, attended by a lieutenant and his detachment. The rest of the 30th Alabama and the 46th Alabama occupied the connecting line south of the redoubt. The 31stAlabama, 23rdAlabama, and 20th Alabama filled out the rest of Lee's sector. The 20th was responsible for Square Fort opposite Osterhaus.[6]

Col. Thomas N. Waul's Texas Legion was held as a reserve just behind Railroad Redoubt. Put together in the spring of 1862, the legion initially consisted of eight infantry companies, four cavalry companies, and a battery of light artillery. Waul had increased it in size until it consisted of eleven infantry companies and "a detachment of mounted scouts, and a battalion of Zouaves, attached to the command." The battalion, known as the 1st Louisiana Zouaves, was led by Capt. J. B. Fleitas. Waul detached his battery to Pemberton's artillery and took the rest of his legion to Stevenson's Division, where it was given to Lee on the afternoon of May 19. On the morning of May 22, with Union artillery pounding the area, Waul sent two companies under Maj. O. Steele north of the railroad and held the remaining nine companies plus Fleitas's battalion south of the tracks, just behind the open gorge of Railroad Redoubt.[7]

Railroad Redoubt, May 22

Railroad Redoubt. Taken from the northeast angle of the Confederate work, near where a small brass artillery piece was located, this photograph looks toward the approximate location of Battery Maloney's thirty-pounder Parrots and McClernand's command post in the distance, where the Iowa Monument is now located. (Photograph by Earl J. Hess)

LAWLER

Eugene A. Carr committed one brigade and Andrew J. Smith another opposite Railroad Redoubt on the morning of May 22. Lawler's troops formed in two lines, with the 11th Wisconsin on the left and the 22nd Iowa on the right of the first line. The 23rd Iowa on the left and the 21st Iowa on the right constituted the second line. Lawler divided authority between the two wings, assigning Col. William M. Stone of the 22nd Iowa to lead the right wing (22nd Iowa and 21st Iowa) and Col. Charles L. Harris of the 11th Wisconsin to lead the left wing (11th Wisconsin and 23rd Iowa). Behind Lawler, Col. William J. Landram positioned his 19th Kentucky on the left and the 77th Illinois on the right of his first line and the 130th Illinois on the left and the 48th Ohio on the right of his second line. The 97th Illinois took position as a reserve, although a detail of twenty men and a commissioned officer were detached to skirmish. The formation was located south of the railroad so that the right wing, led by Stone's 22nd Iowa, would hit Railroad Redoubt squarely. The

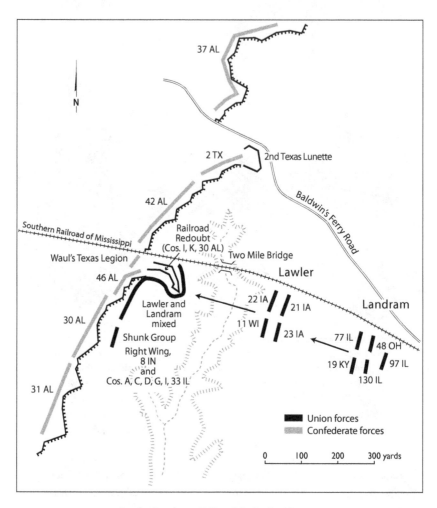

N

37 AL

2 TX   2nd Texas Lunette

Baldwin's Ferry Road

42 AL

Southern Railroad of Mississippi

Railroad Redoubt (Cos. I, K, 30 AL)

Two Mile Bridge

Waul's Texas Legion

Lawler

46 AL

Lawler and Landram mixed

22 IA   21 IA   Landram

30 AL

11 WI   23 IA   77 IL   48 OH

Shunk Group Right Wing, 8 IN and Cos. A, C, D, G, I, 33 IL

19 KY   97 IL

130 IL

31 AL

Union forces
Confederate forces

0   100   200   300 yards

Lawler-Landram, Railroad Redoubt, May 22

left wing, led by Harris's 11th Wisconsin, would hit the connecting line south of the redoubt. Lawler had so much confidence in his troops that he did not bother to deploy skirmishers, telling Landram that "his men could accomplish anything."[8]

Aware of his important role in leading the main effort, Stone was eager to better his chances of success. He wakened the men of the 22nd Iowa at midnight of May 21 and moved them forward under cover of darkness until they were only fifty yards from the redoubt. Stone completed the move just before dawn. He then sent Companies A and B to positions where they could skirmish and cover his advance. Company F had already been detached from the 22nd Iowa to provide guards at headquarters and to look after prisoners.

As a result, only seven companies, about 200 men, were poised to conduct the attack that morning.[9]

Lt. Col. Cornelius W. Dunlap also sent Companies A and B of his 21st Iowa to the skirmish line. He told the two company commanders to "partially cover, and at least distract or draw the fire of the enemy from the advancing columns as they charged." Dunlap issued orders for the 21st Iowa to fix bayonets and wait for the word to go.[10]

Lawler sent Bluford Wilson, his assistant adjutant general, to give final instructions to Stone and Harris a short time before 10:00 A.M. Wilson found, however, that the two men had developed an idea about how to conduct the attack. Rather than in a formation of two lines, Stone and Harris now wanted to organize the entire brigade into one column of regimental or even company front. The entire mass should advance on Railroad Redoubt rather than spread out along the Confederate line. They wanted, in Wilson's words, to "hurl the whole weight of the brigade directly against the point of the rebel works nearest to us, to be the quickest reached and with the least loss."[11]

Wilson was open to the idea. He told the two colonels that they could do it on their own and he would support them, but Stone and Harris were reluctant to take on the responsibility. As it turned out, ten o'clock neared while they were still pondering the change, so both decided to keep the current formation. Wilson estimated that no more than 1,000 men constituted Lawler's attack force. With the benefit of hindsight, he came to the conclusion that the Stone-Harris plan of massing the brigade in one column would have had a better chance of success than Lawler's formation.[12]

The mood in Lawler's brigade as the men waited for the attack varied with each individual. George A. Remley of Company F, detailed to the provost guard at Carr's headquarters, chafed at not being able to support his comrades of the 22nd Iowa. On the other hand, Hiram J. Lewis found no eagerness for the assault in the 11th Wisconsin. "It looked like a forlorn hope," he wrote. "Every man moved in the work with firmness but with doubt."[13]

The Federal artillery pounded away until the moment came for the infantry to go in. Inside Railroad Redoubt, Pearson asked permission of his superior to evacuate the fort but was told to stay and make the best of it. Some of his men took shelter behind the traverse while the rest remained at the forward parapet. McClernand gave instructions for the bugler to blow his signal at 9:55 A.M., allowing five minutes for officers to issue orders to their commands. At 10:00 A.M., Lawler and Landram started out. The men of the 22nd Iowa shouted, "Remember Kinsman," referring to Col. William H.

Kinsman of the 23rd Iowa, who had been killed at the Big Black River five days earlier.[14]

Two blue-coated brigades rose up and made their way toward the fort, creating a vision of martial power in the rugged landscape. "The enemy were on the alert," wrote Adj. Samuel D. Pryce of the 22nd Iowa, "and as our colors rose above the crest of the hill, a thousand bayonets glistened in the sunlight above the parapet of Fort Beauregard." It seemed to Samuel C. Jones of the same regiment that "our army arose at once as if by magic out of the ground."[15]

From the Confederate perspective, the sudden appearance of two Union brigades was unforgettable. Pearson recalled the sight nearly forty years later. "They seemed to be springing from the bowels of the earth[,] a long line of indigo." With Federal cheers adding to the excitement, Stephen D. Lee stood in awe of the view. "The scene was a grand one, the rough hills and valleys turning blue and appearing alive with the assaulting Federals. The enemy seemed to be full of confidence, their ranks opened because of the rough ground."[16]

The Confederates began to fire almost immediately upon seeing Lawler's men. A correspondent of the *New-York Daily Tribune* who was standing near Carr's tent witnessed the result. "The redoubts are all alive with heads and muskets and jets of smoke," he reported. Pearson's men fired and loaded but on glancing around the lieutenant noticed that the gun crew at the brass piece was running away. "Why don't you shoot your cannon Lieutenant?" Pearson yelled. "I have no lanyard," the artillery officer replied as he scampered to the rear. Pearson estimated that only fifteen of his twenty men fired at the oncoming Federals. He later admitted that some of those men might have run back with the artillery detachment but could hardly blame them. "I had a very strong inclination myself to retire at that time, and nothing but a fear of disastrous consequences resulting from such a course prevented me." The killing field was open except for the undulating terrain, and the fire had its effect. The Federals also caught some unintended rounds from the rear. A projectile from an Ohio battery hit Lt. Matthew A. Robb of the 22nd Iowa and killed him as he advanced.[17]

The Federals found the terrain nearly as disconcerting as the Rebel fire. They had to negotiate felled timber immediately in front of their staging area. The obstructions "literally covered the ground," according to Samuel Pryce. Then they encountered the abatis forty yards from Railroad Redoubt. After working through it, the 22nd Iowa stopped to re-form ranks before continuing to move forward.[18]

Railroad Redoubt, May 22

As the 22nd Iowa marched steadily on, the intensity of Rebel fire forced the regiment to split in two. The left wing "was driven into the hollow on the left of the fort," reported Stone, while the right wing continued moving directly toward Railroad Redoubt. By about 10:30 A.M. Stone reported that the right wing of his regiment had lodged on the terrace 150 feet east of the redoubt. Stone and about fifty of his men went farther and lodged in the ditch of the work. Two men planted the state flag of the 22nd Iowa on the parapet. One of McClernand's aides carefully noted that the color was placed "immediately outside the [crest] of the parapet, barely low enough to secure protection to the color-bearer."[19]

Those men who remained at the terrace found that it offered only limited protection from projectiles descending from right and left. They huddled behind its slim profile and tried to scoop out holes with their bayonets.[20]

The left wing of the 22nd Iowa veered left and followed the left wing of Lawler's brigade as it moved toward the connecting line south of Railroad Redoubt. Led by the 11th Wisconsin, which was followed by the 23rd Iowa and then the left wing of the 22nd Iowa, this group of Federals came to a ravine that lay between their staging area and the target. They had no idea it existed and found that it was absolutely filled with cut timber and brush. It took some time to snake through the entanglement.[21]

The Federals lost much cohesion while struggling through the timber-engulfed ravine. The 11th Wisconsin "seemed to be scattered like chaff before the wind," thought George Crooke of the 21st Iowa, "and soon went to cover in all directions; many of them falling headlong into the blind ditch at the bottom of the ravine and remaining there." Crooke did not follow them. "By a miracle which I do not understand," he survived the harrowing trip through the timber, crossed the ditch, and made his way up the opposite slope. Crooke stopped fifty yards short of the connecting line south of Railroad Redoubt. Here he found fifteen other Federals scattered about but forming no line. Half of these fifteen stalwarts were members of his regiment.[22]

According to Bluford Wilson, these men could not go farther because of heavy fire delivered at short range in front of the works. They found some shelter among the "rough and rounding contour of the hill," as Crooke put it. "The thickness of the rebel works protected us from the fire of the enemy, but almost any motion of the body was likely to be observed." Some men of the 11th Wisconsin managed to come up to Crooke's position. Occasionally a Confederate stood up to take a shot at these men but he risked his life to do so.[23]

Lawler's brigade had broken up during its ten-minute advance to high tide. Clearly he needed help from Landram's brigade. Landram, who had been a fervent abolitionist though he lived in the slave state of Kentucky, was awake to his duties. He had formed on Porter's Chapel Ridge 600 to 800 yards from the Confederate line and thus was some distance back from the advanced starting point of Stone's 22nd Iowa. Moreover, a ravine "filled with fallen timber and thick undergrowth of brush, brambles and cane" lay just in front of Landram's men. As a result, Stone's Iowans reached their high tide in only a few minutes, while Landram's men had to struggle for longer. His troops snaked their way through the crowded ravine, negotiated "a deep gully" at the bottom, and then crawled up the opposite slope through tangling undergrowth. At times the men pulled themselves up the slope by grabbing on to bushes. According to Lt. Col. Lysander R. Webb of the 77th Illinois, it took his troops at least a half hour to advance out of the ravine and be in position to help Lawler.[24]

Despite the terrain, Landram's command remained intact. The 77th Illinois got out of the ravine and moved a short distance toward the target a few minutes before the rest did. Webb noted that the men stopped to catch their breath and continued, about sixty of them getting into the ditch with Stone's fifty men of the 22nd Iowa and the rest taking shelter at the terrace. Fifteen to twenty minutes later, the 48th Ohio and 130th Illinois arrived on the scene and lodged with the group already occupying the terrace, although that terrain feature was not large enough to harbor all of them.[25]

It was now time to plant flags on the parapet of Railroad Redoubt. The national colors of the 22nd Iowa went up. Sgt. David Vore of the 48th Ohio raised the regiment's "bullet-riddled" flag onto the works. Close by, Cpl. James P. Black of Company C and Cpl. John Griffith of Company A, 77th Illinois, put that regiment's national flag and regimental colors on the parapet.[26]

Col. Nathaniel Niles's 130th Illinois approached the works, but the color-bearer hesitated to push forward . When Lt. Frank Parker of Company C called for a volunteer to replace him, Frank Dunn answered. Described as "a pale faced Irish boy" only eighteen years old, Dunn impressed Parker with his willingness to carry the flag. "All right, if you take it to-day Frank, you shall carry it as long as it belongs to the regiment." Dunn managed to place the flag on "the counter-scarp of the ditch" at Railroad Redoubt. According to a newspaper correspondent who signed himself Mack, the flag of the 19th Kentucky also was planted on the redoubt.[27]

As early as 10:10 A.M., even before Stone lodged at the ditch of Railroad Redoubt and long before Landram closed on the fort, Lawler and Landram dashed off a note to McClernand. "The enemy are massing their forces in our front. No movement of our troops on our left. We ought to have reenforcements." It is probable that both men were aware they had too few troops to accomplish the task and were already alarmed that Osterhaus was not making headway to the south. They probably also were aware that bringing up reinforcements in a timely way was essential in conducting an attack and wanted to prod McClernand as early as possible. In this they were disappointed because the corps commander had no ready reserves to offer them. He had given his only reserve unit, Col. William T. Spicely's brigade, to Osterhaus.[28]

Lawler and Landram had to battle it out on their own for many hours under difficult circumstances. "We were now exposed to an enfilading fire from the right and left, which was thinning our ranks at a fearful rate," according to the historians of the 48th Ohio. Cpl. Isaac H. Carmen used his bayonet to scoop out a small hole and hid in it as a member of the 77th Illinois took cover in a shell hole nearby. The 77th Illinois man agreed to reload Carmen's musket as the Ohioan fired round after round at the enemy.[29]

A bit before 1:30 P.M. McClernand instructed Landram to place two regiments behind the right wing of Lawler's brigade. Along with instructing Burbridge to place two of his regiments behind Benton's two left regiments, this was McClernand's effort to even out troop dispositions between the 2nd Texas Lunette and Railroad Redoubt. These instructions indicate that McClernand had little awareness of how jumbled his troop positions had become. Benton's brigade was hopelessly fractured rather than in a neat formation, and neither Landram nor Burbridge could detach any units without endangering their positions.[30]

Landram made no attempt to obey McClernand's order. Instead he offered advice to Thirteenth Corps headquarters at 1:50 P.M.: "If General Osterhaus, on my left, will press forward, I think the works can soon be cleared." Osterhaus did not do so. Fifty minutes later, at 2:40, Landram wrote to his division leader, A. J. Smith. "Our men are holding the flanks of the fort in front of us. There is a heavy cross-fire upon us. They are hurling hand-grenades upon us, and hurting us considerably in that way." In providing this status report, Landram failed to offer a suggestion about how to break the stalemate.[31]

The only slim hope for breaking the stalemate rested with a handful of daring men in the 22nd Iowa. A Federal soldier crawled out of the ditch at Railroad Redoubt and exposed himself to take a shot. He was a noncommissioned officer and seemed to Pearson to be six feet tall. The man fired his musket at the connecting line just south of the redoubt. Someone handed him a second musket and he fired it too but then was "shot down on the parapet," in Lee's words. More Federals got into the work but soon either were shot by Pearson's troops or retreated. Pearson was certain that only three Yankees managed to escape this initial penetration of Railroad Redoubt.[32]

Pearson had been knocked down and stunned during the repulse of this first Union penetration of the work. By the time he recovered his senses and peeked across the parapet, the ground close to the work "was literally blue." He thought 1,000 Federals were lying within a few yards of the work held by his dozen men, with only the parapet and ditch separating the two groups. He fully realized that if they came inside in any number, his small command could not hold them. So Pearson concentrated on keeping his men down to save their lives and prayed for help to arrive.[33]

Soon after, the second penetration of Railroad Redoubt took place. A group of thirteen men of the 22nd Iowa, out of approximately fifty who had lodged in the ditch, crawled up and through the deep furrows ploughed by Federal artillery in the angle of the parapet. They initially got out of the ditch "by raising one another up the wall" and once in the furrows could crawl through them and into the work. Sgts. Joseph E. Griffith and Nicholas C. Messenger of Company I led the group. Griffith, born in Wales and at the time of the attack only nineteen years old, would garner most of the credit for this exploit. When the group entered Railroad Redoubt is uncertain. Stone bragged that "within ten minutes from the time we started my men entered" Railroad Redoubt, but that seems to be an exaggeration. Bluford Wilson thought it was 10:20, while Lt. Col. Harvey Graham of the 22nd Iowa estimated the time to be between ten thirty and noon.[34]

The few Confederates who occupied the small compartment at the angle where the furrows were located immediately fled. In fact, Capt. Frank H. Mason, one of McClernand's aides, noticed from the Union line these men leaving the redoubt. Stone also saw that Rebel troops holding the connecting line north of the fort and up to the railroad seemed to be evacuating their posts. The men of Waul's Texas Legion, positioned at the open gorge of the

Railroad Redoubt, southeast angle. This photograph shows the place where Federal artillery degraded the parapet enough to allow Joseph Griffith and his party to enter Railroad Redoubt, giving rise to expectations that the Union attack might succeed. (Photograph by Earl J. Hess)

redoubt, now received fire from Federals lodged south of the work and had to scurry for cover.[35]

Griffith's small group became the only Federals able to penetrate an enemy fortification on May 22. They could do very little after getting into it, for the compartment was quite small, only about eighteen by twenty-four feet large. In fact, Griffith's twelve men were about all that could fit into it. Moreover, Waul's men at the gorge now noticed them and began to fire into the work from a distance of 100 yards or more. Griffith's men took cover on the ground of the compartment as stalemate once again characterized Lawler's attack on Railroad Redoubt.[36]

By 11:45 A.M., Lee reported the situation to Stevenson. He stated that the attack had been repulsed even though a number of enemy troops had lodged near Railroad Redoubt. "I can't reach them in the ditch. They made a grand assault, and have lost a great many men." At that time, Lee did not mention Griffith's small group inside one compartment of the redoubt—it is possible he did not know of it. Pemberton became worried when Lee's report reached army headquarters. "It is absolutely necessary that they be dis-

William M. Stone. Colonel of the 22nd Iowa, Stone was wounded in the arm soon after reaching Railroad Redoubt and later parlayed his fame into a successful run for the office of governor of Iowa. (Vol. 112, 5778, Massachusetts Commandery, Military Order of the Loyal Legion and the U.S. Army Military History Institute)

lodged," he wrote of the Federals in the ditch. "It may be done by throwing into them shrapnel with short fuses, say two seconds."[37]

At about this time, Stone gained enduring fame for being shot. He had been serving as a circuit court judge in Iowa when the war broke out and he raised a company of the 3rd Iowa. Wounded in a fight at Blue Mills Landing, Missouri, in September 1861, Stone was captured on the first day of fighting at Shiloh. The Confederates paroled him to serve as a liaison with the Federals for the exchange of Benjamin M. Prentiss and other Union captives. Ironically, Stone traveled to Confederate-controlled Vicksburg for this purpose. When negotiations stalled, he honored the terms of his parole and returned to Richmond, but the Confederates sent him north again to finalize the exchange.[38]

Back home, Stone was elected colonel of the 22nd Iowa, and at midday of May 22 his men seemed on the verge of entering Railroad Redoubt. Not long after reaching the ditch, Stone was joined by Lt. Col. Cornelius W. Dunlap of the 21st Iowa. The two officers stood up "on the highest and most exposed point near the fort," Stone reported. They observed Confederates scurrying about to leave the redoubt as Griffith's men entered it. After a short conversation between the two, Stone sent Carr a message "to send me a brigade, and I would hold the works. I regarded the thing as easily done." In fact, Stone later boasted that he "regarded the door to Vicksburg as opened." He had no idea whether his message reached Carr, but Stone and Dunlap continued to stand in their exposed position to observe further developments.[39]

It was a foolhardy gesture. The two men were "congratulating ourselves upon our success, when I was shot in the arm by a sharpshooter from the woods beyond their rifle pits," Stone wrote. Dunlap, who still found it difficult to walk because of a wound received at Port Gibson on May 1, was now "shot through the head and instantly killed," in the words of his major, Salue G. Van Anda.[40]

Stone estimated it was about noon when he started for the rear. Along the way he told several men that if Carr had sent a fresh brigade he could have broken the Rebel line wide open. *"There were no interior works at that time,* in rear of the line we held, as I could see far beyond," he later wrote.[41]

Lt. Col. Harvey Graham replaced Stone as commander of the 22nd Iowa and supported his colonel's assessment of the situation. The Confederates in and near Railroad Redoubt seemed to be "panic stricken," and fresh troops could have busted up the enemy line if they had arrived in time.[42]

The party that Griffith and Messenger led into Railroad Redoubt was too small to achieve a breakthrough. How long the Federals remained there is a bit murky. The major of the 22nd Iowa claimed they stayed one to two hours, while Graham reported that the group occupied the compartment from about ten thirty to noon. Messenger got out of the redoubt before Griffith. "I fired a few rounds in the fort [and] then [retired] to the outside as [did] most of the men who could get out," he reported four months later. It was about noon when he emerged from the fort, about the time Graham replaced the wounded Stone. Graham instructed Messenger "to take a post of much danger as well as of importance on top of the fort, where I lay some four hours under the floating stripe of the Gallant Old Flag," Messenger wrote.[43]

Griffith and his compatriots remained in the compartment, waiting for developments to signal what they should do. The Confederates responded to their presence at about noon, when Col. Charles M. Shelley of the 30th Alabama called on his men for volunteers to rout them out. About fifteen to twenty men responded, and Capt. Henry Penn Oden and Lt. William Wallis stood up to lead them. The thirty-nine-year-old Oden led the group through the open gorge at about 1:00 P.M. and was distracted. Off to the side, taking shelter behind the traverse that defined one side of the Federal-occupied compartment, he saw a handful of comrades. Lt. John M. Pearson and about a dozen men of the 30th Alabama had remained in the second compartment when Griffith and Messenger's group entered the redoubt. The Federals had no idea that Pearson's group huddled only a few feet away on the other side of the covering traverse.[44]

Oden was surprised to see Pearson. "Why are you not fighting?" he yelled. Pearson replied, "You will not be fighting long if you don't get in the trenches and you had better get there quick." Just then a Federal shot Oden in the head and he died instantly. Wallis was shot by another Federal, who had gone beyond the forward line of the salient along the north side of the redoubt. The rest of Oden's group suffered similar fates. Literally every man was shot within a very short time by fire coming from Griffith's group as well as from Federals outside the fort. The decimation of the Oden group stunned and demoralized the Confederates who witnessed the awful scene. "It took some time to get up a new assaulting party," reported Lee, "as the troops saw the fate of the first party."[45]

While Confederate officers tried to organize another counterattack, the Griffith party dwindled to nearly nothing. According to Capt. Charles N. Lee of the 22nd Iowa, about half the men who had gone into the redoubt left the compartment and returned to the ditch. They did so individually. As we have seen, Messenger was one of these men. Sometime after the killing of Oden's group, only Griffith remained inside the work.[46]

When Griffith realized he was alone, he began to crawl back through the furrowed section of parapet to get out as well. By that time, Pearson and his dozen men of the 30th Alabama had begun to explore what lay inside the Federal-occupied compartment. They made their way cautiously around the end of the traverse, for here was a passage wide enough for men to move from one compartment to another.[47]

Pearson and his men found Griffith in the furrows. A moment of truth was now presented to the young Welshman. Griffith noticed an unusual weapon lying in the furrows. Described as "a Peabody sporting rifle," a civilian weapon probably owned by a Federal who had dropped it accidentally, Griffith, thinking quickly, grabbed it. The gun was a repeater and multiplied his power to deal death and injury to the thirteen Confederates who had suddenly presented themselves. Lying prone in the furrows, Griffith aimed the Peabody at Pearson and told everyone to drop to the ground. He then crawled backward through the hole in the parapet and ordered his prisoners to crawl forward as he continued to cover them with the rifle. His daring ploy worked; Griffith got out alive and with thirteen prisoners, one of them an officer.[48]

Graham was so impressed by the sight of these prisoners filtering into the ditch that he told Griffith to take them to McClernand's headquarters. Griffith did so, but one of the prisoners was hit by Confederate fire between the ditch and terrace and was killed. Imagine the impression created when Griffith brought the rest of his captives to McClernand at about 2:00 P.M. Engineer Hains overheard the short discussion that ensued at headquarters and chided Pearson for giving up a dozen of his men to this lone Federal. "Is it true that all of your men surrendered to this boy in the manner he states?" Hains asked him. Pearson grew red in the face "and in an insolent tone replied, 'What could we do? He got that loaded rifle, and ours had all been discharged.'"[49]

STANDOFF AT RAILROAD REDOUBT

Griffith's exploit made him a hero, but the brief and limited penetration of Railroad Redoubt had come to an end. McClernand and everyone at headquarters remembered only that some Yankees had gotten into a Rebel fort and captured a dozen Confederates. Perhaps a larger effort by fresh troops, supported by renewed attacks elsewhere along the line, could take advantage of the opening Griffith's men had explored to achieve a breakthrough.

There were some tentative signs of hope that such a scenario could play out. According to Landram, Griffith's exploit counteracted reports that Lawler's brigade had lost heavily in a futile effort to breach the opposing line. A correspondent for the *New-York Daily Tribune* used his field glass to observe a Confederate officer "moving backward and forward among the men, with drawn sword, vainly attempting to get them up to the support of their comrades." Capt. William F. Patterson, who commanded an independent company of Kentuckians that served as engineer troops, assigned Lt. Nicholas Steinauer to work on cutting down the Rebel earthworks on both sides of the railroad that had been temporarily evacuated by defending Confederates. Steinauer belonged to the 60th Indiana in Burbridge's brigade, but he had been detached to the pioneers of the Thirteenth Corps and was under Patterson's orders. Another pioneer detachment under Cpl. Hendry contributed to Steinauer's detail and lost one man in the process of digging down the works.[50]

But there were no fresh troops to break the standoff at Railroad Redoubt. Ironically, Col. David Shunk's group was in the vicinity but neither Lawler nor Landram noticed it. The unplanned movement of the right wing of the 8th Indiana accompanied by Companies A, C, D, G, and I of the 33rd Illinois, failed to provide added impetus to Federal operations against Railroad Redoubt. It is unclear exactly where this improvised group of men from Benton's brigade lodged. Some sources indicate that three color-bearers of the 8th Indiana were shot and at least one flag was planted on the Confederate works, but the information is unconfirmed by other reports and highly suspect. Albert O. Marshall of Company A, 33rd Illinois, reported that after the Shunk group finished its advance, the men of the 33rd were still not on the Rebel works. "By the time our charge was ended all company and regimental organizations were destroyed. All were mingled together. No attempt to reform was thought of. Each held the ground they had taken."[51]

Marshall was among a group of men lodged fairly close to the connecting line south of Railroad Redoubt. A truce ensued on that part of the battlefield, and some Confederates stood up above the parapet to see what was happening. The Federals refrained from firing at them, and the opposing warriors exchanged some words. When Marshall also stood up he caught a glimpse of a Rebel hiding behind his comrades and carefully pointing his rifle directly at him. Marshall ducked just in time to avoid the bullet, which grazed the head of David R. Curtis of Company A and badly injured another man in the chest. The "wind jar" knocked Curtis insensible for a time. The "spontaneous truce" ended the moment this Confederate fired his round, and the battle continued on that part of the field. When he recovered, Curtis was angry for the rest of the day and tried to shoot any Rebel who appeared.[52]

There appeared to be no way for the Federals to recharge their effort against Railroad Redoubt, but the Confederates could reach much of the ditch with their rifle fire. They eventually cleared all of it from roughly where the furrows had been ploughed all the way to the railroad. There were still a few dozen Federals lodged in the ditch at and near the furrows, but no Confederate fire could reach them and the regimental flags still waved in that area. As word of the situation spread, Confederate reinforcements moved toward the redoubt. The 39th Georgia of Brig. Gen. Alfred Cumming's Brigade, Stevenson's Division, marched toward the threatened work "through a perfect shower of shot and shell," in the words of Robert Magill.[53]

The stalemate at Railroad Redoubt was nearly as solid as the one at the 2nd Texas Lunette, but a misreading of Griffith's limited penetration of the work excited McClernand. Moreover, McClernand could see several Union flags flying from the redoubt. Both bits of information led the corps leader to request reinforcements and cooperative assaults by the other two corps. His urgency, which led to slightly inflated reports of his success, became a turning point in the battle of May 22 and in McClernand's career as a field commander in the Civil War.

{ 11 }

I Don't Believe a Word of It

GRANT, SHERMAN, and McCLERNAND, MAY 22

By noon it had become apparent to most observers that the Federal assaults had ended well short of a breakthrough. If Grant had called off further effort, the battle of May 22 would have been counted as a good try with acceptable losses and a siege would have been the only option. But McClernand wrote a series of messages to Grant requesting help and urging further attacks by his colleagues to support what he thought were promising signs that his men could break through the opposing line. He based those requests on slim and confusing information about those promising signs. Furthermore, he deliberately exaggerated the prospects in those messages. McClernand played a crucial role in prompting a renewal of heavy assaults that largely increased the Union casualty list but failed to produce a breakthrough. He set up a situation that inadvertently ruined his career as a general. A controversial pivot point had been reached in the battle of May 22.

MCCLERNAND

McClernand relied on a flow of information coming from his subordinates who were heavily involved in conducting the attack, observations by his staff members, and his own view of the attack obtained from a command post opposite Railroad Redoubt. The flow of news began with a joint message from Lawler and Landram, written at 10:10 A.M. and routed through

Andrew J. Smith, warning the high command that the enemy was massing in their front and requesting aid. According to Capt. Frank H. Mason, serving as an aide to McClernand, the corps leader wanted to send help. He dispatched another aide to tell Carr that Benton should divert Confederate attention from Lawler or help Lawler directly in assaulting Railroad Redoubt. But as we have seen, Benton had lost control of his brigade almost immediately after the advance began and could not respond to this directive. Very soon after McClernand sent the aide, word arrived at his command post that Smith's men had lodged in the works at the 2nd Texas Lunette, but the information was imprecise. Did they enter the lunette itself or just lodge in the ditch? "A part of the language of the officer bringing the report was that 'our flag is planted on the enemy's works,'" recalled Mason.[1]

If the flow of information did not keep McClernand well informed, could he have supplemented it with personal observation? The corps commander had established his command post a bit to the left and rear of Battery Maloney, named for Maj. Maurice Maloney, who commanded some men of the 1st U.S. Infantry trained to handle thirty-pounder Parrotts. The battery was located 600 yards from Railroad Redoubt on a prominent rise of ground that offered what everyone agreed was the best view of the Rebel lines on the corps front. The command post was spotted on lower ground, but the corps leader often walked up to the battery to obtain the best observation he could.[2]

McClernand was located at the prime spot to observe corps activity, but there was a limit to what he could see given the smoke of battle and the rugged terrain. Moreover, he had to sift through the incomplete reports streaming toward Battery Maloney. Mason was careful to note that at exactly 11:46 A.M. an officer arrived to report that the 22nd Iowa had captured Railroad Redoubt and the Federal artillery should cease firing on it. "You seemed incredulous," Mason later recalled in writing to his commander.[3]

The officer who brought this amazing news was Lt. Col. Henry Clay Warmoth, another Thirteenth Corps staff officer, who had made his way through enemy fire to Railroad Redoubt. Warmoth managed to return safely, stopping to see Lawler first and then proceeding to Battery Maloney to ask McClernand for reinforcements. Warmoth recalled forty-seven years later that McClernand struck "a heroic figure, alert, erect, cool, in full possession of himself but with the fire of battle in his eye and all his Irish fighting blood aroused." When Warmoth informed him that Lawler's troops were on Railroad Redoubt, McClernand replied, "Show me[,] my son." Warmoth asked him to move a few yards to a better place for observing, where it was pos-

Railroad Redoubt and the Iowa monument. This photograph, taken about 1910, shows the remnants of Railroad Redoubt in the right foreground and the Iowa Monument in the left background. McClernand's command post was near Battery Maloney, which was about where the Iowa Monument now stands. The absence of tree cover vividly illustrates the lay of the ground between the monument and the fort. Haines Photo of Conneaut, Ohio, was responsible for this and other panoramic photographs of the new Vicksburg National Military Park. (Library of Congress, panorama no. 5, pan6a07050)

sible to see the regimental flags on the work as the smoke of battle allowed it. "Run my boy," McClernand told him excitedly, "tell Lawler I haven't a man to give him but to hold—hold to the death! If there are any reserves on the line he shall have them."[4]

But according to Mason, McClernand was not fully convinced. McClernand "sent me to Colonel Landram" to confirm the report, Mason wrote. Landram did so, producing a note by Lt. Col. Harvey Graham that "was written inside the fort," according to Landram. The note was written on a torn piece of envelope. Mason returned and showed it to McClernand. Capt. Ambrose A. Blount of the 17th Ohio Battery heard Carr give the order to cease firing on Railroad Redoubt. But as time rolled on, further evidence that the news had been exaggerated began to develop. Mason saw Sgt. Joseph E. Griffith and his dozen Confederate prisoners leave the redoubt ditch and head toward Battery Maloney. McClernand saw this as further proof that his boys were having a good deal of success, but Mason felt it was not so. "Yes, General, there are prisoners coming in sure, but we have not possession of the works."[5]

The evidence was far from clear as to whether the Federals had taken any portion of Railroad Redoubt. Even though he was only 600 yards away, McClernand's knowledge of events on the Rebel line was murky at best. Yet he tended to interpret the information from the most hopeful perspective, occasionally toned down by Mason's objective evaluation of the evidence.

McClernand can be forgiven, to a degree, for his desperate enthusiasm. By 11:00 A.M. his available units (except Col. William T. Spicely's brigade) had been fully committed to the assault. At the very least, there were reports of some success portending a possible breakthrough. "Failure and loss of my hard-won advantages became imminent," he later reported. At 11:15 he sent his first note to Grant informing him of the situation and asking for aid. "I am hotly engaged with the enemy. He is massing on me from the right and left. A vigorous blow by McPherson would make a diversion in my favor." The idea that the Confederates were "massing on" him was derived from the Lawler-Landram note he had received an hour earlier, but as we have seen, there was no true massing by the Confederates. Only two or three regiments were in motion toward the Thirteenth Corps sector. Of course, McClernand could not know the reality, only what was reported to him by subordinates, who had no evidence that what they said was true.[6]

Grant replied to this note at 11:50 A.M. "If your advance is weak," he advised, "strengthen it by drawing from your reserves or other parts of the lines." This was not the reply McClernand wanted. As a result, he penned a second dispatch to his commander but failed to indicate the time it was written. "We have gained the enemy's intrenchments at several points, but are brought to a stand." McClernand also told Grant that he had no opportunity of pulling troops out of position to reinforce one part of the corps sector, forgetting that Spicely's brigade was unemployed behind Osterhaus's division. Brig. Gen. John McArthur's lone brigade was available but located several miles away on the east bank of the Mississippi near Warrenton. Instead of communicating with Spicely, who was but a few hundred yards from Battery Maloney, McClernand asked McArthur "to re-enforce me if he can."[7]

McClernand's biographer believes the corps leader had come to the conclusion that his men were on the verge of rupturing the Rebel line and he needed help to make that happen. His first dispatch was Grant's initial hint that Thirteenth Corps operations might have gone further than those of the Fifteenth or Seventeenth Corps. Grant felt that his own command post, located along Jackson Road on McPherson's front, offered him the best opportunity to see the battle as far as one person could do so. According to geographer Warren Grabau, that command post near Mount Ararat was located 1,000 yards east of the 3rd Louisiana Redan, 1,400 yards southeast of Stockade Redan, and 2,600 yards northeast of Railroad Redoubt. Although battle smoke obscured the view at times, Grant had a good view of most key objectives in the grand assault.[8]

Still, Grant had a tendency to rove about the battlefield to obtain different perspectives and to consult with subordinates. Between noon and 1:00 P.M. he rode to Sherman's command post near Graveyard Road. Grant dismounted in a hollow because of enemy fire and walked up to Sherman, who greeted his friend and commander with the truth. "I pointed out to him the rebel works, admitted that my assault had failed, and he said the result with McPherson and McClernand was about the same."[9]

As the two men sat on the grass and talked, a courier arrived with McClernand's second dispatch. Grant shared it with Sherman. "I think the writing was in pencil," the corps commander recalled, "on a loose piece of paper." The purport of the dispatch was that Thirteenth Corps troops had lodged on the enemy parapet and raised flags and needed diversionary attacks. "I don't believe a word of it" was Grant's first reaction, according to Sherman, who took a completely different tack in assessing the note. "Not dreaming that a major-general would at such a critical moment make a mere buncombe communication," Sherman took the dispatch seriously and tried to convince Grant to do the same. "I reasoned with him, that this note was official, and must be credited, and I offered to renew the assault at once with new troops." Sherman's opinion counted with Grant. He acquiesced to his subordinate and told him he would ride along the line to the Thirteenth Corps. If Grant did not send word to abort the renewed attack by 3:00 P.M., Sherman could "try it again."[10]

This was a fateful moment in the battle of May 22. Objectively there was no need for diversionary assaults, because the Confederates did not have the option of shifting large numbers of troops from one point to another. Fresh men coming in soon after the first wave of Thirteenth Corps troops might have helped, but time was fast running out on that option. McClernand was operating mostly on the initial Lawler-Landram note of 10:10 A.M., which stated that reinforcements were needed—he had none, so he thought to ask for help from other corps.

One of the problems lay in the rather vague and overly hopeful wording of his second message to Grant. "We have gained the enemy's intrenchments at several points," he wrote with a good deal of deliberate exaggeration. No wonder that Grant initially reacted with skepticism, for he had been in a position to see that such did not seem the case. Sherman played the key role in translating the second dispatch into a renewal of attacks, mostly because he had no opportunity to personally observe Thirteenth Corps operations and could not believe McClernand would be so irresponsible as to exaggerate his success. It is interesting to speculate what would have happened if McClernand's second note had been delivered before Grant arrived at Sherman's command post—Grant most likely would not have ordered additional assaults by the other two corps without Sherman's urging.

Complicating the situation, both Grant and Sherman misremembered small details of McClernand's second dispatch. Grant later reported that the Thirteenth Corps leader wrote of having possession of two forts, while Sherman recalled that he'd written of taking three forts. These differences in memory meant little except to indicate how far both men were impressed by what they later learned was an exaggeration. It has been pointed out by several historians that the bad blood that had long before developed between Grant and McClernand must have played a role in the army commander's reluctance to take the second dispatch seriously. There is no doubt of that, but it cannot account entirely for Grant's reluctance. As noted, he had some opportunity to see Thirteenth Corps operations and had noticed nothing to support McClernand's contention.[11]

Before Grant left Sherman's command post, he authorized Fifteenth Corps reserve units to renew the assault. "If we are not successful," he further told Sherman, "we will have to proceed with a regular siege." Grant then returned to his horse in the hollow, mounted, and rode south. Along the way another courier found him and delivered a third dispatch from McClernand, which was written about 1:00 P.M. It contained similar news as the second note: Thirteenth Corps troops held small portions of the enemy line and needed help. Grant did not want the army to lose any chance of success "through fault of mine." Sherman's admonition had had its effect on Grant's thinking.[12]

Arriving at Seventeenth Corps headquarters, Grant showed McClernand's dispatches to McPherson as a way of justifying renewed effort. Interestingly, he then ordered McPherson to either renew the attack on the Seventeenth Corps sector or send Brig. Gen. Isaac F. Quinby's division to help McClernand. McPherson probably displayed no enthusiasm for renewing attacks on the 3rd Louisiana Redan or Great Redoubt, and Grant must have felt uncomfortable forcing him to do so. Quinby was relatively near McClernand's sector, but it would take some time for him to move his three brigades. As with Sherman, Grant failed to issue written orders to McPherson for the renewal of operations.[13]

At this point Grant changed his mind about riding to the Thirteenth Corps and instead wrote to McClernand. "McPherson is directed to send

Quinby's divison to you if he cannot effect a lodgment where he is," he wrote at 2:30 P.M. "Quinby is next to your right and you will be aided as much by his penetrating into the enemy's lines as by having him to support the columns you have already got. Sherman is getting on well."[14]

Grant can certainly be faulted for failing to consult with McClernand in the same way he had met with Sherman and McPherson, but both men had come to dislike the other and neither seemed interested in staging an unpleasant meeting. Grant remained in full written communication with McClernand, however, reminding him during the course of the day that McArthur's brigade at Warrenton was available (although many miles away) and urging the Thirteenth Corps leader to use whatever ready reserve he possessed (Spicely's brigade).[15]

MCCLERNAND

McClernand received Grant's 2:30 P.M. note at 3:15 and was delighted to see that his repeated requests were having an effect. He immediately wrote back expressing enthusiasm and hope at the thought of having four fresh brigades when McArthur and Quinby reached him. "As soon as they arrive I will press the enemy with all possible dispatch, and doubt not that I will force my way through. I have lost no ground. My men are in two of the enemy's forts, but they are commanded by rifle-pits in the rear. Several prisoners have been taken, who intimate that the rear is strong. At this moment I am hard-pressed." Grant received this fourth and final message from McClernand at 3:50 P.M. but there was no need for a reply.[16]

McClernand's biographer wonders why the general did not make better use of Spicely's brigade and assumes he forgot it was available. The truth was, however, that McClernand had never forgotten Spicely but had the odd idea that only Osterhaus could order the brigade around. He also was fully aware that Osterhaus had done relatively little to promote the corps attack. "You must advance and assault the enemy," McClernand wrote to Osterhaus at some point during the day, "and thereby make a diversion." If he failed to do so, McClernand wanted Osterhaus to act on the defensive and send Spicely to help Carr. "One or other of these things must be done," he forcefully concluded. In the end Osterhaus failed to take either course of action and thereby let McClernand down. Spicely's men were underused in a situation where McClernand needed all the help he could get. The corps commander bore equal responsibility with the division leader for this result.[17]

The Lawler-Landram attack on Railroad Redoubt was the only Federal

Grant, Sherman, and McClernand, May 22

effort on May 22 that went beyond the ditch of a Rebel earthwork, but Griffith's small penetration of one compartment of the fort was at best a tentative hope. Nevertheless, it was true that Railroad Redoubt was the only part of Pemberton's line that weakened dangerously. It is possible that a large number of fresh troops pushing rapidly through the narrow opening very soon after the Confederates evacuated the compartment might have broken the line, but the Federals could not know that at the time and had no such reserve handy to shove into the breach at the right moment.

It took four hours for slow communications to produce a willingness on the part of army headquarters to respond to the glimmer of success at Railroad Redoubt. Communications always lagged far behind events on every Civil War battlefield. It took time for couriers to convey written dispatches from one point of a confusing field to another, and May 22 was no exception. Another factor lay in Grant's innate distrust of McClernand, which had built up for months before the battle. That distrust was justified because McClernand did not accurately report his progress in his several messages that day. Both Grant and Sherman had difficulty accepting the content of those dispatches. In short, McClernand misrepresented his true situation to Grant, deliberately exaggerating his prospects out of a sense of desperation to get the army commander to take seriously his opportunity to break the opposing line. McClernand suffered from a confusing stream of sometimes contradictory information from his own troops, even though his command post was located within easy sight of the engagement. His emotions tended to influence the tone and detail of his important messages to Grant that day. Whether the renewal of effort during the latter half of the afternoon had any hope of creating victory was to be seen.

{ 12 }

Am Holding Position but Suffering Awfully

BLAIR, RANSOM, and TUTTLE, MAY 22

McClernand's messages and Sherman's reaction to them led Grant to authorize renewed assaults on the afternoon of May 22. Sherman took this renewed effort very seriously. Up to that time, only one brigade of the Fifteenth Corps had launched an assault and it was repulsed without making a dent in the fortifications. During the latter half of the afternoon, however, five brigades tried their hand in three separate attacks, with the cooperation of one brigade from the Seventeenth Corps.

It would have been better if Sherman had been able to coordinate these efforts, but that level of coordination was not possible at this stage of the day's operations. Col. Giles A. Smith's and Col. Thomas Kilby Smith's brigades needed a good deal of time to move from Graveyard Road south into the maze of hollows and ravines, meeting Brig. Gen. Thomas E. G. Ransom's Seventeenth Corps brigade and then taking position in preparation for an assault by 2:00 P.M. Brig. Gen. James M. Tuttle's reserve division rested along Graveyard Road and could be called into action relatively quickly, but Maj. Gen. Frederick Steele's division off to the right also needed a good deal of time to move attacking units to what Sherman thought was the best target. The rugged terrain and sprawling front of the Fifteenth Corps inhibited coordination of three assaults widely spread across the ground. They went in when ready and largely alone at 2:15 P.M., 3:00 P.M., and 4:00 P.M.[1]

Maj. Gen. Frank P. Blair explained why Giles A. Smith and Kilby Smith took so long to gain a position from which to attack by blaming it on "the nature of the ground." He also pointed out that the Confederates had cut a lot of timber in the ravines the Federals were forced to use. This "artificial entanglement" delayed his brigades longer than the lay of the land.[2]

GILES A. SMITH

By midafternoon the two brigades had worked their way 300 yards south of Graveyard Road and 100 yards from the target, contacting Ransom's right flank. Giles A. Smith posted the 8th Missouri on the left with the 116th Illinois next to it, then the 113th Illinois, and the 6th Missouri on the right. The 1st Battalion, 13th U.S. Infantry, had been detached since the battle of May 19 to serve as Sherman's headquarters guard.[3]

For a few minutes the officers tried to encourage their men for the trial ahead. J. J. Kellogg of the 113th Illinois saw an example of this in the next regiment to the left, the 116th Illinois, where Col. Nathan W. Tupper exhorted his troops. It appeared to Kellogg, however, that Tupper was drunk. The colonel began to make a mess of the exhortation. Smith happened to be near and noticed Tupper's condition. "Three cheers for Colonel Tupper," Smith yelled. Fortunately, the men of the 116th Illinois took the cue and responded, cutting off Tupper's inane comments, but the explosion of a Confederate shell silenced the men partway into their second cheer.[4]

At 2:00 P.M. Sherman sent an order for Smith to advance in conjunction with Ransom, and by two fifteen the order reached its recipient. Smith relayed it to his regimental commanders and the brigade set out. The men moved at the double-quick and with fixed bayonets. In fact, from his position in the first rank of the 113th Illinois, Kellogg glanced back to see a row of bayonets close behind him in the second rank. It spurred him to move even faster. "I feared the front far less than the rear," he recalled.[5]

Impelled by the presence of friendly bayonets, Kellogg's attention was drawn more and more toward the target. "The nearer the enemy we got the more enthusiastic we became," he reported, "and the more confidence we had in scaling their works." Accompanying his men, Smith yelled encouragement. "Boys, they'll give us one volley; before they can reload, we'll be inside their works. Forward, double-quick, march! And hurrah like ——!"[6]

But it would not be that easy. The defending Confederates could tell that an attack was imminent for a few minutes before the Federals started, and they were ready. "Just look at the rascals on that hill," cried a man in the

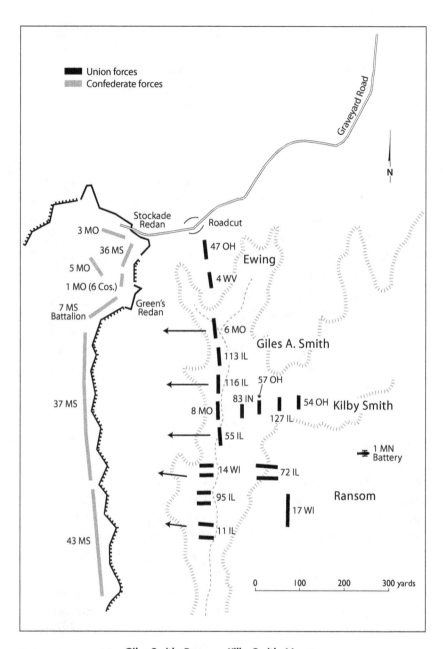

Union forces
Confederate forces

3 MO

36 MS

5 MO

1 MO (6 Cos.)

7 MS
Battalion

Green's
Redan

Stockade
Redan

Roadcut

Graveyard Road

N

47 OH

Ewing

4 WV

6 MO

Giles A. Smith

113 IL

116 IL

57 OH

83 IN

54 OH Kilby Smith

8 MO

127 IL

55 IL

1 MN
Battery

14 WI

72 IL

37 MS

95 IL

Ransom

17 WI

11 IL

43 MS

0   100   200   300 yards

Giles Smith–Ransom–Kilby Smith, May 22

37th Mississippi when the Federals set out. They waited until the enemy was within easy range before opening fire. "As they came down the hill one could see them plunging headlong to the front," reported J. H. Jones of the 38th Mississippi, "and as they rushed up the slope to our works they invariably fell backwards, as the death shot greeted them."[7]

For the time, the Confederates in Stockade Redan were not employed, so they delivered long-range enfilading fire toward Smith's brigade. But the fire coming directly from the front was the most devastating. The Federals ground to a halt about twenty-five yards short of Lockett's line. Two color-bearers fell in the 116th Illinois and two more in the 113th Illinois. Pvt. John B. Bartholomew, the color-bearer of the 8th Missouri, was killed. Sgt. Amos E. Hilton took the flag and was wounded, dropping it as the regiment retired from its high tide. Maj. Dennis T. Kirby was reluctant to tell one of his men to retrieve it, so he gathered the colors himself, later receiving a Congressional Medal of Honor for the exploit.[8]

The hopelessness of a further advance was palpable. After some time, the troops of Smith's brigade made their way toward the rear, stopping at the first rise of ground, which was about seventy-five yards from the Confederate line. The shallow ridgetop saved many lives, but the slope was so steep some men had to cling to stumps, roots, and grapevines to keep from sliding down. Kellogg lay on his back on the east slope of the ridge and could see Federal batteries firing in his direction. One round hit a sapling and deflected downward, hitting the line; it killed a soldier in Company H, 113th Illinois. When another man stood to fire his musket, a Union projectile decapitated him.[9]

"Our regiment came out safe to what sum of them did," reported Frederick W. Russell of the 113th Illinois. He had been told that the regiment lost a total of six killed and twenty-four wounded. Ebenezer Werkheiser thought his 116th Illinois was "agane batley youst up."[10]

RANSOM

Giles Smith's attack was repulsed with relative ease due to the alert and ready defender. To Smith's left, Ransom's brigade went in with him but fared no better. Ransom had been in place since 11:00 A.M. but made no move forward until Giles Smith and Kilby Smith arrived and readied their brigades. To prepare for the assault, Ransom shifted the 72nd Illinois from his far right to the rear of the 14th Wisconsin, which was just to its left. Four of his regiments (11th Illinois on the left, 95th Illinois in the center, 14th Wisconsin on the right, and 72nd Illinois behind the 14th) arrayed in double column. The 17th Wisconsin formed in line behind the brigade as a support. Ransom positioned the 1st Minnesota Battery 300 yards from the Confederates to provide fire support.[11]

Ransom set out with Giles Smith at 2:15 P.M., the men of both brigades cheering for the first few steps of their attack. The Minnesota gunners fired away as did the skirmishers nearby, but they failed to counter what Ransom called "one continuous blaze of musketry" that greeted his men at short range. Lt. George Carrington of the 11th Illinois described it vividly. His comrades "were fairly swept off their feet by the most deadly, concentrated, cross and enfilading fire, we were ever under." Contributing to the cross fire were the gunners commanded by T. Jeff Bates of Capt. J. F. Waddell's Alabama Battery, who sighted a ten-pounder Parrott from the 3rd Louisiana Redan. Bates's men had a "beautiful enfilade" on Ransom's formation.[12]

From the position of the 1st Minnesota Battery the scene was grand and terrible. "O such an awful withering fire was poured upon his brave heroes," wrote Capt. William Z. Clayton of Ransom's men. Lt. Henry Hurter of the same battery agreed with Clayton. "It was dreadful to see the effects of the enemy's bullets fired into the ranks of the infantry at such close interval."[13]

Ransom's formation mostly dissolved. Carrington blamed this on the slope combined with the deadly fire. Lt. Col. Garrett Nevins was killed, which depressed the members of his 11th Illinois. "Entirely disheartened we just seemed to flatten out and as a Regt dropped back to the shelter of the ravine," Carrington admitted. In the view of a staff officer with Brig. Gen. John E. Smith's brigade to the south, it seemed like Ransom's men "were shot down like dogs."[14]

The 95th Illinois lost its colonel in a peculiar manner. Col. Thomas W. Humphrey led the way several steps in front of his regiment without glancing back. The men tried to follow him but found the going too difficult because of the heavy fire descending on their path. Most members of the regiment stopped several yards short of the Rebel line, but they lost sight of Humphrey and assumed he was killed. This "cast a heavy gloom over our spirits," recalled Sgt. T. A. Rollins, "and checked our ardor." Wales W. Wood estimated that close to 100 of the 367 men in the regiment had fallen by that time.[15]

To counteract the deadening of morale, Ransom urged his staff members to encourage the men to continue moving forward. They were able to get some laggards up to the line, but the brigade came to a halt short of the target. The first six companies of the 14th Wisconsin stopped several yards away from the ditch. The last four companies were halted by Col. Lyman M. Ward when it became apparent that Giles Smith's brigade to the right was stalled. The color-bearer planted the regimental flag, and soon three other unit banners were raised as each regiment reached its high tide.[16]

For twenty minutes Ransom's men held on at their close position to the Rebel works. "We had almost 3000 men within 15 yards of the foot of the wall," reported Captain Clayton to his mother. "They could not retire nor advance but kept the enemy behind the wall" by firing at the top of the parapet. Clayton argued that about 150 of Ransom's troops left the ranks and climbed up the parapet but only about a dozen returned. This claim is not substantiated and Clayton, it must be remembered, merely observed the fighting from a distance of 300 yards. The brigade was hammered by enfilading fire that "came crashing through the ranks," according to Blair.[17]

Ransom was desperate to get his men out of this place and into the enemy works. He "shouted, threatened, swore, and used every effort," wrote Lt. Benjamin W. Underwood of the 72nd Illinois. Finally, Ransom scribbled a penciled note to McPherson. "I cannot get the move forward until that damn gun on the left is silenced. Am holding position but suffering awfully . . . terrible loss. I have done all man can do to get over the works." Buffeted by rifle fire from the front and punishing artillery fire from the flanks, Ransom decided to fall back. Giles Smith's brigade had failed to keep pace with him and was stalled farther back.[18]

Frustrated, Ransom allowed his men to retire but only "if we would do it in good order." According to a newspaper correspondent named Bod, Ransom gave instructions to his command before starting the withdrawal. "Men of the Second Brigade! We cannot maintain this position. You must retire to the cover of that ravine, one regiment at a time, and in order. The 17th Wisconsin will remain to cover the movement. The 72d Illinois will move first, and move now. Move slowly. The first man who runs or goes beyond that ravine shall be shot on the spot. I will stand here, and see how you do it."[19]

This was a remarkable display of calm under pressure on Ransom's part. He claimed the fallback took place "in perfect order" some forty yards to the rear and into the shelter of a ravine. The forward six companies of the 14th Wisconsin remained behind because they "occupied a position of comparative safety directly under the rebel works, and from which it was unsafe" to move until darkness provided cover. After dusk, not only were these six companies removed, but McPherson told Ransom to pull his entire brigade back from the ravine and rejoin the rest of the Union line. Ransom reported that he brought "most of my dead and all of my wounded from the field."[20]

The brigade lost 57 killed, 275 wounded, and 32 missing for a total of 364 men on May 22. The 95th Illinois lost 109 men out of 367 men engaged, or 29.7 percent. According to one report, that amounted to 36 percent of the officers and 28 percent of the enlisted men. The 14th Wisconsin took a bit less than 300 men into action and lost 107 of them, or 35.6 percent. As Clayton put it, "Our loss was frightful. Many & Many of my dear friends of this Div have fallen."[21]

But one man thought to be lost showed up after dark. Col. Thomas W. Humphrey surprised everyone when he wandered back to the 95th Illinois in the night. He had been stunned by a shell explosion soon after losing contact with the regiment during the advance. After that he "lay down closely upon the ground" for several hours, with bullets and artillery rounds throwing dirt onto him. Humphrey was well enough to resume command of the 95th Illinois and made a wry comment in the third person when penning the regimental report. "Colonel Humphrey (supposed to be killed) was so far in advance of his regiment as to be unable to return or render his command any assistance."[22]

In contrast to Humphrey, Col. Frederick A. Starring of the 72nd Illinois nearly lost his reputation on May 22. He was well liked by the regiment but acted in an unsteady manner during the buildup to the attack. Many thought he was drunk—"more bad whiskey," as Benjamin Underwood put it. Starring claimed he was suffering from sunstroke, and at least some members of the regiment accepted that explanation. Ransom himself saw Starring was incapable of leading the regiment and relieved him of command, telling the adjutant to move the 72nd from the far right to its position behind the 14th Wisconsin in stages just before the assault began. Maj. Joseph Stockton took command of the regiment for the forward movement.[23]

Starring created a bad impression for the regiment by his action. Even if he was a genuine victim of sunstroke, he had a reputation for drinking that would not go away. Underwood and many other officers were convinced he was intoxicated. They prepared charges against him but showed the colonel these charges before submitting them. Starring denied being drunk, argued that a combination of poor health and the stinging sun had caused his debility on May 22, and gained a good deal of sympathy from the officers. Yet he also pledged to swear off liquor so this question would never come up again. Underwood knew that several men had suffered from the sun that day, so Starring may have been telling the truth. Ransom filed what an officer of the regiment called a "white washing report" about Starring's case in September 1863, but it hardly made a difference in the minds of many who continued to

Blair, Ransom, and Tuttle, May 22

Frederick A. Starring. Born in Buffalo, New York, educated at Harvard University, and working as a lawyer and in the railroad industry before the war, Starring became colonel of the 72nd Illinois. On the afternoon of May 22, he nearly came to grief because of a controversy about whether he was drunk or merely suffering from sunstroke. Ransom relieved him of command just before the attack began, but Starring recovered his reputation and served ably during the rest of the war. (Vol. 73, 3630L, Massachusetts Commandery, Military Order of the Loyal Legion and the U.S. Army Military History Institute)

think that not only Starring but other officers of the 72nd Illinois had been drunk on the day of battle.[24]

Ransom's was the last attack on the Seventeenth Corps sector that day. It was as vigorous as any launched by Logan's division that morning or that attempted by Brig. Gen. Isaac F. Quinby's division on the Thirteenth Corps sector later in the afternoon. But it had ended similarly as all the rest. Merely getting to a point a few yards away from the Confederate ditch was an act of courage, but it fell far short of what was needed to break through the opposing line.

KILBY SMITH

Giles A. Smith and Ransom were supported by Thomas Kilby Smith's brigade, which advanced behind Giles Smith's men. Kilby Smith initially had formed his command with the 55th Illinois in line to the left of Giles Smith's 8th Missouri. He kept the rest of his brigade in column of regiments behind the 8th Missouri. The 83rd Indiana was first in that column, followed by the 57th Ohio, 127th Illinois, and 54th Ohio. Although Kilby Smith did not say so, he must have deployed those four regiments into line just before or just after the advance began, because numerous members of those units reported that they delivered fire at the Confederates during the attack and that could only be done when in line rather than column.[25]

Kilby Smith's troops were unable to do anything except take a position and fire over the prone members of Giles Smith's command at high tide. Lt. Col. Samuel R. Mott of the 57th Ohio thought his men lodged "within easy range of the works" after their advance had ground to a halt. For Samuel J. Oviatt of the 57th Ohio, that meant about fifty yards from the sputtering rifles behind the parapet. Here the Federals received as well as delivered fire. "My rite hand man was shot through the head with a muskett ball," Oviatt told a correspondent. "He threw up his hands and said oh god[;] he fell over torge me so i laid him on the ground and fell back and called for the drumers and fifers to come and carry him off the field."[26]

Kilby Smith's men settled into a static fire fight at close range. "We fired and kept the reb down as mutch as we could," asserted Oviatt. Before long he could see three or four Confederates climbing a tree that stood just behind Lockett's line. From their perch, these Rebels posed a deadly threat to the Federals. Oviatt and four men of the 57th Ohio, in addition to eight men of the 55th Illinois, targeted these sharpshooters. The Federals "pord to or three volleys of musketry in the tree[;] the first volley i Saw too of them fall out of the tree but whether we killed them or not I cant say."[27]

The Federals soon fired enough to cause fouling in the musket barrels of some of Kilby Smith's men. This usually happened after about twenty-five rounds. Kilby Smith singled out Maj. Frank S. Curtiss of the 127th Illinois because the major helped his troops with this problem. "He was ever in the

Blair, Ransom, and Tuttle, May 22

foremost ranks, and even exceeded his duty in assisting soldiers with their guns when from frequent firing they became foul."[28]

As dusk descended, Kilby Smith's men received orders to retire. Within the 57th Ohio, that fallback was accomplished by one company at a time. The regiment lost fifteen killed and wounded, while the 55th Illinois suffered the loss of 41 men out of 250 engaged, or 16.4 percent. "I thought that i had a hart Stronger than a stone," lamented Oviatt, "but it cut me down to see so many good men shot down and the way they laid cutt to peeces by musketry and grape and canester sollid shot and shell."[29]

With that action, Blair's division ended its participation in the battle of May 22. It had shouldered almost all of Sherman's effort on May 19 and now again bore a large share of fighting on May 22. The bloodletting by Giles A. Smith, Ransom, and Kilby Smith had failed to draw off Confederate troops from the Thirteenth Corps sector, the primary reason for renewing Fifteenth Corps action that afternoon. But Sherman was by no means finished. He held an entire division in reserve, commanded by James M. Tuttle, and was willing to try another attack along Graveyard Road with one brigade.

MOWER

Cloyd Bryner of the 47th Illinois claimed to have been close to the group of officers when Grant visited Sherman's command post at 2:00 P.M., and he overheard some of the conversation. "Have you a brigade that can carry that point?" Grant asked Sherman when the latter offered to renew his attacks. "I have one that can do it if it can be done," Sherman answered. "Then send it in," Grant ordered. Sherman sent an aide to fetch Brig. Gen. Joseph A. Mower to his command post when Grant left. Sherman then grilled the brigade leader, and we again rely on Bryner's testimony for the details. "'General Mower, can you carry those works?' Shaking his head from side to side in his peculiar way, he answered simply, 'I can try.' 'Then do it,' said Sherman."[30]

Mower's command had already formed in a column of regiments as had Brig. Gen. Hugh Ewing's brigade before him. Mower placed the 11th Missouri in the lead with the 47th Illinois next and then the 8th Wisconsin. The 5th Minnesota brought up the rear. Brig. Gen. Charles L. Matthies's brigade formed behind Mower, and Brig. Gen. Ralph P. Buckland's brigade formed behind Matthies. If Mower could make a lodgment in Stockade Redan, Matthies was available to go in and lend support. Buckland was told to protect the concentration of artillery near Graveyard Road, but he could also be called

Joseph A. Mower. Born in Vermont, Mower moved west and served in the Mexican War. He then obtained a commission in the U.S. Army without a West Point education and served as colonel of the 11th Missouri early in the Civil War. As a brigadier general, Mower displayed both ability and personal courage in his brigade's attack on May 22, and he went on to command a division and a corps before the war ended. (Library of Congress, LC-DIG-cwpb-06128)

on to support the other two brigades. Mower and Matthies were in a column of four men abreast, "charging endways," as many of the enlisted men quaintly put it. Like Ewing, Mower formed in a ravine off Graveyard Road with the intention of swinging into the roadway when it was time to go.[31]

Mower conducted a personal inspection of the ground he was to charge over before setting out. Robert McCrory recalled seeing him stand on top of the south bank of the roadcut only a few feet away, deliberately exposing himself to examine the ground toward Stockade Redan. "Move your men out of the road," he told Lt. Col. George H. Hildt of the 30th Ohio, "that I may bring my brigade in, and I will take that fort in FIVE minutes." Ewing had a different memory, stating after the war that Grant himself told him another division would try the fort. "Impossible" was Ewing's answer, but he offered to clear the road of his men and let the others have a clear run at the target.[32]

As Mower's men prepared for the charge they fixed bayonets. According to orders, they retained their haversacks with one day's rations rather than drop them to lighten their load. The troops were cautioned to make as little noise as possible in the vain hope that they could take the Confederates by surprise when they appeared rushing along Graveyard Road. But according to at least one Confederate, it was possible to detect that something was in the making because of the activity evident along the road. "Every one eager for the charge," noted Edwin Farley of the 8th Wisconsin, "impatient to be ordered forward." Because no one else in the brigade mentioned their mood just before the attack, we cannot be sure if everyone felt the same way as Farley.[33]

Mower's brigade started at 4:00 P.M., long after Smith, Ransom, and Kilby Smith ended their assault. The head of Mower's column emerged from the ravine and swung onto Graveyard Road, passing "a little group," in the words of Robert J. Burdette of the 47th Illinois. The group consisted of Sherman, Tuttle, and Mower, who were watching the men go by. "As we passed, Mower detached himself from the group and placed himself at the head of his own men," Burdette recalled. Once on the roadway, the troops moved at the double-quick.[34]

The men of the 11th Missouri had the same experience Ewing's brigade had had that morning. Their approach was no secret to the watchful garrison of Stockade Redan. From the Rebel viewpoint it seemed as if "the dark masses then rolled forward to the onslaught." In fact, according to Brig. Gen. Francis A. Shoup, it was "a terrible beautiful scene."[35]

But when the head of the column entered the roadcut, already littered with bodies of the slain and wounded from Ewing's assault, the Confederates opened a raging fire. From the viewpoint of Col. Lucius F. Hubbard in the 5th Minnesota, the 11th Missouri "was . . . melted down, by the fire in front and on both flanks." With that terrible volley, confusion ensued in the Missouri column and the color sergeant refused to go on. Lt. Menomen O'Donnell of Company A grabbed the colors and exhorted the troops to follow him. According to one survivor's account, forty-four Missourians did so. O'Donnell tried to persuade the color-bearer to retake the flag, but he continued to refuse. Cpl. Wesley S. Warner of Company I volunteered to take

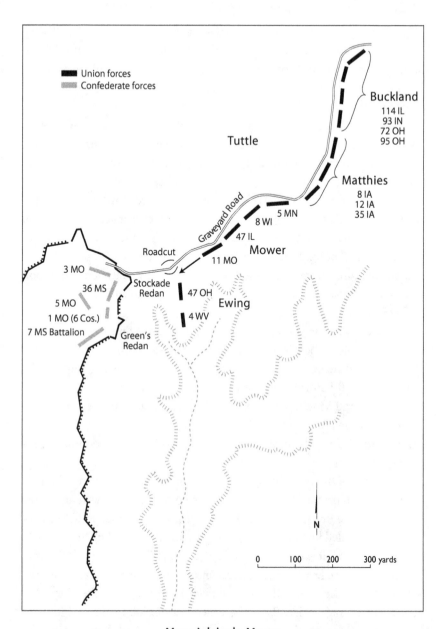

Mower's brigade, May 22

the emblem, and the little group continued through the storm of bullets and shells a short distance to Stockade Redan. Only twenty-four of the forty-four men made it to the ditch of the Confederate work.[36]

Col. Andrew J. Weber was among the small group of men who reached the ditch, but most of his regiment milled behind at the roadcut. Nevertheless, Warner placed the regimental flag next to Ewing's headquarters flag, which had been planted hours before by Pvt. Howell G. Trogden. The 11th Missouri men mingled with the survivors of the Forlorn Hope in the ditch and on the parapet, huddling between Union and Confederate waves of fire. Those men who continued to brave a position on the parapet exposed themselves to harm. Lt. Charles H. Brookings was mortally wounded "while actually on the ramparts of the enemies works," commented his friend Edwin Loosley, "which act was well in keeping with his brave and dauntless spirit." Weber remained in the ditch but was nearly killed by a shell rolled down by the Confederates as a hand grenade. It exploded and "tore off the front of his cap, doing him no other injury," recalled a member of the 11th Missouri.[37]

Mower's attack had already ground to a halt. The 47th Illinois, the next regiment in the brigade column, also got stuck at the roadcut, which by now was far too crowded with the living and the dead to serve as a portal through which to gain the target.[38]

John Merrilles of Battery E, 1st Illinois Light Artillery, had a perfect opportunity to observe Mower's attack. He had helped to manhandle projectiles from the caissons up to the battery position to support the opening of artillery fire at 3:00 P.M. as a way to soften up Stockade Redan. Only half of the ammunition had been moved forward when Blair's batteries roared into action, but Merrilles continued to haul rounds through a ravine and up a slope to the battery as the guns pounded away for an hour.[39]

"I was on my way to the caissons when [Mower's] column started, and by the time I got round to the road, the third regiment, the 8th Wisconsin, was passing." The 11th Missouri and 47th Illinois already had left the ravine and were heading for the roadcut. Then "a perfect roar of musketry had commenced, above the noise of which the cheering would swell out distinctly at intervals."[40]

Merrilles noticed that as the 8th Wisconsin reached Graveyard Road, "all at once the flight of bullets came sweeping through" it and also sailed into the 5th Minnesota behind it. Those two regiments continued to move forward slowly until they caught up with the stalled 47th Illinois and what was left of the 11th Missouri in and near the roadcut. Then all forward progress stopped. The column formation of the 8th Wisconsin and 5th Minnesota broke apart as most of the men retired rather than lie exposed on and near the open roadway. Soon Merrilles saw nothing but a scene of "inextricable confusion" as the men of the various regiments mingled going down the slopes to either side of the road, seeking shelter in ravines.[41]

Sherman, who keenly observed Mower's attack from his command post, was ready to call it off as soon as it seemed the effort had no chance of success. According to Cloyd Bryner, Sherman told Tuttle, "This is murder; order those troops back." Bryner did not indicate exactly when this occurred, but Tuttle sent his chief of staff, Maj. John D. McClure, to recall the troops.[42]

Amid the confusion one thing stood out for Thomas H. Barton. The hospital steward of the 4th West Virginia walked far enough forward to see the action because his dressing station was not yet busy. He saw Old Abe, the eagle mascot of the 8th Wisconsin, "flapping his wings and croaking, appeared to be as lively as any of the soldiers." But John Melvin Williams of the 8th Wisconsin reported that Old Abe had a rough time on May 22. He was hit by a spent ball, which did not hurt him much. But the eagle was startled and flew from his perch, to which he was connected by a strong cord. Abe flew with such force that he lifted his handler, Edward Homiston, a few inches off the ground and deposited him on top of a brush pile. Adolph Pitwch, assigned to help Homiston if needed, aided in the effort to get Abe back on his perch. Then a shell exploded nearby and Abe tried to fly again. This time Homiston managed to control the bird. Abe was rewarded when a member of the regiment caught a rabbit and gave it to the eagle. Abe devoured it under fire. That evening Homiston noticed that the spent ball had scratched Abe's neck and breast, cutting off some feathers, and another ball had penetrated "the web of his left wing, making a round hole in it."[43]

The troops of Ewing's brigade also had a good position from which to observe and evaluate Mower's attack. The surviving members of the 30th Ohio pulled out of the roadcut to make room for Mower's advance. Under heavy Confederate fire they took shelter behind the ridge that already covered other units of the brigade to the south of the cut.[44]

From here, the men of Ewing's brigade watched Mower advance. The 11th Missouri "swept past us on the double quick," wrote Wayne Johnson Jacobs of the 30th Ohio. Henry R. Brinkerhoff was very impressed by the Missourians. "With arms at a 'right shoulder shift,' at an ordinary double quick, . . . no running, no excitement, and their ranks closed up beautifully," they gave a martial show to be remembered.[45]

Ewing's troops took some solace in concluding that Mower's men did not make as much progress as they had hours earlier. That conclusion would have stung Mower's troops if they had known of it, but Ewing's men were right. The clutter inside the roadcut, matched with an alert and highly motivated defending force in Stockade Redan, spelled doom for the assault.[46]

Many of Mower's troops made their way to the rear on their own and others had to be helped. Robert J. Burdette of the 47th Illinois helped the wounded Lt. Christopher Gilbert to the rear with the aid of a comrade named Robley D. Stout. Gilbert recovered and many years later moved to Los Angeles, where Burdette happened to be pastor of Temple Baptist Church. When Gilbert was ready to be married, he asked Burdette to perform the ceremony. "Bob, do you recall the hot afternoon on the slopes before the bastion at Vicksburg?" Gilbert asked Burdette after the wedding. "I was just thinking of it, Lieutenant. And I was wondering if now you might ever blame me for helping to drag you out of the range of Pemberton's sharpshooters?" Gilbert had to admit that life had its strange meanderings. "'Indeed, no,' he said, 'I never will. I've often wondered why the dear Lord sent you back after me. But this is the 'Why.'"[47]

Only with the passage of many years could the "why" of Mower's attack make sense to Gilbert and Burdette. For a while after the failed assault, all that mattered was picking up the pieces. Mower suffered 17 killed, 136 wounded, and 29 missing for a total of 182 casualties. The 11th Missouri lost the most, with ninety-two casualties, and the 47th Illinois had the second-highest loss, with thirty-eight men down.[48]

Matthies's supporting brigade never had a chance to go in behind Mower. He advanced until the men were 400 yards from Stockade Redan and then stopped because of the wreckage of Mower's command. After a while Matthies moved his troops to the right of Graveyard Road behind a ridge and supported the 2nd Iowa Battery. He remained there the rest of the day, losing five men on May 22.[49]

Assigned to support batteries, the men of Buckland's brigade stood as astonished spectators of the fighting. Buckland told his wife that "we had for a short time during the assault the most terrific fire of artillery and musketry I ever heard." When Mower went in, Samuel Estill of the 114th Illinois was awed by the sight. "I was staning whare I could see the men as they made the charges. . . . Men fell like grass before a sythe som had booth legs shot off some one arme others was shot through the boddy and some shot through the head and was still able to walk."[50]

The 72nd Ohio was detached from Buckland's brigade and positioned close to the scene of Mower's attack. Harkness Lay therefore had a ringside seat for the event. He clearly saw the colors of the 11th Missouri move to Stockade Redan and rise above the dirt bank. "It was shot down and blown to pieces by the enemy's cannon," he contended. "But the bearer took it waved it three times above his head and stuck it again where it remained until dark." Because of its role as support for the batteries, Buckland's brigade counted only nine casualties on May 22.[51]

Mower failed to draw off Confederate troops from the Thirteenth Corps sector and had no chance of breaking into Stockade Redan. He also was unable to offer aid to the stranded members of Ewing's Forlorn Hope. The fifty or so Forlorn Hope men had a good view of Mower's attack. Lt. William C. Porter recalled that thirty troops of the 11th Missouri, including Colonel Weber and both regimental flags, made it to the ditch of the redan. "The bearing of the two color-bearers was all that bravery and true courage could do, waving their colors in defiance of enemies and traitors, marching straight and unwavering to the fort through the most murderous fire I ever experienced."[52]

STANDOFF AT STOCKADE REDAN

But this small accomplishment only added more stranded men to the group. For the rest of that long, frustrating day, the fifty troops of the Forlorn Hope and the twenty-four men of the 11th Missouri clung to their foothold on Pemberton's works and hoped to survive until night. They were so close that conversations between enemies sprang up. The Missourians inside the redan called out, promising to take in the stranded Yankees after dusk. Or they simply yelled, "Surrender, Yanks!" to which the Federals responded, "Come and get us."[53]

However, the Confederates began to use hand grenades on their enemy, which were more deadly than words. According to one source, these were real hand grenades, light enough to be thrown by a man. Some of them were thrown too hard and landed outside the ditch, exploding harmlessly.[54]

But then the Confederates began using artillery shells, setting the fuses very short and rolling them down the parapet into the ditch. Exactly who started this became a matter of opinion. According to Col. Francis M. Cockrell, Col. W. R. Gause of the 3rd Missouri had the idea, but according to W. J. Ervin, the credit belonged to Lt. King Hiram Faulkner of the same regiment. Faulkner procured some shells from the magazine of a nearby battery that had been silenced and told his men to cut the fuses at three seconds. He then directed the rolling of forty shells over the parapet. When Faulkner called on the Yankees to give up or endure more "shelling," they yelled, "Go to h———."[55]

The Federals managed to throw some of the lighted shells back into the redan before they exploded. This indicated that Faulkner's men cut the fuses much longer than three seconds. At times the Federals used bayonets on their rifles to stop the shells before they rolled very far down and pushed them back over the top. In fact, Lieutenant Porter contended that at least three shells were averted from rolling into the ditch in this fashion. They "burst on the inside, causing the same effect they intended for us."[56]

It was impossible for the Federals to take care of all the rolling shells in this way; many fell into the ditch and exploded with deadly effect. One shell decapitated a man a few feet from Orderly Sgt. George Theodore Hyatt of the 127th Illinois. Another killed Sgt. Richard Haney of the 55th Illinois and wounded four privates at the same time. The rolling shells caused the Federals to dig more and deeper holes in the parapet slope and use ladders to cover them, which seems to have been effective.[57]

The number of Federals estimated to have been killed and wounded by this shelling ranged from twenty-one to twenty-seven. In contrast, the 3rd Missouri (C.S.), which was most directly involved in this unusual fight with the stranded members of Ewing's Forlorn Hope and the 11th Missouri, lost fifty-six men killed and wounded on May 22.[58]

Some fortunate members of the stranded party managed to escape. Andrew E. Goldsberg of the 127th Illinois and a friend agreed to run back when powder smoke from the heavy firing provided some degree of cover. They waited for an opportune moment and then ran for their lives, reaching a log 100 feet from the Confederate work. Here they plopped down and fired back at the enemy for a while until a Federal shell landed uncomfortably close. Then the pair ran back, reaching the Union line in safety.[59]

Thus far, Fifteenth Corps efforts to renew pressure on the enemy had failed. But Steele's yet-unengaged division was finally getting into position to launch an attack on an untested part of the Confederate line.

{13}

It Made the Tears Come to My Eyes

STEELE, MAY 22

When Sherman persuaded Grant to renew assaults in an effort to help McClernand, he was thinking mostly of Blair's and Tuttle's divisions as the units to call on. Sherman had earlier given Steele wide latitude to conduct operations along the north face of Lockett's line as he saw fit, only recommending a possible point of attack. That point was the place Thayer's brigade had approached without an attack on May 19. The ground at the foot of Fort Hill Ridge and at the bottom of Mint Spring Bayou offered a large sheltered spot for the assembly of an assault force because the ridge happened to bulge out considerably here, shielding a considerable area from Confederate view. Steele consumed most of the day in moving troops to that point and was not ready to assault until Blair and Tuttle had nearly finished their work that afternoon.[1]

Simply moving to the attack point proved to be dangerous because portions of the route were exposed to Confederate fire. Col. Charles R. Woods left behind the 76th Ohio to hold the brigade line near the river while moving his other five regiments in a roundabout way to the left. He was careful to choose a route that was covered from Confederate view as much as possible and in the process consumed several hours of precious time. Col. Francis H. Manter also left behind some troops—the 27th Missouri, 29th Missouri, and 32nd Missouri—before taking his other three regiments to the left behind Woods. Manter started later but had a shorter distance to move.[2]

As these troops made their way to the assembly area, batteries on both sides maintained a spirited exchange of fire along Steele's sector. Brig. Gen.

William E. Baldwin was hit "rather severely" in the shoulder by an artillery burst about noon. Col. Allen Thomas of the 28th Louisiana took control of his brigade for the rest of the day. Thomas's regiment returned to Brig. Gen. Francis A. Shoup's Brigade on May 23, whereupon Col. Robert Richardson of the 17th Louisiana managed Baldwin's Brigade until Baldwin recovered and returned to duty by June 13.[3]

MOVING TO POINT OF ATTACK

When Woods began his movement to the left, he placed Col. George A. Stone's 25th Iowa in the lead of his column. The Iowans found the day had already grown "very hot." Most of the men assumed "we are going to charge," and that led some of the troops to "give out," as Pvt. Calvin Ainsworth of Company H put it. For much of the distance from Woods's sector to Thayer's position, about two and a half miles, the Federals negotiated the irregular contour of Indian Mound Ridge, crossing three high pieces of ground fully exposed to the Confederate line. Here is where the trouble started. Ainsworth noted that Company H had comparatively little difficulty crossing the first piece of high ground, suffering no losses even though "the balls fly thick and fast." As he crossed a small and muddy creek at the bottom of the slope, bullets were "plowing the mud all around me." His company managed to cross the second bit of high ground without loss as well.[4]

The third piece of high ground, however, was the worst. Ainsworth estimated that he had to rush along a quarter of a mile before descending into Mint Spring Bayou, all the while seen by Confederates along a full mile of Lockett's line. For about 150 to 200 yards of that quarter mile, the Federals would be most dangerously exposed to enemy fire. Lt. William A. Simons received orders to halt Company H at the brow of the ridge and send men down the most exposed part singly or in small groups. Simons told Ainsworth to drop back to the rear of the company and make sure no one straggled.[5]

According to Ainsworth, Simons folded under the pressure. Instead of leading from the front, Simons took shelter and shouted orders to move. The men stood still because of this, ignoring the orders, until several began to fall. "Why don't you take this company down," Ainsworth asked of Simons. "I used two or three very emphatic words, for I was mad, and at any other time it would have cost me a court martial, but everything goes in battle." No one moved, so Ainsworth took matters into his own hands. He walked past the stalled column and made his way down the exposed slope. Later he had the impression that no Confederates fired at him, probably because their attention was diverted toward the massed company visible on the top of the ridge.[6]

Ainsworth made it to the bottom to find a perfectly sheltered place and a handful of his company comrades who had preceded him. John Parent, who had gotten down to this spot before him, "said he knew it was certain death to remain there and so ran." Still, it took Simons another five minutes to move after Ainsworth reached the bottom, and then the lieutenant ran "very swiftly" down the exposed slope. He slipped and fell thirty feet from the bottom and rolled the rest of the way down the ridge and into a small creek. The rest of the company quickly ran down the slope too.[7]

When Ainsworth walked to the lieutenant he discovered that Simons had been hit in the back "just over the hip," which had caused his fall. Some cynical comrades assumed he had been shot deliberately by one of his own men, because he was quite unpopular. Ainsworth, however, judged Simons leniently. He did not believe the lieutenant was a coward, but he may have been unnerved by a premonition of injury or death. Moreover, Ainsworth admitted that the ridgetop "was a mighty hard place to stay in and a mighty hard place to leave." Company H lost one man killed and a dozen wounded while descending the exposed slope of Indian Mound Ridge.[8]

The rest of the 25th Iowa suffered as well. James Thomas of Company F, the next company in the regimental column, noted that each succeeding company had a tougher time of it because the Confederates now were alert to Woods's movement. Finding safety at the bottom of Mint Spring Bayou, Thomas was appalled to look back and see "many of our soldiers shot down, while they were running down the other hill."[9]

Each regiment in Woods's column duplicated the trial experienced by the 25th Iowa. They had to "run the Blockade as the Boys call it," wrote Thomas. They all did it the same way, singly or in small groups. Col. Hugo Wangelin's 12th Missouri followed the 25th Iowa. "It was always one company after the other," wrote Lt. Henry A. Kircher, "so that there was no crowding." At one point Kircher had to urge a reluctant member of his Company K by threatening him with the tip of his sword before he got down the exposed slope. The 12th Missouri also lost one of its officers, Capt. Christian Andel, who was killed by a shell fragment that "went into his right shoulder and came out between the last rib and the hip. It must have taken heart, liver, lungs and almost everything."[10]

"It was exciting for us to watch the other Regiments of the division come over the ridge in our rear under a galling fire," reported John W. Niles of the 9th Iowa in Thayer's waiting brigade. Woods thought the 25th Iowa and 12th

Missouri lost more men in moving to Thayer's position than the rest of the brigade. He also estimated that a total of sixty men fell while closing in on the assembly area at Thayer's position, an estimate that seems conservative.[11]

Manter's brigade did not go through this last gauntlet of fire. Having passed through the previous exposed places along the march, the 13th Illinois, which led Manter's column, prepared to brave this last and worst exposure. But Col. James A. Williamson, whose 4th Iowa had been detailed by Thayer to sharpshooting duty on the ridge, stopped the regiment and urged it to stay put. Williamson took responsibility for this disobedience of orders and sent word to Steele, who replied with instructions for Manter to stay where he was and act as a reserve for Thayer and Woods.[12]

FORMING FOR THE ASSAULT

The assembly area offered shelter from Confederate fire, especially from the 26th Louisiana Redoubt nearby, but to reach the enemy the Federals had to climb a very steep incline. The slope of Fort Hill Ridge at this point rose 110 feet in elevation in less than 200 yards of distance, presenting a formidable obstacle to an assault. Thayer formed his units with the 30th Iowa on the left, the 9th Iowa in the center, and the 26th Iowa on the right of his first line. These three units, aggregating a front of about eighty yards, were sheltered in trenches dug earlier in a semicircular fashion, with the 9th Iowa much farther up the lower slope of the ridge than its neighbors. In fact, once the 9th Iowa men emerged from their earthwork and stood up, they would be able to catch a glimpse of the enemy works on top of the ridge. The rest of Thayer's brigade was held in reserve. Woods formed his two lead regiments, the 25th Iowa and 12th Missouri, to support Thayer while the rest of his brigade continued to make its way to the area.[13]

As the troops prepared for the attack, hurried instructions were relayed down the chain of command. "The order was to march up the steep hill where we stand," reported James Thomas of the 25th Iowa, "then charge on the fort that was about 300 yards from us." The left wing of the Iowa regiment was supposed to act as sharpshooters as soon as it reached a place on top of the ridge where a feasible position could be found to do so and wait for the right wing to continue advancing. If successful, the left wing would also advance to support the right wing's attack.[14]

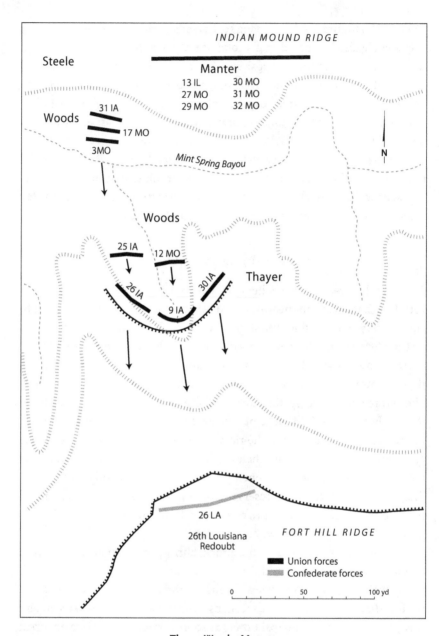

INDIAN MOUND RIDGE

Steele

Manter

13 IL	30 MO
27 MO	31 MO
29 MO	32 MO

Woods

31 IA

17 MO

3 MO

N

Mint Spring Bayou

Woods

25 IA 12 MO

26 IA 30 IA Thayer

9 IA

26 LA

26th Louisiana
Redoubt

FORT HILL RIDGE

Union forces
Confederate forces

| 0 | 50 | 100 yd |

Thayer-Woods, May 22

There could be no possibility of a surprise in this effort. It was obvious that Steele was massing near the 26th Louisiana Redoubt. Exactly when the Thayer-Woods attack started is a matter of disagreement. Some participants and observers reported it as 3:00 P.M. and others as 5:00 P.M. — obviously the synchronization of watches that Grant wanted did not seep down to lower-level commanders.[15]

Struggling up the steep slope, Thayer's first line emerged onto the uneven top of Fort Hill Ridge. As soon as the Federals became visible to the waiting Confederates, hell broke loose. "We started up the hill, & Oh, what a fire they pored in to us," moaned Robert Bruce Hoadley of the 26th Iowa. "We were Swept down like Grass before the Sythe." Hoadley was not seriously injured, although a spent ball struck his forehead just above the left eye and raised a mighty bump.[16]

Woods's men in the second line of the assault formation reached the top very soon after Thayer's regiments. Wangelin's 12th Missouri "moved forward over the crest of the hill in gallant style," reported Woods, "exposed to a withering fire." The climb up had been difficult not only because of the steep slope but also due to the uneven nature of the ground and the scattering of cut trees and brush. "It was impossible to move forward with any regularity," Woods explained of the 12th Missouri.[17]

Henry Kircher recalled that his Company K, 12th Missouri, was positioned directly behind the colors of the 9th Iowa and very close to the Iowa battle line. "How those who survived survived God knows, I can't comprehend it," he wrote. Pvt. Benjamin Dallmer of the 12th Missouri was shot six times during the assault but lived. Benjamin Codd, an Englishman, tripped during the advance and hit his chest on a stump, leading to his discharge from the service within a few months.[18]

The charge became an intensely emotional experience for Kircher. "But I can tell you that there were tears in my eyes when I saw the brave 9th Iowa advancing and the 12th, with heap upon heap dead or wounded, making one last energetic thrust, sometimes into the bayonet of a friend, falling to the ground and still crying out in a firm and loud voice 'Forward!' to his friends. That has to unnerve anybody," he told his mother, "no matter how tough he might be." "It made the tears come to my eyes," Kircher wrote in his diary, "as I was urging my brave company forward and seeing them drop one after the other like flies from the first frost."[19]

26th Louisiana Redoubt, Federal view. This incredibly steep slope was considered the best place for Steele's division to launch its assault on May 22 because the terrain bulged forward to create a protected staging area at the foot of Fort Hill Ridge. Three regiments of Thayer's brigade, supported by two regiments of Woods's brigade, made the attempt on the afternoon of May 22 and lodged surprisingly close to the 26th Louisiana Redoubt on top of the ridge. (Photograph by Earl J. Hess)

Despite the steep slope, the scattered brush, and the heavy fire at close range, Thayer and Woods got closer to the Rebel line than one could have expected. The 9th Iowa in the center of Thayer's first line lodged only ten to fifteen steps from the works. From the Confederate perspective, the distance seemed more like thirty steps. Lt. Lewis Guion in the 26th Louisiana Redoubt noted that his regiment "behaved finely, men mounting on top [of] the parapet to receive the enemy." For some of the Federals, it seemed as if the Rebels might sally forth and attack them. Col. Milo Smith, commander of the 26th Iowa, pointed his revolver at the top of the earthworks and muttered, "Let them come over, damn them, if they want to."[20]

Four color guards in the 9th Iowa were shot along with the bearer—the flag fell to the ground within "a few feet from the rebel works," thought Alonzo Abernethy. Otis Crawford was wounded close to the works but was able to make his way back to where most of his comrades were planted. He saw the abandoned flag and passed it downslope. Crawford was particularly motivated by the fact that the flag had "Pea Ridge" inscribed on it to commemorate the regiment's first battle. With a good deal of effort, Crawford

26th Louisiana Redoubt, Confederate view. Taken from the top of Fort Hill Ridge, where the 26th Louisiana Redoubt once stood, it is easy to see how the forward bulge of the terrain prevented the Confederates from fully seeing the Unionists while they remained at the foot of the ridge. Once the Thayer-Woods assault crested the bulge, however, the Federals were in easy range of the Confederates. (Photograph by Earl J. Hess)

and several other men managed to secure the banner. The rest of the 9th Iowa took shelter behind logs and undulations of the ground.[21]

While the 9th Iowa advanced straight up the slope between two ravines, the other two regiments in Thayer's formation encountered much difficulty because of the terrain. On the left the 30th Iowa crowded into the left wing of the 9th and caused some confusion. Then Col. Charles H. Abbott was shot near the top of the slope and that "seemed to paralyze the [men of the 30th Iowa] so that they did not advance." Maj. James P. Milliken was then mortally wounded, and the senior captain had gone missing. Capt. Robert D. Creamer of Company G took command and moved the 30th Iowa a few feet farther up the slope, where the men lay down to avoid the devastating fire bursting from the works. On Thayer's right, the 26th Iowa was compelled to go mostly into a ravine, where the men naturally preferred to seek shelter than to move toward the sputtering earthworks, and many members of the 12th Missouri did the same.[22]

The Thayer-Woods assault ground to a halt as the men took shelter on the sloping ridgetop. "When we stoped," wrote Robert Bruce Hoadley of the 26th Iowa, "a man went a head of me stoped & looked around[;] in less than a minuet he was *dead*, as I lay I could just reach his feet." Hoadley remembered the fate of Charles Butler, "a fellow I got acquainted with in Iowa & a first rate fellow to[o; he] was to my right he was shot threw the head ball went in just above the right eye made a hole as larg as my thumb he lived about 1 hour it was hard to see him lye there groning but their was no help for him."[23]

Calvin Ainsworth thought the attack had lasted no more than seven minutes—he probably meant from the moment the Confederates opened fire until the Federals grounded short of the works. Participants blamed the topography. The ridgetop was uneven and the space between the southern edge of the top and the blazing fortifications was so constricted it prevented full deployment or maneuvering. Federal survivors recalled the searing, close-range musketry. James Thomas told a friend, "The rebels made a cross fire on our men and Slaughter them awfully so it was impossible to make a charge." The uneven ground and a few scattered tree stumps and logs came in handy as shelter for the Federals.[24]

Survivors of the attack blamed supporting troops for failing to come to their aid. The right wing of the 25th Iowa, according to Ainsworth, "never got up" to the top of the ridge. At least part of the 3rd Missouri lodged on its top, but the 17th Missouri "stayed way back," according to Henry Kircher. "The other regiments more or less left us completely in the lurch," he bitterly complained. "They just shot one of us here and there in the back, the wretched ones." The lack of support was understandable considering the topography. There was no room for additional units on the battlefield atop the ridge. Most of Thayer's and Woods's troops remained at the bottom of the slope.[25]

The Confederate defenders had a clear view of the action and were impressed with the spirit of the Federals. Many Yankees were lodged too near the works for the Confederates to fire at them, but there was no possibility they could cross the parapet. Lt. Jared Young Sanders of Company B, 26th Louisiana, watched with fascination as one Federal soldier "stooped behind a stump within 20 yards of us" and calmly smoked his pipe. After the battle, Confederate soldiers went forward under cover of darkness and found this man dead. Francis Shoup, whose brigade held this part of the line, reported that the Union attack utterly failed. "It is slaughtered, and flies in confusion," he wrote. The Rebels estimated that Thayer and Woods lost 600 men in the charge, an inflated number bolstered by the excitement of victory. In contrast, the 26th Louisiana, which was the target of this Union thrust, lost six killed and three wounded.[26]

Thayer lost 155 men, mostly suffered among the three regiments that led the attack. Seventy-eight troops out of fewer than 300 engaged, or 26 percent, fell in the 9th Iowa. Woods's brigade suffered 190 casualties, with the 12th Missouri accounting for 108 losses out of 360 men engaged (30 percent). That represented the highest regimental loss rate in the division. The regiment's left wing suffered more heavily than the right, which had a more covered position on the ridgetop. Members of the 25th Iowa counted twenty-eight holes in their regimental colors, but the cloth was still intact and recognizable as a flag. Manter lost only seven men, and Steele's artillery lost one man. The total casualties of Steele's division amounted to 353 men. It is not known where Steele positioned himself during the attack, but he was grazed on the ankle by a shell fragment. Stunned for a while, he retained command of the division.[27]

Survivors of the Thayer-Woods attack counted it "a memorable bayonet charge." Calvin Ainsworth refused to call it a battle but characterized the assault as a "destruction." John T. Buegel of the 3rd Missouri bluntly termed it "a slaughter" and wondered that "the whole division was not destroyed on the spot. What had been accomplished? Nothing at all."[28]

It is impossible to argue against these bitter assessments. Even though Steele's artillery fired relentlessly during the day, exhausting stocks of ammunition, the division's efforts on May 22 failed to draw troops from other parts of the Confederate line.[29]

None of Steele's men were more emotional in assessing the attack than Henry Kircher. "It was a sade scene to see so many brave boys slaughtered without having accomplished any thing," he confided to his diary. "It very *foolish* of our Commanders to take all these troops by three blockades during daylight[;] in doing so he of course notified the enemy of our coming and showed the strength of our attacking party so it could not be any surprize for the enemy which if it had been we could have carried the works." Kircher admitted that as good soldiers they had to obey the order to charge. "But may this be the last fit of insanity that our commanders will ever have." In writing to his mother, Kircher did not hesitate to name the officer he most blamed for the attack. "A third of the entire 12th regiment murdered, only because Sherman thinks that everything can be forced by the stormers without knowing the terrain or testing it out." He was not alone. "The rash move the boys all attribute to Sherman's 'hot headed' ambition," commented Henry I. Seaman of the 13th Illinois.[30]

To some degree these criticisms were justified. If it was true that Thayer's position held the best (or perhaps only) prospect for an assault, then Woods and Manter were compelled to move to it. They cannot be blamed for the terrain or the watchful Confederates who saw them moving along the way to Mint Spring Bayou. But the slope up Fort Hill Ridge toward the 26th Louisiana Redoubt is incredibly steep. Climbing up that ridge into the teeth of waiting riflemen was the toughest attack plan of any Federal troops on May 22.

As for Sherman's culpability in this bloody outcome, it must be remembered that Steele's attack was originally scheduled to be part of the general assault planned for 10:00 A.M. The long time needed for Woods and Manter to move two and a half miles to the staging area prevented that from happening. The two brigades happened to arrive just in time to participate in the renewal of Sherman's assaults during the late afternoon. If it were not for McClernand's urgent request for support, presumably Thayer and Woods would not have attacked that afternoon. Because Sherman was keen on helping McClernand (a desire that McClernand never appreciated), Kircher was right to identify Sherman as the prime mover behind the Thayer-Woods assault.

END OF A TRYING DAY

At three key points along the Fifteenth Corps sector, harried troops who had lodged close to enemy works prayed for night to fall. The men holed up in the ditch of Stockade Redan had been there the longest, since 10:00 A.M. Lt. William C. Porter of the 55th Illinois, who assumed command of the Forlorn Hope when Capt. John H. Groce was wounded, received a verbal order from Blair at 7:30 P.M. to get his men away. Porter made sure they carried the wounded back too. Pvt. Howell G. Trogden also made sure he took away Brig. Gen. Hugh Ewing's flag, the same he had planted in the parapet nine and a half hours earlier. It was "perfectly riddled with bullets" but still intact. When the flag was returned to Ewing, the brigade leader displayed it in the parlor of his Lancaster, Ohio, home for the rest of his life. Crouching Confederates inside Stockade Redan heard the enemy leave and fired at them, hitting several men as the Federals made their way back.[31]

Porter felt responsible for the Forlorn Hope and wanted to document the unit's suffering. Over several days he visited almost all the regiments of Col. Thomas Kilby Smith's brigade that contributed troops to the 150-man detail and tabulated the casualties. Porter could not consult with officers of the 127th Illinois because it had been detached from the brigade, but the other four regiments contributed forty-one men to the detail. They lost sixteen of them on May 22, for a loss ratio of 39 percent. Of nine men sent from the 57th Ohio, only five returned to duty on the night of May 22. Porter was unable to visit the regiments of Blair's other two brigades and thus had no data on them.[32]

When he recovered from his wound, Groce provided a full accounting of the detail's numbers and losses. He listed a total of 158 officers and men, of whom fourteen were killed, twenty-six wounded, and two listed as missing. This totaled forty-two casualties, or a loss ratio of 26.5 percent.[33]

Porter frankly reported on an unnamed lieutenant of the 127th Illinois who had volunteered for the storming party but flinched at a critical moment. The lieutenant "did not reach us till dark, remaining about 4 rods from the fort, on the road, protected by its high banks, without attempting the march to the fort." That officer "kept back from the assailing party 10 men, who remained where he did during the entire day on the road." Porter's frankness did not extend to actually naming the lieutenant, and there is no evidence that any disciplinary action was taken in his case.[34]

Ewing noted that with the withdrawal of the Forlorn Hope, his brigade was concentrated only 100 yards from the enemy behind a good rise of ground. Here the men stayed, dug in, and contributed to pending siege operations. Ewing lost 144 troops. In contrast, Col. Giles A. Smith suffered 102 casualties and Kilby Smith counted fifty-six losses. Blair's total casualties for May 22 amounted to 304 men.[35]

Col. Francis M. Cockrell, whose Missouri Rebels were primarily responsible for the defense of Stockade Redan, lost 123 men on May 22. The 3rd Missouri suffered a dozen killed and fifty-two wounded because it endured a good deal of enfilade fire into the redan, "against which there was then no protection or defenses," Cockrell reported.[36]

As the Forlorn Hope pulled away just after dark, Steele's troops also fell back from the 26th Louisiana Redoubt. Robert Creamer, in charge of the 9th Iowa, received a written order to retire, but it was too dark for him to read it. "The Boys held a Gum blanket over me that I might strike a match," he recalled. Then after the moon went down the regiment quietly pulled away. For the exhausted troops of Thayer and Woods, the night was consumed with efforts to retrieve their wounded comrades and carry them a mile over rough country, some of the way exposed to enemy fire, until they arrived at field hospitals. Although Henry Kircher reported bitterly that the Confederates fired at them, Lewis Guion made a point in the record book of the

26th Louisiana that this was not so. In fact, the Confederates sallied out in front of their line to pick up wounded Federals who lay so close to the works that their comrades could not reach them. When the task of removing the wounded was done, Woods's people returned to their former position on the far right of Grant's line "dead tired and hungry," as John T. Buegel of the 3rd Missouri noted with some irony, but "richer in experience."[37]

"We have had a hard day's work, and all are exhausted," Sherman told Grant that evening. Grant's mind, however, was already on the next step. "Would it be advisable to mine and blow up the salient near where you now have the flag planted on the enemy's parapet? I am sending after powder and expect to have it here some time during the night." Sherman was hopeful. "From Ewing's position a sap may be made to reach the right bastion, and it may be we can undermine and blow it up." Based on Grant's suggestion, Sherman told Blair to keep Ewing's brigade behind the ridge that lay 100 yards from Stockade Redan and keep Smith's men in place as well, "close up to the enemy's works." He requested 1,000 entrenching tools and wanted his men to dig in as near the target as possible. Those instructions were formalized in General Orders No. 39, issued later that evening, which mandated that Ewing and Smith construct "a rifle-pit or breast-height of logs" to secure their positions. Those orders also instructed officers to remove all wounded to the rear and bury the dead.[38]

The Fifteenth Corps suffered 150 killed, 666 wounded, and 42 missing on May 22, for a total of 858 men. Edwin C. Bearss has criticized Sherman for failing to throw large masses against the enemy works, dribbling out his manpower in separate and uncoordinated assaults at 10:00 A.M., 2:15 P.M., 3:00 P.M., and 4:00 P.M.[39]

None of those four attacks achieved anything like coordination with the others, but to be fair to Sherman it was not entirely his fault. The three afternoon assaults took place when they did because of circumstances beyond Sherman's control and because of his legitimate desire to help Thirteenth Corps operations based on McClernand's plea for assistance. The many difficulties of moving masses of troops over the rugged terrain and within sight of enemy defenses largely accounts for the uncoordinated timing of these assaults.

{ 14 }

Boys, Don't Charge Those Works

LOGAN and QUINBY, MAY 22

Grant instructed McPherson to renew offensive efforts on the Seventeenth Corps sector that afternoon, but true to his performance of the morning, the corps commander displayed little willingness to take those instructions seriously. He agreed to do what he could along Jackson Road and sent his reserve division under Brig. Gen. Isaac F. Quinby to help McClernand. The Thirteenth Corps commander could not have expected more of his colleague, but in the end neither of McPherson's efforts helped him. Logan did not press his men forward with any effect, and Quinby's fine division was frittered away by McClernand himself in piecemeal advances.

LOGAN

Logan ordered Brig. Gen. Mortimer D. Leggett to prepare his reserve brigade for a charge. Leggett maneuvered the men through ravines south of Jackson Road to obtain a position close to the Rebel line and then waited behind the crest of a ridge for orders to advance.[1]

While they waited, Leggett told Col. Manning F. Force of the 20th Ohio that "upon entering the enemy's works a line of troops, or a second line of works, would be found close to hand, which must be promptly charged." Force relayed that gruesome information to his men. "They all earnestly promised to keep closed ranks and make the charge."[2]

Force insisted that his men were ready to attack if they were ordered to do so. But it is obvious that many of them were grateful they were not called on to do so. Before the advance on May 22, William David McClure scribbled in his diary, "Oh! how many brave boys will fall in the Charge. *May God* protect *us*, and His Guardian hover over us." After the fighting died down on May 22, McClure expressed relief that his regiment "did not make the Charge."[3]

For unexplained reasons Logan never issued the attack order to Leggett, and his brigade remained in place the rest of the day. As Edwin C. Bearss has put it, McPherson's attempts to renew offensive efforts on the Seventeenth Corps sector were "feeble," or in the words of Michael Ballard, "halfhearted." McPherson never explained his lack of resolve to help the common cause, but it stands in stark contrast to Sherman's efforts.[4]

Capt. Stewart R. Tresilian, Logan's engineer officer, did what he could to achieve something on May 22. After it became apparent that the fighting had ended for the day, he moved half of the division pioneer corps to the advanced Union position and started to construct a sap. During the course of the night his men dug sixty feet forward. Their work came to naught because the next day Confederate sharpshooters made it too hot for them to continue.[5]

The Confederates holding this part of the line received reinforcements that afternoon. Maj. Gen. Martin L. Smith sent two regiments to help Maj. Gen. John H. Forney. One of them, the 29th Louisiana, wound up at the Jackson Road sector. When Col. Allen Thomas took charge of Brig. Gen. William E. Baldwin's Brigade after Baldwin was wounded that day, he assigned Capt. James W. Bryan to lead the 29th Louisiana. Bryan received orders to move toward Forney's Division from his position near the city graveyard but soon after was diverted by Maj. Charles Pollard Ball. The major "piloted me to a ravine in the rear of" Col. Richard Harrison's 43rd Mississippi. Harrison wanted only five companies, so Bryan remained with the right wing of his regiment and sent Capt. William F. Norman off with the left wing to another part of the line.[6]

Harrison had very definite ideas about how to deploy Bryan's men. He wanted four companies to be placed on Jackson Road between the 3rd Louisiana on the north and the 21st Louisiana on the south. He directed Bryan's largest company to enter the redoubt held by part of the 43rd Mississippi.[7]

At the end of McPherson's efforts that day, casualty figures told the tale of his corps' work. John E. Smith's brigade lost eighty-one men, and Leggett's brigade suffered six casualties. Stevenson's brigade lost a great deal more with 34 killed and 238 wounded. The 7th Missouri, which drew the lion's share of attention because of its drive to Great Redoubt, lost 102 men, the highest regimental loss in the corps. The 81st Illinois suffered ninety-eight casualties, the second-highest regimental loss in the corps.[8]

QUINBY

The only other contribution McPherson made to Federal efforts that day was to dispatch Quinby's division to the Thirteenth Corps by 3:00 P.M. McClernand was very happy upon receiving the news. "As soon as they arrive," he informed Grant at 3:15 P.M., "I will press the enemy with all possible dispatch, and doubt not that I will force my way through. I have lost no ground. My men are in two of the enemy's forts, but they are commanded by rifle-pits in the rear. Several prisoners have been taken, who intimate that the rear is strong." Grant received this message at 3:50 P.M.[9]

It would take some time for Quinby to move his men. Meanwhile Col. Ashbel Smith continued to hold the 2nd Texas Lunette. He directed his men to light spherical case rounds with five-second fuses and roll them down the parapet into the ditch. This tactic seemed to work, because Federal fire slackened for the next hour or so. The Confederates were still plagued by smoldering cotton bales used as revetment, obscuring vision "for any considerable distance," according to Cpl. Charles I. Evans.[10]

The Federals could do little more than hold on to their toeholds at both the 2nd Texas Lunette and Railroad Redoubt until help arrived. The tension remained high among the troops at the advanced positions and at Thirteenth Corps headquarters; everyone was compelled to wait for Quinby. At about 5:00 P.M. McClernand lost the services of an energetic staff officer when Lt. Col. Henry Clay Warmoth was hit. "I was receiving an order to carry to Genl. Osterhaus," he wrote in his diary, when "a Ball hit me in the shoulder inflicting a mean wound. If it had not been quite so fully spent it would have Cut my juggler vein & Killed me." Warmoth fell so close to McClernand that the Thirteenth Corps commander caught the falling officer in his arms.[11]

Quinby took care when planning to move his division. He detailed the 18th Wisconsin to remain in position, hoping it could distract the Confederates by its fire. Then he used a ridge to the east to screen his march, plotting a route of two miles in length. As a result, even though he set out at 3:00 P.M., he did not report to McClernand at Battery Maloney until 5:00 P.M. In a controversial move, McClernand parceled out the division to different parts of his line rather than use it as a single unit. One brigade, under Col. John B. Sanborn, received orders to take the 2nd Texas Lunette; another, under Col.

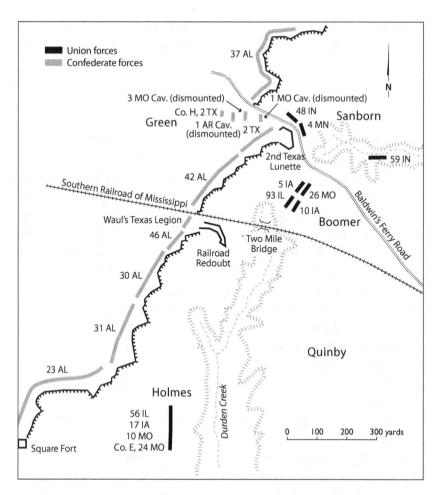

Quinby's division, May 22

George B. Boomer, headed toward the Confederate line between the 2nd Texas Lunette and Railroad Redoubt; and the third brigade, under Col. Samuel A. Holmes, was told to move south and help Osterhaus. In this way McClernand violated his own principle, expressed to Grant the evening before, that the Federals should attack in concentrated rather than dispersed formation.[12]

SANBORN

Quinby's men knew why they had shifted to the left. "It was said [McClernand] had got a foothold on the works," as Maj. Edward Jesup Wood of the

48th Indiana put it. An aide of McClernand's pointed out Sanborn's assembly area, which used the same ravine that Benton had used to launch his attack at 10:00 A.M. Sanborn placed the 4th Minnesota on his left, the 48th Indiana in the center, and the 59th Indiana on the right. Because of the narrow width of the ravine, the three regiments formed a column of four men abreast.[13]

When the head of Sanborn's column debouched from the ravine and onto Baldwin's Ferry Road, it was greeted with heavy small-arms and artillery fire. Sanborn maintained better control over his men than Benton had and led the column toward the right so that the 4th Minnesota, the last unit in the column, wound up "hard against the lunette." The 59th Indiana stayed inside the ravine for unexplained reasons.[14]

"We found a few brave fellows, clinging to the edge of the parapet," recalled Edward Jesup Wood. "The stars & stripes [were] planted half way up on the breastwork, and the little band themselves only saved from complete annihilation by the steady stream of fire which they poured over the top of the fort." Those Federals belonged to Burbridge's brigade and were nearly out of ammunition. Sanborn's men took position with them and opened fire, "raking the top of the fort, and sweeping everything that appeared on it." Wood noted that his comrades were but thirty feet from the enemy, the parapet separating the opposing forces. Here his men remained for the next one and a half hours.[15]

But a miscommunication now occurred that weakened the Federal position. For some reason Burbridge assumed that Sanborn was to relieve his brigade rather than reinforce it for further effort. A correspondent of the *New-York Daily Tribune* charitably called it "one of those mistakes which are liable to occur in the confusion of the battle-field." Word circulated to Col. Henry D. Washburn's band of the 18th Indiana, Benton's brigade, and at least the 16th Indiana and 83rd Ohio of Burbridge's command to fall back as soon as the new men arrived. They did not hesitate to do so. Presumably the 60th Indiana and 96th Ohio also fell back, although information is unclear on that point. In contrast, the 23rd Wisconsin of Burbridge's brigade never received an order to retire and remained with Sanborn's men. In his hasty and unauthorized departure, Burbridge left behind the 67th Indiana (which also did not receive an order to retire). His men also left behind the six-pounder gun of the Chicago Mercantile Battery that had earlier been rolled forward to fire at point-blank range into the 2nd Texas Lunette.[16]

Sanborn never found out whether Burbridge's command retired "by positive orders or the result of the impulse of the men." But for close to two hours his troops held on where Burbridge had held for the past seven hours, and they found it a far from pleasant task. "I can see the men on each side of me drop," wrote Richard S. Reeves of the 4th Minnesota in his diary. "We keep firing till we get out of Ammunition it is a sickening sight to behold so many falling on every side of you they completely cover the ground." Back in the ravine from which the 4th Minnesota and 48th Indiana had emerged, the men of the 59th Indiana took shelter from artillery fire in numerous sink-holes. When that fire slackened near dusk, the Indianans "reformed at the head of the ravine behind some hillocks," noted James Curtis Mahan.[17]

Rather than wage a battle-winning assault, Sanborn managed to bring forward only two regiments to the Union force outside the 2nd Texas Lunette. Because of Burbridge's misunderstanding, most Federal manpower was stripped from that position before Sanborn could do anything. In fact, the Union posture at the 2nd Texas Lunette was weaker than it had been be-fore Sanborn arrived.

Moreover, the Confederates took measures to counterattack and drive away what few Federals remained near the fort. Ashbel Smith could see the approach of Sanborn's two regiments despite the smoke that lingered around the lunette. Smith had earlier in the afternoon called for help, which now began to arrive. As a result, Brig. Gen. Martin E. Green's Missouri Brigade of Maj. Gen. John S. Bowen's Division left its reserve post and headed for the 2nd Texas Lunette. Green placed the 19th Arkansas and 20th Arkansas in the lunette. The 1st Missouri Cavalry, 3rd Missouri Cavalry, and 1st Arkansas Cavalry, all dismounted, took position just north of the work to protect the 100-yard gap in the line that the Federals seemed interested in approaching. Smith now had considerably more force than he had when Burbridge first approached the lunette that morning.[18]

Smith apparently expected Green's units that were positioned north of the lunette to counterattack immediately, but they did not. The harried Texas colonel concluded that the Missouri and Arkansas troops were hesi-tant about advancing. In fact, he noted that "a most gallant lieutenant" in one of the regiments moved twenty paces ahead of his men. Smith must have based this on reports coming from his own troops, for there is no evi-dence of hesitation coming from the Missouri and Arkansas units. Smith got excited and stood on a rise of ground near the lunette, calling on the re-inforcements to "come and help my boys." He also ordered Capt. Jerome T. McGinnis's Company H, 2nd Texas, to move from the right of his regimen-tal sector and across the gorge of the lunette to reinforce Green's three regi-ments. He hoped in this way to jump-start a counterattack.[19]

But Smith need not have worried. If there was any hesitation among the dismounted Missouri and Arkansas cavalrymen it soon evaporated and the three regiments advanced with spirit through the 100-yard gap in the line. McGinnis's company of the 2nd Texas arrived just as Green's troopers started out. Col. Thomas P. Dockery, who later commanded Green's Brigade, called this counterattack "a short but desperate fight." Smith thought it lasted about half an hour. Twilight was now descending; cotton bales in the connecting line north of the lunette caught fire from the muzzle flashes of Smith's Texans, who were dispersed along the line. Charles Evans recalled the eerie scene "lighted up by the bright flames" that "presented a grand and brilliant spectacle from the elevated position" of the 2nd Texas Lunette.[20]

Isolated, Sanborn's 4th Minnesota and 48th Indiana resisted Green's advance for a while, then slipped away. Edward Jesup Wood reported that the 48th Indiana fell back in stages, one company at a time, until only two were left on the firing line when he told both to make their way back as best they could. Burbridge's 67th Indiana also retired, as did the 4th Minnesota. According to Sanborn, Company C of the 4th came across the Chicago Mercantile Battery's six-pounder gun and brought it back to Union lines. According to members of the 48th Indiana, however, Pvt. James Andrews of Company F persuaded men of their regiment to pull it back to safety.[21]

"So ends one of the greatest slaughters of the war," concluded Richard S. Reeves of the 4th Minnesota. He estimated his regiment lost eighty-four men in the abortive attack. Many members of Burbridge's command complained that Sanborn's troops had allowed themselves to be driven off from the advanced position so soon after "taking over" from them. In their view, Burbridge had held on for seven hours; Sanborn had held on for only two. The 83rd Ohio received orders to retrace its steps and try to help Sanborn when word of the enemy counterattack reached its commander, but it was too late to help the Seventeenth Corps troops hold the advanced position. Charles F. Smith of the 83rd Ohio unfairly called Sanborn's troops "miserable soldiers as they all run before they had been there half an hour."[22]

The failure of Sanborn's assault can hardly be attributed to poor performance by the rank and file. When Burbridge took most of the troops away from the advanced position, any hope of jump-starting a push through the Rebel works vanished. There was little purpose in keeping Sanborn and the 67th Indiana in that vulnerable position after the less than brilliant performance by Burbridge. Green's counterattack merely hastened a foregone conclusion: Sanborn would have retired under cover of darkness.

George B. Boomer. Born in Massachusetts but living much of his life in Missouri before the war, Boomer became colonel of the 26th Missouri and later was elevated to brigade command. Like corps commander James B. McPherson, Boomer was widely respected for his character and personality but displayed little military talent on the battlefield. He was killed during the advance of his command on the afternoon of May 22. (Vol. 5, 224, Massachusetts Commandery, Military Order of the Loyal Legion and the U.S. Army Military History Institute)

BOOMER

The next brigade from Quinby's division to try its hand was George B. Boomer's. After "winding round hills" in double column formation, the brigade reached McClernand's sector and set out to hit the line between the 2nd Texas Lunette and Railroad Redoubt.[23]

Boomer was a widely respected officer but not because of any stellar battlefield exploits. Like McPherson, Boomer impressed everyone with his character rather than his military accomplishments. Born in Massachusetts thirty-one years earlier, he moved to Missouri early in the 1850s, developing the town of Castle Rock on the Osage River and setting up lumber mills to support the bridge-building business he and his brother established. Boomer was known as an intelligent, cultured, and sensitive man. He raised and became colonel of the 26th Missouri and was wounded at the battle of Iuka on

September 19, 1862. Upon recovery he took command of a brigade and led it well enough at Champion Hill to prompt Missouri governor Hamilton Gamble to recommend his promotion to brigadier general.[24]

When word of the pending attack circulated on the evening of May 21, Boomer was confident. He thought it would probably succeed and with comparatively little loss of life. Like Grant, he based this assessment on the assumption that the Confederates were demoralized. But by noon of May 22, after the initial attacks had failed, Boomer lost all hope of success. He expressed fear that his superiors would continue attacking and lose half the men to no purpose. Just when he considered expressing those views to McPherson, the order arrived for the division to move south. This was the last moment that Sanborn saw Boomer, departing with a wan smile on his face as if he had no faith in the mission.[25]

When Boomer reported at 5:00 P.M., Brig. Gen. Eugene A. Carr took him and his regimental commanders to a point where all could see the approach to the target. According to Henry G. Hicks of the 93rd Illinois, Carr's instructions were explicit: "To rest, directly in the rear of the intervening hill, then take breath for a few moments and then charge." It was possible to see some of the men belonging to the 99th Illinois and Company E, 33rd Illinois, lodged close to the works. But, according to Hicks, everyone could also see "the utter folly" of the planned attack. Capt. Benjamin D. Dean, who commanded the 26th Missouri, thought Boomer was happy that Carr gave instructions about how to conduct the assault because it "relieved himself of the responsibility for the order to charge."[26]

Regardless of his personal views, Boomer put on a "cool and collected" attitude. He formed his brigade in two lines, spaced fifty yards from each other, and placed himself between them 600 yards from the Confederate works. The 5th Iowa held the right of the first line with the 26th Missouri to its rear. The 93rd Illinois occupied the left of the first line, and the 10th Iowa took place behind it.[27]

The terrain to be traversed was clearly in view. The brigade had to cross two ridges, the crests of which were between 160 and 220 yards apart from each other. The Confederate line lay more than 200 yards west of the second ridge. Boomer instructed his regimental commanders to cross the first ridge and the valley between but stop behind the crest of the second ridge to gather strength for the last leg of the advance. "If a soldier might at any time ... weigh his life, in the scales, against his honor, that was a time to determine which he would lose," commented a veteran of the 93rd Illinois.[28]

"Attention Third Brigade!" Boomer shouted when his command was ready at 6:00 P.M. "Shoulder Arms! Right shoulder shift, arms! Forward, Common time, March!" The men started across the rugged terrain, up and down the slopes, exposing themselves to enemy view much of the way. "With lines well aligned," wrote Henry Hicks, "the brigade swept down through the peach orchard, to the valley below." Because of heavy fire, the line began to break up halfway down the slope, but the men quickened their pace until they entered the ravine. Here they found fallen trees and brush that slowed their advance. After working through it, they moved up the slope of the next ridge. Hicks believed the brigade received fire from Rebel infantry along a half mile of trenches, which forced the Federals to pick up the pace from common time to quick time and then to double-quick time before they came to a halt on top, about 200 yards from the Confederate works.[29]

Boomer's advance was also visible to thousands of Federal soldiers. The men of Col. David Shunk's group (right wing of 8th Indiana and Companies A, C, D, G, and I of the 33rd Illinois), lodged close to the Confederate line somewhere south of Railroad Redoubt, had received word to expect reinforcements. They assumed fresh troops would move forward by snaking through the cover of ravines. Instead, they were surprised to see Boomer's men racing along a direct line over the undulating landscape.[30]

"Of all the sights I ever beheld," wrote Albert O. Marshall of the 33rd Illinois, "none were more heartrending than to see those Union soldiers destroyed in such a useless and aimless manner." He heard "many exclamations of horror" among his comrades. "Mismanagement seemed to rule the day upon our part of the line," Marshall concluded.[31]

The brigade stopped on the second ridge to catch its breath. Lt. Col. Ezekiel S. Sampson wanted to dress the line of his 5th Iowa, and Boomer thought of adjusting the entire formation. That involved moving the 5th Iowa and 26th Missouri from the right of the brigade line to form a column behind the left wing. The 5th Iowa moved about eighty yards in this shift, and its left extended a bit farther than that of the 10th Iowa.[32]

At this point, before the 26th Missouri completed its shift, Boomer was hit in the head with a musket ball while standing in front of the 5th Iowa. Historians assume someone near Railroad Redoubt fired the shot. Boomer "shouted 'Attention!' as if to resume the charge," according to Dean, just before the ball found its mark. But other officers on the scene told a different story. According to reports relayed to Carr, Boomer's last words before expiring were "Boys, don't charge those works."[33]

Col. Holden Putnam of the 93rd Illinois took control of the brigade and prepared to continue the advance. According to Hicks, Putnam began to give the order but his regimental commanders refused "to obey the command, . . . protesting that it was murder to go further." Then Maj. Nathaniel McCalla of the 10th Iowa told Putnam Boomer's last words. That made the colonel pause. He consulted with his subordinates, and their opinion was summed up by Benjamin Dean, who said he "would not move without positive orders as it was impossible to do anything under the terrible artillery fire." Putnam replied that he was fully aware of this but Carr wanted the brigade to make a vigorous attack. Dean countered with the idea that "the situation had changed," and the other regimental leaders agreed with him. Dean suggested the brigade stay where it was and pull back at dusk. Putnam agreed. To cover that decision, Dean sent one of his lieutenants from the 26th Missouri to report to Quinby. The division commander sent word confirming that waiting and retiring at dusk was the right thing to do.[34]

This ended Boomer's attack at a point fully 200 yards short of the enemy works. Carr's decision to send the brigade along the shortest but most exposed route of advance was the chief cause of its failure. Although Putnam reported that the brigade suffered ninety-five casualties, a modern estimate places the toll at 14 killed and 100 wounded for a total of 114 men. Sampson's 5th Iowa lost two killed and seventeen wounded for a total of nineteen men out of 250 engaged (7.6 percent). Putnam's 93rd Illinois lost fifty-five men in the afternoon attack plus a dozen more in the morning operations.[35]

The brigade retired after dusk, bringing along Boomer's body. "I saw two men bringing back his corpse," wrote JRSC of the 16th Indiana, acting as an aide on Andrew J. Smith's staff. Boomer's clothes were "torn and dirty, blood running from his mouth and ears; he died like a hero should." S. H. M. Byers of the 5th Iowa also saw the body after it was taken back to the Union line. It lay on the grass with a handkerchief covering the face. Byers lifted the covering to confirm it was his respected brigade commander.[36]

"He was a man beloved by all who knew him," wrote Henry Hicks, "and his loss was keenly felt." But Hicks also knew that in his death Boomer bequeathed life to many of his men. While alive, he had felt it was his duty to fulfill the attack order at any cost. When mortally wounded, all commitments to his duty evaporated, and in his last breath he told the men not to go on. Boomer probably knew he would not live to suffer the consequences of arbitrarily calling off the assault. As Hicks put it, Boomer's "death unquestionably saved the brigade from practical annihilation."[37]

To his credit, Carr also came to realize that calling off further effort was wise. He nevertheless defended his initial decision to push the brigade forward in the most direct manner. "The only chance to secure the lodgement made by my Division on the enemies works was evidently to send reinforcements to them," he wrote to Quinby, "and though it entailed the loss of brave men, I felt that the importance of the object made it absolutely necessary to try." Carr never admitted that the manner in which he moved the troops forward was a mistake, but many other men thought it was unnecessary. The brigade could have "moved around the ravine as the other troops did, concealed as long as possible," thought JRSC.[38]

Boomer's attack ended with a whimper. The men waited until 9:30 P.M. and then fell back in the dark, working until midnight to gather their wounded. After that the darkness "was painfully silent."[39]

HOLMES

Sanborn and Boomer failed to provide the fresh manpower McClernand needed to exploit his tenuous hold on the Rebel works. Holmes's brigade accomplished nothing as well. Sent to Osterhaus, Holmes reached the left-most division of the Thirteenth Corps late in the evening. Osterhaus did nothing with the brigade because of the lateness of its arrival. McClernand's decision to send Holmes to Osterhaus essentially nullified one-third of Quinby's division, which could have been better employed elsewhere. While McClernand's biographer roundly criticizes Osterhaus for this failure to employ Holmes, the real cause of that failure must be borne by McClernand.[40]

Osterhaus ordered Holmes's brigade to take a position for the night, and the men struggled for several hours trying to find it, finally landing on a spot in the early morning hours of May 23. Osterhaus's two brigades retired under cover of darkness on the evening of May 22. The troops were "a very much discouraged body of men," reported W. F. Jones of the 42nd Ohio.[41]

When the men retired they were greeted with rations that had just arrived from the Federal landing at Chickasaw Bayou. The boxes of food were thrown from wagons onto the ground, and the men scrambled for them. "It would not have been possible to deal them out to the men," recalled Henry P. Whipple. "They were too hungry to wait."[42]

Similar feelings of hunger, frustration, and exhaustion characterized Burbridge's men after they fell back that evening. "It seems a wonder now that one of us escaped," wrote Charles F. Smith of the 83rd Ohio. Charley Palmer grew so ill under the strain that "by evening [he] was entirely senseless" and Smith and one or two comrades were compelled to take him back "in our arms, leaving our guns behind us."[43]

JRSC saw Burbridge soon after the brigade fell back, and his appearance betrayed a dire emotional state. "His eyes [were] glaring, and the perspiration standing thick upon his haggard face." It had indeed been a "miserable day" for the command. "The men came back with clothes torn and dusty, and faces blackened with powder. They had lived years in those few hours," thought JRSC. Thomas Townsend of the 23rd Wisconsin was ill in the hospital and thus missed the battle, but reports of the casualties stunned him. "It was a Murderous thing and many a hundred good and Brave men Yielded up there lives on that day," he wrote his wife. When he was informed of comrades killed and wounded, the news "was a little more than I could bear for all at once things looked dark to me and I fainted away."[44]

McClernand really mishandled the fresh troops that arrived in time to be employed in the battle of May 22. Although he knew that the only fort his men had penetrated was Railroad Redoubt, he did not direct Boomer to that spot. McClernand put a spin on his mistake, informing Grant that Quinby arrived "too late to be properly formed and successfully applied," which was stretching the truth. It is true that there were only about two hours of daylight left when Quinby reported to McClernand, but there is no reason his men could not have been employed in a more concentrated and effective way. Dividing this fine division into three parts and sending them in with no support was the worst way to use it. McClernand was "of a nervous, sensitive temperament," thought JRSC, and "seemed much depressed at the slaughter of his men." One can sympathize with McClernand's despondency at the loss of his troops, but he played a significant role in that loss.[45]

All McClernand could do now was pick up the pieces. He worried about the security of his right flank, which was still in the air, and asked McPherson to extend his left and cover it for the night. McClernand knew that Brig. Gen. John McArthur's lone brigade was on its way to his sector — McArthur had a long way to march and could not reach the Thirteenth Corps before dark. That fresh brigade could be used to extend the Thirteenth Corps line the next day, replacing the troops McPherson had extended into the gap. McClernand also sent Quinby's division back to McPherson.[46]

Thirteenth Corps losses for the day amounted to 202 men killed, 1,004 wounded, and 69 missing, for a total of 1,275 men. Osterhaus's casualties came to 180 men, while Carr suffered 709 losses and A. J. Smith counted 385. Carr's division bore the brunt of Thirteenth Corps killed, wounded, and missing because it had vigorously pressed forward against the 2nd Texas Lunette and Railroad Redoubt. Smith's supporting division suffered almost half the loss rate of Carr's.[47]

Quinby had nothing to show for his division's effort except casualties.

Sanborn lost 36 killed, 176 wounded, and 2 missing, for a total of 214. In contrast, Boomer suffered 114 casualties, and Holmes lost twelve. Quinby's total loss of 340 men was quite high considering that most of his division never got close to the enemy.[48]

McClernand frankly reported to Grant on the condition of his men. "I have had a hotly contested field all day," and every division leader informed him that troops were "exhausted by fatigue and a want of sufficient food and rest. I doubt if a considerable portion of their commands will be qualified for efficient action to-morrow." In a bizarre twist of logic, McClernand again told Grant of his idea to "mass a strong force upon some one or two points" of the enemy line if there was any thought of mounting another attack. In this letter, McClernand completely ignored his dispersal of Quinby's division only a short time before. Finally, McClernand issued a circular to his troops instructing them to hold their ground, dig in, bring up rations, and await further orders.[49]

{ 15 }

It Is Absolutely Necessary That They Be Dislodged

RECLAIMING RAILROAD
REDOUBT, MAY 22

Federal efforts to storm Vicksburg ground to a halt on the evening of May 22, but Confederate efforts to reclaim the one fort that was compromised by those attacks began to play out. Railroad Redoubt essentially was a small bit of no-man's-land. Some of its tiny garrison had fled on the initial approach of Lawler's brigade, and the rest had been captured by Sgt. Joseph E. Griffith. The Oden group's effort to restore Confederate control of the work ended in shocking failure. Neither party in the struggle tried to assert control of the fort for hours after Griffith backed out through the degraded parapet.

But a couple of dozen Federals were still ensconced in the ditch of the work. Confederate troops covered the open gorge of the redoubt so there was no true gap in the line. "It is absolutely necessary that they be dislodged," Pemberton's assistant adjutant general wrote to Forney about the Federals who had been hugging the exterior of the 2nd Texas Lunette. The same idea applied to Railroad Redoubt.[1]

The sight of Col. George B. Boomer's brigade moving across the landscape prompted Brig. Gen. Stephen D. Lee into action. As his men opened fire on the Federals, Lee told Col. Thomas N. Waul, whose Texas Legion constituted his reserve, to organize a counterattack into the redoubt. Nearly thirty years later, however, Waul tried to take credit for initiating this effort. He claimed that the 30th Alabama, which was responsible for the work, had failed to respond to Lee's repeated orders for a counterthrust. "I drew Gen'l Lee's attention" to the delay and Lee authorized him to jump-start the effort, leaving it to Waul's discretion as to whether he would use his own troops or work with the Alabamians.[2]

Waul tried to gather more glory than he deserved, for two months after the battle he reported that Lee initially ordered Col. Charles M. Shelley of the 30th Alabama and Col. Edmund W. Pettus of the 20th Alabama to take control of the redoubt. Lee also offered these units any Yankee flags they may capture in the process. When these regiments failed to respond, Lee then turned to Waul for help.[3]

On one level, it is immaterial who deserves credit for starting the final effort to reclaim Railroad Redoubt. Both Lee and Waul cooperated in it. Waul naturally turned to his own men. Two companies, under Capt. L. D. Bradley (Company B) and Lt. James Hogue (Company C), already were on the scene, positioned to the rear of the work. Both officers responded when told of the mission. Waul then suggested that Bradley choose twenty of his best men, and Hogue selected fifteen of his own, because a smaller group could better infiltrate the work without drawing fire. Waul placed Bradley in command of the special group and held the rest of his legion as a reserve. "The angle was narrow and I did not think there was fighting room for more," he wrote in 1891.[4]

A handful of additional troops now came forward to help. Three men of the 30th Alabama broke ranks with their reluctant comrades and volunteered to take part in the mission. More important, Edmund W. Pettus also stepped forth "with his belt and musket," according to Waul, to lend his aid as a guide to the group. Pettus found himself in an anomalous position. He held a commission as lieutenant colonel of the 20th Alabama, but when Col. Michael Woods of the 46th Alabama was captured at Champion Hill, Pettus was detailed to lead that regiment. Pettus knew the works around Railroad Redoubt very well, better than the Legion men, yet no one in the 20th, 30th, or even the 46th Alabama seemed interested in trying to clear them of the enemy. Pettus told Waul "that the men were worn down and exhausted and in addition were cowed by their defeat on Big Black River." Waul later thought that Pettus's sense of "chivalry and courage was no doubt much excited by the fact, that he was unable to stimulate his command to an exploit requiring less than forty men."[5]

Waul agreed to let Pettus serve as guide for Bradley. When Pettus approached Bradley to coordinate their efforts, he was immediately taken with the Texas officer. Born in Alabama, Bradley had practiced law in Dallas County in partnership with N. H. R. Dawson, whom Pettus in turn had worked with when he moved to Dallas County after Bradley left the area. Missing each other in this way before the war, the two men met for the first time under fire on the evening of May 22 when they began to coordinate the details of their counterthrust into Railroad Redoubt.[6]

One of the first things Bradley said to Pettus reflected the demoralized state of the Alabama troops. "Did you see that whole Alabama company killed trying to take it?" Bradley said, referring to the Oden group. "'Yes,' I replied; 'but the captain and all of his men were killed before they got to the back door of the redoubt,'" Pettus explained. "I expect to kill them before they know I am coming."[7]

Pettus tried to claim credit for organizing the select group of men designed to execute the thrust. In 1907, he asserted that Waul let him manage the organization of the counterattacking force. According to Pettus, when Bradley asked how many men were wanted, he told him that thirty troops were "as many as could be used in so small a place." Then Pettus authorized Bradley to count off fifteen men from the right of his company and Hogue the same with his company. It makes more sense that Waul would have made the decision as to how many men should constitute the party given that he, rather than Pettus, commanded the legion. Giving preference to Waul's account, a total of forty-one men would essay the dangerous task of retaking Railroad Redoubt. They were ready to start by 5:30 P.M.[8]

COUNTERATTACK

Pettus devised a plan to cover his party's approach until it could spring into the "corner section" of the fort, the small enclosure whose angle had been breached and which Griffith's party had entered. Pettus led the men along the connecting infantry line south of the redoubt. They crouched so as not to be seen by watchful Yankees. When he got to the southwest corner of the redoubt, where the connecting line attached to the work, he and Bradley stopped to allow the line to close up on their position. Then, according to his prearranged signal, Pettus dropped a red bandanna to tell the Texans posted along the open gorge of the work to stop firing.[9]

As soon as they had done so, Pettus sprang into the enclosure and raced for the eastern end of the work at 5:50 P.M. The enclosure was empty, but there were a number of Federals in the ditch where the breach had been opened. As Pettus neared he could see them, but they hardly noticed him or his party. "They had their heads down to avoid the firing" by Waul's men at the gorge and still had not raised them up to look around. "Not one of our assaulting party was scratched," Pettus remembered years later. Lee recalled, however, that three Confederates were wounded, but none killed, in the endeavor. Taking position close to the breach, Pettus called on the Federals to give up and many of them did so. He gathered up three officers and thirty-three enlisted men.[10]

The Confederates also secured the flag of the 77th Illinois, but the Federals saved the other colors planted nearby. Cpl. Isaac H. Carmen of the 48th Ohio saw Pettus's men and reacted quickly enough to grab the regimental colors before they could reach the flag. He was unable to snatch the regimental flag of the 77th Illinois. Carmen threw his body in the ditch of the redoubt so hurriedly that he ran accidentally into the bayonet of a comrade in his own company. The bayonet inflicted a nasty wound, penetrating the small part of his thigh. "I had enough presence of mind to run the shaft of the flag into the dust and hang on to it," he later recalled of the 48th Ohio color. His friends managed to get him into the ditch, take out the bayonet, and secure the flag in the process. They later carried him back to the Federal line.[11]

Pettus had conceived and executed a good plan to get his small party into the empty part of the fort with minimal losses. Oden's mistake had been to advance from the gorge in the open against a fresh enemy. That had been several hours before Pettus's counterattack. By late afternoon the Federals were exhausted and their spirits had considerably waned. Their only thought was to hang on, crouching in the ditch, and Pettus took them completely by surprise. He "won the admiration of every one by his daring on May 22," Lee reported two months later. "Too much praise cannot be awarded to every-one engaged in" the effort.[12]

The Texans who composed most of the men Pettus led into the enclosure certainly agreed with Lee. "As soon as anything could be heard," Pettus wrote more than forty years later, a man of Bradley's Company B who wore "buckskin breeches" called out, "What fellow was that brought us into this hell's hole?" Bradley refused to say. "I move we elect him a Texan, name or no name, rank or no rank," continued the buckskinned Texan. When Bradley called for a vote, everyone agreed. "So I was unanimously elected a Texan," Pettus mused, "the greatest honor I have ever received, although I have had many beyond my deserving."[13]

"The angle is carried and the enemy's colors taken," Lee reported to Carter L. Stevenson. "It was a gallant affair." But Lee was also frank in reporting that the victory was not complete. A significant number of Federals still huddled in the ditch of Railroad Redoubt farther north of the breach in the southeast angle and on ground near the redoubt. In fact, McClernand's artillery opened a concentrated fire on the enclosure now that it was obvious that the Confederates occupied it. With shells falling within a few feet of the huddled Yankees in the ditch, Pettus called on his men to take cover. For fifteen to twenty minutes, Federal gunners spent their frustration at the turn of events, but they apparently brought down no Confederates. At least the barrage forced the Pettus group to pause rather than seek ways to get the rest of the Federals out of the ditch.[14]

But the guns could not keep the Confederates at bay forever. When the barrage ended Waul took action to clear the ditch. He sent two companies of his legion to move forward into the work and fill it with more troops. "Many of the men mounted the parapet and fired into the ditch," he reported, "subjecting themselves to the aim of its occupants and the concentrated fire from the enemy's lines." Col. James W. Gillespie's 43rd Tennessee, dispatched at noon from Col. Alexander W. Reynolds's Brigade of Stevenson's Division, supported these two companies of Waul's Legion.[15]

Firing into the ditch alone did not clear the Yankees. Only when Waul's men began to use ten-pound shells as hand grenades did the final act in the long drama at Railroad Redoubt begin. Jesse Sawyer and his comrades were preparing to leave the ditch, when the first few shells rolled in. They killed a couple of men "and nearly paralyzed the rest of us." When Rebel voices asked if they wished to surrender, the Federals said yes. "We were fished out of the ditch by the Confederates," Sawyer recalled.[16]

As some Federals called out their willingness to surrender, many of their comrades broke out of the ditch and ran toward the Union line. Members of the 48th Ohio and 77th Illinois fell back only a short distance—Lt. Col. Lysander R. Webb of the latter regiment thought it was no more than twelve feet. Webb credited "the prompt action" of his officers with steadying the men for the next couple of hours. According to one source, some spades and shovels were brought up and the men started to dig in but then received an order at 10:00 P.M. to retire to the Union line.[17]

A number of Federals were captured in the ditch. Joseph Griffith believed that about fifteen members of the 22nd Iowa fell into Confederate hands, including Lt. Col. Harvey Graham, who had been wounded. Col. Charles L. Harris of the 11th Wisconsin remembered that Graham asked his men to surrender with him but many refused. Harris placed the number of captives at twenty-eight men of the 21st and 22nd Iowa. J. D. Harwell, a member of Lee's brigade staff, estimated that thirty Federals were captured in the ditch of Railroad Redoubt, while Jesse Sawyer put the number at twenty-five of his regimental comrades and fifteen from other regiments. Pettus tabulated the number as three officers and thirty-three enlisted men. The Confederates also found the regimental flag of the 22nd Iowa lying in the ditch and took possession of it. Waul credited Lt. Col. James Wrigley with retrieving this color, which had been flying for hours over the redoubt, but apparently no Union soldier took responsibility for it in the rushed retreat. A total of at least fifty-one Federals had been captured in the Confederate effort to reclaim Railroad Redoubt.[18]

Included in the haul were two more Union flags. Pettus's initial charge secured the national colors of the 77th Illinois. The staff of the regiment's other color, the state flag, had earlier been shot in two, and it fell into the ditch. Some men claimed the Federals buried it in the floor of the ditch during the Union bombardment that followed Pettus's counterattack, but Sawyer thought it was covered when part of the scarp fell in. "We are in hopes to get it yet," Lysander Webb asserted two days later.[19]

Lee was so proud of his men's achievement in reclaiming Railroad Redoubt that he wanted to reward them with the captured colors. Pettus sent the flag of the 77th Illinois to Waul, who forwarded it to Lee with a note about its capture. Lee sent the flag to Stevenson with a note of his own. "It was as gallant an act as I have ever seen during the war. I have pledged myself to give it to its captors. I beg that you and general Pemberton will bear me out." Lee sent the message and the flag with Lt. H. N. Martin, an acting aide, who had been wounded. Stevenson supported Lee's request when he sent the flag to Pemberton's headquarters. What became of this color, which Waul described as "a rich and heavy silk flag and finely decorated," is a mystery. One story had it that, after the fall of Vicksburg, Pemberton told an officer of the 77th Illinois that it was so battered and torn his staff members discarded it as worthless. Veterans of the 77th Illinois searched for information about its whereabouts but without luck. Waul also sent the captured flag of the 22nd Iowa up the chain of command.[20]

Just after dark, Pemberton and Maj. Samuel H. Lockett visited Railroad Redoubt. They were pleased at the resolution of the crisis and issued orders for the fort to be repaired that night. Waul and his staff also visited the redoubt. Pemberton reviewed Pettus's attacking party as a way to show respect for their deed.[21]

EVENING OF MAY 22

As dusk descended, all elements of McClernand's corps lodged forward of the Union line now returned. The left wing of the 22nd Iowa, positioned a short distance south of Railroad Redoubt, waited until darkness allowed each man to fall back. "Many of us got a parting shot," recalled Samuel C. Jones. The first thing they did was look for food because they had had eaten nothing since early morning. Jim Sterling, the regimental quartermaster, made sure rations were readily available for everyone.[22]

"The outlines of our faces were pale and rigid," recalled Jones. "Our hearts were sad, many friends had fallen since morn, and the end was not yet. After washing our dirt and powder stained faces, and eating supper, we strolled together, one after another, and went into camp for the night."[23]

Other units also fell back in the twilight. Members of the 11th Wisconsin in Lawler's brigade collected their wounded until midnight, but they left the dead on the field. Charles L. Harris, commander of the 11th, was surprised to find members of the 97th Illinois who had hidden in a ravine all day instead of supporting their comrades. "They informed me 'that they knew too much to go into that charge,'" he later wrote.[24]

Col. David Shunk's group, consisting of the right wing of the 8th Indiana and Companies A, C, D, G, and I of the 33rd Illinois, fell back under cover of night. "This has been a sad day for the 33d as well as for this whole army," Cpl. Charles E. Wilcox mused in his diary. Of the 250 men in these companies, plus Company E, which went in with the 99th Illinois, seventy-five men had been killed and wounded. Company E, along with the 99th Illinois, also fell back that evening. Col. George W. K. Bailey's 99th Illinois lost 103 men out of 300 engaged in the action, amounting to a loss ratio of a little more than one-third.[25]

The failed assault had exacted a high price. Lawler's brigade suffered 54 killed, 285 wounded, and 29 missing for a total of 368 men. The 22nd Iowa suffered the most: 164 casualties, which represented the highest regimental loss in Grant's army that day. The 21st Iowa lost 113 men. The 77th Illinois in Col. William J. Landram's brigade took 275 men into action and lost 114 killed, wounded, and missing for a loss ratio of 41.4 percent.[26]

CLEANING UP AT THE 2ND TEXAS LUNETTE

As day turned into dusk, Col. Ashbel Smith worked to clear up the area around the 2nd Texas Lunette. He estimated that at least 400 Federals had fallen within range of his fort. "The ground in our front and along the road, and either side of the road for several hundred yards way to the right, was thickly strewn with their dead." In several places "two and three dead bodies were piled on each other. Along the road for more than 200 yards the bodies lay so thick that one might have walked the whole distance on them without touching the ground."[27]

The Confederates came into possession of two stands of Union colors near the 2nd Texas Lunette. Those of the 99th Illinois fell into their hands because of the single-minded effort of color-bearer Cpl. Thomas J. Higgins to keep going no matter what happened. The other flag has not been identified.[28]

After dusk, Smith sent details to pick up abandoned small arms, securing about 200 rifles before dawn. These men reported that the Federals had dug many small holes in the glacis of the work during the course of the day. These holes became their slim protection from enemy fire. Maj. George W. L. Fly organized details to fill in the holes as a way of maintaining the integrity of the work. The Confederates also placed twenty-seven bodies of slain Federals in the holes before covering them up.[29]

The 2nd Texas suffered relatively few casualties on May 22. According to Cpl. Charles I. Evans, seventeen men were lost inside the lunette and a handful in the connecting lines north and south of the work. Alex Frazier of Company E recorded that the 2nd Texas lost twelve killed and thirty-nine wounded.[30]

As the defending party, the Confederates along McClernand's sector lost fewer troops than the Federals. In the 31st Alabama, for example, one man named J. W. Carroll in Company K was killed. Two men were assigned the duty of carrying his body to the rear for burial after dark. One of them, William Lewis Roberts, remembered the trip because he and the other man could hardly see where to step. They "fell in a ravine with [Carroll's body] on top of us[;] we had to go down it to the distance of 3 hundred yards before we could get him out" of the ravine. Finally, after an awful struggle, they delivered Carroll's body to the burial detail well to the rear.[31]

The Confederates could count themselves lucky that the fortunes of war favored them on May 22. Firing continued on many parts of the line until darkness put an end to it; then "all quiet at these points now," Forney told Pemberton. "We still hold our position," wrote William Lowery of the 20th Alabama in his diary, and "hope God will help us to continue to hold it until some relief comes."[32]

{ 16 }

An Ardent Desire to Participate in the Capture of Vicksburg

GRANT, PEMBERTON, PORTER, and McARTHUR, MAY 22

Fought at key points along the line of Confederate works, the battle of May 22 took place in an environment that maximized people's ability to see the action. It was fought on a largely open arena of bare ridgetops that offered stunning sights of combat. Observers located at many different places not only saw but heard the fierce fighting.

Some of those observers were Federal signal officers assigned the task of reporting the course of events. William J. Pittenger of the 93rd Illinois had been detached to the Signal Corps and spent the day peering at the battle through field glasses. He "could see the Rebel Sharp Shooters in their forts" and ducked whenever Confederate guns sent a shell or two over his signal post. "Was in a Position to see the fighting going on," Pittenger confided to his diary, "which was desperate."[1]

Other observers had little to do with the action but were spectators of the drama. Alfred A. Rigby of the 24th Iowa was detached from his regiment to guard a cattle herd to the rear of Grant's line. Late in the day he joined a group of comrades who gained a spot where "we had a fine view of the fight in progress. Stayed until the time we were admonished by the close proximity of stray shots to seek safer quarters."[2]

Another sightseer was Lt. Aquilla Standifird of the 23rd Iowa, who took a break from guarding prisoners at Young's Point to join a group that walked along Grant's Canal to its southern end. From there they had a good view of Porter's gunboats as the vessels bombarded Vicksburg. "The rebs would send Shell at the Boats Striking the water or coming across in the timber which made it necessary to keep back of the levee. Looked until tired and returned to Camp." Anson R. Butler, ward master on the hospital boat *Nashville*, did more than just sight-see. He joined two surgeons, a major, and a woman on a picnic at the end of De Soto Point, where they obtained a good vantage point to observe Porter's fleet in action. "We took a bottle of wine and something to eat and had a picnic dinner in a good shade there. I saw more than if I had been in the fight," Butler reported.[3]

For those men positioned too far from the action to see it, the sound of combat carried far enough to reach many ears. Alexander McDonald of the 33rd Wisconsin heard the artillery firing eight miles away while stationed at Haynes' Bluff, and Henry H. Boynton of the 28th Iowa also heard it at the Big Black River Bridge. Federal soldiers at various locations around Vicksburg heard many rumors about the progress of the fight, casualties suffered, and prisoners taken. Far away from the battlefield, a report that Vicksburg had fallen to Grant gained wide currency in some Northern towns. "To-day nearly every public building and many private ones have the United States flag displayed," declared a newspaper correspondent in Springfield, Illinois, on May 25. "The Copperheads say it is a d——d Republican lie."[4]

GRANT

Not only was Grant positioned to see, hear, and probably smell the battle smoke, but he also shouldered the responsibility of gauging how far to press the attack. He bore that awesome weight stoically. George D. Reynolds of Battery K, 2nd Illinois Light Artillery, had been detached from his company as an aide to an officer on Grant's staff. Reynolds had ample opportunity to observe the army leader. "He made no comment, expressed neither chagrin or anger," when reports of Federal failure came streaming into the command post.[5]

Grant projected outward calm but his mind, of course, was working. At one point during the day he wrote to Sherman asking if he thought mining the salient at Stockade Redan would work. "I am sending after powder and expect to have it here some time during the night." In short, Grant was thinking of the next step to be taken after admitting that the attacks had failed.[6]

Pemberton did not go forward to observe the action and thus relied on a stream of dispatches sent him by division commanders. Maj. Gen. John H. Forney tended to write much more than anyone else, and his short messages were accurate and to the point. He kept Pemberton informed of enemy attacks and spelled out the disposition of reserve units. "The men are standing to the work," he informed headquarters at one point. During the course of May 22, Maj. Gen. John S. Bowen sent a message to his headquarters spelling out how many men he had in his division. It amounted to 2,569 effectives plus 100 servants.[7]

There also was a stream of dispatches emanating from Pemberton's headquarters at 1018 Crawford Street. He tended to worry more about a major Federal push along Jackson Road than along Graveyard Road. Pemberton warned Maj. Gen. Martin L. Smith that, in addition to Bowen's division, acting as a reserve, he might have to pull one or two of his regiments out of line to reinforce a threatened point. Bowen and Smith shifted units about during the day in response to perceived needs. Often the men simply marched to those points, fired a couple of rounds, and then realized there was no need for them after all. There certainly was an air of anxiety in Pemberton's messages. His handling of reserve forces probably was the best he could do under the circumstances, but some Confederate soldiers complained about fruitless marching about.[8]

In the end, Pemberton and his staff were quite satisfied with the results of the day. "They came up in good style," the department commander noted in his diary, "but were repulsed with heavy loss." Not every Confederate soldier covered himself with laurels. Martin L. Smith ordered Brig. Gen. John C. Vaughn to detail two men from each of his Tennessee regiments "to gather to your command all stragglers in town or the vicinity."[9]

PORTER AND THE NAVY

The navy tried to support Grant's attack, but the best aid Porter could offer was of a logistical nature. His boats transported Col. William Hall's brigade of Brig. Gen. John McArthur's division, Seventeenth Corps, across the Mississippi by early morning of May 22. Hall then operated along the east bank of the river toward the southern end of Pemberton's line. Porter laid out a plan to attack the river batteries early that day, forcing one after another to respond to his bombardment and then silencing them. "The Army attacks the town at 10 o'clock to-morrow," he told Lt. Cdr. James A. Greer on May 21, "and we must, with our small force, be heard from."[10]

In fact, if Greer could spare USS *Benton*, USS *Mound City*, and USS *Carondelet* during the night of May 21–22, Porter wanted him to begin bombing Vicksburg in the dark. Greer was to steam in as close as possible and "throw in rapid broadsides and bow guns without any particular aim, and not too high. Keep dropping down and going ahead to shift position." He was to fire rapidly for an hour and reduce to moderate fire during the whole night, "so as to annoy the enemy all we can before the attack in the morning." Greer did a little of what he was told. He sent the *Benton* up at 1:00 A.M. to fire only twenty-four rounds before dropping back. The boat received one or two rounds of return fire, which did no damage.[11]

In addition to the *Benton*'s work, Porter managed to get six of his mortar boats to fire into Vicksburg during the night of May 21–22. Then he began to bombard the town from 9:30 A.M. to 10:30 A.M. with the mortars. The *Mound City* started to fire on the river batteries located opposite the southern end of Grant's Canal by 7:00 A.M. and was joined by the *Benton*, *Tuscumbia*, and *Carondelet* an hour later. These four ironclads silenced the guns at South Fort and most of the pieces at Widow Blakely Battery, although Porter admitted that the *Mound City* was responsible for most of the success.[12]

After that, the *Benton*, *Mound City*, and *Carondelet* steamed farther upriver to engage the Marine Hospital Battery, leaving the *Tuscumbia* behind to watch that the pieces at South Fort and Widow Blakely Battery did not resume firing. The three boats stood 450 yards from the Marine Hospital Battery and pounded it for more than two hours, taking heavy return fire all the time. After a while, the *Tuscumbia* also steamed up to support the other vessels at a distance of 800 yards from the target. A Confederate round hit the pilothouse on the *Tuscumbia*. Other rounds loosened bolts that allowed iron plates to shift and jam gunports at the vessel's forward battery. The *Tuscumbia* therefore broke contact and steamed downriver. Porter ordered the other three vessels to do the same.[13]

It had been a sharp fight with blows felt by both sides. The *Benton* was engaged from 8:23 A.M. to 10:40 A.M., firing 283 rounds in that time. Of 430 rounds fired by the Confederate heavy guns that day, thirteen hit the *Benton*. Four of those Confederate rounds struck the boat at the waterline. "At first the vessel leaked some," reported Greer, "but we have it now completely under control." No one was hurt on board. The *Carondelet* also was hit by two rounds, one of which tore out ten feet of planking dangerously close to the waterline. The *Mound City*, which was engaged longer than any other vessel, received sixteen hits and suffered bent iron plates and damage to two guns and had some equipment destroyed. Four men on board were wounded. The *Tuscumbia* suffered considerable damage to its "fighting pilot house" when a Rebel round hit it.[14]

"I have an ardent desire to participate in the capture of Vicksburg," Acting Lt. John McLeod Murphy of the *Carondelet* told Porter, but he admitted his ship needed repair and maintenance work. The river battle of May 22 was among the more severe naval actions to be seen in the Vicksburg campaign. The four gunboats mounted a total of forty-six pieces and fired at least 508 rounds at three forts. They received return fire from fourteen Confederate pieces in those forts. Three Rebel guns, including the famous Whistling Dick, were temporarily disabled during the fight, and the Rebels lost two men wounded. For that, Porter's boats endured a total of thirty-four hits and five men wounded.[15]

At best one can say that Porter's attack was a tactical draw that failed to help Grant's infantry assault. Col. Edward Higgins, commander of the river batteries, had ample artillery and gunners deployed in good earthworks; this Confederate sector could take care of itself.

But Pemberton could not prevent the Federals from dropping rounds into the city of Vicksburg. There had been no naval action from the upper Union fleet on May 22, but the mortar boats firing from the river just north of town damaged buildings, stressed the people, and seemed unstoppable. The entire crew of the gunboat *Signal* had been detailed to man the mortar boats the night before, and "they enjoyed the work very much," according to Symmes E. Browne. Grant's artillery east of town also fired into Vicksburg. In fact, Porter contended after the war that his sailors could distinctly hear "the shriek of the shells from the army field-pieces" when the roar of the naval guns paused. Some Confederates were astonished to realize they were hemmed in by enemy fire. "We are penned in two miles square and are fighting all around," declared surgeon Joseph Dill Alison. "If this is not a hot place, I hope I may never see one."[16]

Unlike the soldiers, the civilians had to endure this cross fire without fighting back. Their coping strategy was to seek shelter in the earth. Dentist Rowland Chambers stayed in his house early on May 22 until a shell exploded in the backyard. Then he scampered to a cave and stayed there until the shelling slackened enough to come out. Civilians were hit, although the exact number is unknown. A Confederate deserter told Grant's staff that 109 women and children had been killed by mortar shells by May 28, but that was probably an exaggerated report based on rumor rather than calculation.[17]

The only direct aid Porter could give Grant's plan was to assist the movement of McArthur's men up the east bank of the Mississippi. At 2:00 P.M. Porter assured Grant that McArthur's infantry had advanced to within striking distance of South Fort. Porter frankly told Grant that his gun crews were exhausted, he wanted to save ammunition, and the Marine Hospital Battery was "a hard nut to crack." Later that evening, he reported that his sailors were "much used up, but we will bombard all we can. There is no danger of our firing into you, as we know exactly where you are."[18]

Sherman was keen on getting the navy to cooperate with the army. He urged Grant on May 22 to have Porter bring the gunboats that were positioned north of Vicksburg in to shore and help Maj. Gen. Frederick Steele clear the Confederates from the bluffs. He suggested Grant send a staff officer to consult with Porter and feed the naval officer information about his position. "A gunboat fleet should attend each flank of our army," Sherman continued, "and his mortars should come within easy range and drop shell by the thousand in the city."[19]

Apparently Sherman was unaware that Porter already was doing most of what he suggested, except using gunboats as fire support for Steele. Grant informed Porter that his grand assault had failed. Later in the day he adjusted his earlier report to assure Porter that some Federal troops had gained a foothold in a couple of Rebel forts. His attack was "not an entire failure." He relayed the gist of Sherman's suggestions and begged Porter to employ every gunboat and mortar boat "to bear upon the city."[20]

In explaining his operations on May 22, Porter argued that the swift current of the Mississippi was too much for his underpowered gunboats. They could not deal with it and with Confederate fire at the same time and became "perfect targets for the enemy." But he felt obliged to tell Grant, "I fought the batteries one hour and a half longer than you asked me to do." Porter told Secretary of the Navy Gideon Welles that the army had "terrible work before them, and are fighting as well as soldiers ever fought before, but the works are stronger than any of us dreamed of."[21]

The navy played only a marginal role in the battles of May 19 and 22 through no fault of Porter's. There were severe limitations to his resources and his opportunities. The army generals did not arrange a major push along the riverbank. Sherman himself suggested Steele attack a mile and a half from the riverbank on the far left of the division's sector rather than on the far right, and Grant had placed no more than one brigade of McArthur's division on the riverbank south of Vicksburg. Although he urged McArthur to push that brigade forward, McArthur's force was too small to accomplish much.

Porter managed to silence the Rebel guns in South Fort, but those guns were heavy pieces trained on the river and could not have been used to fire on McArthur. Moreover, the Confederates had substantial infantry forces to protect South Fort and the southern approach to Vicksburg that could bar the Federal infantry's progress.

MCARTHUR

Whether McArthur could contend with the forts and the Rebels who manned them remained to be seen. Hall's Iowa brigade had been shifted to various points for several days before marching across De Soto Point to Bowers' Landing, where Porter's boats transported it across the river to Warrenton on the night of May 21. The Confederates had earlier abandoned Warrenton, located about three miles south of Vicksburg, so the lodgment was uncontested.[22]

With McArthur along to direct his movements, Hall set out early on May 22 and reached the Confederate picket line by 9:00 A.M. He detailed five companies of the 16th Iowa to skirmish and drive the enemy pickets back, dispatching the other five companies of the 16th Iowa to cover his right wing and flank. Making steady progress, the Federals came within range of four Confederate batteries by 11:00 A.M., an hour after Grant had launched his grand assault. Hall then established an aggressive stance. He advanced his skirmish line until it was as close as forty yards from the Rebel works. Hall also sent out several companies from the 11th Iowa, 13th Iowa, and 16th Iowa to act as sharpshooters, pinning the Rebels down in their works. He then waited for orders.[23]

Brig. Gen. Seth M. Barton's Brigade of Georgia troops opposed Hall's advance. "Enemy advancing in force on the Warrenton road," Barton told division leader Maj. Gen. Carter L. Stevenson. When Stevenson forwarded the message to Pemberton, the department commander tersely told Barton, "I can only say to you to hold the place."[24]

As events transpired, the Confederates had little need for worry. McArthur hesitated before pushing on. He scouted the terrain and prepared to attack with the 11th Iowa in the lead. But McClernand's effort to find fresh troops influenced affairs along the Warrenton Road. Grant had not forgotten

Grant, Pemberton, Porter, and McArthur, May 22

McArthur; he had authorized McClernand to call on him for help. But some-time during the day Grant reneged on the offer and encouraged McArthur to push his drive along the Warrenton Road. Grant knew there was a possibility that Maj. Gen. Nathaniel P. Banks might bring his troops up from the vicinity of Port Hudson and could arrive as early as May 23. If so, Banks and Hall would constitute a force big enough to break through the Rebel line.[25]

But Grant's views conflicted with those of McClernand, who wrote an urgent request to McArthur for help. McArthur canceled all attack plans in favor of sending Hall eastward.[26]

Porter believed that McArthur was not very serious about attacking along the Warrenton Road anyway. He told Grant that McArthur had advanced too cautiously before McClernand's plea arrived. The Iowa troops "were seen straggling along the top of the hills," he told his army colleague. "I think we lost a fine chance" to break through the Confederate line, Porter wrote Grant the next day. He exaggerated a bit when asserting that "it is a pity they did not assault, for they would have taken the place without any trouble, as there were not 20 men in it." Porter referred to South Fort, the most visible portion of the Confederate line south of Vicksburg. "It is the most important fort along that range of hills," he continued, "[and] commands the big rifle-gun fort [Widow Blakely Battery], which we damaged and silenced, and the latter commands the rest of the batteries."[27]

To be fair to McArthur, Porter had a good view of the riverbank but no view of what lay a few hundred yards beyond it. McArthur's front was the width of Hall's brigade, and thus his zone of responsibility extended beyond the riverbank. Porter ignored the fact that Barton's Brigade, in size probably equal to Hall's command, barred the way. Moreover, Porter did not take into account that McArthur had to contend with more than just South Fort.

Also to McArthur's credit, he did not respond to McClernand's first message for help because it contradicted his instructions from Grant. When a second message arrived, and another dispatch from Grant authorized him to respond to the Thirteenth Corps commander, McArthur sent Hall east along a system of roads a bit after dusk. But the Iowans had to move about eight miles along dimly understood roads, and the day was fast ebbing away. The brigade did not even make it to McClernand that night, for it stopped to bivouac after marching only four miles. Hall's command finally reached McClernand's headquarters at 10:00 A.M. on May 23. Ironically, Hall failed to help the Thirteenth Corps and failed to attack South Fort. All the blame for this has to rest on McClernand for insisting that the brigade move such a long distance to his sector.[28]

Of course, there is no guarantee that Hall would have succeeded if he had attacked South Fort. As Porter noted, it would have been better if at least two brigades, rather than one, had advanced along the Warrenton Road. But veterans of Hall's brigade felt for the rest of their lives that they had a good chance of breaking Barton's line if they had been ordered to try. At least Hall suffered light losses — only one man killed and two wounded.[29]

There was little that men outside of the Federal line fronting Lockett's earthworks could do to make Grant's attack a success. Porter's resources were geared for river action and could not overpower the well-sited water batteries. McArthur's small command was too far away from McClernand for effective support. Grant's attack columns had to rely on their own resources, and Pemberton's men, huddled in well-sited earthworks, were able to stop those columns without interference from outside forces. Men along the periphery of the scene of action mostly watched, listened, and wondered as the drama of May 22 unfolded.

{ 17 }

I Feel Sad but Not Discouraged

MAKING SENSE OF MAY 22

After a day of frenzied action, survivors of the battle of May 22 turned to evaluating what had happened and making conclusions about the significance of its outcome. This process was most intense among the defeated Federals, but it also took place among the successful Confederates. An important fallout of the failed attacks was a worsening relationship between Grant and his troublesome commander of the Thirteenth Corps; this led to McClernand's dismissal. Grant also had to accept that storming Vicksburg was no longer an option, at least for the foreseeable future. Siege operations were the only recourse, even though Johnston still hovered around Jackson with an unknown force, presumably getting ready to pounce on the Federals and save Vicksburg.

EVALUATING MAY 22 — THE FEDERALS

The immediate results of Grant's offensive on May 22 were clear and decisive. Everyone knew the assaults had failed and in many cases with high casualties. When Grant's men surveyed the battlefield on May 23, the sight of hundreds of bodies greeted their vision. "It looks awfull dead all around, some heads off Some legs off Arms off by canon Balls," wrote Capt. Henry Schmidt of the 37th Ohio.[1]

Yet Federals in position of authority tended to put a good deal of spin on the situation. "Our army is in the best spirits," reported Charles A. Dana to the secretary of war, "though impatient at the delays. Our position was somewhat though not much improved by the day's operations." In fact, Col. Manning F. Force of the 20th Ohio woke up on May 23 assuming that another assault would be made that morning. "The 20th will run against a brick wall, if ordered, and stand against it till shot down," he asserted in a letter to a family friend.[2]

Initial reports in Northern newspapers proclaimed that Vicksburg had fallen, but that false news soon was corrected. While some midwestern newspapers put a positive spin on the results of May 22, others frankly reported the lack of success. Before long, Federal assessments of May 22 fully admitted the day's failure. No one in the ranks pretended it was anything other than "a useless expenditure of life." Lt. John Reese could only refer to the battle of May 22 as "a Slaughter" because his 81st Illinois suffered so much and did so little. In fact, it was not until June 4 that Reese reported his regiment had "nearly Recovered from the Repulse of the 22nd." Henry Ankeny of the 4th Iowa asserted that "no one had any confidence in the successful end of the assault, but it has satisfied our generals that the enemy works cannot be taken by storm."[3]

Grant's first dispatch to Henry Halleck in Washington admitted that the attack "was not entirely successful. We hold possession, however, of two of the enemy's forts, and have skirmishers close under all of them. Our loss was not severe." That day, even before the battle had completely stopped, Grant told Halleck that he would have to besiege the place. In a burst of incredible optimism, Grant estimated it would take no more than a week to capture it. His only worry was Joseph E. Johnston. "I learn that Jeff Davis has promised that if the garrison can hold out for fifteen days he will send 100,000 men, if he has to evacuate Tennessee to do it."[4]

Grant's headquarters issued instructions on May 23 that "any further assault on the enemy's works will for the present cease." Grant now adopted a plan to minimize casualties. "I intend to lose no more men," he told David D. Porter, "but to force the enemy from one position to another without exposing my troops."[5]

Grant ordered McClernand to return the units sent to him the day before. As a result, Brig. Gen. Isaac F. Quinby's battered division marched back to the Seventeenth Corps. Col. William Hall's brigade reached McClernand's headquarters at 10:00 A.M. on May 23 and rested awhile. When Grant came to the area and saw Brig. Gen. John McArthur, he was surprised to find the Iowa brigade here rather than on the Warrenton Road. John A. Rawlins, Grant's assistant adjutant general, reminded Grant that he had given McClernand

Making Sense of May 22

authority to call on McArthur, but that did not help his mood very much. "Go back to where you came from," Grant told McArthur, "and hereafter obey no orders in future, except from your own Corps Commander or myself." Grant then referred to McClernand when he told Rawlins, "We can never succeed with such insubordinate officers." McArthur interjected his own view, "saying that I wished I had had that order yesterday, that we had lost the best opportunity along the whole line." Hall started on the trek back to the Warrenton Road, reaching his former position by 4:30 P.M.[6]

Porter supported the pending siege operations. "I sent you all the powder I had today and 200 feet of safety fuse," he told Grant. "If you want more, telegraph and I will send it." He also relayed the news that Maj. Gen. Nathaniel P. Banks would not join him after all. Instead, Banks was using Grant's boats to ferry his army across the Mississippi and attack Port Hudson. Most of Porter's gunboats were below Vicksburg and it was impossible to push them against the current, pass the river batteries, and support Sherman's infantry north of the city. But Porter made sure his mortar boats, which were already north of the city, would help. "Depend that I am doing everything that can be done with my small means."[7]

Grant continued to interpret the fighting on May 22 in further dispatches to Halleck. He estimated Pemberton's numbers at 10,000 to 20,000 men and noted the natural strength of the Confederate position, arguing that his troops "simply failed to enter the works of the enemy." On May 24, he also informed Washington authorities that McClernand's repeated calls for support led the other corps to renew their efforts in the afternoon and the result doubled Union casualties.[8]

It was not until May 25 that Grant issued general orders for the Army of the Tennessee to "commence the work of reducing the enemy by regular approaches." While communicating with Benjamin M. Prentiss, who commanded the garrison of Helena, Arkansas, Grant admitted it would take some time to reduce the fortress, "contrary to my expectations when I first arrived near it."[9]

In his official report and memoirs, Grant continued to justify the attack on May 22 as a better way to capture Vicksburg than initiating siege approaches. Its failure therefore served a purpose. "The troops being now fully awake to the necessity of [conducting a siege], [they] worked diligently and cheerfully." He displayed a striking lack of awareness of his men's emotions for, as we have seen, many Federals had no confidence that the attack would succeed.[10]

The Federals were happy to resort to siege approaches after May 22, but that does not mean they needed the pain of failure to convince them a siege was necessary. Col. Thomas Kilby Smith thought Lockett's earthworks were "masterpieces of skill in military engineering" that could only be reduced by sapping. "I hope they will not sacrifice any more life by Storming," wrote Capt. William Z. Clayton of the 1st Minnesota Battery. The consensus in Union ranks was that all officers had learned their lesson on that score.[11]

Despite the bloody repulse of May 22, the overwhelming majority of Federals retained a strong and abiding faith in Grant's leadership. "The Soldiers have all Confidence in our *Generals*," asserted Orin England of the 72nd Ohio. The basis of that confidence rested on Grant's brilliant handling of the march from Port Gibson to the Big Black River. A strange rumor circulated through Federal ranks on May 24 that Pemberton had offered to surrender on the condition that his men could march away without interference but Grant refused. He "will not be Satisfied without an unconditional Surrender of evry thing," asserted Captain Clayton.[12]

Whether by assault or siege, Grant's men were sure Vicksburg would fall in the near future. "I feel sad but not discouraged," wrote Hiram J. Lewis of the 11th Wisconsin. "We will have the town yet. It is only a question of time. We work, work, work, but feel that it is amounting to something and our one desire is to see this thing put through." Clayton told his mother that "the fate of Vicksburg is sealed. We will have it God, justice and Liberty must prevail."[13]

As time offered them a longer perspective to evaluate the attack of May 22, many Federals criticized the tactics employed. To them, the assault seemed to be a huge reconnaissance based on inadequate knowledge about the Confederate position. They were not impressed by the minimal planning that underlay the effort and wondered that the casualties were not heavier.[14]

Many men thought Grant should have massed an entire corps to bust through one section of the enemy works. Still others preferred extended lines rather than massed columns or thought scaling ladders should have been provided for everyone. Other men blamed the breakdown in coordination that left many units unsupported at critical moments, while some criticized bad small-arms and artillery ammunition. Granville McDonald of the 30th Illinois wished Grant had not announced the attack to his troops the day before. It produced a lot of worry, "thinking that the 22nd of May would probably be their last." Inevitably, some Federals blamed everything on liquor-loving generals but did not name anyone.[15]

A number of Federals cited the landscape as a major factor in the battle. "The area all around is Switzerland, as many who could know call it," remarked Lt. Henry A. Kircher of the largely German 12th Missouri. Brig. Gen. Hugh Ewing also blamed the terrain for the failure of his brigade to take Stockade Redan. "Charging Fortifications looks very Romantic on paper and will do to read about," asserted Clark Wright of the 6th Missouri Cavalry, "but it is quite a different thing, when you come to the practical part of it."[16]

There was plenty of postbattle analysis but one unanimous verdict: no more storming. "From any more charges or assaults — Good Lord deliver us!" wrote Maj. Edward Jesup Wood of the 48th Indiana. "I don't think another will be attempted." Edwin A. Loosley of the 81st Illinois agreed. "We got such of whipping the last time that I guess our leaders had enough of that kind of a business."[17]

Despite their clear view of May 22 as a bloody failure, the rank and file refused to openly blame Grant for it. In fact, higher-ranking officers and staff members tended to justify his decision to assault. He "would have been called all sorts of names for being slow and over cautious," thought Capt. David Herrick Gile, one of McPherson's aides. "We none of us believed the enemy would make a very vigorous defense." Grant's staff members supported their chief's decision to attack by arguing that the army was not yet ready to conduct siege approaches on May 22. Several men noted that Johnston posed an ominous threat to the Federal army. Many soldiers understood that Grant seemed to have a golden opportunity to whip Pemberton in the wake of the battles at Champion Hill and the Big Black River. This idea "blinded Gen. Grant to the true state of affairs here, so difficult it is to find a man who is a perfect General," wrote Brig. Gen. Eugene A. Carr.[18]

Grant's own view of the assaults of May 19 and 22 remained simple. He wanted to end the campaign as quickly as possible so as to send troops into the interior of Mississippi and pacify the entire state, not just open up Mississippi River navigation. If the assault on the second day had succeeded, Grant informed his father nearly a month later, he was confident that objective could have been achieved.[19]

In his official report, dated July 6, Grant noted this reason for his desire to capture Vicksburg quickly and asserted that his men would not have accepted the drudgery of digging Pemberton out if he had not tried to take the town by storm. He believed that the losses did not cripple his army and blamed McClernand's misleading messages for the afternoon attacks, which added "fully 50 per cent" to the day's butcher bill. The rugged terrain inhibited the massing and maneuvering of his men. Halleck supported Grant's explanations in his annual report to the secretary of war later that year.[20]

Grant and his friends continued this line of argument long after the war. Adam Badeau, who wrote a military history of the general's career, rationalized his chief's decision to attack by noting that he could not have known Confederate morale had improved since the battle at the Big Black River. Broken ground prohibited troop massing, the only real hope, Badeau thought, for a successful assault. Grant continued the line of reasoning he had established in his official report when penning his memoirs during the last months of his life more than twenty years later.[21]

Sherman also cited the rugged terrain and the strength of Lockett's line as the primary reasons for defeat. "We were compelled to feel and assault Vicksburg as it was the only way to measure the amount of opposition to be apprehended," he informed his wife. "We now Know that it is strongly fortified on all sides and that the Garrison is determined to defend it to the last." After the war he visited Sebastopol and examined the Russian defensive position in this famous siege of the Crimean War in 1854–55. "Without hesitation I declare [the Confederate position] at Vicksburg to have been the more difficult of the two."[22]

GRANT AND MCCLERNAND

The battle of May 22 was a turning point in the relationship between Grant and McClernand. Grant set the mood. Correspondent Sylvanus Cadwallader claimed to have been the first witness of McClernand's attack on Railroad Redoubt to report accurately just how faintly the Federals had penetrated that work. "I . . . shall never forget the fearful burst of indignation from [Rawlins] and the grim glowering look of disappointment and disgust which settled down on Grant's usually placid countenance." Lt. Col. James H. Wilson noted in his journal that 1,000 Federals fell on the afternoon of May 22 due to McClernand's faults. When high-ranking officers discussed this idea late that evening, Rawlins told Lt. Col. Theodore S. Bowers "to open the record book and charge a thousand lives" to McClernand.[23]

On May 24, Grant explained to Halleck that McClernand was "entirely unfit for the position of corps commander, both on the march and on the battle-field. Looking after his corps gives me more labor and infinitely more uneasiness than all the remainder of my department." On the same day, Dana told Secretary of War Edwin M. Stanton that Grant had decided to relieve McClernand of his command the day after the failed assault but then changed his mind. "My own judgment is that McClernand has not the qualities necessary for a good commander, even of a regiment," Dana concluded.

Making Sense of May 22

Sherman agreed, viewing McClernand as "so envious and selfish that he cannot harmonize with any where he does not command." In Sherman's view, McClernand was a "dirty dog."[24]

The most serious blow to the Grant-McClernand relationship before May 22 had been a foolish act by the corps commander during the march along the Louisiana side of the Mississippi. Governor Richard Yates was visiting the army at the time and so was McClernand's wife. According to Dana, the baggage of these visitors "somewhat delayed" troop movements along the narrow lines of march. McClernand also insisted on reviewing his Illinois troops for Yates's approval, and he fired an artillery salute in violation of Grant's order to conserve ammunition. Grant was incensed. Acting on Dana's report, Stanton wired authority for Grant to relieve McClernand on the spot if he disobeyed orders. "He has the full confidence of the Government," Stanton told Dana about Grant.[25]

McClernand went on to do well in the battle of Port Gibson on May 1, a key engagement that established a Federal lodgment east of the Mississippi River. Rawlins and Wilson urged Grant to make up with McClernand by congratulating his command for the victory, but the army commander refused. From that point on, Grant "not only maintained the most formal attitude toward McClernand, but, so far as practicable, refrained from meeting him in person or giving him written orders." He preferred to send Wilson "with discretionary authority to see that he did the proper thing."[26]

One can criticize Grant for allowing this relationship to develop even though McClernand was the wellspring of ill feeling between the two men. It played a role in the events of May 22; Grant never visited McClernand's command post even though the corps commander's dispatches clearly suggested the need to do so.

Responding to rumors, many Federal soldiers blamed McClernand for the failure of May 22. McClernand heard those rumors and became nervous. Writing to Jonathan B. Turner, a professor at Illinois College in Jacksonville and an agricultural reformer, McClernand reported "that there are those who are trying to saddle upon me the responsibility of the attack. I am not responsible for it. I privately pronounced it 'absurd' before-hand." McClernand asked Turner to counter the rumor if it spread as far as his home state. McClernand also informed Governor Yates of these same "senseless and mendacious" rumors that were "the spawn of petty, prejudiced partisans" of Grant. He now began to lobby for an official investigation of the entire campaign. The desperate general bothered Abraham Lincoln with his personal troubles, decrying "the monstrous injustice that meanness would do to me and my command" as he requested a court of inquiry. McClernand tried to pin the blame for the attack's failure on Grant alone.[27]

By June 4, McClernand wrote directly to Grant. "What appears to be a systematic effort to destroy my usefulness and character as a commander" compelled him to do so. Rumors that he had been relieved were floating up and down the Mississippi, and McClernand asked Grant to issue an order contradicting them. According to the corps commander, Grant agreed to do so but later reneged on his promise.[28]

Matters stood at this impasse until McClernand made his last foolish error. He penned a congratulatory order to the Thirteenth Corps that was not only bombastic but utterly unnecessary. It was easily interpreted as claiming for his own corps all the credit for Grant's success in the long campaign against Vicksburg. The order stemmed not only from McClernand's overpowering ego but also from Grant's reluctance to say anything about calming the rumors of his relief from command. In other words, McClernand let his sensitivity get the better of his judgment. It was bad enough to write such an unseemly order for internal circulation within the corps, but the order was released for publication in Northern newspapers without the permission of department headquarters. That represented a violation of standing orders. Apparently McClernand had not intended for this to happen. It appears that the publication of the congratulatory order was the result of a mistake by some of his staff members.[29]

This was the last straw for everyone who had grown tired of McClernand's presence in the army. Blair, Sherman, and McPherson wrote very strongly worded protests about it, and Grant had no intention of ignoring the incident. He sent copies of the published order to verify that it was true, and McClernand, who now was caught in a vise, had to admit it was an accurate copy of his order. Grant now had a supportable reason for relieving him of command on June 18. Of course McClernand was bitter toward Grant for the rest of his life, but he would never return to the field except in the backwaters of the war for a few months in 1864.[30]

Grant's relationship with McClernand has become a matter of divided opinion among historians. While some, such as Edwin C. Bearss, fully back up Grant's views, others argue that McClernand had real ability as a commander, a view that even James H. Wilson conceded. Michael Ballard views both commanders as letting their personal sensitivity get the better of them. Neither man "exhibited gentlemanly qualities, the positive traits of character that put the job at hand above personal feelings." As William L. Shea and Terrence J. Winschel have pointed out, in many ways McClernand had achieved more battlefield success than either Sherman or McPherson. Grant may have declined to relieve the Thirteenth Corps leader on May 23 for fear it might depress soldier morale in that corps.[31]

McClernand's biographer, Richard L. Kiper, criticizes Grant for his distant attitude toward the Thirteenth Corps leader. Grant's failure to personally observe conditions in McClernand's sector was a failure of command in favor of personal convenience. Kiper also believes that massing strength offered a better chance of success and blames both Grant and McClernand for not doing so. Finally, Kiper correctly points out that McClernand exaggerated his political capital in Washington, relying on his personal connection with Lincoln to compensate for the growing trust and support Grant received from all authorities in the nation's capital.[32]

There is no doubt that McClernand possessed admirable qualities as a corps commander. It is also true that the Thirteenth Corps achieved stellar success on several occasions during the Vicksburg campaign and McClernand deserved credit for those successes. But it is equally true that McClernand was a royal pain in everyone's side, and that is not an unimportant factor in assessing a general's worth to a field army. In the end McClernand pushed everyone too far while giving free rein to his unchecked ego and ambition. Grant put up with him longer than many other commanders would have been willing to do. McClernand's mistakes in dealing with superiors and colleagues alike, including his inaccurate and misleading messages of May 22, justified his relief.

EVALUATING MAY 22 — THE CONFEDERATES

The gray-clad men who repulsed the attacks on May 22 enjoyed quiet and rest the next day, basking in the awareness that they had turned an emotional corner in the Vicksburg campaign. Having endured crushing defeats only a week before, they now stopped the enemy in their tracks and regained a measure of confidence and hope that Vicksburg could be held for a while.[33]

Confederate soldiers noted the unusual quiet that prevailed on the morning of May 23 and interpreted it as a sign that Grant had had enough of fighting. Pemberton thought the Federals were "evidently staggered by the severe repulse of the day previous." Rebel troops thoroughly agreed. William Lewis Roberts of the 31st Alabama asserted that "we made them willing to behave their selves."[34]

Rebel soldiers merely had to glance at the battlefield to see evidence of their success. In front of every point of attack lay bodies that were beginning to emit odors. Morale rose dramatically among the Confederates along with their opinion of Pemberton, who deserved credit for managing the repulse. Lida Lord Reed, one of the women trapped in Vicksburg, wrote that the battle of May 22 sparked "the moral reconstruction of our army." When a local truce developed on the skirmish line of Maj. Gen. John A. Logan's sector, Seth J. Wells found the Confederates in a mood to talk. "They appeared quite confident of holding the place," he wrote.[35]

Many Confederates were quick to evaluate the battle of May 22 as a "grand though disastrous assault" by their enemy. Brig. Gen. Stephen D. Lee was careful to calculate the statistics after the war, asserting that Grant had attacked along a front of three and a half miles with 30,000 troops while Pemberton had only 9,938 men and thirty-three artillery pieces to defend that line. He may have exaggerated these details, but the truth was that Pemberton's army had done very well in holding the fortifications against the most determined efforts to break into Vicksburg. Many Confederates believed the most exaggerated estimates of Yankee losses even though they were ready to praise the gallantry of their foe. "Surely no more desperate courage than this could be displayed by mortal men," remarked J. H. Jones of the 38th Mississippi.[36]

Praising the enemy for determination and courage was merely a way of accentuating their own success. "This defeat of the enemy gave our army great satisfaction," remarked Capt. Joseph Boyce of the 1st Missouri. It "restored us to our usual good spirits, and strengthened our determination to hold the place." Col. Ashbel Smith could not resist viewing May 22 as a special vindication of his state's contribution to the Confederate army. His regiment "utterly destroyed any prestige which the enemy might have heretofore felt when the soldiers they should encounter should be Texans." He saw this in the "marked and special respect with which the enemy, officers and men, after the surrender, during our stay in Vicksburg, were wont to treat and speak of the members of the Second Texas Infantry."[37]

Acknowledging the significance of their victory on May 22, the Confederates then settled down for a long siege. Union mortar boats continued to throw shells into the city all day and into the night of May 23 as Rebel officers made arrangements to repair earthworks damaged by Federal artillery fire the day before. Smith requested permission to fill up embrasures in the 2nd Texas Lunette, given that the two guns normally stationed there had been silenced so readily by McClernand's gunners.[38]

Pemberton redistributed his artillery to counter Grant's siege approaches. Col. Edward Higgins moved eleven light guns from the riverfront to the landline east of town and sent detachments of his artillerymen to man them. From May 24 to 26 Higgins also moved heavier pieces to the siege lines, including an eight-inch siege howitzer, a smoothbore thirty-two-pounder, and an English Whitworth rifle, including their gun crews.[39]

Pemberton insisted on strict economy concerning rations. A circular issued on May 24 mandated that reports of men on duty had to be whittled down to the essential personnel in the trenches. All civilian employees not absolutely needed in the various departments would receive no food. He also restricted officers to no more than one personal servant each.[40]

How long the Confederates could hold out at Vicksburg was a matter of grave concern. Although Pemberton's men had repelled Grant's attempt to storm the place, they knew everything depended on whether Johnston would come to the rescue. A few Federal prisoners taken on May 22 told Pemberton of rumors that Johnston was approaching Grant's army. "Prospect brightens," noted John Cowdry Taylor.[41]

JOHNSTON

If Taylor knew the real story, he would not have been so optimistic. Johnston was very far from a serious attempt to relieve Vicksburg. In fact, he was still busy forming a field army when the attack of May 22 took place. The next day, May 23, a dispatch arrived from Pemberton, which Johnston telegraphed to Richmond. It offered news only up to May 21, but Johnston heard rumors of the failed Federal attack the day after it happened. "This gives me confidence in Pemberton's tenacity," he told Jefferson Davis. "If army can be organized and well commanded, we shall win." Davis agreed that the news seemed good, but the key point was Johnston's ability to move quickly toward the enemy. In fact, everyone in Johnston's command heard optimistic reports that Grant had lost up to 30,000 men in no fewer than six assaults at Vicksburg.[42]

Relaying more reports of the May 22 battle, brought by a man Carter Stevenson sent through the lines, Johnston told Richmond of Pemberton's estimate that Grant had an army of 60,000 men. He further told Davis that only 13,000 troops had been sent to Jackson and the total he could expect would amount to a relief force of 23,000 men. "We have tremendous odds against us," the general told Davis. "I respectfully urge, therefore, thorough

organization." That, of course, would take time. Meanwhile, Johnston arranged to smuggle percussion caps for small arms into Vicksburg.[43]

It is true that the Richmond authorities were well behind the curve of
events. In addition to Maj. Gen. William W. Loring's Division, Johnston
could count on only three infantry brigades as of May 21, with another arriving at Jackson on May 23 and a fifth brigade reaching the place by May
25. Davis asked Gen. Braxton Bragg if he could spare men from the Army
of Tennessee, which defended what was left of Confederate Middle Tennessee. Although he had already dispatched units, Bragg promised to send
more. When Maj. Gen. John C. Breckinridge's Division arrived in Jackson,
Johnston could count on an army of 23,000 men, but he was not confident
of his ability to lift the siege. Johnston continued to point out that Grant had
up to 80,000 men by May 27 (a gross overestimate at that time). Moreover,
"his troops are worth double the number of Northeastern troops." Johnston wanted at least 30,000 Rebels to have a hope of succeeding, and "even
that force would be small for the object." Davis countered by noting that
his people had already sent Johnston more men than originally requested.
When Johnston asked for two major generals to command newly created
divisions, Davis had great difficulty finding them.[44]

Beyond arranging for reinforcements, Davis could only console and encourage his men in the field. "I made every effort to re-enforce you promptly,"
he told Pemberton, but "was not successful." This dispatch was smuggled
into Vicksburg along with the 200,000 percussion caps Johnston had sent.
Davis contemplated going personally to Jackson to see if he could help the
cause but felt his health was too weak. He did send Gabriel J. Rains with
orders to plant torpedoes where he thought they might prove useful against
either Federal troops or river steamers. Upon arriving at Jackson, Rains felt
it was impossible to sneak his land mines into Vicksburg and dismissed the
idea that he could at that stage of events put submarine mines in the Mississippi. In short, beyond sending a few brigades, Davis felt powerless.[45]

Brig. Gen. States Rights Gist, one of Johnston's brigade leaders, temporarily took charge of 12,000 troops at Canton while Johnston managed affairs
in Jackson. Gist kept his former commander, Gen. Pierre G. T. Beauregard,
informed of events transpiring in Mississippi. He noted the widespread criticism of Pemberton, still not abating despite the successful defense on May
22. Everyone seemed to have their spirits and hopes buoyed by the fact that
Johnston was in charge of the relief effort. Meanwhile, reports indicated that
Pemberton's garrison had enough food and ammunition to hold out some

Making Sense of May 22

time. In short, there seemed to be a real prospect of holding Vicksburg and saving Pemberton's army at the same time.[46]

But the man most responsible for rescuing the town and the army felt the weight of that responsibility. "Pemberton can be saved only by beating Grant," Johnston told Davis. "The odds against us will be very great."[47]

{ 18 }

I Am Surfeited, Sick, and Tired of Witnessing Bloodshed

CASUALTIES, WOUNDED, PRISONERS

The battle of May 22 created much work for the survivors that demanded intense effort during the immediate aftermath of the assaults. They had to count the losses and clear up the battlefield as far as possible, given that neither side entirely controlled it. Trophies were there to be collected and thousands of wounded men were in desperate need of care. The few prisoners demanded attention as well. For both armies, many days of work were required to pick up the pieces.

CASUALTIES

The Federals lost 3,199 men on May 22, divided into 502 killed, 2,550 wounded, and 147 captured or missing. These losses occurred in a force of roughly 40,000 men according to some estimates and thus amounted to 7.9 percent of the total. But one must keep in mind that many Federal regiments were not engaged, so the percentage of loss would have been higher among the troops that actually fought that day. By comparison, Grant's casualties in the victory at Champion Hill amounted to 2,441 men, and all Federal losses from May 18 to 21, excluding the small battle of May 19, amounted to only 239 troops. Grant lost 942 men on May 19, making a total of 1,181 casualties during the four days preceding the grand assault of the twenty-second. For the Federals, May 22 was the bloodiest day of the Vicksburg campaign from July 1862 to July 1863.[1]

Blair's division bore a huge burden of the cost. It lost 890 troops in the attacks of May 19 and 22. McPherson's Seventeenth Corps racked up losses of 1,966 men on May 22, after having done very little fighting on the nineteenth. McClernand's Thirteenth Corps posted losses of 1,521 men on May 22, with Carr's division bearing the lion's share, at 725 casualties. Smith's division lost 485 men, and Osterhaus and Spicely together suffered 311 casualties. Lawler's brigade lost more men than any other Federal brigade that day.[2]

Those losses were bad enough, but rumors placed them even higher. Estimates ranged from 5,000 to 10,000 even among Union soldiers. A wild rumor that a regiment of 500 men lost all but ninety-six of them in the futile assault was widely credited. The Confederates believed an even wilder report that Grant had lost 40,000 men in the assault of May 22.[3]

Pemberton's losses were far lower than Grant's. Estimates range around the 500 mark out of about 14,000 men engaged, or 3.5 percent. Forney's Division posted casualties of 159 men despite the fact that it held a heavily targeted part of the line. In Martin L. Smith's Division, the 26th Louisiana lost eighty-five men from May 19 to June 29, but only nine of them fell while defending its redoubt against Steele's attack on May 22. Total Rebel losses on that day, compared to Pemberton's casualties in the defeat at Champion Hill, offer a stark contrast. A total of 3,840 Confederates fell on May 16 as the price of defeat but only 500 as the price of victory on May 22.[4]

CLEANING UP THE BATTLEFIELD

As soon as the battle of May 22 ended, the task of cleaning up the field began. Pemberton's headquarters instructed division leaders to collect abandoned ammunition and small arms in front of the fortifications. The Confederates wanted percussion caps because they had 1 million more cartridges than caps in store. Regimental officers detailed men for the task, which had to be undertaken during the night of May 22. In front of Stephen D. Lee's Brigade, they found a number of "beautiful Enfields" left on the ground by Thirteenth Corps troops. Col. Ashbel Smith's 2nd Texas gathered 200 rifle muskets near the lunette in addition to 9,000 rounds of cartridges and 1,500 caps.[5]

The Confederates collected trophies as well as guns and ammunition. The most valuable of these trophies were enemy flags. The 27th Louisiana claimed one and sent it through the chain of command to Pemberton's headquarters. The flag of the 99th Illinois, captured when color-bearer Cpl.

Thomas J. Higgins literally carried it into the Confederate works, also was sent to headquarters. "Some of Gen. Pemberton's staff gave Miss Rebecca a piece of Yankee flag that was put on our fortifications," wrote Emilie Riley McKinley after the siege. "It has blood on it. I have a piece of it." It is not known which Federal flag McKinley referred to, but the fact that this took place after Vicksburg's fall indicates the Confederates refused to give up the captured banner when they surrendered the town. In fact, these staff members met McKinley and Miss Rebecca as they crossed the Big Black River on their march to parole camps.[6]

FEDERAL WOUNDED

Federal officials shouldered an enormous responsibility in taking care of their wounded comrades who needed treatment on May 22. The surgeons of A. J. Smith's division located their hospital four miles from the scene of battle at the farm of a Mr. Swett. The attendants who waited for the wounded could hear the sound of McClernand's artillery at that distance and knew there would be many casualties. The ambulances began to arrive by 2:00 P.M., according to Charles Benulyn Johnson of the 130th Illinois. So many ambulances arrived that attendants had to unload several of them simultaneously and rush the patients into tents. Surgeons bypassed those who were mortally wounded and those with simple injuries, concentrating on the serious but savable cases. Surgeon John B. Rice of the 72nd Ohio took care of 120 wounded men who streamed in during the first two hours of the battle on May 22. By midnight he and his attendants had performed all necessary operations and had "properly dressed" all wounds. A medical inspector named John E. Summers reached the Army of the Tennessee by May 27 to observe the quality of medical care. He reported that supplies were abundant and the worst cases were being transported to Memphis while division hospitals handled the rest.[7]

Surgeon Thomas S. Hawley provided information about the wounded he treated in Tuttle's division hospitals. According to records collated by his assistants, 107 men had the cause of their injury noted and 87.8 percent of them were hit by small-arms projectiles. Only 12.2 percent of the wounds were caused by artillery rounds. Of the artillery wounds, fully 75 percent were caused by shells rather than canister. Only 8.9 percent of the wounded endured amputation of a limb.[8]

Hawley's information tells us what type of weaponry was more effective on the battlefield, but the emotional experience of the hospital was a dif-

Casualties, Wounded, Prisoners

ferent matter. Col. Thomas Kilby Smith visited his hospital on May 23 and was aghast at what he saw. "God help us—a fearful, fearful sight. I have seen agony and death in all its phases. Oh, that horrid, horrid, damnable hospital!" he wrote his mother. "Rather a thousand deaths in the glorious enthusiasm of battle than an hour's torture on that table."[9]

The story was similar throughout Grant's army. Logan's hospital in the Seventeenth Corps treated 300 wounded men as of May 31. James K. Newton of the 14th Wisconsin asked permission to work at the hospitals in part so he could write home about the losses of May 22. "I will enclose a copy of the report sent in to the Regimental H'd Qrs.," he told his parents, "and the wounded boys want you to send it round so that there friends will not worry on their accounts. Hardly any of them are able to write and otherwise it would be a long time before their folks would hear from them." Informing loved ones was essential, because misinformation often plagued civilians at home. George D. Kellogg's name erroneously was added to the list of killed in the 23rd Wisconsin, and when told of it Kellogg hastened to write to his family. "So I am not dead I know, but I am very dirty and covered with gray backs." Seventeenth Corps hospitals were located so close to the lines that Patrick Heffron of the 14th Wisconsin was bothered by the noise of artillery. It made "the very earth to tremble and causes my hands to tremble that I scarcely can write."[10]

Jordon Carroll Harriss of the 81st Illinois visited Logan's hospital after the battle and "saw horrible scenes[,] The amputating knives busily employed in taking off the limbs of my *comrades*." Harriss noted that attendants had found an old wheelbarrow and placed it next to the porch of the house within which the surgeons were operating. When the wheelbarrow was filled with amputated feet and hands, they wheeled it away and buried the severed limbs somewhere.[11]

Surgeon Benjamin Franklin Stevenson of the 22nd Kentucky took charge of Osterhaus's hospital and worked feverishly for days. He told his wife about amputating legs for three soldiers, resecting the bones of arms for several others, and conducting so much minor surgery that he could not recall all of it. "I am surfeited, sick, and tired of witnessing bloodshed," he confessed on May 23, "but nothing short of it would satisfy the insane men who would overthrow the government."[12]

Seven surgeons organized their efforts to care for the wounded of Carr's division, 498 men. They divided responsibilities with Dr. James K. Bigelow of the 8th Indiana, who was in charge of the wounded from his own regiment, the 18th Indiana, and the 1st Indiana Battery. There was so much to do that most of the surgeons stopped at 10:00 P.M. on May 22, too exhausted to continue. But Bigelow and Dr. William L. Orr of the 21st Iowa, assisted by Chaplain Henry C. Skinner of the 8th Indiana, stayed up all night to work on the wounded. These injured men waited for hours, lying on beds of raw cotton spread out under trees, until the surgeons managed to tend to all of them by dawn of May 23.[13]

Most men who visited Thirteenth Corps hospitals found the conditions acceptable. Arbors of brush were erected to shield wounded men from the sun while they lay about in the yards of civilian homes turned into hospitals. Charles Benulyn Johnson was astonished when the hot, humid weather led to a maggot infestation of open flesh in A. J. Smith's division hospital. "This looked horrible, but was not deemed specially detrimental," he recalled after the war. Many surgeons knew that maggots ate damaged or decayed flesh but left healthy tissue alone.[14]

Grant never forgot that he had left a large number of wounded men behind during the overland march to Vicksburg. In fact, a medical inspector reported that 2,161 wounded Federals and nineteen medical officers had been left at various places where battles had taken place. These people were now struggling to survive in places not fully controlled by either army and eking out an existence without a secure source of supplies. Grant had sent five wagons of medical stores to Champion Hill on May 19 and thirty days' rations for the wounded two days later. The dispatch of these needed articles required contact with Confederate commanders and a plea for cooperation. Fortunately the Confederates responded well, and wagons loaded with 30,000 rations set out for the Federal wounded located at Champion Hill, Jackson, and Raymond. Only half of the meat ration could be sent, and Grant's chief of staff suggested that desiccated vegetables make up the other half.[15]

Ironically, Grant could better aid the wounded left miles behind his army than he could aid those shot down in the assault of May 22 who had been left on the field. Stephen D. Lee reported on May 24 that quite a few of the enemy still lay near his brigade line and "seem to be suffering very much." If the sight bothered Lee, imagine how much it hurt the comrades of these helpless men. "It is horrible, indeed, to think of the wounded being left there," wrote George Crooke of the 21st Iowa.[16]

The Confederates were able to get to some of the wounded Federals under cover of darkness and bring them in. Capt. Thomas Hayes of the 30th Ohio fell twenty feet from Stockade Redan and was taken in after lying for two days in the broiling sun. His thigh was "shattered by a ball, and mortifi-

Casualties, Wounded, Prisoners

cation had ensued." Hayes gave his money and papers to the surgeons and asked that they be sent to his wife; he then soon died.[17]

The majority of Federal wounded, however, ended up in Union hands, where facilities for treatment were managed with commendable efficiency. Now that Grant was reestablishing his river-based supply line it was possible to move many cases north to hospitals in Mississippi River towns. The *City of Memphis* and *Nashville* had been fitted up as hospital boats for this purpose. Three hundred wounded men boarded the *Nashville* on the night of May 24, and attendants were kept busy the next day taking care of them. They mostly seemed to be lightly wounded, thought Anson R. Butler, with injuries in the arms and legs. But Butler must have had the wrong impression, for as many as twenty of these men died each day over the next week and a half. Butler worked with the surgeon in charge of the boat to send notifications to eighty-five regiments that had members on board who had died by June 2.[18]

Stories concerning medical inefficiency and shortages of supplies circulated in the North following the battles of May 19 and 22. They led many concerned citizens to arrange for the donation or purchase of medical stores, the mobilization of volunteers, and the contracting of steamboats to move the material and personnel to Grant's assistance. Mostly those people found to their surprise that the army was doing a pretty good job of handling things on its own resources. James Yeatman of the Western Sanitary Commission left St. Louis with 250 tons of supplies and fifty-five surgeons, nurses, and attendants, enough to care for 1,000 men, on May 26. He found on arrival a few days later that Grant's medical staff had 4,500 wounded on their hands. They had already shifted 1,900 north and were caring for 2,000 slightly wounded in field hospitals, with a few hundred men too badly hurt to be moved. Division hospitals were in the process of being consolidated into corps hospitals. The army did not need Yeatman's hospital boat but accepted his surgeons, nurses, and attendants. Army surgeons were very grateful for the medical stores.[19]

The story of medical care in the period of May 18 to 22 can also be told through individual cases. Lt. Noble Walter Wood of the 26th Iowa was shot in the head while on picket duty the night of May 18 and suffered a fractured skull. When he came to, Wood was able to walk to the rear with some assistance, where he was placed in a small house crowded with other injured men. "My wound is painful and I am quite weak," he wrote in his diary on May 20. "I have been as comfortable as I should expect," he wrote. Although surgeons sent many others north, they kept Wood in the house. "Sleep on the floor, eat off dirty dishes & suffer all night from the candle light and tramping nurses over the floor." By May 28, Wood complained that "flies swarm around us, and many wounds get maggots in, in spite of care. They are doing all they can for the wounded but that is not much, amid the filth & inconveniences of camp life."[20]

Finally, Wood was moved out of the house to Thayer's brigade hospital, which was set up on May 28. "My head stinks awful bad," he wrote in his diary the next day. "Maggots got in it. Had dressed about noon, not very painful." By May 31 the flies and heat oppressed Wood. Surgeons found that a bone was pressing against tissue in his wound and contemplated cutting it out but eventually decided not to operate.[21]

Wood was well enough for transport north by June 8 and wound up on the *Hiawatha* at Young's Point, which also carried the governor of Iowa and several other dignitaries to their northern homes. Wood was weighed and found he had lost twenty-five pounds since May 18. The trip north was not pleasant. "This is a very slow, dirty old boat & the fare is worse," he complained in his diary. Upon reaching Memphis, Wood transferred to the *Continental*, where he found the conditions more crowded but the food much better. He reached Cairo by June 15 and St. Louis the next day. Upon debarking at Davenport, Iowa, Wood finally was able to go home to recuperate.[22]

Levi Shell of the 23rd Wisconsin was a late casualty of the battle on May 22. When his regiment was pulling away from its position near the 2nd Texas Lunette, he rose to one knee while capping his musket and a Rebel bullet went through his nose. The ball went on to cut a piece of his jawbone, take out some teeth, and finally cut through his shoulder. The wound looked awful but Shell maintained a positive attitude. "I have good care here," he informed friends from Memphis on June 10. He could not chew solid food but subsisted on a special diet. "Everything is kept neat and clean and I can have any thing I want as far as care is concerned. I am as well off as I could ask for." Discharged from the army, Shell arranged for an artificial jaw and teeth to be made by a Dr. Moody of Madison, Wisconsin, by March 1864. He was so satisfied with them that he provided a testimony for Moody that ran in the state's newspapers, asserting that the government paid the cost of the prosthetics.[23]

Of course not all Federal wounded survived. William J. Kennedy was hit while getting ammunition up to the 55th Illinois on May 22, suffering a broken left arm. While being carried in an ambulance toward the rear, the vehicle upset and he suffered additional injuries. Initially his arm seemed to improve, and Kennedy wound up on the *Nashville* with hundreds of other wounded men. After Kennedy reached Gayoso Hospital in Memphis, his condition worsened. He developed typhoid fever and became "flighty and wandering part of the time," according to Emeline B. Rose, who had gone to the hospital to nurse her brother whose cot was placed near Kennedy's. Rose gave Kennedy drink and fanned him whenever she had a chance to do so. Kennedy also suffered from severe diarrhea, his arm wound began to bleed again, and gangrene set in. He continued to be delirious and sank rapidly, dying on June 22.[24]

CONFEDERATE WOUNDED

Despite the resources available to Union authorities, they could not keep all their wounded alive. In contrast, the Confederates, cut off as they were by Grant's army, had no opportunities to transport wounded to other locations and had only limited medical supplies within Vicksburg. But they had far fewer cases to care for as well.

Confederate surgeons used any civilian structure that was handy as a field hospital. Near Railroad Redoubt, that meant the McRaven House. In addition, dentist Rowland Chambers saw that several wagonloads of wounded entered Vicksburg on May 23. Chambers glanced into one of them and saw a captured Federal soldier with a bullet hole in his head, and "his brains was running out of it."[25]

Confederate wounded suffered the added stress of bombardment in their hospitals located in the city. Benjamin D. Lay, surgeon of the City Hospital, reported on May 24 that the various houses holding wounded men had been hit twenty-one times by Porter's gunboats and mortar boats and that six injured men suffered additional wounds as a result. "Men in their condition, whose nerves are already shattered by wounds, bear this very badly, and I shall have great mortality among my amputations and serious operations," Lay warned army headquarters.[26]

Some wounded officers could escape the hospital. Col. Winchester Hall had been hit by a Yankee bullet on May 19 that tore the calf of his leg and fractured the bone. He was initially taken to the home of a Mrs. Hansford at the corner of Jackson Road and Graveyard Road, where his wife and children were already staying, but the area was exposed to shelling. After some consultation the surgeons decided against amputation. Instead, they administered chloroform, cut a slit three inches along the shinbone, and took out the ball, which had split into two lumps of lead. They had to take out several small pieces of bone too. It was officially listed as "a compound, comminuted fracture of the tibia."[27]

After the operation, Hall and his family moved out of the building and into tents in the backyard because the shelling was too heavy. When a projectile killed a soldier at the house, the family trekked to a structure closer to the river. Even there the bombardment was so heavy that Hall's wife and children retreated into a nearby cave, but Hall could not be moved. Mrs. Hall rigged up a system to drip water onto his wound to keep down inflammation. This arrangement soaked the mattress that Hall used for three weeks of painful, tedious recovery. He whiled away the time by reading novels.[28]

Conditions for the Confederates who filled Pemberton's hospitals in Vicksburg could be grueling. Chaplain William Lovelace Foster of the 35th Mississippi was absolutely stunned by what he witnessed in Moore's brigade hospital. He visited the place a day or two after the battle of May 22 and found the wounded scattered in tents located in a hollow. One man had his leg taken off, and Foster learned that he never really recovered from the effects of chloroform, remaining "stupid and drowsy" until he died a week later. An artilleryman suffered badly when a caisson exploded and burned his hair and eyebrows until he seemed "scarcely human" in appearance. Another man's head had been mutilated by a bullet that entered under one eye and lodged in a facial bone. He could not chew or open his eyes. Soldiers had been shot clean through the chest, some were armless or legless, and others had their shoulder mangled by an artillery round. "There is one who has had a pair of screw drivers driven into his jaw and temples. He floods his bed with his blood," Foster reported. "Every part of the body is pierced. All conceivable wounds are inflicted. The heart sickens at the sight."[29]

The conditions in the hospital also appalled Foster. He observed that flies bothered the wounded by the million. They were worse around the men who had suffered the more horrible injuries, attracted by the smell and exposure of injured flesh. "The vile insect finds its way into the wounded part," Foster wrote, and thus maggots became a common presence. Unfortunately, only one nurse was available for every eight wounded men, making it difficult to provide proper care for everyone.[30]

PRISONERS

The fighting on May 19 and 22 produced a lot of Union casualties and a modest number of Confederate wounded. But it did not lead to a large number of Federal prisoners in Southern hands. Thomas J. Higgins was taken to the rear about 1:00 P.M. of May 22 after his solo advance to the Confederate works. After dark he was taken into town, where Pemberton questioned him, "but I never told him one word of the truth." Cpl. William Archinal of the 30th Ohio had participated in the Forlorn Hope advance and was captured in the evening while trying to return to Union lines. A Confederate officer interrogated him. "See here, young man, weren't you fellows all drunk when you started this morning?" Archinal denied it. "Well, they gave you some whiskey before you started, didn't they?" the officer continued. "No Sir, that plan is not practiced in our army," Archinal answered. "Didn't you know it was certain death." "Well, I don't know, I am still living." "Yes," the officer concluded, "you are living, but I can assure you that very few of your comrades are."[31]

The Confederates sent Archinal to town, where he joined sixty other prisoners in tents erected on the lawn of the jail compound. They were restricted by a brick wall fifteen feet high that encompassed the compound, and they could not get any sleep that night due to Porter's bombardment. In fact, at daylight a mortar shell hit the slate roof of the jail and a piece of slate cut the rim of Archinal's hat as he dodged behind a tree. The prisoners' breakfast consisted of cornbread and something the black cook told them was mule meat, all of it passed to the Federals through a hole in the wall.[32]

The Confederates had no intention of keeping unwounded prisoners, because they wanted to conserve food for their own men. On May 23 the Rebels paroled their Federal captives and transported them across the Mississippi to De Soto Point. Union gunboats fired at the flotilla of small boats until the guards raised their truce flag high. Upon landing the Federals into the care of a cavalry patrol, the guards shook their hands and rowed back across the river to Vicksburg. Archinal's prisoner experience had lasted about twelve hours by the time he reached Union lines on the Louisiana shore. The parolees gathered at Young's Point, where the wounded Lt. Col. Harvey Graham of the 22nd Iowa was put in charge of the group, reporting to Grant's provost marshal. Some of the other Federal prisoners testified "that the rebels had no food; and our men had nothing to eat during the time they were in Vicksburg." The paroled prisoners were moved to Benton Barracks near St. Louis until they were exchanged after the fall of Vicksburg, when they returned to their units in the field.[33]

In contrast, Lt. John M. Pearson, captured by Sgt. Joseph E. Griffith at Railroad Redoubt, never returned to his comrades. After Griffith delivered him to McClernand, the lieutenant went to Lawler's headquarters tent, where he was grilled for information. Pearson told the Federals that Pemberton had three lines of earthworks and lots of food, showing them fourteen biscuits he had received that morning for breakfast. That evening Pearson was taken to the Yazoo and transported to Cairo on a steamer, winding up at Johnson's Island until he was released on parole in March 1865. He was never exchanged, because the war came to an end the next month.[34]

{ 19 }

No One Would Have Supposed That We Were Mortal Enemies

BURIAL, MOURNING

Both armies faced a huge task in clearing the battlefield of May 22 of its human carnage. Hundreds of bodies, possibly a handful of wounded barely surviving among them, littered the terrain between the lines. Union and Confederate details worked during the night of May 22 to accomplish what they could in this way, but it was dangerous work. The Confederates fired at any sound they detected in the dark.[1]

BURIAL BEFORE MAY 25

At least one local truce was arranged at midnight of May 23–24 to allow the Federals more latitude in burying their comrades. It took place near the 26th Louisiana Redoubt. "The dead was stinking," recorded Lt. Jared Young Sanders, and "we hallowed to them to come over and bury their dead." By this time the bodies had putrefied to the extent that many "burst as they were moved." Even without a local truce, J. J. Kellogg and a colleague from the 113th Illinois sneaked into no-man's-land on the night of May 24–25. They "could only bury them by throwing dirt upon the bodies just as they lay upon the ground," but Federal pickets fired at Kellogg and his friend on the way back.[2]

On some parts of the line, watchful Confederates allowed Unionists to retrieve their own. Members of the 9th Iowa buried twenty-three of their comrades on May 23 but were not allowed to reach others. On some sectors, Unionists found a wounded comrade still alive. When Isaiah Richards and two men of the 17th Ohio Battery heard groaning, they ventured out to search for the man and were able to get him back to the Union line. The wounded soldier was in very bad shape and pleaded with Richards to write his mother about his pending death. Growing weaker, he asked them to sing "Jesus, Lover of My Soul." Richards and several battery men complied, "although I thought my heart would break." The man died before they even finished the hymn.[3]

A general truce was required to clear the battlefield, but that was difficult to arrange. McClernand urged Grant to ask Pemberton for a truce on May 23 to bury the dead and recover the wounded. Grant ignored the suggestion, and even members of the rank and file understood why: such a request "would be acknowledging our repulse as a defeat," according to Charles Wilcox of the 33rd Illinois.[4]

An unidentified member of the 17th Ohio Battery reported that Grant was emotionally distraught by the dead and wounded. The general came to the battery on May 23 because it was located close to the enemy line. "He stood contemplating the scene, then steping back with tears trickling down his face, he uttered in sad and sorrowfull tone; it is horid, horid indeed." If Grant refused to be the first to ask for a truce, then it was only through some personal suffering on his part. But Confederate officer Simeon R. Martin of the 46th Mississippi called this ploy by Grant an "unqualified piece of brutality" because of the prolonged suffering it caused.[5]

The wounded continued to languish, and the dead continued to deteriorate. Many Confederates witnessed the former and grew disgusted with the latter. Members of the 2nd Texas called out to Federal pickets to come forward and help their wounded near the lunette, but the Yankees refused. In fact, according to Rebel sources, the Federals fired on any Confederate who ventured out to offer aid. One Texan waved his handkerchief until the Unionists agreed to hold fire, and then he went forward with canteens for several wounded men. Upon returning to the Confederate line, some Federals fired at him but fortunately missed.[6]

William Lewis Roberts of the 31st Alabama estimated that 700 dead and wounded Unionists lay unattended for several days in front of Pemberton's position. That probably was an exaggeration, but the reality was bad enough. The sight of the killed became an absolute horror to the living as the hot sun did its worst, causing the bodies to swell and turn black. Cpl. Charles I. Evans of the 2nd Texas claimed that many of his comrades became physically ill from smelling the effluvia. As Theodore D. Fisher of the 2nd Missouri (C.S.) put it, the bodies "were almost stinking us out of the works." Decay had so bloated them that many assumed grotesque poses, with arms "extended as if pleading to Heaven for the burial that was denied them by man." A Tennessean in the Vicksburg trenches wondered if Grant refused to ask for a truce in order to make his enemy suffer as much as possible from the smell.[7]

MAY 25

If Grant wanted Pemberton to make the first move toward a burial truce, he got his wish on May 25. That day dawned unusually hot and sunny. Disturbed by continued reports of the smell, Pemberton's adjutant general asked division leaders if they thought it was justified to ask Grant for a burial truce. Maj. Gen. Carter L. Stevenson thought it did, adding that the Confederates might be able to gain some information about Federal plans as a side benefit. Ironically, Maj. Gen. Martin L. Smith replied that a truce was not necessary, even though he had requested Pemberton's headquarters to seek one only the day before. He offered no explanation for this abrupt change of opinion.[8]

How Maj. Gen. John H. Forney and Maj. Gen. John S. Bowen responded we do not know, but Pemberton asked Grant for a truce. "In the name of humanity I have the honor to propose a cessation of hostilities for two hours and a half." Pemberton offered to send his own details out to bury the dead if he could be assured the Federals would not open fire.[9]

The Confederate commander prepared to deliver the message as his staff instructed division leaders to have their men cease fire while negotiations were pending. In passing on these instructions to brigade leaders, Martin L. Smith also told them that, if a burial truce was arranged, they should send details to move bodies away from the points of attack and not allow the Federals to come near.[10]

Pemberton sent three flags of truce into no-man's-land at about 3:00 P.M. One of them appeared at Stockade Redan, carried by Stephen C. Trigg of Company C, 3rd Missouri (C.S.). It took a few minutes for the surprised Federals to round up the appropriate officer to receive it. He met the flag party halfway between the lines along Graveyard Road while men on both sides stood up and crowded the works to see what was going on. The second truce flag appeared where Jackson Road crossed the Confederate line. Maj. Gen. John A. Logan personally greeted the party and negotiated with Col. L. M. Montgomery of Pemberton's staff. Montgomery insisted on seeing Grant personally but Logan refused, sending Pemberton's message to army headquarters. A third flag was reported appearing along Baldwin's Ferry Road and was met by Brig. Gen. Stephen G. Burbridge, who sent the message to Grant's headquarters.[11]

Grant did not hesitate to respond to Pemberton's request. At 3:30 P.M. he wrote a letter proposing 6:00 P.M. as the start time and ending at 8:30 P.M. Pemberton readily agreed and spread the word to his subordinates. Grant's staff also spread the word to Federal officers. The rank and file on both sides had the advantage of a cease-fire from 3:00 P.M. until 8:30 P.M.[12]

Many men speculated about Pemberton's motives for arranging a truce. Most Confederates assumed it was due to the awful stench of the dead and the threat their decomposition posed to the health of his men. Charles A. Dana also wondered if the Confederates hoped to gain information about the Union position during the truce. A few days later a Rebel deserter told Lt. Col. James H. Wilson that his former comrades wanted to bury dead animals near their lines that they could not reach for fear of being shot.[13]

BURIAL

Federal details moved into the disputed ground and began their gruesome work at 6:00 P.M. They found bodies that had decayed so badly they were hardly recognizable as human. Most had turned black and many had "fingers like birds claws." Decay had caused the skin and hair to become loosened, and it "would slip off, as if scalded." They were bloated, black, "and alive with worms & maggots," Charles F. Smith put it, "almost ready to fall to pieces." Flies swarmed by the millions around them. Thomas B. Marshall of the 83rd Ohio counted twenty-six bodies while standing on one spot at the place where Burbridge's brigade had fought. Literal piles of corpses were seen where Brig. Gen. William P. Benton's brigade had emerged from the ravine in plain sight of the 2nd Texas Lunette.[14]

The condition of most bodies was such that all the Federals could do was cover them where they lay. They dug a shallow hole and literally shoveled the disintegrating remains into it. In many cases the details just shoveled some dirt over the remains without moving them. As a result, no-man's-land was dotted with small mounds of dirt scattered across the uneven landscape. If a member of the burial detail happened to recognize someone, they fashioned a crude marker for the mound. Charles Benulyn Johnson observed at least one burial marked with "a piece of board put at the head, upon which, in rude letters," was the name and unit of a fallen soldier. Brig. Gen. Thomas E. G.

Ransom's men constructed a picket fence around fifteen comrades whose remains they buried. James K. Darby of the 8th Indiana could identify his friend Thomas S. Smith's body, burying it "on a beautiful hill close to a peach tree."[15]

Nicholas Miller, also of the 8th Indiana, was detailed to bury Orderly Sgt. Frank Mays, a friend of his, and he found the remains near Railroad Redoubt. "Such a fearful sight. He was as black as a negro." As his comrades dug a hole next to the body, Miller found a photograph of a young lady from Cincinnati in Mays's pocket. Then using sticks, they shoved him into the hole. Miller's lieutenant corresponded with the lady and asked her what to do with the picture. She asked him to bury it with Mays. True to their charge, Miller and the lieutenant crawled into no-man's-land one night, found the grave, and dug enough at its head to deposit the photograph.[16]

Intact bodies were removed for better burial. Confederate details mostly took on the responsibility for carrying them to an established line halfway across no-man's-land for delivery to the Federals. Where it was feasible, Union details dug trenches for common burial. Sometimes they put a blanket over the remains but mostly had none to spare.[17]

At some points Union burial details came very close to the earthworks. Five men of the 83rd Ohio found the body of Douglas Hutchins of Company K, but it was so decayed they could not carry it to the middle of no-man's-land. As they interred Hutchins, a number of Rebels came out of the 2nd Texas Lunette to chat. Their talk was characterized by "cheerful boasting on one side, and good natured defiance on the other." But at other points on the battlefield, Confederate soldiers called out not to approach too close to the works because "they would take care of those left," as Sherman put it. The Federals also retrieved abandoned guns wherever they found them and so did the Confederates.[18]

The Federals saw many bodies lying at a small pond near Benton's brigade, indicating their comrades had crawled to it for water before expiring. A number of wounded Unionists had crawled into bushes or patches of felled timber where they died. Their remains were not easy to locate. Many Confederates claimed they could smell them from as much as a quarter of a mile away, which was the only way burial details had a hope of tracking them down.[19]

Sherman required his surgeons to be on call with stimulants and stretchers in case any wounded survived on the field. Indeed, a number of men were found still clinging to life. Two soldiers belonging to Company D, 33rd Illinois, were among the number, but their injuries were horrible and they died within a few days. A correspondent of the *Chicago Daily Tribune* named Bod listed by name at least six men belonging to the 21st Iowa, 8th Indiana, 33rd Illinois, and 99th Illinois who were found alive. Their wounds "were in a frightful condition and filled with maggots an inch long," wrote Bod. A diarist of the 17th Ohio Battery reported finding Capt. Andrew O'Daniel, 8th Indiana, but his mangled leg was "badly fly blown hence it was a putrid moving creeping mass" of rotting flesh.[20]

While they were allowed to roam about, many Federals plundered the dead. J. J. Kellogg saw several men rip open the pockets of deceased comrades to pilfer knives, watches, cash, and anything else of value, even though the bodies were absolutely disgusting. They seemed to think nothing of this bizarre and callous action. Kellogg restricted himself to picking up abandoned items left on the field rather than robbing the dead. He found a tintype of a woman and two children as well as a Springfield rifle musket. Charles E. Wilcox found the coat he had thrown off during the heat of the attack three days before, but the contents of its pockets had been pilfered by some Federals.[21]

The Confederates had also robbed many of the Union dead they had buried before the truce on May 25. Comrades of Israel M. Piper of the 99th Illinois could not locate his body and only after diligent search found a Rebel soldier who not only told them he had already been interred but offered them a diary and two letters taken from Piper's body. This man had enough heart to show the Federals where Piper was buried.[22]

There were still many abandoned weapons littering the field on May 25. One Rebel noted that the Union burial details did not bother to remove accoutrements from the dead before interring them, probably because of the condition of the bodies.[23]

FRATERNIZATION

As the main business of the truce continued, many Union and Confederate soldiers mingled with their enemy. The works "were literally swarming with soldiers" when the truce went into effect at 6:00 P.M. To Lt. George Carrington of the 11th Illinois, it was "just like 'gophers' popping up out of the ground in all directions." Brigade commander Col. James R. Slack marveled at what happened next. "They very soon began to hollow at each other & very soon began to visit shake hands and talk, trade knives, exchange papers. Our boys gave them some crackers, whiskey & c." For the first time in a week men in both armies had a chance to get out of the works and they were "prepared to enjoy it." In fact, many Confederates called it a "recess."[24]

For the most part the meeting was cordial and friendly, so much so that many observers found it to be "rather a strange sight, no one would have supposed that we were mortal enemies." Being able to observe the enemy close up, speaking with them and observing them face-to-face, was a common objective of these meetings. Soldiers wanted to gauge their opponents in a personal way. "I saw several of the Feds," wrote John Harvey Fryar of the 34th Georgia. "They are fine looking men," he concluded.[25]

Other soldiers gained a good deal of information from the enemy. Confederates told Federals that the wells in Vicksburg had mostly become dry and they lived on Mississippi River water. The battle of May 22 convinced them they could hold out until Gen. Joseph E. Johnston came to the rescue. Many Confederates asserted that they intended to fight to the bitter end, no matter what the outcome.[26]

Rebel soldiers also gained information from the Yankees during their conversations. Most of the Federals expressed their disappointment at the result of the attack and admitted they had assumed Pemberton's army would fold easily. But the Federals assured their opponents that Grant would starve them out and keep Johnston at bay.[27]

There were plenty of jibes by one side against the other. Members of the 2nd Texas jeered the Federals by inquiring "if they had all gotten negro wives yet & how they liked them." When the Federals asked these Texans how many men Pemberton had in Vicksburg, they replied, "A million."[28]

Trading items of value to soldiers was probably the most common form of interaction. Coffee for tobacco, Northern newspapers for Southern newspapers, even some whiskey, if reports can be trusted, changed hands. In addition, knives and canteens were in demand. Almost anything that could be had was traded by someone.[29]

Despite their mutual animosity, the common soldiers of both armies tended to treat each other with respect, even kindness, during the burial truce. Many Federals noticed that Confederate officers were extremely watchful of their men as if they did not trust them. It is true that most Rebel officers tried to put up a show of bravado, bragging to the Federals that Pemberton had enough food to feed his garrison for six months. But deserters had already alerted the Federals to their short rations. In other words, they did not believe these boasts and felt sorry for the rank and file in gray. "We gave them from our own rations some fat meat, crackers, coffee and so forth," recalled Osborn Oldroyd, "in order to make them as happy as we could."[30]

Unusual acts of thoughtfulness were surprisingly common. Whether it was expressed in the gift of food or in friendly talk, there was more goodwill than bitterness. According to William G. Christie of the 1st Minnesota Battery, Logan "was a little sprung, so he told a secesh officer, that when they saw a man on a white horse with a mustache ridding along the line they must not shoat him for he was a Damned good man, meaning himself." Logan was not alone. "The Officers of both Armies took drinks together and felt hilarious," reported a corporal in the 30th Ohio.[31]

The feelings of goodwill became so strong that in some cases Federal soldiers invited Confederates to enter their lines. Obviously this violated standing orders. Often the invitation was for the purpose of feeding hungry Confederates. In another case a group of Rebels evaded the sentinels and penetrated the Union side of no-man's-land to take ripe fruit from a plum tree. They found a group of Federals doing the same thing and shared the bounty while having a good conversation to boot. When officers realized that intimate mingling of this kind was taking place they broke it up.[32]

In a small number of cases, the burial truce offered an opportunity for family members serving in opposite armies to visit each other. The 6th and 8th Missouri in Col. Giles A. Smith's brigade held a number of men whose brothers served in gray, and at least two of them found their siblings in the Confederate Missouri units near Stockade Redan. They exchanged family news and shared letters from home as long as the truce lasted. They also agreed not to discuss war issues but to make the visit purely personal.[33]

Maj. Arthur Platt of the 11th Wisconsin clearly went too far in his generosity toward the enemy. He allowed a Confederate commissary of subsistence to enter the Union line during the truce and took him to Lawler's headquarters to talk to an officer on the brigade staff. The Rebel officer therefore had a wonderful opportunity to examine the Federal defenses. McClernand was angry at Platt's indiscretion and refused to let the Confederate officer return to Pemberton's army. With Grant's approval, McClernand sent him north to Kentucky, where he had to fend for himself.[34]

Capt. Andrew Hickenlooper, chief engineer of the Seventeenth Corps, gained a lot of information without getting into trouble. McPherson had tasked him with running a sap across no-man's-land, and it had been difficult for him to understand the terrain while enemy skirmishers fired at him. During the burial truce, Hickenlooper walked about within the zone of Union control and was able to observe what he needed to know about digging the sap. Based on this observation, he also decided where to place key artillery positions along the way toward the 3rd Louisiana Redan.[35]

In a few cases, men took advantage of the burial truce to send letters across the lines. Col. Orlando S. Holland of the 37th Mississippi met Lt. James D. Vernay of the 11th Illinois in a ravine where they could have a private talk. Holland gave Vernay a packet of letters to mail, and the lieutenant fulfilled his charge at the first opportunity.[36]

Sherman used this ploy to occupy Maj. Samuel H. Lockett so the Confederate engineer could not observe his siege approaches during the burial truce. Lockett was standing on the parapet at Stockade Redan when a Federal orderly approached him with an invitation from Sherman to have a chat. He went forward to where Sherman was standing about 200 yards in front of the fort. Sherman had observed Lockett's demeanor and guessed he was visually surveying no-man's-land. He had a packet of letters from people outside Vicksburg who wanted to communicate with Confederate friends and relatives inside the city and decided to entrust them to Lockett for delivery.[37]

The conversation involved some playful jibes. "I thought this would be a good opportunity to deliver this mail before it got too old," Sherman told Lockett. "Yes, General," replied Lockett, "it would have been very old, indeed, if you had kept it until you brought it into Vicksburg yourself." When the general asked if the engineer thought he was "a very slow mail route," Lockett retorted, "Well, rather, . . . when you have to travel by regular approaches, parallels, and zigzags." Sherman had the last word when he admitted that these were indeed slow but they were sure, "and I was determined to deliver those letters sooner or later."[38]

Then Sherman invited Lockett to sit on a log and have a long talk. It was a friendly conversation in which the general congratulated the engineer on constructing a good defense line on admirable ground. Lockett repaid the compliment by noting that the Federals had already begun to construct effective siege approaches. In this way the two whiled away the time until eight thirty, when the burial truce ended. "Intentionally or not," Lockett concluded after the war, "his civility certainly prevented me from seeing many other points in our front that I as chief engineer was very anxious to examine."[39]

Another way to take advantage of the truce was to use it as a venue for desertion. Charles E. Wilcox noted that "a great many of the enemy" tried to do so. "One man deserted the rebs and came over here," noted Job H. Yaggy of the 124th Illinois. "I do not know whether he is upright or not." Confederate officers seemed worried about the mingling because they knew it might encourage desertion.[40]

In fact, a handful of Rebel rank and file disliked the mingling altogether. "I did not care to have any conversation with them," wrote James West Smith about the Yankees. He stayed in the works and watched the proceedings. Critical of the "general mixing-up of our boys with the Yankees," Smith bitterly concluded that it "never should have been admitted and must ever lead to disastrous results."[41]

Smith was not the only soldier to hang back during the truce. Surprisingly, a number of Federals and Confederates did not know why it had been called. Most of this confusion stemmed from the fact that the cease-fire started at 3:00 P.M., followed by quiet negotiations. Many men wondered if Pemberton wanted to surrender.[42]

It also is unclear what Pemberton meant when he reported that 100 prisoners "were captured" on May 25. These probably were Federals who had walked beyond the line of demarcation in no-man's-land and were taken captive. If so, they were the unlucky victims of the too-free mingling of the armies.[43]

There also were a number of violations of the truce. "I had one man shot in the Calf of the leg after the order 'Cease firing' was given," reported James R. Slack to his wife. "Presume it was a mistake." During the middle of the truce Lt. Charles Williams of Company A, 1st U.S. Artillery, was walking on top of the parapet until some Rebel shot him in the chest. Just when the truce ended and most men had gone to cover, Lt. Jared Young Sanders of the 26th Louisiana lingered a bit on top of the parapet until a Yankee "took a *deliberate fire* at me—the ball passed harmlessly by. It was an infamous act. Their men were in full view, & one of my men hallowed to them—'If *ye* do that again we will fire a volley into *ye* & it will take all day tomorrow to bury ye're carcasses!'"[44]

At 8:30 P.M. everyone said goodbye and left their enemy with parting thoughts. "We had a long talk over matters and things in general," reported James K. Newton of the 14th Wisconsin. "They agreed with us perfectly on one thing. If the settlement of this war was left to the Enlisted men of both sides we would soon go home."[45]

Everyone marveled at the quiet of the burial truce. Except for an occasional violation of the cease-fire there was no artillery or small-arms fire. Grant had not forwarded news of the truce to Porter, so the navy knew nothing of it. As a result, the mortar boats continued to fire shells into Vicksburg.

But along the siege line every soldier enjoyed "a few hours of rest & free breathing," as Sanders put it. "The spirits of all went up," thought a man in the quartermaster department of Stephen D. Lee's Brigade.[46]

The Federals failed to tally the number interred, but there were many inflated reports. Col. Ashbel Smith insisted that his men had counted at least 100 bodies buried near the 2nd Texas Lunette. In addition, his own men had buried twenty-seven Federals on the night of May 22 and he could only guess how many bodies had been carried away. In fact, Smith insisted that his regiment had killed 500 Unionists in the assault of May 22 and relayed a report given him by the major of the 33rd Illinois after the fall of Vicksburg that the tally actually was 600 killed and 1,200 wounded at the lunette.[47]

Grant lost a total of 502 killed and 2,552 wounded all along the line on May 22, so the dead and injured near the 2nd Texas Lunette could not have been as high as Smith noted. Perhaps Lt. Maurice Kavanaugh Simons came much closer to the truth when he estimated that a total of 300 bodies were buried on May 25.[48]

For some time after 8:30 P.M. quiet reigned along the siege lines. "After such a meeting it was with seeming reluctance that the firing was resumed," noted William Pitt Chambers of the 46th Mississippi.[49]

Union soldiers often encountered reminders of the burial truce during the ensuing siege. As the Federals worked their way forward by digging saps and advancing skirmish lines, they came to pockets of graves. Louis Bir of the 93rd Indiana stepped on a grave one night while on picket duty. "My foot Went Down in to the Decayed body and the awfull Smell it made me So Sick." The stench on the picket line was terrible some nights. Even after the fall of Vicksburg these graves continued to dot the landscape.[50]

MOURNING

Mourning the dead started immediately after the battle of May 22. Edward H. Ingraham of the 33rd Illinois had been on detached duty and did not participate in the assault, but he was haunted by "the loss of more than one intimate friend who seemed like a brother." In the 81st Illinois, Edwin A. Loosley referred to "the fatal 22nd of May, the sad day that sent mourning in so ma[n]y houses in Illinois."[51]

The rank and file mourned the loss of valued officers such as Maj. John C. Jenks of the 18th Indiana, who died of wounds a few days after the battle. "We all regret [his loss] as though it had been our own father," wrote Louis Knobe. Capt. Thomas Hayes of the 30th Ohio "was the model of a Christian soldier," thought Brig. Gen. Hugh Ewing. "He fell in the front rank of honor, where he lived and still lives."[52]

Col. George B. Boomer had been widely admired for his character and personality. Because it was not possible to send his body north or to embalm his remains, Boomer was buried at Young's Point until a group of his St. Louis friends arranged for his removal north on June 21. His remains lay in state at the Planter's House, and then a memorial service was held at a Baptist church in St. Louis, followed by a funeral parade and shipment to his father's home in Worcester, Massachusetts. There another service took place on June 28 before final burial.[53]

When Boomer's sister published a memorial book about her brother, many of Boomer's comrades contributed letters. Brig. Gen. Isaac F. Quinby recalled viewing Boomer's body just before dusk on May 22 "and was impressed by the natural and composed posture and expression of the face. There was no distortion, and but little disfigurement, so that it was difficult to persuade myself that he was really dead, and not sleeping after the fatigue of the day."[54]

"All who knew Boomer loved him," wrote an anonymous friend from Castle Rock, Missouri. "There was a strength and tenderness in his nature that made him a universal favorite where he went." When a new line of Federal works was built to protect Vicksburg from Confederate attack in late 1863 and early 1864, an artillery emplacement at Jackson Road was named Battery Boomer in his memory. It was the only fort on the Union defense line of Vicksburg to be named for a deceased officer.[55]

Burial, Mourning

{ 20 }

They Ought to Be Remembered

HONORS, INFAMY, LIFE STORIES

The process of honoring the participants of the battle of May 22 began on many levels after that day. The less pleasant task of identifying those who failed the test of courage also began. Honor and infamy coexisted in the aftermath of battle, but most survivors preferred to praise than condemn, overlooking the faltering of their comrades. For a selected few, moments of battlefield conduct stuck in the public mind and made heroes of obscure soldiers. The life trajectories of these people changed dramatically because of the battle of May 22.

FEDERAL HONORS

Although Col. Peter J. Sullivan was not in command of the 48th Ohio during the assault of May 22, he thought it was important when writing the regimental report to honor every man of the color guard on that fearful day. They "ought to be remembered and held up as true heroes by the brave and the true," he wrote as justification for giving their full names, ranks, and company affiliations in the report.[1]

In a similar vein, many officers of Blair's division thought it was important to immortalize the Forlorn Hope, which had been organized to lead the strike against Stockade Redan. Lt. William C. Porter of the 55th Illinois had taken command of the ad hoc unit when its initial commander fell. Porter wrote a separate report for the Forlorn Hope even though it was no more than a temporary detachment. His men "would have cleared the ramparts had they seen one particle of support," he bitterly stated. Brig. Gen. Hugh Ewing seconded the effort to immortalize the Forlorn Hope by forwarding a list of men from his brigade who had volunteered. At least some survivors of the temporary unit received a special furlough for volunteering. Blair went further than that and urged Sherman to recognize their bravery by awarding each member the new Congressional Medal of Honor. Sherman supported Blair's recommendation and suggested a "more substantial reward" in terms of money.[2]

Sherman's hope never materialized, but Blair's did. A total of 122 Medals of Honor were awarded for the Vicksburg campaign, and seventy-eight of them went to members of the Forlorn Hope. As of 1905, a little more than one-third of the members were still alive, including Pvt. Howell G. Trogden of the 8th Missouri, who had planted Ewing's flag on the ramparts of Stockade Redan. Although not a member of the Forlorn Hope, the youngest recipient of the Vicksburg Medals of Honor was fourteen-year-old Orion P. Howe for his acclaimed interaction with Sherman on May 19.[3]

The troops involved in the small but sharp battle of May 19 were not ignored when it came to commendations. On August 15, 1863, more than a month after the fall of Vicksburg, Sherman created a board to follow through with a circular issued four days earlier by Grant that mandated proper commendation be accorded all troops involved in the reduction of Vicksburg. It was a complicated process because the campaign had involved several different phases and not every regiment had participated in every phase. Sherman appointed four men to the board, including his foster brother Hugh Ewing, to determine which regiments could place "Vicksburg Siege and Assault, May 19th and 22nd" on their regimental banners. Those units that had not participated in the attacks could place "Siege of Vicksburg" on their flags, and those units involved in other phases of the campaign were entitled to just "Vicksburg."[4]

But Sherman wanted to single out his battalion for special commendation. He authorized the board to verify which unit "in force planted its colors on the parapet, and suffered the greatest relative loss." The board certified that only the 1st Battalion, 13th U.S. Infantry, deserved this honor and authorized it to place "First at Vicksburg" on its flag. This was done immediately. When Sherman's wife, Ellen (sister of Hugh and Charles Ewing), visited her family at Fifteenth Corps camps near the Big Black River in late August or early September, she formally presented a brand-new flag to the battalion with "First at Vicksburg" displayed on it. The phrase became part of the regiment's heritage, and members of the descendant units that evolved from it even today wear "First at Vicksburg" on their shoulder patches.[5]

LIFE STORIES

Several Federal veterans of May 22 gained unusual fame for what they did that day. Col. William M. Stone, who was wounded in the arm, became an object of admiration for many people. The basis of this seems to have been the fact that some of his men managed to worm their way into Railroad Redoubt, which became big news in the North. He spent several days in a field hospital before recuperating in Iowa, where he was nominated by the Republican Party for governor of the state. Stone accepted the nomination but returned to the field in time to lead the 22nd Iowa in the latter stages of Sherman's campaign against Johnston's troops at Jackson in mid-July 1863. Stone also led his brigade for a short while before attending to his political future. Ironically, he ran against Brig. Gen. James M. Tuttle, division commander in the Fifteenth Corps, who campaigned on the Democratic ticket. Stone won by a large margin and defeated Tuttle again in the next gubernatorial election.[6]

As one of the 22nd Iowa men who entered Railroad Redoubt, Sgt. Joseph E. Griffith also achieved a good deal of fame for the exploit. Lt. Col. James H. Wilson, one of Grant's staff officers, described Griffith as "a fine, hearty Iowa lad of great courage." He was exactly the type to become "a popular hero." Grant gave him a field commission as first lieutenant to replace the officer of that grade who was lost in his company on May 22. The governor of Iowa confirmed this promotion. By October 1863, Griffith was further rewarded with an appointment to the U.S. Military Academy. A sharp-minded and good natured young man, Griffith was "full of deviltry . . . once climbing into the Academic Building and abstracting the examination programs for the benefit of his duller classmates," Wilson reported. Griffith graduated fifth in the class of 1867 and was commissioned in the Corps of Engineers. He wound up serving as one of Wilson's assistants during improvements on navigation along the Upper Mississippi, but he was not fully satisfied with a military career. Griffith resigned on December 25, 1870, and entered the railroad business. He had married in 1867 and left his wife and a young son behind when disease struck him down in 1877.[7]

Another man who gained some degree of recognition for crawling into Railroad Redoubt was Sgt. Nicholas C. Messenger. He was captured on that day and released the next by the Confederates. Messenger received a promotion to first lieutenant of Company I, 22nd Iowa, and was severely wounded at the battle of Cedar Creek in the Shenandoah Valley of Virginia on October 19, 1864. The bullet broke a bone in his left arm "just above the wrist." Because surgeons failed to set the break "naturally" (they twisted it so that his thumb was "too far turned in"), Messenger had trouble with that arm for the rest of his life. He made a living selling fruit trees. After his death on January 8, 1894, in Omaha, his widow received a pension based on her thirty-year marriage to Messenger. Pvt. David K. Trine was also mentioned in accounts of the attack on Railroad Redoubt. He died of consumption, brought on through exposure while serving in the war, on May 28, 1871, in Iowa City. Trine left behind a widow and two children.[8]

Lt. John M. Pearson, who experienced firsthand the effects of Griffith's, Messenger's, and Trine's exploits at Railroad Redoubt, lived for many years in McKinney, Texas, after the war. Being captured by Griffith on May 22 at age nineteen had been "the most terrible experience of my life," he told Stephen D. Lee in 1902. For a long while he had no desire to visit the scene of that experience even though he traveled to Vicksburg by boat and train, preferring not even to get off those conveyances to set foot in the city. But by 1902 that had worn off and he was eager to see what was left of Railroad Redoubt. Whether he ever fulfilled that desire remains unknown.[9]

Two other Federal survivors of May 22 did not wish to capitalize on their fame that day. Howell Trogden lived quietly in Chicago until at least 1890, and Cpl. Thomas J. Higgins modestly downplayed his fame in carrying the colors of the 99th Illinois into the waiting arms of 2nd Texas infantrymen. He moved to Hannibal, Missouri, after the war and found himself in a nest of trouble. "You had a quiet time over there," Higgins told Charles A. Hobbs, who continued to reside east of the Mississippi in Illinois, "but we over here had to fight it over and over again and to stand up before a lot of old stay-at-home Rebels and be called 'A damned nigger thief.'" This was too much for Higgins's Irish blood. "Well, you know how hard it is for me to keep my tongue still, but sometimes I have to take a knock down with them and I never got whipped yet."[10]

INFAMY

Fame came to some but failed to find others for what they did or did not do on May 19 and 22. For those who failed the test of courage, and there were more than a few, it was rare to be publicly identified as a slacker. Capt.

James O. Hawkins of Company G, 22nd Iowa, resigned his commission on May 26, 1863, to avoid being dishonorably dismissed for cowardice in the assault. In Blair's division, Hugh Ewing named Lt. James H. Ralston of the 4th West Virginia as one who failed the test. He mentioned "absence without cause on the day of battle" and recommended that Ralston be reduced to the ranks. Nothing was done about this case until Ralston tendered his resignation on July 28, 1863, citing illness in his family. Col. James H. Dayton heartily endorsed the request by characterizing Ralston as "entirely incompetent and also very dissipated." The resignation was accepted within a couple of weeks.[11]

Lt. Col. Job R. Parker of the 48th Ohio also ran afoul of the authorities because of what they characterized as his dereliction of duty on May 22. Parker, "by some means or other, received a very slight flesh wound on the cheek-bone," noted Col. Peter J. Sullivan, "merely breaking the skin." Parker soon retired from the field and let someone else handle the regiment. He received a twenty-day leave of absence on May 31 but still had not returned to the field by the time Sullivan complained about him on August 4. In fact, Parker had not reported his whereabouts or status to regimental headquarters.[12]

Parker could not be counted as the only man who transformed a slight wound into an excuse for not returning to duty, and their cases often were more complicated than was apparent. That is exactly why M. Ebenezer Wescott of the 17th Wisconsin felt it was important to explain to his parents what happened to him on May 22. "I came out all right," he told them in a letter five days later. "May be you think because I was not killed or wounded I skipped out. Well you just ask the Captain. He is coming home. He got a ball through the calf of his leg and he promised me he would come and see you as soon as he was well enough."[13]

CONFEDERATE HONORS

Compared to Federal efforts to commemorate brave deeds on May 22, the Confederates did little to bolster the spirits of their men after the battle. Maj. Gen. Martin L. Smith wrote a circular to his division. "You have been the first to meet the shock of the enemy's assault upon Vicksburg, and he has again recoiled before your admirable steadiness and courage. Your country's admiration and gratitude await you."[14]

Pemberton tried to boost his men's spirits as well. "You have met the enemy and have repulsed him with heavy loss," he proclaimed in a circular. "The Commdg Genl is proud of his troops and tenders them his sincere thanks." Pemberton specially mentioned Lee's Brigade, the Texas troops, and Col. Edmund W. Pettus. He soon regretted this and recalled the order, explaining that it had not been the intention to single out any units or people. This resulted from a mix-up among his staff members — Pemberton meant to congratulate Lee, the Texans, and Pettus in a special message rather than in the circular issued to the entire Army of Mississippi and Eastern Louisiana. Not surprisingly, other Confederate troops complained, and Pemberton was forced to act quickly. R. W. Memminger, his assistant adjutant general, wrote privately to each division leader. "It was not intended to compliment General Lee's brigade to any greater extent than any of the troops engaged in the trenches," Memminger wrote. "No distinction can be drawn, all the troops having behaved with the greatest gallantry." Nevertheless, the army commander's stock among his troops rose after May 22. "Even the strong prejudices against Pemberton began to soften down," thought Chaplain William Lovelace Foster of the 35th Mississippi.[15]

But the elevated spirits produced by the Confederates' defensive victory on May 22 did not last long. As they faced an increasingly stressful siege and suffered ultimate defeat with the surrender of Vicksburg on July 4, the entire experience of Grant's operations against the city became a subject to ignore rather than celebrate in their minds for decades to come.

Honors, Infamy, Life Stories

{21}

Eventful on the Page of History

COMMEMORATION

With the passage of time, veterans of the battles at Vicksburg gained valuable perspective on their experiences. For most, bitterness and disappointment continued for some time but eventually lessened. More and more they felt the need to cloak the events of May 22 in nostalgia. They never entirely forgot the hard touch of combat but had increasing opportunities to master the memories and move on with their lives in productive and fulfilling ways. Commemoration became vitally important to them as they grew older.

WARTIME REMEMBRANCES

Many Federal soldiers remembered May 22 as "a terrible day," one that would remain "eventful on the page of history." Writing of Col. George B. Boomer's attack twenty-three years later, W. T. Clark, McPherson's assistant adjutant general, called it "simply murder and slaughter." Survivors of the attack on May 22 compared it with other battles in their experience. "I must tell you that Shiloh fight was nothing compared to this," concluded Patrick Heffron of the 14th Wisconsin. From McClernand down to the privates, the words "sad" and "memorable" cropped up repeatedly in discussions about the action on May 22. Long after the war, Grant's veterans continued this theme. "The 22d of May, 1863, is a dark spot in the memory of many of us," wrote Pvt. Charles D. Morris of the 33rd Illinois in 1884.[1]

Efforts to commemorate the battles of May 19 and 22 started almost immediately after the guns fell silent. As early as June 12, 1863, Sherman wanted souvenirs of the fight on the nineteenth because his 1st Battalion, 13th U.S. Infantry, distinguished itself for the first time in battle that day. He arranged for a dozen canes to be cut from near the scene of action and sent them to Lancaster, Ohio, for his son Willie, who was barely nine years old. Sherman gave him instructions to distribute the canes, which could be used as fishing poles, to Willie's friends and relatives. "Every cane has vibrated to the sound of near fifty thousand cannon balls fired with intent to kill," Sherman told the boy, "and it may be that more than one poor fellow has crawled to the Shadow of their leaves to die. Each cane is therefore a precious memento."[2]

Sherman also considered the bullet-riddled flag of the 13th U.S. Infantry a memory-laden symbol of the fight on May 19. That is why he kept it flying in front of his tent during the siege, after he detailed what was left of the battalion to serve as his headquarters guard. "I wish you could see it for a minute," he informed Willie about the flag on June 21, "but it is not right for children to be here, as the danger is too great."[3]

SPEECHES, POETRY, AND PAINTING

Peace offered greater opportunities for veterans to commemorate their experiences near Vicksburg, and many of them did so in a variety of ways. Quite a few spoke of May 22 in public speeches, including Albert O. Marshall of the 33rd Illinois. In an Independence Day speech at Lockport, Illinois, only three years following the fall of Vicksburg, Marshall told the audience that "the desperate charge of the twenty-second of May [could] never be forgotten. Words would fail to describe the scene. One might as well try to paint on canvas the fearful sound of roaring thunder, as to attempt to fully describe a battle."[4]

Pemberton's men rarely commemorated their victories of May 19 and 22. Their efforts tended to be oriented toward defending the entire cause rather than boasting about individual days of success on the battlefield. For example, when Col. Thomas N. Waul corresponded with Charles Colcock Jones, Jr., of Savannah about a speech Jones gave in 1889, the former commander of Waul's Texas Legion praised it highly as unrepentant. He liked men who knew "the cause was holy." Ironically, Federal survivors of Grant's defeat on May 19 and 22 were far more active in commemorating the battles than the victors. Perhaps the true reason for this is that Vicksburg ultimately was a lost cause for Pemberton's army—individual successes within that long campaign failed to shine as brilliantly as engagements involved in a successful campaign.[5]

Commemoration

A few Federals turned their hand to poetry as a way to commemorate the battles. Five days after the attack on May 22, W. H. Bentley of the 77th Illinois wrote of his fallen comrades.

How great was the sacrifice made,
How precious the blood that was shed,
How sacred the spot where your bodies are laid
And sacred the ground where you bled.

No bugle trump heralds your fame,
No martial display, pomp or pride
But this record emblazons each name,
"For his country he lived and he died."

Written only two days after the burial truce of May 25, Bentley's pedestrian rhymes and imagery, which mimic the style of popular poetry of the day, become a painful reflection not only on the loss of friends but on the hope that someone will remember and care about their sacrifice.[6]

Former sergeant Charles A. Hobbs of the 99th Illinois commemorated Grant's campaign against Vicksburg in a book-length poem published in 1880. Totaling 299 pages, the book obviously was a labor of love even though it lacks poetic grace. Hobbs's main purpose in the effort was "to present a faithful picture of that campaign . . . and especially to make vivid the life of the soldiery during the siege of Vicksburg." Hobbs did his homework, quoting from dispatches and trying to be faithful to history. But he sacrificed poetic license and even included the Orion P. Howe incident as part of May 22 instead of May 19. In the end, one must admit that Hobbs failed to fulfill his mission; his poem has almost no literary merit and it hardly qualifies as a history of the attacks. But it meant something to Hobbs to write it, and we should view its significance within that context — as a personal expression of one man's reaction to May 19 and 22.[7]

Hobbs was not the only aspiring poet to deal with the storming of Vicksburg. Tom E. Fulgham read a poem he wrote about the May 19 assault to a reunion of the 1st Battalion, 13th U.S. Infantry, at Des Moines, Iowa, in 1888. Consisting of six stanzas, the poem began:

In front of Vicksburg's frowning heights
The First Battalion formed in line;
Impelled by love of human rights
And liberty, man's right divine,
There were no craven spirits there,

Each was a hero in the First;
Whatever men would do or dare,
Each one of them had braved the worst.

Obviously Fulgham's objective was not only commemoration but praise for the character of every man in the battalion and an assertion that, in his reference to human rights, they were fighting for an end to slavery. Whether either of these assertions was literally true for every member of the battalion is highly questionable, but a reunion of the unit was no place to doubt the morals or motives of its veterans.[8]

The battle of May 22 became the subject of a major painting, a cyclorama. It was one of only seven battles to be thus commemorated by 1890. Spearheaded by the painters Louis Kindt of Germany and Thomas Gardner of the United States, the cyclorama was entitled *General Grant's Assault on Vicksburg.* It opened to the public in Milwaukee by July 1885. After only two and a half years, the cyclorama closed in late 1887 and has disappeared from view—no photographs or diagrams of it remain.[9]

A second cyclorama immediately followed the Kindt-Gardner effort. Spearheaded by Joseph Bertrand and Lucien Sergent, it was painted on canvas in Paris and New York. The pair had previously executed cycloramas of Gettysburg and Waterloo. They spent several months at Vicksburg, consulting veterans, scouting the landscape, and researching official records before taking eighteen months to create the painting. Other artists worked on the three-dimensional foreground for the circular painting in preparation for its debut in New York in May 1886. This cyclorama was entitled *The Panorama of the Land and Naval Battles of Vicksburg* and was moved to San Francisco in July 1887. Housed at Mason and Eddy Streets, it was open each day from 9:00 A.M. to 11:00 P.M.[10]

The focus of the Bertrand-Sergent cyclorama was the battle of May 22. The viewer's platform was placed at Railroad Redoubt. Visitors praised the three-dimensional designer for using metal foil to represent the gleam of bayonets, but they also criticized the painting for too much focus on events surrounding Railroad Redoubt. Quite a few veterans of the Vicksburg campaign saw it, including Samuel H. Lockett, R. W. Memminger, George W. Hale of the 29th Wisconsin, Henry Clay Warmoth of McClernand's staff (who was severely wounded on May 22), Frederick A. Starring of the 72nd Illinois, and brigade leader Thomas Kilby Smith. The cyclorama enjoyed only a short life. It folded in late 1889 or early 1890 but reopened in Tokyo in

"The Louisiana 'Tigers,' Under the Command of General Pemberton, Defending Their Works." Artotype 42 of *The Panorama of the Land and Naval Battles of Vicksburg (May 22nd, 1863)*. Reflecting the nonspecific nature of this cyclorama, this image looks like a generic representation of an attack on a redoubt rather than an accurate portrayal of the assault on Railroad Redoubt. No unit in Pemberton's army was known as the Louisiana Tigers, and Railroad Redoubt was not attacked in the way depicted. The work was not constructed in this fashion, and it is impossible to see the Mississippi River from the site of Railroad Redoubt, even though the artists included the mighty stream in the background. (Series 1, folder 5, Artotypes from the San Francisco News Letter, 1887–1902, Special Collections, Stanford University)

May 1890, where it remained on display until July 1891. With the exception of the cycloramas depicting Pickett's Charge at Gettysburg and the battle of July 22 during the Atlanta campaign, all other cycloramas of Civil War battles have disappeared.[11]

Fortunately, some images of the Bertrand-Sergent cyclorama have survived. Four scenes of the circular painting were reproduced in the form of cabinet cards. One scene depicts the forward placement of a piece from Capt. Patrick H. White's Chicago Mercantile Battery near the 2nd Texas Lunette. A second scene depicts the entry of 22nd Iowa men into Railroad Redoubt. The third image shows Porter's fleet bombarding what probably

"The Main Confederate Fort on the Mississippi Shore." Artotype 51 of *The Panorama of the Land and Naval Battles of Vicksburg (May 22nd, 1863)*. The artists outdid themselves in poetic license with this apparent depiction of the Marine Hospital Battery, one of the major works defended by Confederate heavy artillerymen along the Mississippi River. With the stonework and thatched roof, this looks much more like a pastoral scene in Europe than one of Pemberton's river batteries under fire by Porter's vessels. (Series 1, folder 6, Artotypes from the San Francisco News Letter, 1887–1902, Special Collections, Stanford University)

was the Marine Hospital Battery and the Castle, while the fourth image depicted Confederate gunners, probably at the Marine Hospital Battery, returning Porter's fire.[12]

But there are serious problems with the cyclorama. The painters failed to properly identify the Confederate water batteries involved in the third and fourth scenes, and they failed to accurately depict the details of the first and second scenes. There is a detached aura in these illustrations; they lack emotional punch and historical accuracy. Unlike the cycloramas of Gettysburg and July 22, there is little sense of movement in these largely static pictures, which resemble technical drawings. They have less emotive force than one would expect from such a grand attempt to convey the meaning of battle to an audience consisting of both veterans and civilians. Perhaps that is the primary reason for the financial failure of this and other cycloramas of the Civil War.

Public knowledge of the panorama disappeared. When tourist Patricia M. Terrell found a print of the Chicago Mercantile Battery gun firing at the 2nd Texas Lunette, she asked rangers at the Vicksburg National Military Park to identify its origin. Writing in 1964, the rangers could not do so, displaying no knowledge of the painting and not even knowing that veterans and visitors of the nineteenth century typically referred to the 2nd Texas Lunette as Fort Pemberton.[13]

Despite the failure of both cycloramas to carry on a public memory of the battle of May 22, it is remarkable that the engagement became the subject of not one but two larger-than-life circular paintings. Both of them disappeared after a disappointing experience with the public, leaving behind only those four individual scenes from the last cyclorama to attempt an immortalization of the human experience of battle on that fateful day outside Vicksburg.

Flags inevitably carried with them a load of emotion for Civil War soldiers. This was by design, for regimental colors were the center of official life for them. These flags guided their massed movement while in formation, inspired their fighting spirit, and symbolized what they enlisted to defend. For the 22nd Iowa men, flags became particularly important as a memorial to the regiment's deeds on May 22. Their national colors were taken away from Railroad Redoubt "torn and riddled to shreds." The flag was initially ordered to be condemned, but Adj. Samuel D. Pryce took it upon himself to disobey that order and sent it home, where the torn banner wound up in the State Historical Society of Iowa. That organization officially delivered it to the adjutant general's office of the state government years later. The state color had been captured at Railroad Redoubt, but the wife of an Iowa congressman found it among captured flags in Washington years after the war and arranged for its return to Iowa.[14]

According to a resolution passed by the officers of the 77th Illinois on October 31, 1863, both flags of the regiment had been captured at Railroad Redoubt. But decades later some regimental veterans were not so sure. They asked the War Department to search its files and see if it had a list of flags captured on May 22, but the department could not offer any assistance.[15]

Flags played such an important part in soldier life during the war and in veteran awareness after the conflict that they became symbols of many values vested in military life. The same level of emotion was vested in efforts to preserve Vicksburg for future generations. Physical evidence of the battles that took place on May 19 and 22 impressed many men beginning just a few days after the engagements. Chaplain Nathan M. Baker, who was not present with the 116th Illinois when it advanced on May 19, saw the ground on June 13, 1863, when visiting picket posts. Trees, logs, and bushes "are everywhere cut, torn, and splintered with balls. One large oak tree standing on the crest of the hill, is literally riddled. There is scarcely a space three inches square from the ground upward for 30 feet, but what contains a ball." On July 3, Baker came across a grave of someone killed on May 22 and noticed "a long hand reaching out" from the dirt. The ground was still littered with debris of the battle: "Broken guns, cartridge boxes, canteens, and haversacks were lying about."[16]

Pinpointing locations of important actions during the battles became increasingly important. Immediately after the siege that was not difficult to do. Charles A. Hobbs of the 99th Illinois not only found the exact spot where he lay during a part of the day on May 22 but even found a letter that had fallen out of his pocket on the ground, although badly deteriorated by the weather. After the war, when James A. Grier saw the field across which his 33rd Illinois advanced on May 22, it had been converted into a cotton field. Grier considered the attack a "bloody, and foolish, and fruitless Charge" and ventured the poetic idea that a huge cotton plant was feeding on the remains of every Federal soldier who was still buried there.[17]

Civilian development intruded on the battlefield soon after the war, making it more difficult for veterans to recognize terrain. A Jewish cemetery was located on the high spot occupied by the 2nd Texas Lunette about 1869, necessitating the destruction of its ditches and parapets. When the Vicksburg National Military Park was created in 1899, returning Union veterans were appalled at the destruction of this important landmark.[18]

Survivors of the assault on Stockade Redan found that the fort had been taken over as a Sunday School picnic ground, and a postwar growth of trees obscured the vista surrounding the work. The oak tree that had grown on the north side of the cut in Graveyard Road had been so riddled by shot during the siege that it died, but new growth was popping out of its roots when Robert McCrory visited in 1890.[19]

When Lt. William Titus Rigby, a veteran of the campaign, became a

Railroad Redoubt, 1899. Taken from a position just north of what had been the Southern Railroad of Mississippi thirty-six years earlier (then called the Alabama and Vicksburg Railroad), this view shows how much clearing of trees and underbrush had already been done once the Vicksburg National Military Park was created in 1899. Railroad Redoubt stands out on the highest ground in the distance, surprisingly intact. (Vol. 111, 5722, Massachusetts Commandery, Military Order of the Loyal Legion and the U.S. Army Military History Institute)

member of the park commission, he embarked on several years of effort to enlist the aid of veterans in the placing of unit markers. When asked to remember details of May 22, many veterans asserted that they could never forget what happened on that fateful day even though more than thirty-five years had passed. Even so, a visit to the ground often refreshed their memory, or converted it, or left them confused. The landscape changed in places, weeds and bushes tended to obscure lines of sight if a veteran visited during summertime, and poor health also limited some veterans' ability to explore the rugged landscape. For those who could not afford to travel to Vicksburg, Rigby mailed a blueprint of a map prepared by his engineer to jog recollections, and often it helped.[20]

Rigby and the park commission adopted a rigorous process for determining unit placements, including the high-water marks of the attacks on May 19 and 22. They gleaned information from official reports, solicited copies of wartime letters and diaries, and even paid expenses for selected veterans to visit Vicksburg and give personal testimony. C. E. Henry of the 42nd Ohio told a newspaper reporter how the last named tactic was done after he returned home. Rigby and his engineer took him by carriage out to the field, and the trio walked around until Henry could positively identify the spot where the 42nd Ohio had stopped in its advance. "Here is where the regiment and brigade was halted," he told them. "They looked at their maps and examined their notebooks and drove a stake for the monument." Henry then took them to another spot where he personally could see far to the right and left. "They drove an iron stake there. They then informed me that my testimony agreed with the known facts on . . . records."[21]

But Rigby and his informants did not always agree so readily. Many veterans became heatedly interested in the place where their regiment's assault on May 22 should be marked and drove their agenda in the face of Rigby's resistance. For example, veterans of the 22nd Iowa argued with him about where their monument should be located and threatened to seek permission from the War Department to place a private marker, bypassing the Vicksburg Park Commission entirely.[22]

Rigby had to handle these disagreements with tact and generally managed to smooth them over with some compromise and gentle persuasion. "We all want to be right," wrote Capt. Asa C. Matthews of the 99th Illinois to Rigby, "and we all want to be heard, and when we have all been heard, and it has been decided, I feel sure there will be no 'insurrection.'" Matthews recognized that Rigby required "an immense amount of patience, and a great deal of diplomacy," to complete the complicated task of siting hundreds of markers and monuments within the confines of the park.[23]

But it is a matter of great importance that Rigby, a veteran of the campaign, cooperated so closely with hundreds of fellow veterans, Union and Confederate, to commemorate the assaults of May 19 and 22. Visitors to the park today should be aware that most markers were placed with input by men who had actually experienced those bloody days.

CONCLUSION

The bloody failure of May 22 did not erase all thought of storming Vicksburg from the minds of Union commanders. William T. Sherman continued to view it as a viable method of winning the city. The general whom Lt. Henry A. Kircher had called "the great charger" was not ready to call off attacks. Because Joseph E. Johnston loomed as a threat to the east, Sherman told his wife on May 29 that "we may try and assault again." On June 2, he seemed ready to go. "In about three days we ought to be able to make another assault, carrying our men well up to the enemy's ditch under cover."[1]

Sherman represented the tension in Federal tactics during this phase of the long campaign for Vicksburg. As soon as Grant's army closed in on May 18, the question revolved around whether he should opt for a quick solution by assault or adopt the long process of siege approaches. Each option promised positive and negative consequences. Sherman supported assault even more than did Grant on May 22. After that, he counted on preparing the way for an attack by constructing siege approaches so the men could move across no-man's-land under cover of saps and mines. In Sherman's view there was no immutable boundary between assault and siege — he correctly saw them as connected tactics in the struggle to take Vicksburg. Grant, too, thought another attack was necessary, even if there was to be a siege. He authorized McPherson to conduct a limited follow-up assault after blowing a mine at the 3rd Louisiana Redan on June 25. That attack failed. Soon after, Grant contemplated a major assault scheduled for July 6. This move never happened because starvation brought Vicksburg down two days before, on the nation's eighty-seventh Independence Day.

Could the attacks of May 19 and 22 have succeeded? To address that question demands an awareness of the tactical context of Civil War operations. The old interpretation among historians has been that rifle muskets wielded by troops ensconced behind earthworks spelled inevitable defeat for any attacking force, no matter how large or ably led. This view holds that modern weaponry largely nullified the effectiveness of frontal attacks, shifting the weight of advantage to any force acting on the defensive. In this view, the attacks of May 19 and 22 were doomed to failure.[2]

But a newer interpretation discounts the old view by noting that rifle muskets, although capable of much longer range, were rarely used by Civil War soldiers for long-range firing. They correctly understood that short-range rifle fire was more effective and continued to prefer to use the new musket in an old way. There is no reason to believe that the weight of advantage shifted to the defending force in the Civil War any more than it had in any previous or subsequent conflict. Rather than considering how general rules affected military operations, we need to understand each operation within its own context. In other words, every battle had a set of contingencies affecting its outcome that were far more important in explaining that outcome than any general tendency.[3]

For storming Vicksburg, the contingencies included the character of Lockett's earthworks, the morale of defending Confederate troops, and the ability of Grant's army to mount an assault in rugged terrain.

The battle of May 19 was little more than an exploratory effort as far as most Federal units were concerned. Only one division seriously attacked the Stockade Redan sector — and was bluntly repulsed — because the Confederates had a good position that was well manned. But the battle of May 22 was far bigger and more seriously pressed. Although meant to be a major assault by all elements of Grant's force, it did not turn out that way. Many units failed to contribute, and those that participated often failed to maintain enough cohesion for a real chance of succeeding.

While acknowledging the supreme act of bravery represented by the Federal attack, we have to admit that Grant's army did not conduct the assault well. May 22 represented the largest, most ambitious tactical offensive launched by the Army of the Tennessee in its history. Its troops had mounted attacks at Belmont, Fort Donelson, Davis's Bridge, Chickasaw Bayou, Port Gibson, Raymond, Jackson, Champion Hill, and the Big Black River, but they were all limited, small-scale operations. The army launched no assaults at Shiloh. Any competent field force of the Civil War could manage offensive action by one brigade or one division at a time, targeting a discrete segment of the enemy position. But managing a large-scale, general assault was beyond the ability of most Civil War commanders. Throughout the Civil War, corps- and army-level assault coordination tended to be very unreliable.[4]

Grant's army ranked high in its ability to penetrate enemy territory, live off the land, and march anywhere at any time. Those were immensely important skills, and the Army of the Tennessee played a key role in Union military victory during the war by using them. The army's accomplishments during the other phases of the Vicksburg campaign provide a sterling example of these skills.

But the Army of the Tennessee ranked low compared to other field armies in terms of its ability to bring massive weight of numbers to bear on the battlefield. It could not match the Army of the Potomac when it came to coordinating large-scale assaults. The Army of the Tennessee was poorly prepared for the task on May 22. Peter J. Osterhaus, who commanded a division in that army for most of his Civil War career, hinted that something was wrong with the Army of the Tennessee. When commenting on the failed attack against the Confederate line at Kennesaw Mountain on June 27, 1864, he cryptically noted in his diary, "The whole thing utterly unprepared!" and "General arrangements of Army of Tenn very poor." While Osterhaus failed to explain what he meant, he certainly felt that something was lacking when it came to thorough planning and execution of offensive action in that army.[5]

As Edwin C. Bearss estimates, Grant had 49,500 men under his command on May 22. Some 7,500 of them were stationed at Grand Gulf, Snyder's Bluff, and the Big Black River, leaving a total of 42,000 available for the attack. Only four Confederate brigades held the 3.75-mile sector of Lockett's line that was targeted. While a total of 28,000 Confederate troops were available to Pemberton, only 14,000 held the targeted sector.[6]

But the Army of the Tennessee failed to bring its numerical advantage to bear on the Army of Mississippi and Eastern Louisiana. Bearss goes too far in characterizing Sherman's and McPherson's operations of May 22 as "an embarrassment." Those attacks were in some ways vigorous and sincere but not well coordinated. Bearss castigates Sherman for the fact that only one brigade got seriously involved in the morning action and only four brigades took part in serious efforts during the afternoon. Bearss also notes that McPherson used only two of his seven brigades in a serious attack during the morning. In the afternoon, McPherson sent off three other brigades (Brig. Gen. Isaac F. Quinby's division) to operate on the Thirteenth Corps sector.

McClernand used all but one of the seven brigades available to him, but as we have seen there were serious problems of command and control in several of those brigades, especially Brig. Gen. William P. Benton's command.[7]

Historians have tended to support the idea that massing troops would have had a better chance of success on May 22 than spreading them out along a wide sector. But they also note that the terrain inhibited Grant's ability to mass his men. McClernand also thought it would have been better to push a large column at a single point, but when he had the chance to try, he failed to make it work. Unlike the other two corps commanders, McClernand made a halfhearted attempt to mass. He placed Brig. Gen. Andrew J. Smith's division behind Brig. Gen. Eugene A. Carr's division when targeting the 2nd Texas Lunette and Railroad Redoubt. Limited massing in this case failed to provide any dividends, suggesting that a larger effort to mass even more troops on a more limited front might have failed as well.[8]

It is striking that so many of the Federal attacks on May 22 fell apart before they reached the target. The disintegration of Benton's brigade in the advance toward the 2nd Texas Lunette is the most visible example, and it tended to be blamed on Benton himself, who was, in the words of Isaac H. Elliott of the 33rd Illinois, "no good."[9] In Brig. Gen. John M. Thayer and Col. Charles R. Woods's attack on the 26th Louisiana Redoubt, supporting regiments to the rear were conspicuous by their absence once the forward units closed on the target. Most of Brig. Gen. Hugh Ewing's brigade failed to get past the cut in Graveyard Road, leaving members of the Forlorn Hope stranded for hours in the ditch of Stockade Redan. In other units, brigades remained relatively intact but simply stopped upon receiving heavy fire so the men could protect themselves. This happened in Osterhaus's division on the Seventeenth Corps sector and in Quinby's division during the afternoon fight.

These examples display a weakness of command and control by officers in addition to a common phenomenon in warfare: the insistence by common soldiers that they had a right to decide how far they could be pushed into the cauldron. The latter is a phenomenon only barely recognized by military historians. One is tempted to call it a legitimate right of the rank and file. Not only can it be seen on May 22, but it happened on many other battlefields of the Civil War. The action of those common soldiers made it appear as if the brigade tried hard but simply could not accomplish the impossible; in reality, they made a show of charging and then stopped after their bravery could be verified by their commanders. Officers at all levels of command accepted the men's decision and either ignored the issue in their reports or supported their troops in this universal military ritual.[10]

John Henry Hammond, Sherman's assistant adjutant general, had noticed the same thing about Fifteenth Corps troops in the battle of Arkansas Post the previous January. "Men and officers especially very backward," he wrote about the advance against Rebel fortifications, compelling Hammond to urge many units forward in order to keep the pressure on.[11]

Recognizing that soldiers made their own decisions to stop an attack partway through its execution is not a criticism of their morale. The fact that they were willing to go partway across no-man's-land rather than refuse to go at all was an act of heroism in itself. And of course there were many Federals who did not stop partway but went on to lodge in the ditches of Stockade Redan and Railroad Redoubt and near the 2nd Texas Lunette, where they stayed dangerously exposed for the rest of the day.

An exploration of the unpublished letters and diaries of Union soldiers reveals that Grant was wrong when he thought his men would not be content to lay siege to Vicksburg unless they had a chance to storm the bastion. In fact, the overwhelming majority of Federals who said anything about their mood just before the attack on May 22 were dead set against the idea of storming Vicksburg. Grant knew that his men enjoyed an unusually high state of morale, but he failed to understand that this did not necessarily mean they wanted to attack earthworks.

In reality, Grant was swayed by his own sense of impatience at laying siege to Vicksburg before trying one more time to quickly end the campaign. He was driven by his own estimate of the situation, not by his understanding of the men's mood. Grant correctly reasoned that if he could capture Vicksburg early in the summer, he would be able to clean out a good deal of central Mississippi before the hot weather became unbearable. Citing his men's mood was merely a rationalization for justifying a risky attack based on his desire to move the pace of operations forward as fast as possible.

"Grant had no idea of the severe challenges his men faced trying to overcome the Vicksburg defenses," Michael Ballard has written. That is certainly true; Grant seems to have had little detailed information about those defenses and especially what kind of troops held them. The truth was that his army had defeated only three Confederate divisions at Champion Hill and the Big Black River. One of those divisions broke off from Pemberton and failed to retire to Vicksburg, but Pemberton had two fresh divisions in and around the city to call on. He deftly placed them in the most likely sectors of Lockett's line to receive an attack while positioning the defeated divisions in a less threatened sector or using the troops as reserves. Ironically, Grant assumed that all Confederate troops facing him in that line had suffered from the demoralization of May 16 and 17, but the Rebels who held those key sectors were fresh and in good spirits.[12] One wonders if Grant would have attacked on May 22 if he had been aware of this fact.

Pemberton outgeneraled Grant during the May 18–22 phase of the Vicksburg campaign. Rebounding from one of the most humiliating defeats any Civil War general suffered, Pemberton began quickly to pick up the pieces and smartly placed his best units where they could do the most good. Lockett's fortifications, by no means perfect, were good enough to serve Pemberton's needs. Combined with the natural reluctance of many Federal soldiers to risk their skins attacking a strong position, the result of May 22 does not emerge as a surprise to the student of military history.

This is not to say that Pemberton was a better general than Grant. Overwhelmingly, Grant outgeneraled him in key phases of the Vicksburg campaign. The Federal general had been in his element during the overland march to Vicksburg. He excelled in grand strategic movement, boldly striking deep into enemy territory with a hardy group of campaigners under his control. When faced with a Gibraltar like Vicksburg, where his tactical choices were limited instead of wide open, he employed trial and error to figure out what to do. In a way, the same thing happened after he maneuvered Robert E. Lee from the Wilderness down to the James River and then was confronted with another Confederate Gibraltar called Petersburg. In fact, it took Grant ten months to figure out what to do about that city and only six weeks to accomplish his mission at Vicksburg.

In the end Grant emerged as the nation's great hero when Vicksburg fell on July 4, 1863. He deserved the accolade. Although the repulse of his May 19 and 22 attacks inspired the citizens of Vicksburg and encouraged them that Pemberton might be able to save their town, the surrender of their city blasted that brief period of optimism.[13] Pemberton sank into the pits of public opinion on the fall of the river city. No one wanted him as a subordinate and his name became anathema in the South. Eventually he gave up his commission as lieutenant general and accepted one as a lieutenant colonel in the artillery service. He continued to serve and after the war struggled with a failed farm until he wound up teaching at a little school in Warrenton, Virginia. For the rest of his life Pemberton blamed Johnston for the loss of Vicksburg. If Johnston had been able to drum up the courage to strike Grant early in the siege, there would have been a chance of holding the place and saving the garrison.[14]

In fact, the potential threat posed by Johnston emerges as the best explanation for Grant's desire to break into Vicksburg by storm soon after he neared the city. He had little to fear from Pemberton, but Johnston's force was an unknown quantity, Johnston had a high reputation for generalship, and Grant could not know exactly where he was at any given moment. He did not know it then, but Grant had little to fear from Johnston. The latter's force was far too small in late May to pose a real threat to his army, and the Confederate general's willingness to engage in hard and risky fighting was very low. By the time he accumulated enough troops to pose a significant threat, Grant received massive reinforcements (thanks to Henry Halleck) and was more than ready for him.

Could the navy have helped Grant capture Vicksburg on May 22? The answer clearly is no, despite Porter's almost desperate efforts to aid Grant in any way. The Confederate water batteries were too powerful for even his heaviest ironclads to silence with any finality. All Porter could do for the rest of the siege was bombard the town and make life miserable for its inhabitants. The most important task Porter could achieve was to protect the steamboats Grant's army relied on for food, ammunition, and all manner of supplies while they awaited the slow workings of a siege.

The most basic reasons for the results of May 22 are related to Lockett's line of earthworks combined with the willingness to defend them. Finding good ground, building defenses on it before those works were needed, and placing the right troops in the right sectors spelled defensive success for the Confederates on May 22. The Federals tried to take Vicksburg by storm but failed. As the subsequent siege unfolded, the period of May 18 to 23 lost its potential significance as the end point of the long campaign for Vicksburg. It started to be viewed as an interim period between the overland march and the siege.

If the Federals could have exploited genuine weak points in the Confederate position (such as Railroad Redoubt), if the Army of the Tennessee had been managed better by its subordinate commanders, and if more Confederates had suffered from a low will to fight (again as at Railroad Redoubt), the outcome of May 22 could have been very different. Vicksburg might have fallen that day instead of on July 4, 1863.

ORDER OF BATTLE

ARMY OF THE TENNESSEE: MAJ. GEN. ULYSSES S. GRANT

Thirteenth Corps: Maj. Gen. John A. McClernand

NINTH DIVISION: BRIG. GEN. PETER J. OSTERHAUS

First Brigade: Brig. Gen. Albert L. Lee (wounded); Col. James Keigwin
118th Illinois: Col. John G. Fonda
49th Indiana: Maj. Arthur J. Hawhe
69th Indiana: Col. Thomas W. Bennett
7th Kentucky: Lt. Col. John Lucas
120th Ohio: Col. Marcus M. Spiegel

Second Brigade: Col. Daniel W. Lindsey
54th Indiana: Col. Fielding Mansfield
22nd Kentucky: Lt. Col. George W. Monroe
16th Ohio: Capt. Eli W. Botsford
42nd Ohio: Lt. Col. Don A. Pardee
114th Ohio: Col. John Cradlebaugh

Ninth Division Artillery
7th Michigan Battery: Capt. Charles H. Lanphere
1st Wisconsin Battery: Lt. Oscar F. Nutting

TENTH DIVISION: BRIG. GEN. ANDREW J. SMITH

First Brigade: Brig. Gen. Stephen G. Burbridge
16th Indiana: Col. Thomas J. Lucas
60th Indiana: Col. Richard Owen
67th Indiana: Lt. Col. Theodore E. Buehler
83rd Ohio: Col. Frederick W. Moore
96th Ohio: Col. Joseph W. Vance
23rd Wisconsin: Col. Joshua J. Guppey

Second Brigade: Col. William J. Landram
77th Illinois: Col. David P. Grier
97th Illinois: Col. Friend S. Rutherford
130th Illinois: Col. Nathaniel Niles
19th Kentucky: Lt. Col. John Cowan
48th Ohio: Lt. Col. Job R. Parker

Tenth Division Artillery
Chicago Mercantile Battery: Capt. Patrick H. White
17th Ohio Battery: Capt. Ambrose A. Blount

TWELFTH DIVISION: BRIG. GEN. ALVIN P. HOVEY

First Brigade: Col. William T. Spicely
11th Indiana: Lt. Col. William W. Darnall
24th Indiana: Unknown
34th Indiana: Col. Robert A. Cameron
46th Indiana: Col. Thomas H. Bringhurst
29th Wisconsin: Col. Charles R. Gill

FOURTEENTH DIVISION: BRIG. GEN. EUGENE A. CARR

First Brigade: Brig. Gen. William P. Benton
33rd Illinois: Col. Charles E. Lippincott
99th Illinois: Col. George W. K. Bailey
8th Indiana: Col. David Shunk
18th Indiana: Col. Henry D. Washburn
1st U.S. (Siege Guns): Maj. Maurice Maloney

Second Brigade: Brig. Gen. Michael K. Lawler
21st Iowa: Lt. Col. Cornelius W. Dunlap
22nd Iowa: Col. William M. Stone
23rd Iowa: Col. Samuel L. Glasgow
11th Wisconsin: Col. Charles L. Harris

Fourteenth Division Artillery
Battery A, 2nd Illinois Light Artillery: Lt. Frank B. Fenton
1st Indiana Battery: Capt. Martin Klauss

Order of Battle

Fifteenth Corps: Maj. Gen. William T. Sherman

FIRST DIVISION: MAJ. GEN. FREDERICK STEELE

First Brigade: Col. Francis H. Manter
13th Illinois: Col. Adam B. Gorgas
27th Missouri: Col. Thomas Curly
29th Missouri: Col. James Peckham
30th Missouri: Lt. Col. Otto Schadt
31st Missouri: Col. Thomas C. Fletcher
32nd Missouri: Maj. Abraham Jefferson Seay

Second Brigade: Col. Charles R. Woods
25th Iowa: Col. George A. Stone
31st Iowa: Col. William Smyth
3rd Missouri: Lt. Col. Theodore Meumann
12th Missouri: Col. Hugo Wangelin
17th Missouri: Col. Francis Hassendeubel
76th Ohio: Lt. Col. William B. Woods

Third Brigade: Brig. Gen. John M. Thayer
4th Iowa: Col. James A. Williamson
9th Iowa: Col. David Carskaddon
26th Iowa: Col. Milo Smith
30th Iowa: Col. Charles H. Abbott (killed); Maj. James P. Milliken
(mortally wounded); Capt. Robert D. Creamer

First Division Artillery
1st Iowa Battery: Capt. Henry H. Griffiths
Battery F, 2nd Missouri Light Artillery: Capt. Clemens Landgraeber
4th Ohio Battery: Capt. Louis Hoffmann

SECOND DIVISION: MAJ. GEN. FRANK P. BLAIR

First Brigade: Col. Giles A. Smith
113th Illinois: Col. George B. Hoge
116th Illinois: Col. Nathan W. Tupper
6th Missouri: Lt. Col. Ira Boutell
8th Missouri: Lt. Col. David C. Coleman (missing); Maj. Dennis T. Kirby
1st Battalion, 13th U.S. Infantry: Capt. Edward C.
Washington (missing); Capt. Charles Ewing

Second Brigade: Col. Thomas Kilby Smith
55th Illinois: Col. Oscar Malmborg
127th Illinois: Col. Hamilton N. Eldridge
83rd Indiana: Col. Benjamin J. Spooner
54th Ohio: Lt. Col. Cyrus W. Fisher
57th Ohio: Col. Americus V. Rice

Third Brigade: Brig. Gen. Hugh Ewing
30th Ohio: Lt. Col. George H. Hildt
37th Ohio: Lt. Col. Louis von Blessingh
47th Ohio: Col. Augustus C. Parry
4th West Virginia: Col. James H. Dayton

Second Division Artillery
Battery A, 1st Illinois Light Artillery: Capt. Peter P. Wood
Battery B, 1st Illinois Light Artillery: Capt. Samuel E. Barrett
Battery H, 1st Illinois Light Artillery: Capt. Levi W. Hart
8th Ohio Battery: Capt. James F. Putnam

THIRD DIVISION: BRIG. GEN. JAMES M. TUTTLE

First Brigade: Brig. Gen. Ralph P. Buckland
114th Illinois: Col. James W. Judy
93rd Indiana: Col. De Witt C. Thomas
72nd Ohio: Lt. Col. Le Roy Crockett
95th Ohio: Col. William L. McMillen

Second Brigade: Brig. Gen. Joseph A. Mower
47th Illinois: Lt. Col. Samuel R. Baker
5th Minnesota: Col. Lucius F. Hubbard
11th Missouri: Col. Andrew J. Weber
8th Wisconsin: Col. George W. Robbins

Third Brigade: Brig. Gen. Charles L. Matthies
8th Iowa: Col. James L. Geddes
12th Iowa: Col. Joseph J. Woods
35th Iowa: Col. Sylvester G. Hill

Third Division Artillery
Battery E, 1st Illinois Light Artillery: Capt. Allen C. Waterhouse
2nd Iowa Battery: Lt. Joseph R. Reed

Seventeenth Corps: Maj. Gen. James B. McPherson

THIRD DIVISION: MAJ. GEN. JOHN A. LOGAN

First Brigade: Brig. Gen. John E. Smith
20th Illinois: Maj. Daniel Bradley
31st Illinois: Lt. Col. John D. Rees
45th Illinois: Col. Jasper A. Maltby
124th Illinois: Col. Thomas J. Sloan
23rd Indiana: Lt. Col. William P. Davis

Second Brigade: Brig. Gen. Mortimer D. Leggett
30th Illinois: Lt. Col. Warren Shedd
20th Ohio: Col. Manning F. Force
68th Ohio: Col. Robert K. Scott
78th Ohio: Lt. Col. Greenberry F. Wiles

Third Brigade: Brig. Gen. John D. Stevenson
8th Illinois: Lt. Col. Robert H. Sturgess
17th Illinois: Maj. Frank F. Peats
81st Illinois: Col. James J. Dollins (killed); Lt. Col. Franklin Campbell
7th Missouri: Capt. Robert Buchanan
32nd Ohio: Col. Benjamin F. Potts

Third Division Artillery
Battery D, 1st Illinois Light Artillery: Capt. Henry A. Rogers
Battery L, 2nd Illinois Light Artillery: Capt. William H. Bolton
8th Michigan Battery: Capt. Samuel De Golyer
3rd Ohio Battery: Capt. William S. Williams

SIXTH DIVISION: BRIG. GEN. JOHN MCARTHUR

Second Brigade: Brig. Gen. Thomas E. G. Ransom
11th Illinois: Lt. Col. Garrett Nevins
72nd Illinois: Col. Frederick A. Starring (sick); Maj. Joseph Stockton
95th Illinois: Col. Thomas W. Humphrey
14th Wisconsin: Col. Lyman M. Ward
17th Wisconsin: Lt. Col. Thomas McMahon

Third Brigade: Col. William Hall
11th Iowa: Lt. Col. John C. Abercrombie
13th Iowa: Col. John Shane
15th Iowa: Col. William W. Belknap
16th Iowa: Lt. Col. Addison H. Sanders

Sixth Division Artillery
Battery F, 2nd Illinois Light Artillery: Capt. John W. Powell
1st Minnesota Battery: Capt. William Z. Clayton
Battery C, 1st Missouri Light Artillery: Capt. Charles Mann
10th Ohio Battery: Capt. Hamilton B. White

SEVENTH DIVISION: BRIG. GEN. ISAAC F. QUINBY

First Brigade: Col. John B. Sanborn
48th Indiana: Col. Norman Eddy
59th Indiana: Col. Jesse I. Alexander
4th Minnesota: Lt. Col. John E. Tourtellotte
18th Wisconsin: Col. Gabriel Bouck

Second Brigade: Col. Samuel A. Holmes
56th Illinois: Col. Green B. Raum
17th Iowa: Col. David B. Hillis
10th Missouri: Maj. Francis C. Deimling
24th Missouri, Company E: Lt. Daniel Driscoll
80th Ohio: Col. Matthias H. Bartilson

Third Brigade: Col. George B. Boomer (killed); Col. Holden Putnam
93rd Illinois: Col. Holden Putnam; Lt. Col. Nicholas C. Buswell
5th Iowa: Lt. Col. Ezekiel S. Sampson
10th Iowa: Col. William E. Small
26th Missouri: Capt. Benjamin D. Dean

Seventh Division Artillery
Battery M, 1st Missouri Light Artillery: Lt. Junius W. MacMurray
11th Ohio Battery: Lt. Fletcher E. Armstrong
6th Wisconsin Battery: Capt. Henry Dillon
12th Wisconsin Battery: Capt. William Zickerick

ARMY OF MISSISSIPPI AND EASTERN LOUISIANA (ARMY OF VICKSBURG): LT. GEN. JOHN C. PEMBERTON

STEVENSON'S DIVISION: MAJ. GEN. CARTER L. STEVENSON

First Brigade: Brig. Gen. Seth M. Barton
40th Georgia: Lt. Col. R. M. Young
41st Georgia: Col. William E. Curtiss
42nd Georgia: Col. R. J. Henderson
43rd Georgia: Capt. M. M. Grantham
52nd Georgia: Maj. John Jay Moore

First Brigade Artillery
Hudson's Mississippi Battery: Lt. Milton H. Trantham
Company A (section), Pointe Coupée Louisiana Artillery: Lt. John Yoist
Company C, Pointe Coupée Louisiana Artillery: Capt. Alexander Chust

Second Brigade: Brig. Gen. Alfred Cumming
34th Georgia: Col. James A. W. Johnson
36th Georgia: Maj. Charles E. Broyles
39th Georgia: Lt. Col. J. F. B. Jackson
56th Georgia: Lt. Col. J. T. Slaughter
57th Georgia: Col. William Barkuloo

Second Brigade Artillery
Cherokee Georgia Artillery: Capt. M. Van Den Corput

Third Brigade: Brig. Gen. Stephen D. Lee
20th Alabama: Col. Edmund W. Pettus
23rd Alabama: Col. Franklin K. Beck
30th Alabama: Capt. John C. Francis
31st Alabama: Lt. Col. T. M. Arrington
46th Alabama: Col. Edmund W. Pettus (temporarily)

Third Brigade Artillery
Waddell's Alabama Battery: Capt. J. F. Waddell

Fourth Brigade: Col. Alexander W. Reynolds
3rd Tennessee (Provisional Army): Col. N. J. Lillard
39th Tennessee: Col. William M. Bradford
43rd Tennessee: Col. James W. Gillespie
59th Tennessee: Col. William L. Eakin

Fourth Brigade Artillery
3rd Maryland Battery: Capt. John B. Rowan

Waul's Texas Legion: Col. Thomas N. Waul
1st Battalion (Infantry): Maj. Eugene S. Bolling
2nd Battalion (Infantry): Lt. Col. James Wrigley
Cavalry Battalion: Lt. Thomas J. Cleveland
Artillery Company: Capt. J. Q. Wall

Stevenson's Division Artillery
Botetourt Virginia Artillery: Lt. James P. Wright

FORNEY'S DIVISION: MAJ. GEN. JOHN H. FORNEY

Hébert's Brigade: Brig. Gen. Louis Hébert
3rd Louisiana: Maj. David Pierson
21st Louisiana: Lt. Col. J. T. Plattsmier
36th Mississippi: Col. W. W. Witherspoon
37th Mississippi: Col. Orlando S. Holland
38th Mississippi: Capt. D. B. Seal
43rd Mississippi: Col. Richard Harrison
7th Mississippi Battalion: Capt. A. M. Dozier

Hébert's Brigade Artillery
Company C, 2nd Alabama Artillery Battalion: Lt. John R. Selater
Appeal (Arkansas) Battery: Lt. R. N. Cotten

Moore's Brigade: Brig. Gen. John C. Moore
37th Alabama: Col. J. F. Dowdell
40th Alabama: Col. John H. Higley
42nd Alabama: Col. John W. Portis
35th Mississippi: Lt. Col. C. R. Jordan
40th Mississippi: Col. W. B. Colbert
2nd Texas: Col. Ashbel Smith

Moore's Brigade Artillery
Sengstak's Alabama Battery: Capt. H. H. Sengstak
Company B, Pointe Coupée Louisiana Artillery: Capt. William A. Davidson

SMITH'S DIVISION: MAJ. GEN. MARTIN L. SMITH

Baldwin's Brigade: Brig. Gen. William E. Baldwin
17th Louisiana: Col. Robert Richardson
31st Louisiana: Lt. Col. James W. Draughon
4th Mississippi: Capt. Thomas P. Nelson
46th Mississippi: Col. Claudius Wistar Sears

Baldwin's Brigade Artillery
Tobin's Tennessee Battery: Capt. Thomas F. Tobin

Vaughn's Brigade: Brig. Gen. John C. Vaughn
60th Tennessee: Capt. J. W. Bachman
61st Tennessee: Lt. Col. James G. Rose
62nd Tennessee: Col. John A. Rowan

Shoup's Brigade: Brig. Gen. Francis A. Shoup
26th Louisiana: Lt. Col. William C. Crow
27th Louisiana: Col. L. D. Marks
28th Louisiana: Col. Allen Thomas

Shoup's Brigade Artillery
McNally's Arkansas Battery: Capt. Joseph T. Hatch

Mississippi State Troops: Brig. Gen. Jeptha V. Harris
5th Regiment: Col. H. C. Robinson
3rd Battalion: Lt. Col. Thomas A. Burgin

Smith's Division Artillery
14th Mississippi Light Artillery Battalion: Maj. M. S. Ward

BOWEN'S DIVISION: MAJ. GEN. JOHN S. BOWEN

First Brigade: Col. Francis M. Cockrell
1st Missouri: Col. A. C. Riley
2nd Missouri: Lt. Col. Pembroke S. Senteny
3rd Missouri: Maj. J. K. McDowell
5th Missouri: Col. James McCown
6th Missouri: Maj. S. Cooper

First Brigade Artillery
Guibor's Missouri Battery: Lt. Cornelius Heffernan
Landis's Missouri Battery: Lt. John W. Langan
Wade's Missouri Battery: Lt. R. C. Walsh

Second Brigade: Brig. Gen. Martin E. Green
15th Arkansas: Capt. Caleb Davis
19th Arkansas: Col. Thomas P. Dockery
20th Arkansas: Col. D. W. Jones
21st Arkansas: Capt. A. Tyler
1st Arkansas Cavalry Battalion (dismounted): Capt. John J. Clark
12th Arkansas Battalion (sharpshooters): Lt. John S. Bell
1st Missouri Cavalry (dismounted): Maj. William C. Parker
3rd Missouri Cavalry (dismounted): Capt. Felix Lotspeich

Second Brigade Artillery
Dawson's Missouri Battery: Capt. William E. Dawson
Lowe's Missouri Battery: Lt. Thomas B. Catron

NOTES

ABBREVIATIONS

AC   Augustana College, Special Collections, Rock Island, Illinois

ADAH   Alabama Department of Archives and History, Montgomery

AHC   Atlanta History Center, Atlanta, Georgia

ALPL   Abraham Lincoln Presidential Library, Springfield, Illinois

BHL-UM   University of Michigan, Bentley Historical Library, Ann Arbor

CHM   Chicago History Museum, Chicago, Illinois

CPL   Cleveland Public Library, History Branch and Archives, Cleveland, Tennessee

CWM   College of William and Mary, Manuscripts and Rare Books Department, Williamsburg, Virginia

DU   Duke University, Rubenstein Rare Book and Manuscript Library, Durham, North Carolina

EU   Emory University, Manuscript, Archives, and Rare Book Library, Atlanta, Georgia

FHS   Filson Historical Society, Louisville, Kentucky

GLIAH   Gilder-Lehrman Institute of American History, New-York Historical Society, New York, New York

HL   Huntington Library, San Marino, California

IHS   Indiana Historical Society, Indianapolis

ISL   Indiana State Library, Indianapolis

ISU   Iowa State University, Special Collections, Ames

KHS   Kentucky Historical Society, Frankfort

LC   Library of Congress, Manuscript Division, Washington, D.C.

LSU   Louisiana State University, Louisiana and Lower Mississippi Valley Collection, Special Collections, Baton Rouge

MHM   Missouri History Museum, St. Louis

MHS   Minnesota Historical Society, St. Paul

MU   Miami University, Walter Havighurst Special Collections, Oxford, Ohio

NARA National Archives and Records Administration, Washington, D.C.
NC Navarro College, Pearce Civil War Collection, Corsicana, Texas
NL Newberry Library, Chicago, Illinois
OCHM Old Court House Museum, Vicksburg, Mississippi
OHS Ohio Historical Society, Columbus
OR *The War of the Rebellion: A Compilation of the Official Records of the Union and Confederate Armies.* 70 vols. in 128. Washington, D.C.: Government Printing Office, 1880–1901.
ORN *Official Records of the Union and Confederate Navies in the War of the Rebellion.* 30 vols. Washington, D.C.: Government Printing Office, 1894–1922.
RBHPC Rutherford B. Hayes Presidential Center, Fremont, Ohio
SHSI State Historical Society of Iowa, Iowa City
SHSM-RCC State Historical Society of Missouri, Research Center Columbia
SHSM-RCR State Historical Society of Missouri, Research Center Rolla
SIU Southern Illinois University, Special Collections Research Center, Carbondale
SOR *Supplement to the Official Records of the Union and Confederate Armies.* 100 Vols. Wilmington, N.C.: Broadfoot, 1995–99.
SU Stanford University, Special Collections and University Archives, Palo Alto, California
UA University of Alabama, Special Collections, Tuscaloosa
UCB University of California, Bancroft Library, Berkeley
UGA University of Georgia, Hargrett Rare Book and Manuscript Library, Athens
UI University of Iowa, Special Collections, Iowa City
UNC University of North Carolina, Southern Historical Collection, Chapel Hill
UO University of Oklahoma, Western History Collections, Norman
USAMHI U.S. Army Military History Institute, Carlisle, Pennsylvania
UTA University of Texas, Dolph Briscoe Center for American History, Austin
UTK University of Tennessee, Special Collections, Knoxville
UVA University of Virginia, Special Collections, Charlottesville
UW University of Washington, Special Collections, Seattle
VHS Virginia Historical Society, Richmond
VNMP Vicksburg National Military Park, Vicksburg, Mississippi
WHS Wisconsin Historical Society, Madison

PREFACE

1. Bod to editor, May 23, 1863, *Chicago Daily Tribune*, June 4, 1863.
2. Ulysses S. Grant, *Memoirs*, 588.
3. Hess, *Rifle Musket*, 197–215.

CHAPTER 1

1. Ballard, *Vicksburg: The Campaign*, 129–55, 191–220.

2. Ballard, 221–318.

3. Ballard, *Grant at Vicksburg*, 93.

4. Ulysses S. Grant, *Memoirs*, 358; *OR* 24(1):269.

5. *OR* 24(1):269.

6. Ballard, *Vicksburg: The Campaign*, 294, 296, 298, 300–303, 306–8.

7. Ballard, 310–15.

8. Ballard, 311, 316–18; Ulysses S. Grant, *Memoirs*, 350.

9. John Cowdry Taylor diary, May 17, 1863, Taylor Family Papers, UVA; *OR* 24(1):269.

10. Ballard, *Pemberton*, 3–113; R. H. Chilton to William T. Sherman, October 31, 1872, Sherman Papers, LC.

11. Hess, *Civil War in the West*, 57–60, 75–83.

12. See, for example, *OR* 24(3):1059–60.

13. Lockett, "Defense of Vicksburg," 488; Ballard, *Pemberton*, 165.

14. Lockett, "Defense of Vicksburg," 488.

15. *OR* 24(1):271; Lee, "Siege of Vicksburg," 55.

16. *OR* 24(1):271.

17. *OR* 24(2):365–66; *OR* 24(1):270–71; Bearss, *Unvexed to the Sea*, 731.

18. "An Autobiography of Louis Hébert," 12, Hébert Papers, UNC; *OR* 24(3):888–89; *OR* 24(2):374–75; Tunnard, *Southern Record*, 235–36.

19. *OR* 24(2):375, 379–80.

20. *OR* 24(2):385; Foster Letter, UA; Willett, Pickens Planters Diary, 53–54, ADAH.

21. *OR* 24(1):271; *OR* 24(2):366.

22. *OR* 24(2):343.

23. *OR* 24(2):343, 401; Bearss, *Unvexed to the Sea*, 733–34.

24. *OR* 24(2):350, 352–53; *OR* 24(3):891.

25. Chambers Diaries, May 16, 17, 1863, LSU; Balfour, *Vicksburg*, unpaginated.

26. Cable, "Woman's Diary," 770–71; Maynard, "Vicksburg Diary," 47.

27. Camp, "'What I Know,'" 64; Hall, *26th Louisiana*, 66.

28. Cable, "Woman's Diary," 771; Nestor, "Inside View of the Siege of Vicksburg," *Memphis Daily Appeal*, July 27, 1863.

29. Ruyle Letter, 32, SHSM-RCR; John Cowdry Taylor diary, May 17, 1863, Taylor Family Papers, UVA; Willis Herbert Claiborne journal, June 7, 1863, Claiborne Papers, UNC; Abrams, *Full and Detailed*, 29; Foster Letter, UA; Moss, "Missouri Confederate," 40.

30. Shoup, "Vicksburg," 172.

31. Balfour, *Vicksburg*, unpaginated; Cable, "Woman's Diary," 771; Fisher Diary, May 17, 1863, MHM; Bevier, *First and Second Missouri*, 199; *OR* 24(2):418, 420.

32. Abrams, *Full and Detailed*, 29; Lida Lord Reed, "Woman's Experiences," 922–23.

33. *OR* 10(2): 430; Lockett, "Defense of Vicksburg," 482–83.

34. Lockett, "Defense of Vicksburg," 484; Bearss, *Rebel Victory*, 121–285; Hess, *Civil War in the West*, 79–82.

35. Lockett, "Defense of Vicksburg," 484; "The Defence of Vicksburg from an Engineering Point of View," folder 9, Lockett Papers, UNC.

36. "The Defence of Vicksburg from an Engineering Point of View," folder 9, Lockett Papers, UNC; Lockett, "Defense of Vicksburg," 484.

37. Lockett, "Defense of Vicksburg," 482–84; "The Defence of Vicksburg from an Engineering Point of View," folder 9, Lockett Papers, UNC; *OR* 24(1):273.

38. Hewitt, Schott, and Kunis, *To Succeed*, 14.

39. *OR* 24(1):273; Lockett, "Defense of Vicksburg," 487; *OR* 24(2):335.

40. Evans, "Second Texas," 596; *OR* 24(2):366, 381, 385; Ashbel Smith to James M. Loughborough, July 8, 1863, Smith Papers, UTA; Foster Letter, UA; "History of Company B," 176–77; Chance, *Second Texas*, 103.

41. Truman, "Memoirs of the Civil War" (web page); Moss, "Missouri Confederate," 40.

42. *OR* 24(1):272; Lockett, "Defense of Vicksburg," 488; Dodd, "Recollections," 2; circular, Headquarters, Department of Mississippi and Eastern Louisiana, May 17, 1863, Order Book, VHS; Ballard, *Vicksburg: The Campaign*, 319–20.

43. *OR* 24(1):213.

44. *OR* 24(1):215, 220–21.

45. Ulysses S. Grant, *Memoirs*, 353; Thomas M. Stevenson, *78th Regiment*, 237.

46. *OR* 24(2):263.

47. *OR* 24(3):321–22.

48. *OR* 24(3):322; Fowler and Miller, *Thirtieth Iowa*, 28; Ulysses S. Grant, *Memoirs*, 353; *OR* 24(2):251, 256.

49. *OR* 24(3):322.

50. Bearss, *Unvexed to the Sea*, 752; *SOR*, 4(1):391.

51. Lacey Diary, May 16–17, 1863, NL; Martin quoted in Alonzo L. Brown, *Fourth Regiment*, 218–19.

52. Osborn, "Tennessean," 357.

CHAPTER 2

1. Spencer Diary, May 18, 1863, SHSM-RCR; diary, May 18, 1863, Smith Papers, NC; diary, May 18, 1863, Patterson Papers, DU.

2. Obenchain to John W. Johnston, March 18, 1904, Botetourt Virginia Artillery Folder, VNMP; Bearss, *Unvexed to the Sea*, 740; *OR* 24(1):273; Lee, "Siege of Vicksburg," 56; S. N. Pickens to William Rigby, April 16, 1902, 27th Louisiana Folder, VNMP.

3. *OR* 24(2):169–70, 330; Lockett, "Defense of Vicksburg," 488.

4. Bearrs, *Unvexed to the Sea*, 743n; Truman, "Memoirs of the Civil War" (web page).

5. *OR* 24(2):169; Young, "Confederate Fort Hill," 3–4, 13, 16, 19–20.

6. Grabau, *Ninety-Eight Days*, 45; Bearrs, *Unvexed to the Sea*, 741, 741n; S. N. Pickens to William Rigby, April 16, 1902, 27th Louisiana Folder, VNMP.

7. Grabau, *Ninety-Eight Days*, 47.

8. Grabau, 45–46.

9. Grabau, 46, 375–76.

10. Grabau, 46–47.

11. Grabau, 21–22, 48.

12. Stephen D. Lee, quoted in T. B. Marshall, *Eighty-Third Ohio*, 83–84; Lee, "Siege of Vicksburg," 56; Lockett, "Defense of Vicksburg," 483; *OR* 24(2):169; Fisher Diary, May 18, 1863, MHM.

13. Ulysses S. Grant, *Memoirs*, 359–60; *OR* 24(2):169; Loosley to wife, June 1, 1863, Loosley Papers, SIU; M. F. Force to "Loula," May 25, 1863, Force Papers, UW.

14. Grabau, *Ninety-Eight Days*, 22.

15. Grabau, 47–48; *OR* 24(2):169; J. H. Jones, "Rank and File," 19; Bearss, *Unvexed to the Sea*, 761.

16. *OR* 24(1):271; Lee, "Siege of Vicksburg," 56–57.

17. George H. Frost to Lockett, September 11, 1885, Lockett Papers, UNC.

18. *OR* 24(1):272; *OR* 24(3):889.

19. *OR* 24(1):272.

20. *OR* 24(1):272–73; *OR* 24(3):890; Stephen D. Lee, "Siege of Vicksburg," 1, folder 33, Claiborne Papers, UNC.

21. *OR* 24(1):272; *OR* 24(3):890.

22. Shoup, "Vicksburg," 172; *OR* 24(2):405–6.

23. Frost to Lockett, September 11, 1885, Lockett Papers, UNC; *OR* 24(2):406.

24. Oldroyd, *Soldier's Story*, 26; Lay Diary, May 18, 1863, RBHPC; diary, May 18, 1863, Warmoth Papers, UNC.

25. Ballard, *Grant at Vicksburg*, 11; Shea and Winschel, *Vicksburg Is the Key*, 142; Wilson journal, *SOR*, 4(1):267–68.

26. *OR* 24(2):256.

27. Diary, May 18, 1863, Kimbell Papers, CHM; Wood Diary, May 18, 1863, UCB; Ainsworth Diary, May 18, 1863, BHL-UM; Kellogg, *War Experiences*, 35; Heath Diary, May 18, 1863, OCHM; H. S. Keene diary, May 18, 1863, 6th Wisconsin Battery Folder, VNMP; Dillon to wife, May 22, 1863, Dillon Papers, HL.

28. *OR* 24(2):256–57; Sherman, *Memoirs*, 1:324; Pitzman, "Vicksburg Campaign," 114; Bearss, *Unvexed to the Sea*, 749.

29. Bearss, *Unvexed to the Sea*, 749; *OR* 24(2):266–67, 274, 276–77; Andrew McCormack to parents and sisters, May 24, 1863, McCormack Papers, NC; "Military History of Capt. Thomas Sewell, Co. G, 127th Ill. Vol. Inf. during the War of the Rebellion, 1861 to 1865," Sewell Papers, DU.

30. *OR* 24(2):263.

31. Bearss, *Unvexed to the Sea*, 749; Fowler and Miller, *Thirtieth Iowa*, 28; Sherman, *Memoirs*, 1:325; Strong, "Campaign against Vicksburg," 328.

32. *OR* 24(2):251; Robert Bruce Hoadley to cousin, May 29, 1863, Hoadley Papers, DU; Wood Diary, May 18, 1863, UCB.

33. *OR* 24(2):397, 401, 406; *SOR*, 4(1):414; Sanders, *Diary in Gray*, 19; Sears Diary, May 18, 1863, Mississippi Department of Archives and History, Jackson; Bearss, *Unvexed to the Sea*, 737–38, 750.

34. *OR* 24(2):414; Bevier, *First and Second Missouri*, 200–201; Anderson, *Memoirs*, 327; Fisher Diary, May 19, 1863, MHM; Leach Diary, May 18, 1863, SHSM-RCR.

35. *OR* 24(2):397; Frost to Lockett, September 11, 1885, Lockett Papers, UNC; Stamper Diary, May 18, 1863, CPL; Bearss, *Unvexed to the Sea*, 737–38.

36. *Story of the Fifty-Fifth Regiment*, 234–35; Wood Diary, May 18, 1863, UCB; Ainsworth Diary, May 18, 1863, BHL-UM.

37. Ulysses S. Grant, *Memoirs*, 353–54.

38. *OR* 24(3):324; Bevier, *First and Second Missouri*, 200; *OR* 24(2):375; James West Smith, "Confederate Soldier's Diary," 295; [Newsome], *Experience in the War*, 28; Edwin A. Loosley to wife, June 1, 1863, Loosley Papers, SIU.

39. *OR* 24(3):324; *OR* 24(1):153; *OR* 24(2):33, 387; Webb quoted in Bentley, *77th Illinois*, 148–50.

40. McClernand to Abraham Lincoln, May 29, 1863, Lincoln Papers, LC; Bond, *Under the Flag*, 63; Erickson, "With Grant at Vicksburg," 476.

41. Diary, May 18, 1863, Connor Family Papers, UGA; Champion to wife, May 18, 1863, Champion Papers, DU.

42. Sanders, *Diary in Gray*, 19; Brotherton to father, May 18, 1863, Brotherton Papers, EU.

43. *OR* 24(3):890.

44. A document purportedly written by Pemberton to allay soldier fears of immediate surrender was printed in Abbott (*Civil War in America*, 2:292), but the content and tone are so unlike the orders genuinely issued by Pemberton's headquarters and printed in the *Official Records* that one must wonder if it is a forgery. See also Ballard (*Pemberton*, 168) on this issue. For genuine orders concerning the feeding of animals and conserving ammunition, see General Orders No. 73; and circular, Headquarters, Department of Mississippi and Eastern Louisiana, May 18, 1863, both in Order Book, VHS.

45. *OR* 24(3):890; *OR* 24(1):271–72; Bearss, *Unvexed to the Sea*, 738.

46. *OR* 24(3):889–90; Johnston to Samuel Cooper, May 18, 1863, Letters Sent, January 28, 1862–July 22, 1863, no. 3, box 4, vol. 4, Johnston Papers, CWM.

47. Johnston to Cooper, May 18, 1863, Letters Sent, January 28, 1862–July 22, 1863, no. 3, box 4, vol. 4, Johnston Papers, CWM; Foster Letter, UA; *OR* 24(3):891.

48. Hogane, "Reminiscences," 292; *OR* 24(1):273.

49. *OR* 24(1):273; *OR* 24(3):890.

50. *OR* 24(3):891; Maynard, "Vicksburg Diary," 47; *OR* 24(2):401.

51. *OR* 24(2):406, 414; Hall, *26th Louisiana*, 67; *OR* 24(3):890; Hogane, "Reminiscences," 292.

52. *OR* 24(2):397; *OR* 24(1):273; John Cowdry Taylor diary, May 18, 1863, Taylor Family Papers, UVA; Shoup, "Vicksburg," 172; Baumgartner, *Blood and Sacrifice*, 75–76.

53. Shoup, "Vicksburg," 172; Balfour, *Vicksburg*, not paginated.

54. *ORN* 25:5.

55. Hearn, *Porter*, 228.

56. Hearn, 226–28; Porter, *Naval History*, 320; Milligan, *From the Fresh-Water Navy*, 178.

57. *ORN* 25:5; Porter, *Naval History*, 319.

58. *ORN* 25:5; Porter, *Naval History*, 320.

59. *OR* 24(3):325.

60. *ORN* 25:5–6; *OR* 24(2):337.

61. Diary, May 18, 1863, Smith Papers, NC; Rigby to brother, May 18, 1863, Rigby Papers, UI.

62. Fike, "Diary," 250–51.

CHAPTER 3

1. Diary, May 19, 1863, Kimbell Papers, CHM; diary, May 19, 1863, Smith Papers, NC; *SOR*, 4(1):269; *OR* 24(1):54; Ulysses S. Grant, *Memoirs*, 354.

2. *OR* 24(3):329; *OR* 24(1):54; Erickson, "With Grant at Vicksburg," 476–77; *OR* 24(2):168–69.

3. Ulysses S. Grant, *Memoirs*, 354; Ballard, *Vicksburg: The Campaign*, 328, 330.

4. *OR* 24(2):257, 267.

5. Merrilles Diary, May 19, 1863, CHM; Brinkerhoff, *Thirtieth Regiment Ohio*, 69;

William A. Simmons, "The Siege and Capture of Vicksburg," *National Tribune,* May 17, 1883.

6. Diary, May 19, 1863, Kimbell Papers, CHM; *OR* 24(2):262, 406; Forney to Lockett, May 19, 1863, 12:45 P.M., "General Maury's Order Book," Confederate States of America Collection, CHM.

7. Sanders, *Diary in Gray,* 19.

8. Hall, *26th Louisiana,* 68.

9. Hall, 68, 72–73; *SOR,* 4(1):414.

10. Bearss, *Unvexed to the Sea,* 761; *OR* 24(2):414; Winschel, "First Honor," 9; Bevier, *First and Second Missouri,* 202.

11. *OR* 24(2):267, 274, 277.

12. Merrilles Diary, May 19, 1863, CHM; *OR* 24(2):257, 274; Kellogg, *War Experiences,* 28; McCormack to parents and sisters, May 24, 1863, McCormack Papers, NC.

13. *OR* 24(2):268, 277; Walter George Smith, *Life and Letters,* 295.

14. *OR* 24(2):257, 268, 280; Robert Oliver to William Rigby, April 6, 1902, 55th Illinois Folder, VNMP; Winschel, "First Honor," 13; Vance, *Report of the Adjutant General,* 6:512.

15. *OR* 24(2):268.

16. *OR* 24(2):268; Andrew McCormack to parents and sisters, May 24, 1863, McCormack Papers, NC; "War Diary," 362; *Story of the Fifty-Fifth Regiment,* 235–36.

17. *OR* 24(2):277.

18. Crumpton, *Book of Memories,* 72; *OR* 24(2):376; Lacey Diary, May 19, 1863, NL.

19. Kellogg, *War Experiences,* 27; *OR* 24(2):264.

20. *OR* 24(2):264; C. H. Smart, "Personal Recollections of Vicksburg, May, 1863," 13th U.S. Infantry Folder, VNMP; Kellogg, *War Experiences,* 28; Temple, *Civil War Letters,* 41.

21. Temple, *Civil War Letters,* 41; Kellogg, *War Experiences,* 28–29.

22. Winschel, "First Honor," 3–4, 7, 9; Noble Warwick to William Rigby, October 25, 1906, and Frank P. Muhlenberg to Rigby, n.d., 13th U.S. Infantry Folder, VNMP; Shea and Winschel, *Vicksburg Is the Key,* 146; McAlexander, *Thirteenth Regiment,* 238.

23. Winschel, "First Honor," 9–10, 12; Nelson to W. W. Gardner, February 2, 1902; Frank P. Muhlenberg to William Rigby, March 11, 1903; and Helm letter, n.d., all in 13th U.S. Infantry Folder, VNMP.

24. Winschel, "First Honor," 12–13; Winschel, *Triumph and Defeat,* 120, 125; clipping, Gardner to Levi Fuller, May 25, 1863, *West Union* (Iowa) *Gazette;* Frank P. Muhlenberg to William Rigby, July 9, 1902, January 21, March 16, 1903; and C. H. Smart, "Personal Recollections of Vicksburg, May, 1863," all in 13th U.S. Infantry Folder, VNMP; Thomas Ewing to Henry W. Halleck, July 24, 1863, Ewing Family Papers, LC; McAlexander, *Thirteenth Regiment,* 235, 237–38; *OR* 24(2):264.

25. Charles Ewing to Thomas Ewing, May 22, 1863, Ewing Family Papers, LC; Robert M. Nelson to Gardner, February 2, 1902; Frank P. Muhlenberg to William Rigby, March 11, 1903; and C. H. Smart, "Personal Recollections of Vicksburg, May, 1863," all in 13th U.S. Infantry Folder, VNMP; *OR* 24(2):257, 359; Temple, *Civil War Letters,* 41.

26. Kellogg, *War Experiences,* 29–30.

27. Kellogg, 30–31.

28. Bock, "Confederate Col. A. C. Riley," 282; Francis A. Shoup to John G. Devereux, July 8, 1863, Devereux Papers, UNC; N. M. Baker to "Comrade," September 27, 1902, 116th Illinois Folder, VNMP; Jeremiah N. Sherman to William Rigby, July 1902, Battery A, 1st Illinois, Folder, VNMP; *OR* 24(2):359, 414.

29. *OR* 24(2):257, 281, 283; *SOR*, 52(2):222; diary, May 19, 1863, Jacobs Diaries and Lists, LSU; Brinkerhoff, *Thirtieth Regiment Ohio*, 69.

30. *OR* 24(2):281–84, 397–98; diary, May 19, 1863, Jacobs Diaries and Lists, LSU; Saunier, *Forty-Seventh Regiment Ohio*, 144; Ballard, *Vicksburg: The Campaign*, 329.

31. *OR* 24(2):257; S. B. McCutcheon to William Rigby, January 21, February 10, 1903, 27th Louisiana Folder, VNMP.

32. *SOR*, 4(1):414; Hall, *26th Louisiana*, 68; *OR* 24(2):406; Thomas T. Taylor to William Rigby, March 19, 1903, 47th Ohio Folder, VNMP; Saunier, *Forty-Seventh Regiment Ohio*, 144–45, 152; Barton, *Autobiography*, 152; Winschel, "First Honor," 13.

33. Anderson, *Memoirs*, 328–29; S. B. McCutcheon to William Rigby, January 21, 1903, 27th Louisiana Folder, VNMP; Synnamon Letter, SHSM-RCR; Fowler Civil War Diary, May 19, 1863, SU.

34. *OR* 24(2):282.

35. *OR* 24(2):282; diary, May 19, 1863, Jacobs Diaries and Lists, LSU; Brinkerhoff, *Thirtieth Regiment Ohio*, 70.

36. Walter George Smith, *Life and Letters*, 295–96, 307, 314, 333; *OR* 24(2):274, 277, 280; *Story of the Fifty-Fifth Regiment*, 236.

37. "Military History of Capt. Thomas Sewell, Co. G, 127th Ill. Vol. Inf. during the War of the Rebellion, 1861 to 1865," Sewell Papers, DU.

38. *Story of the Fifty-Fifth Regiment*, 237–39; Sherman, *Memoirs*, 1:326; clipping, "Youngest Civil War Soldier, Now 83, Visiting Sister in Sioux City," 55th Illinois Folder, VNMP.

39. *Story of the Fifty-Fifth Regiment*, 239–41; clipping, "Story Told by Captain," *Streator Daily Free Press*; and clipping, "Taps Sounded for L. D. Howe, 'Youngest Vet,'" both in 55th Illinois Folder, VNMP; "Where Is He Now?" *National Tribune*, January 7, 1882; "War Diary," 382; Frederick D. Grant, "Boy's Experience," 96.

40. *OR* 24(2):259; Ewing to father, May 22, 1863, Ewing Family Papers, LC; McAlexander, *Thirteenth Regiment*, 235, 238; Winschel, "First Honor," 10n, 17.

41. Werkheiser to brother and sister, August 12, 1863, Werkheiser Papers, NC; Kellogg, *War Experiences*, 33; Temple, *Civil War Letters*, 41–42.

42. *OR* 24(2):283–84; Barton, *Autobiography*, 153.

43. *OR* 24(2):251; Thomas to friend, May 26, 1863, Johns and Thomas Letters, UTK.

44. *OR* 24(2):251, 402; Hogane, "Reminiscences," 292.

45. Bearss, *Unvexed to the Sea*, 755; Simon, *Papers of Ulysses S. Grant*, 8:240n; Diary of Unknown Member, May 19, 1863, Gettysburg College, Special Collections and College Archives, Gettysburg, Pennsylvania; Hoadley to cousin, May 29, 1863, Hoadley Papers, DU.

46. Bek, "Civil War Diary," 509; *OR* 24(2):337; Bearss, *Unvexed to the Sea*, 768–69.

47. Ainsworth Diary, May 19, 1863, BHL-UM; Bennett and Tillery, *Struggle*, 96.

48. Diary, May 19, 1863, Seay Papers, UO.

49. Child Diary, May 19, 1863, UI; Hoadley to cousin, May 29, 1863, Hoadley Papers, DU; *SOR*, 4(1):408; Alonzo Abernethy diary, May 19, 1863, 9th Iowa Folder, VNMP; Fowler and Miller, *Thirtieth Iowa*, 28.

50. Bearss, *Unvexed to the Sea*, 757; Crooker to William Rigby, September 1, 1902, 57th Ohio Folder, VNMP; Brumbach to "Kate," May 20, 23, 1863, 95th Ohio Folder, VNMP; W. M. Mallory diary, May 19, 1863, 72nd Ohio Folder, VNMP; Lay Diary, May 19, 1863, RBHPC.

51. Baumgartner, *Blood and Sacrifice*, 76, 78; OR 24(2):401–2; Sears Diary, May 19, 1863, Mississippi Department of Archives and History, Jackson.

52. OR 24(3):893; diary, May 19, 1863, Bannon Papers, University of South Carolina, South Caroliniana Library, Columbia, South Carolina; John Cowdry Taylor diary, May 19, 1863, Taylor Family Papers, UVA; Shoup, "Vicksburg," 173.

53. Willett, Pickens Planters Diary, 54, ADAH; Lockett, "Defense of Vicksburg," 489; Shoup, "Vicksburg," 173.

54. Simpson and Berlin, *Sherman's Civil War*, 471; Ewing to father, May 22, 1863, Ewing Family Papers, LC; Merrilles Diary, May 19, 1863, CHM.

CHAPTER 4

1. OR 24(2):297; Bearss, *Unvexed to the Sea*, 757.

2. OR 24(2):297, 299.

3. OR 24(2):297, 299–300, 359; Sumner Sayles to not stated, May 29, 1863, Sayles Collection, GLIAH; Bearss, *Unvexed to the Sea*, 769–70.

4. OR 24(2):297.

5. OR 24(2):300; Wood, *Ninety-Fifth Regiment*, 74–75; Sumner Sayles to not stated, May 21, 1863, Sayles Collection, GLIAH; Post, *Soldiers' Letters*, 204–5.

6. OR 24(2):297; L. M. Ward to F. H. Magdeburg, February 27, 1903, 14th Wisconsin Folder, VNMP.

7. Wood, *Ninety-Fifth Regiment*, 75; Sumner Sayles to not stated, May 21, 1863, Sayles Collection, GLIAH; OR 24(2):297.

8. OR 24(2):300.

9. OR 24(2):297, 300.

10. James West Smith, "Confederate Soldier's Diary," 296.

11. Smith, 296–97.

12. [Newsome], *Experience in the War*, 28; Thomas M. Stevenson, *78th Regiment*, 288; William Robert McCrary Diary (website), May 19, 1863; Bearss, *Unvexed to the Sea*, 770; S. R. Tresilian to J. H. Wilson, August 17, 1863, Comstock Papers, LC.

13. J. H. Jones, "History of the Wilkinson Guards," folder 31, Claiborne Papers, UNC; Foster Letter, UA.

14. Byers, *With Fire and Sword*, 88; Oldroyd, *Soldier's Story*, 28–29; Griffith Diaries, May 19, 1863, OHS; diary, May 19, 1863, Hickenlooper Collection, CMC.

15. OR 24(2):292–93, 359; Bearss, *Unvexed to the Sea*, 770n; Molineaux Diaries, May 19, 1863, AC.

16. OR 24(1):153; diary, May 19, 1863, Warmoth Papers, UNC.

17. OR 24(1):153–54; Townsend, *Yankee Warhorse*, 106–7; Grabau, *Ninety-Eight Days*, 356–57; Bearss, *Unvexed to the Sea*, 758–59.

18. OR 24(1):153–54; Bering and Montgomery, *Forty-Eighth Ohio*, 86; diary, May 19, 1863, Warmoth Papers, UNC.

19. OR 24(2):230; OR 24(1):154.

20. McClernand to Lincoln, May 29, 1863, Lincoln Papers, LC; OR 24(1):154; OR 24(2):231; diary, May 19, 1863, Warmoth Papers, UNC.

21. Byrne and Soman, *Your True Marcus*, 278; James Keigwin to William Rigby, March 5, 1902, 49th Indiana Folder, VNMP.

22. *OR* 24(2):17–18, 231–32; diary, May 19, 1863, Dillon Papers, HL.

23. Keigwin to R. W. McClaughry, March 27, 1903, Keigwin's Brigade Folder, VNMP; Keigwin to William Rigby, March 5, 1902, 49th Indiana Folder, VNMP.

24. Byrne and Soman, *Your True Marcus*, 281, 284; James B. Taylor diary, May 19, 1863, 120th Ohio Folder, VNMP; diary, May 19, 1863, Warmoth Papers, UNC; William Rand diary, May 19, 1863, and Rand to brother, May 26, 1863, Rand Family Papers, ALPL; James Leeper to "Mary," May 23, 1863, Leeper Papers, IHS; *OR* 24(2):18, 231.

25. *OR* 24(2):232; Keigwin to William Rigby, March 5, 6, 1902, 49th Indiana Folder, VNMP; Byrne and Soman, *Your True Marcus*, 278–79, 284; Bearss, *Unvexed to the Sea*, 771.

26. *OR* 24(2):18–19; Bond, *Under the Flag*, 64–65.

27. *OR* 24(2):33; Bering and Montgomery, *Forty-Eighth Ohio*, 86; Marshall Diaries, May 19, 1863, MU; Painter, "Bullets, Hardtack and Mud," 151–52; William J. Landram to John Hough, May 25, 1862, and Merrick J. Wald diary, May 19, 1863, 77th Illinois Folder, VNMP; Eddington, "My Civil War Memoirs" (web page).

28. *OR* 24(1):154; diary, May 19, 1863, Warmoth Papers, UNC; Vance, *Report of the Adjutant General*, 2:652.

29. *OR* 24(2):387; Smith to James M. Loughborough, July 8, 1863, Smith Papers, UTA.

30. *OR* 24(3):892–94.

31. *OR* 24(3):892–96; *OR* 24(2):357; *OR* 24(1):273; Phillips, *Personal Reminiscences*, 30.

32. *OR* 24(2):360; *OR* 24(3):896; circular, Headquarters, Department of Mississippi and Eastern Louisiana, May 19, 1863, Order Book, VHS.

33. *OR* 24(1):222, 242; Johnston to Gist, May 19, 1863, Letters Sent, January 28, 1862–July 22, 1863, no. 3, box 4, vol. 4, Johnston Papers, CWM; Bearss, *Unvexed to the Sea*, 748.

34. Johnston to Pemberton, May 19, 1863, and to Gardner, May 19, 1863, Letters Sent, January 28, 1862–July 22, 1863, no. 3, box 4, vol. 4, Johnston Papers, CWM; *OR* 24(3):892.

35. Sanborn, "Campaign against Vicksburg," 132–33; Braudaway, "Civil War Journal," 38.

36. Balfour, *Vicksburg*, not paginated.

37. *OR* 24(3):891–92.

38. Chambers Diaries, May 19, 1863, LSU.

39. Foster Letter, UA.

40. Leach Diary, May 20, 1863, SHSM-RCR; Moss, "Missouri Confederate," 41; Alison Diary, May 19, 1863, UNC; *OR* 24(2):360; Braudaway, "Civil War Journal," 37; Rice Memoir, UTK.

41. James West Smith, "Confederate Soldier's Diary," 296–97.

42. *OR* 24(3):895.

43. Journal, May 20, 1863, Rigby Papers, UI; *OR* 24(2):359.

44. Diary, May 19, 1863, Griffen Papers, ALPL; diary, May 19–20, 1863, McClintock Papers, HL; Grant to Porter, May 19, 1863, Porter Papers, MHM.

45. *OR* 24(3):328–29.

46. Bearss, *Unvexed to the Sea*, 709; Simon, *Papers of Ulysses S. Grant*, 8:240n; ORN 25:17.

47. Bearss, *Unvexed to the Sea*, 708–11; ORN 25:19–20, 26; *OR* 24(2):337.

48. ORN 25:17–18, 26; Bearss, *Unvexed to the Sea*, 711.

49. *ORN* 25:18.

50. *ORN* 25:26.

51. Diary, May 19, 1863, Smith Papers, NC; "Elias D. Moore Diary" (web page), May 19, 1863; Simon, *Papers of Ulysses S. Grant*, 8:240–41; Ainsworth Diary, May 19, 1863, BHL-UM.

52. Andrew McCormack to parents and sisters, May 24, 1863, McCormack Papers, NC.

53. *OR* 24(2):268–69.

54. *OR* 24(2):268–69; Anderson, *Memoirs*, 329; Winter, *Joseph Boyce*, 121; Bearss, *Unvexed to the Sea*, 767.

55. *OR* 24(2):269, 271, 277; David Wilson letter, n.d., 13th U.S. Infantry Folder, VNMP; Winschel, *Triumph and Defeat*, 126–27; *Story of the Fifty-Fifth Regiment*, 236.

56. Kellogg, *War Experiences*, 31–32.

57. *OR* 24(2):359; *OR* 24(3):910.

58. *OR* 24(3):895.

59. Winschel, "First Honor," 17; Winchsel, *Triumph and Defeat*, 127; Nelson to W. W. Gardner, February 2, 1902, 13th U.S. Infantry Folder, VNMP; Simpson and Berlin, *Sherman's Civil War*, 472; Ewing to father, May 22, 1863, Ewing Family Papers, LC.

60. Simpson and Berlin, *Sherman's Civil War*, 472; Lay Diary, May 20, 1863, RBHPC; Frank P. Muhlenberg to William Rigby, February 5, 1903, 13th U.S. Infantry Folder, VNMP; McAlexander, *Thirteenth Regiment*, 238; Winschel, "First Honor," 17. Pvt. James Kephardt of Company C, 13th U.S. Infantry, received the Medal of Honor in 1899 for helping a wounded officer off the field in the May 19 attack. Winschel, "First Honor," 16n.

61. Johnson, *Muskets and Medicine*, 97–100.

62. "Military History of Capt. Thomas Sewell, Co. G, 127th Ill. Vol. Inf. during the War of the Rebellion, 1861 to 1865," Sewell Papers, DU.

63. *OR* 24(2):167; Shea and Winschel, *Vicksburg Is the Key*, 147; Ballard, *Vicksburg: The Campaign*, 332; Bearss, *Unvexed to the Sea*, 774–76, 778; Mumford Diary, May 19, 1863, OCHM.

64. Bearss, *Unvexed to the Sea*, 773; *OR* 24(2):359, 415.

65. *OR* 24(1):54; Ulysses S. Grant, *Memoirs*, 354–55.

66. *SOR*, 4(1):270; diary, May 19, 1863, Warmoth Papers, UNC; journal, May 19, 1863, Rigby Papers, UI; Simpson and Berlin, *Sherman's Civil War*, 471.

CHAPTER 5

1. *OR* 24(2):251; Bearss, *Unvexed to the Sea*, 793; diary, May 20, 1863, Seay Papers, UO; Lay Diary, May 20, 1863, RBHPC.

2. Spencer Diary, May 21, 1863, SHSM-RCR; *OR* 24(2):298; diary, May 21, 1863, Reeves Papers, MHS; Yaggy Diary, May 21, 1863, ALPL; Byrne and Soman, *Your True Marcus*, 279; Bond, *Under the Flag*, 65; Levi Shell to brother, June 23, 1863, Shell Papers, WHS; Albert O. Marshall, *Army Life*, 153–54; Gerard, *Diary*, 47.

3. Way, *Thirty-Third Regiment*, 234, 236; Erickson, "With Grant at Vicksburg," 477–78.

4. *OR* 24(3):332.

5. JRSC, "The 16th Regiment at Vicksburg," *Indianapolis Daily Journal*, June 10, 1863.

6. JRSC; *OR* 24(3):331; Simon, *Papers of Ulysses S. Grant*, 8:239n; Bearss, *Unvexed to the Sea*, 801.

7. *OR* 24(3):332; Bearss, *Unvexed to the Sea*, 800–801; diary, May 20, 1863, Smith Papers, NC; Bering and Montgomery, *Forty-Eighth Ohio*, 86–87; John A. Bering to brother, May 28 1863, 48th Ohio Folder, VNMP; J. M. Hobbs diary, May 20, 1863, 33rd Illinois Folder, VNMP; Painter, "Bullets, Hardtack and Mud," 152; Merrick J. Wald diary, May 20, 1863, 77th Illinois Folder, VNMP.

8. *OR* 24(3):332; diary, May 21, 1863, Warmoth Papers, UNC; Kiper, *McClernand*, 254, 256; Ballard, *Vicksburg: The Campaign*, 335; Simon, *Papers of Ulysses S. Grant*, 8:239n.

9. Brinkerhoff, *Thirtieth Regiment Ohio*, 71; Jacobs Diaries and Lists, May 20, 1863, LSU.

10. McClernand to Hovey, May 19, 1863, and Hovey to McClernand, May 19, 1863, McClernand Collection, ALPL.

11. Simon, *Papers of Ulysses S. Grant*, 8:241n; OR 24(3):331; Bearss, *Unvexed to the Sea*, 803; Ballard, *Vicksburg: The Campaign*, 336; Kiper, *McClernand*, 257.

12. OR 24(3):331–32; Simon, *Papers of Ulysses S. Grant*, 8:242n; OR 24(2):240; OR 24(1):154; Fussell, *34th Regiment*, 32–33; Bearss, *Unvexed to the Sea*, 804.

13. Simpson and Berlin, *Sherman's Civil War*, 471.

14. OR 24(2):19–20; Molineaux Diaries, May 20, 1863, AC; Yaggy Diary, May 20, 1863, ALPL; Thomas Gordon diary, May 20 1863, 1st Minnesota Battery Folder, VNMP; diary, May 21, 1863, Seay Papers, UO.

15. OR 24(3):900–901.

16. James West Smith, "Confederate Soldier's Diary," 297; Fowler Civil War Diary, May 20, 1863, SU; Braudaway, "Civil War Journal," 38; Nestor, "Inside View of the Siege of Vicksburg." *Memphis Daily Appeal*, July 27, 1863.

17. Bearss, *Unvexed to the Sea*, 808; OR 24(3):900, 904; S. Croom to Martin E. Green, May 20, 1863, "General Maury's Order Book," Confederate States of America Collection, CHM; OR 24(2):380.

18. Willett, *Company B*, 34; Ashbel Smith to James M. Loughborough, July 8, 1863, Smith Papers, UTA; Guion Log, May 21, 1863, LSU; John H. Forney to chief of staff, Pemberton's headquarters, May 20, 1863, and S. Croom to not stated, May 20, 1863, "General Maury's Order Book," Confederate States of America Collection, CHM; diary, May 21, 1863, Roberts Papers, ADAH; W. L. Faulk diary, May 20, 1863, 38th Mississippi Folder, VNMP; OR 24(2):387; Abrams, *Full and Detailed*, 32; Phillips, *Personal Reminiscences*, 30; John Cowdry Taylor diary, May 21, 1863, Taylor Family Papers, UVA; Foster Letter, UA; OR 24(3):904–5.

19. James West Smith, "Confederate Soldier's Diary," 297–98; Jared Sanders diary, May 20, 1863, Sanders Family Papers, LSU; Tunnard, *Southern Record*, 238; Braudaway, "Civil War Journal," 38.

20. Bearss, *Unvexed to the Sea*, 802–3; OR 24(3):905; OR 24(2):370–71, 380, 387, 407; John Cowdry Taylor diary, May 21, 1863, Taylor Family Papers, UVA.

21. OR 24(2):330, 402; Lockett, "Defense of Vicksburg," 489.

22. S. Croom to Minor, May 21, 1863, and to Moore, May 20, 21, 1863, "General Maury's Order Book," Confederate States of America Collection, CHM; William Van Zandt diary, May 21, 1863, Van Zandt Family Papers, ISU; OR 24(3):900.

23. OR 24(3):899–901, 905, 907; OR 24(2):402; S. Croom to John C. Moore, May 20, 1863, "General Maury's Order Book," Confederate States of America Collection, CHM; Stamper Diary, May 20, 1863, CPL.

24. OR 24(3):904.

25. OR 24(1):274; OR 24(3):904–5.

26. Balfour, *Vicksburg*, not paginated; Alison Diary, May 21, 1863, UNC; Maynard, "Vicksburg Diary," 48; Fisher Diary, May 21, 1863, MHM.

27. Foster Letter, UA; Jared Sanders diary, May 21, 1863, Sanders Family Papers, LSU; S. Croom to Louis Hébert and John C. Moore, May 20, 1863, "General Maury's Order Book," Confederate States of America Collection, CHM; Sanders, *Diary in Gray*, 20; J. H. Jones, "Rank and File," 20; Tunnard, *Southern Record*, 238; James West Smith, "Confederate Soldier's Diary," 297.

28. *OR* 24(2):187; Bearss, *Unvexed to the Sea*, 717–18.

29. *OR* 24(2):187.

30. *OR* 24(2):187; Bearss, *Unvexed to the Sea*, 791–92.

31. Jenney, "Personal Recollections," 260–61; *OR* 24(2):188; Jenney, "With Sherman and Grant," 205–6.

32. *OR* 24(2):188; Bearss, *Unvexed to the Sea*, 791; Grecian, *Eighty-Third*, 31.

33. *OR* 24(1):54.

34. T. B. Marshall, *Eighty-Third Ohio*, 84; Ulysses S. Grant, *Memoirs*, 355.

35. *SOR*, 4(1):270; Miller Diary, May 23, 1863, LSU; Eddington, "My Civil War Memoirs" (web page).

36. *SOR*, 4(1):385.

37. *OR* 24(1):136.

38. Bearss, *Unvexed to the Sea*, 790, 799; Baughman Diary, May 19, 1863, SHSI; diary, May 19, 1863, Eaton Papers, NC; Vance, *Report of the Adjutant General*, 6:73.

39. Simon, *Papers of Ulysses S. Grant*, 8:242–43; diary, May 21–22, 1863, Eaton Papers, NC; Standifird Civil War Diary, May 20–21, 1863, SHSM-RCR; Boals Diary, May 20, 22, 1863, ALPL; Baughman Diary, May 22, 1863, SHSI; Vance, *Report of the Adjutant General*, 6:73.

40. Robbins to Sherman, May 21, 1863, Sherman Papers, LC; diary, May 20, 1863, Rigby Papers, UI; Edward H. Ingraham to aunt, May 21, 1863, Ingraham and Ingraham Letters, ALPL; McCarty and McCarty, *Chatfield Story*, 163; George Hale diary, May 22, 1863, 33rd Wisconsin Folder, VNMP.

41. Standifird Civil War Diary, May 23, 25, 1863, SHSM-RCR; Dudley, *Autobiography*, 72–73.

42. *OR* 24(1):37; Simon, *Papers of Ulysses S. Grant*, 8:243n, 249n; Sylvester Bartow to "Helen," May 24, 1863, Bartow Papers, NC.

43. Diary, May 25, 28–29, 31, June 2, 1863, Eaton Papers, NC; Boals Diary, May 25, 1863, ALPL; Silas I. Shearer to "Elizabeth," May 23, 1863, Shearer Correspondence, SHSI; Baughman Diary, May 24, 1863, SHSI; James H. Dean statement, November 7, 1903, 23rd Iowa Folder, VNMP; George Washington Huff diary, May 24–June 5, 1863, 80th Ohio Folder, VNMP; Simon, *Papers of Ulysses S. Grant*, 8:250n; Vance, *Report of the Adjutant General*, 6:73; Milligan, *From the Fresh-Water Navy*, 179–80.

44. Bearss, *Unvexed to the Sea*, 721, 725–26, 729; *SOR*, 4(1):410; *OR* 24(2):290.

45. Bearss, *Unvexed to the Sea*, 729; Hale Diary, May 17–20, 1863, WHS; McDonald Civil War Diaries, May 19–21, 1863, WHS; George B. Carter to "Bill," May 21, 1863, Carter Civil War Letters, WHS; Simon, *Papers of Ulysses S. Grant*, 8:238n.

46. Simon, *Papers of Ulysses S. Grant*, 8:238n; Bearss, *Unvexed to the Sea*, 719–20.

47. Bearss, *Unvexed to the Sea*, 721; Ditto Diary, May 20, 1863, ALPL; Sylvester Daniels diary, May 20–21, 1863, Magaw Papers, HL; Olynthus B. Clark, *Downing's Civil War Diary*, 116–17; *History of the Fifteenth Regiment*, 256; Simon, *Papers of Ulysses S. Grant*, 8:248n.

48. *SOR*, 4(1):270.

49. Simon, *Papers of Ulysses S. Grant*, 8:238n, 240n; *ORN* 25:6; Milligan, *From the Fresh-Water Navy*, 179.

50. *ORN* 25:21, 26–27; Bearss, *Unvexed to the Sea*, 712.

51. *ORN* 25:27; Bearss, *Unvexed to the Sea*, 713; *Diary of A. Hugh Moss*, 27.

52. *ORN* 25:6, 20; Bearss, *Unvexed to the Sea*, 711, 713; *OR* 24(2):337; *OR* 24(1):274; John Cowdry Taylor diary, May 20, 1863, Taylor Family Papers, UVA.

53. Balfour, *Vicksburg*, not paginated; Alison Diary, May 20, 1863, UNC; Hale Diary, May 19, 1863, WHS; diary, May 20, 1863, Griffen Papers, ALPL.

54. John Cowdry Taylor diary, May 21, 1863, Taylor Family Papers, UVA; *OR* 24(1):274; Lida Lord Reed, "Woman's Experiences," 923; Alison Diary, May 21, 1863, UNC.

55. Bearss, *Unvexed to the Sea*, 709; Miller Diary, May 19, 1863, LSU; *OR* 24(2):249–50.

56. *ORN* 25:12; Fike, "Diary," 251.

57. Bearss, *Unvexed to the Sea*, 710, 713; *ORN* 25:10; Miller Diary, May 20, 1863, LSU.

58. *ORN* 25:6–8; Dudley, *Autobiography*, 75; Albert Chipman to wife, May 23, 1863, Chipman Papers, ALPL; *SOR*, 4(1):391; Miller Diary, May 20, 1863, LSU; Bearss, *Unvexed to the Sea*, 713–14.

59. Bearss, *Unvexed to the Sea*, 713; *ORN* 25:6, 9–10; Miller Diary, May 21, 1863, LSU; Porter, *Naval History*, 321.

60. George W. Brown, "Service in the Mississippi Squadron," 310–11; Bearss, *Unvexed to the Sea*, 715; *ORN* 25:6–9.

61. *ORN* 25:13; Bearss, *Unvexed to the Sea*, 715–16.

62. *ORN* 25:9–11, 13; Miller Diary, May 23, 1863, LSU; Porter, *Naval History*, 321.

63. *ORN* 25:13.

64. *OR* 24(3):899; *OR* 24(1):242.

65. Johnston to Braxton Bragg, May 20, 1863, Letters Sent, January 28, 1862–July 22, 1863, no. 3, box 4, vol. 4, Johnston Papers, CWM; *OR* 24(3):902–3.

66. *OR* 24(3):899.

67. Sherman, *Memoirs*, 1:325–26.

68. *OR* 24(1):55; Ulysses S. Grant, *Memoirs*, 355; Thomas, *Three Years*, 88.

69. *OR* 24(1):174–75; Grabau, *Ninety-Eight Days*, 368; Ballard, *Vicksburg: The Campaign*, 338; Ballard, *Grant at Vicksburg*, 13.

70. Woodworth, *Nothing but Victory*, 399.

71. Johnson to Major Barton, August 8, 1863, box 3, MC1 Collection, Museum of the Confederacy, Richmond, Virginia.

72. *SOR*, 4(1):271; *OR* 24(3):333; Hess, *Civil War Infantry Tactics*, 153–55.

73. *OR* 24(3):333–34.

74. *OR* 24(1):55; Ulysses S. Grant, *Memoirs*, 355; memoirs, 45, Foster Papers, WHS.

75. Grant to Porter, May 21, 1863, Porter Papers, MHM; *OR* 24(3):334.

76. Sherman, *Memoirs*, 1:326.

77. *OR* 24(3):334–35.

78. *OR* 24(2):278; diary, May 21, 1863, Kimbell Papers, CHM; William Van Zandt diary, May 21, 1863, Van Zandt Family Papers, ISU; Farley Diary, May 21, 1863, KHS.

79. Tresilian to J. H. Wilson, August 17, 1863, Comstock Papers, LC.

80. *OR* 24(1):154, 171, 174; McClernand to Abraham Lincoln, May 29, 1863, Lincoln Papers, LC; Ballard, *Grant at Vicksburg*, 94.

81. *OR* 24(2):20; Frank Swigart, "Vicksburg Campaign: The Gallant but Disastrous Charge of May 22," *National Tribune*, August 9, 1888.

82. Wilson to J. C. Switzer, September 13, 1904, Wilson Letters, ALPL.

83. *OR* 24(1):178; S. C. Jones, *Reminiscences*, 37; Stone to McClernand, September 8, 1863, McClernand Collection, ALPL; *Report of the Adjutant General*, 1129–30.

84. *OR* 24(1):183.

85. McClernand to Jonathan B. Turner, May 27, 1863, Turner Papers, ALPL.

86. Edward H. Ingraham to aunt, May 21, 1863, Ingraham and Ingraham Letters, ALPL; Fussell, *34th Regiment*, 33.

87. Erickson, "With Grant at Vicksburg," 478–79.

88. Carter to "Bill," May 21, 1863, Carter Civil War Letters, WHS.

CHAPTER 6

1. Diary, May 22, 1863, Smith Papers, NC; diary, May 22, 1863, Kimbell Papers, CHM; Jesse Sawyer to William Rigby, February 14, 1903, 77th Illinois Folder, VNMP; *OR* 24(2):262; Bearss, *Unvexed to the Sea*, 794; Bevier, *First and Second Missouri*, 204; Merrilles Diary, May 22, 1863, CHM.

2. *OR* 24(2):285; Jefferson Brumbach to "Kate," May 23, 1863, 95th Ohio Folder, VNMP. For another version of this incident, see J. R. Buttolph, "A Bullet-Swept Field: A Batteryman's Story of May 22, 1863, before Vicksburg," *National Tribune*, May 26, 1898.

3. Bod to editor, May 22, 1863, *Chicago Daily Tribune*, June 1, 1863.

4. Abrams, *Full and Detailed*, 33; diary, May 22, 1863, McGlothlin Papers, USAMHI; J. H. Jones, "Rank and File," 20–21; *OR* 24(2):415.

5. J. H. Jones, "Rank and File," 21; Maynard, "Vicksburg Diary," 48; John Cowdry Taylor diary, May 22, 1863, Taylor Family Papers, UVA; Bevier, *First and Second Missouri*, 204; Ervin, "Genius and Heroism," 497; Payne, "Missouri Troops," 377.

6. Brinkerhoff, *Thirtieth Regiment Ohio*, 71; diary, May 22, 1863, Jacobs Diaries and Lists, LSU.

7. *OR* 24(2):257; Saunier, *Forty-Seventh Regiment Ohio*, 147.

8. Brinkerhoff, *Thirtieth Regiment Ohio*, 72; *OR* 24(2):284; Henry Schmidt to "Cate," May 24, 1863, Schmidt Family Papers, FHS; diary, May 22, 1863, Jacobs Diaries and Lists, LSU.

9. *OR* 24(2):257, 269, 277, 280; *Story of the Fifty-Fifth Regiment*, 245; Grecian, *Eighty-Third*, 31; diary, May 22, 1863, Schweitzer Papers, HL.

10. *OR* 24(2):275; McCormack to parents and sisters, May 24, 1863, McCormack Papers, NC.

11. Clipping, George Theodore Hyatt account, *Sunday Times-Herald* (Chicago), March 21, 1897, 127th Illinois Folder, VNMP; *OR* 24(2):273; *Story of the Fifty-Fifth Regiment*, 242.

12. Kellogg, *War Experiences*, 37–38.

13. Hugh Ewing to John S. Kountz, May 20, 1902, 30th Ohio Folder, VNMP; *OR* 24(2):265, 282; "'Forlorn Hope,'" 191; cards, Trogden Service Record, NARA; Mitchell, *Badge of Gallantry*, 119.

14. Shea and Winschel, *Vicksburg Is the Key*, 149; *Story of the Fifty-Fifth Regiment*, 245; *Ninth Reunion*, 21; Saunier, *Forty-Seventh Regiment Ohio*, 147; "'Forlorn Hope,'" 191; Lay Diary, May 22, 1863, RBHPC; diary, May 22, 1863, Jacobs Diaries and Lists, LSU.

15. Kellogg, *War Experiences*, 37–38; *Story of the Fifty-Fifth Regiment*, 245; *OR* 24(2):282.

16. Barton, *Autobiography*, 153; *Story of the Fifty-Fifth Regiment*, 242; Saunier, *Forty-Seventh Regiment Ohio*, 147–48.

17. Buckland to wife, May 21 [22], 1863, Buckland Papers, RBHPC; Schmidt to "Cate," May 24, 1863, Schmidt Family Papers, FHS.

18. Bearss, *Unvexed to the Sea*, 815, 816n; *OR* 24(2):415; Bock, "Confederate Col. A. C. Riley," 282.

19. Diary, May 22, 1863, Ewing Papers, OHS; *OR* 24(2):282; Kellogg, *War Experiences*, 40; Sherman, *Memoirs*, 1:326.

20. McCormack to parents and sisters, May 24, 1863, McCormack Papers, NC; Robert McCrory to William Rigby, June 16, 1905, and George H. Hildt to Rigby, February 8, 1902, 30th Ohio Folder, VNMP; *OR* 24(2):282; *Story of the Fifty-Fifth Regiment*, 245; Mitchell, *Badge of Gallantry*, 116–17.

21. "'Forlorn Hope,'" 191, 197; *OR* 24(2):273; clipping, George Theodore Hyatt account, *Sunday Times-Herald* (Chicago), March 21, 1897, 127th Illinois Folder, VNMP.

22. *OR* 24(2):257, 265, 282; "Statement of Sergt J. W. Larabee in Relation to Forlorn Hope at Graveyard Fort Vicksburgh May 22 1863," 55th Illinois Folder, VNMP; Saunier, *Forty-Seventh Regiment Ohio*, 148; diary, May 22, 1863, Kimbell Papers, CHM; diary, May 22, 1863, Ewing Papers, OHS; Andrew McCormack to parents and sisters, May 24, 1863, McCormack Papers, NC.

23. Mitchell, *Badge of Gallantry*, 118; *Story of the Fifty-Fifth Regiment*, 245; Anderson, *Memoirs*, 332.

24. Brinkerhoff, *Thirtieth Regiment Ohio*, 72–73; diary, May 22, 1863, Jacobs Diaries and Lists, LSU; *OR* 24(2):257.

25. *OR* 24(2):282; diary, May 22, 1863, Jacobs Diaries and Lists, LSU; McCrory to William Rigby, June 16, 1905, and George H. Hildt to Rigby, February 8, 1902, 30th Ohio Folder, VNMP; diary, May 22, 1863, Schweitzer Papers, HL.

26. Bradley quoted in Gottschalk, *In Deadly Earnest*, 287; McCrory to J. B. Allen, April 15, 1904, 30th Ohio Folder, VNMP.

27. George H. Hildt to William Rigby, February 8, 1902; J. W. McElroy to J. B. Allen, April 16, 1904; and G. C. Lofland to Allen, April 27, 1904, all in 30th Ohio Folder, VNMP; Brinkerhoff, *Thirtieth Regiment Ohio*, 74; diary, May 22, 1863, Jacobs Diaries and Lists, LSU.

28. *OR* 24(2):273; Brinkerhoff, *Thirtieth Regiment Ohio*, 75.

29. *OR* 24(2):282, 284; *Ninth Reunion*, 21.

30. *OR* 24(2):257–58; Robert McCrory to William Rigby, June 16, 1905, 30th Ohio Folder, VNMP; Joseph A. Saunier to Rigby, February 8, 1903, 47th Ohio Folder, VNMP; Schmidt to "Cate," May 24, 1863, Schmidt Family Papers, FHS.

31. Saunier, *Forty-Seventh Regiment Ohio*, 148; *OR* 24(2):258, 282.

32. Merrilles Diary, May 22, 1863, CHM.

33. *OR* 24(2):258.

34. *OR* 24(2):269, 278.

35. *OR* 24(2):269.

36. *Story of the Fifty-Fifth Regiment*, 243–44.

37. *OR* 24(2):280–81.

38. *OR* 24(2):269, 275, 278.

39. *OR* 24(2):258–59, 282; Bearss, *Unvexed to the Sea*, 817; Henry Schmidt to "Cate," May 24, 1863, Schmidt Family Papers, FHS.

40. Trogden quoted in Merrilles Diary, May 22, 1863, CHM; Mitchell, *Badge of Gallantry*, 119–21; Andrew McCormack to parents and sisters, May 24, 1863, McCormack Papers, NC; *OR* 24(2):273.

41. "'Forlorn Hope,'" 196; Mitchell, *Badge of Gallantry*, 113–14.

42. "'Forlorn Hope,'" 196.

43. "'Forlorn Hope,'" 194.

44. *OR* 24(2):273, 282.

45. Clipping, George Theodore Hyatt account, *Sunday Times-Herald* (Chicago), March 21, 1897, 127th Illinois Folder, VNMP; "Statement of Sergt J. W. Larabee in Relation to Forlorn Hope at Graveyard Fort Vicksburgh May 22 1863," 55th Illinois Folder, VNMP; *Story of the Fifty-Fifth Regiment*, 246.

46. *OR* 24(2):277; McCormack to parents and sisters, May 24, 1863, McCormack Papers, NC.

47. Pitzman, "Vicksburg Campaign," 115.

CHAPTER 7

1. Bearss, *Unvexed to the Sea*, 796, 819; Ballard, *Grant at Vicksburg*, 10; Davis Diary, May 22, 1863, ALPL.

2. *OR* 24(2):375; Tunnard, *Southern Record*, 236.

3. Bearss, *Unvexed to the Sea*, 797.

4. Bearss, 795, 796n, 797.

5. Diary, May 22, 1863, McClure Papers, UCB; Molineaux Diaries, May 22, 1863, AC; Griffith Diaries, May 22, 1863, OHS.

6. Oldroyd, *Soldier's Story*, 31; Post, *Soldiers' Letters*, 268.

7. Crummer, *With Grant*, 111; Bearss, *Unvexed to the Sea*, 820; "Real Life in the Civil War," 46–47, Bedford Papers, LC; Morris, Hartwell, and Kuykendall, *History 31st Regiment Illinois*, 69; Ballard, *Vicksburg: The Campaign*, 339.

8. Yaggy Diary, May 22, 1863, ALPL; Post, *Soldier's Life*, 269.

9. Yaggy Diary, May 22, 1863, ALPL; Ballard, *Vicksburg: The Campaign*, 339; Bearss, *Unvexed to the Sea*, 820.

10. Adams, *Indiana at Vicksburg*, 250; "Real Life in the Civil War," 50, Bedford Papers, LC.

11. Bearss, *Unvexed to the Sea*, 820.

12. Post, *Soldiers' Letters*, 268–69; Crummer, *With Grant*, 111–13.

13. Post, *Soldiers' Letters*, 269; Crummer, *With Grant*, 113.

14. "Real Life in the Civil War," 47, Bedford Papers, LC.

15. Howard, *History of the 124th Regiment*, 106–7; Vance, *Report of the Adjutant General*, 2:575, 6:446.

16. Bearss, *Unvexed to the Sea*, 820–21; John Reese to "Tissee," May 25, 1863, Reese Papers, SIU; John D. Stevenson undated report, 81st Illinois Folder, VNMP; F. M. Smith to William Rigby, January 28, 1905, 17th Illinois Folder, VNMP; Buchanan to Rigby, February 21, 1905, 7th Missouri Folder, VNMP.

17. Buchanan to William Rigby, February 21, 1905, 7th Missouri Folder, VNMP.

18. Edwin A. Loosley to wife, June 1, 1863, Loosley Papers, SIU; Reese to "Tissee," May 25, 1863, Reese Papers, SIU.

19. Reese to "Tissee," May 25, 1863, Reese Papers, SIU; Molineaux Diaries, May 22, 1863, AC; John D. Stevenson undated report, 81st Illinois Folder, VNMP; Buchanan to William Rigby, February 21, 1905, 7th Missouri Folder, VNMP; Richard Blackstone to Rigby, January 3, 1904, 32nd Ohio Folder, VNMP; Bearss, *Unvexed to the Sea*, 821, 822n; *OR* 24(2):376.

20. Shea and Winschel, *Vicksburg Is the Key*, 149–50; Bearss, *Unvexed to the Sea*, 821n; *OR* 24(2):361.

21. Edwin A. Loosley to wife, June 1, 1863, Loosley Papers, SIU; Jordon Carroll Harriss to unstated, May 26, 1863, Jordon Carroll Harriss Letters (website); clipping, Oliver Guinand, "Locations at Vicksburg," 81st Illinois Folder, VNMP.

22. Loosley to wife, June 1, 1863, Loosley Papers, SIU.

23. Harriss to unstated, May 26, June 5, 1863, Jordon Carroll Harriss Letters (website).

24. Loosley to wife, June 1, 1863, Loosley Papers, SIU.

25. Loosley to wife, June 1, 1863.

26. Reese to "Tissee," May 25, 1863, Reese Papers, SIU; Whipkey to William Rigby, December 26, 1904, 81st Illinois Folder, VNMP.

27. Reese to "Tissee," May 25, 1863, Reese Papers, SIU; Loosley to wife, June 1, 1863, Loosley Papers, SIU.

28. Loosley to wife, June 1, July 3, 1863, Loosley Papers, SIU.

29. Reese to "Tissee," May 25, 1863, Reese Papers, SIU; [Newsome], *Experience in the War*, 29; Loosley to wife, June 1, 1863, Loosley Papers, SIU.

30. Reese to "Tissee," May 25, June 4, 1863, Reese Papers, SIU; McClure Diary, May 22, 1863, OCHM.

31. Robert Buchanan to William Rigby, February 21, 1905, 7th Missouri Folder, VNMP; John D. Stevenson undated report, 81st Illinois Folder, VNMP; Bearss, *Unvexed to the Sea*, 822.

32. Sayers to William Rigby, February 15, 1905, and Conklin to Rigby, February 22, 1905, 8th Illinois Folder, VNMP; Molineaux Diaries, May 22, 1863, AC; Blackstone to Rigby, January 3, 1904, 32nd Ohio Folder, VNMP; Buchanan to Rigby, December 23, 1904, 7th Missouri Folder, VNMP; Bearss, *Unvexed to the Sea*, 822.

33. OR 24(2):295; Force, "Personal Recollections," 304–5; Force to "Loula," May 25, 1862, Force Papers, UW; Henry O. Dwight to W. P. Gault, September 26, 1901, 20th Ohio Folder, VNMP.

34. W. M. Sleeth to W. P. Gault, October 12, 1901, 68th Ohio Folder, VNMP; R. C. Hunt diary, May 22, 1863, 20th Ohio Folder, VNMP; Steele to Gault, September 29, 1904, 78th Ohio Folder, VNMP; B. F. Boring, "Fighting for Vicksburg," *National Tribune*, August 23, 1894.

35. OR 24(2):297, 300; Henry S. Hurter to William Rigby, November 11, 1903, 1st Minnesota Battery Folder, VNMP.

36. OR 24(2):300.

37. OR 24(2):297; Bearss, *Unvexed to the Sea*, 819.

38. Bush to "Father, Mother, and All," May 29, 1863, Bush Papers, University of Michigan, William L. Clements Library, Ann Arbor, Michigan.

39. Carrington Diary, May 22, 1863, CHM.

40. Bearss, *Unvexed to the Sea*, 798, 822.

41. E. G. Hart to "Comrade," February 12, 1905, 18th Wisconsin Folder, VNMP; diary, May 22, 1863, Reeves Papers, MHS.

42. Diary, May 22, 1863, Reeves Papers, MHS; OR 24(2):316; J. Q. A. Campbell diary, May 22, 1863, 5th Iowa Folder, VNMP.

43. Bearss, *Unvexed to the Sea*, 822; OR 24(2):316; H. M. Trimble diary, May 22, 1863, 93rd Illinois Folder, VNMP; Trimble, *History of the Ninety-Third Regiment*, 35.

44. Bearss, *Unvexed to the Sea*, 822; Ballard, *Vicksburg: The Campaign*, 340.

45. SOR, 13(2):568; Mahan, *Memoirs*, 124; J. Q. A. Campbell to William Rigby, January 12, 1904, 5th Iowa Folder, VNMP.

CHAPTER 8

1. *OR* 24(1):174.

2. Grabau, *Ninety-Eight Days*, 375–77.

3. JRSC, "Description of the Storming of the Vicksburg Forts," *Indianapolis Daily Journal*, June 19, 1863.

4. *OR* 24(1):154; Bearss, *Unvexed to the Sea*, 799; *OR* 24(2):240; Albert O. Marshall, *Army Life*, 154; Isaiah Richards to "Dearly Loved Ones at Home," May 19 and 21, 1863, 17th Ohio Battery Folder, VNMP; W. S. Marshall to William Rigby, July 23, 1907, 11th Indiana Folder, VNMP.

5. Stephen D. Lee, "Siege of Vicksburg," 2–3, folder 33, Claiborne Papers, UNC; Braudaway, "Civil War Journal," 38.

6. *OR* 24(1):154; *OR* 24(2):361; Braudaway, "Civil War Journal," 39; Ralph J. Smith, *Reminiscences*, 13.

7. *OR* 24(2):181; Lee, "Siege of Vicksburg," 61; Hains, "Incident," 71.

8. Ballard, *Vicksburg: The Campaign*, 343; *OR* 24(2):20; Bearss, *Unvexed to the Sea*, 832; Larkin A. Byron to James McNeill, July 5, 1863, Byron Papers, NC.

9. *OR* 24(2):232, 234; Byrne and Soman, eds., *Your True Marcus*, 279; James B. Taylor diary, May 22, 1863, 120th Ohio Folder, VNMP.

10. Byron to James McNeill, July 5, 1863, Byron Papers, NC; diary, May 22, 1863, and Dillon to wife, May 22, 1863, Dillon Papers, HL.

11. Bearss, *Unvexed to the Sea*, 833; Byron to James McNeill, July 5, 1863, Byron Papers, NC; *OR* 24(2):232, 234; Byrne and Soman, *Your True Marcus*, 279; Keigwin to William Rigby, March 5, 1902, 49th Indiana Folder, VNMP.

12. *OR* 24(2):232, 234; James B. Taylor diary, May 22, 1863, and Mahlon Rouch diary, May 22, 1863, 120th Ohio Folder, VNMP.

13. *OR* 24(2):232; Perry to H. C. Adams, February 11, 1909, 69th Indiana Folder, VNMP; John Pickering to W. P. Gault, May 9, 1903, 114th Ohio Folder, VNMP.

14. *OR* 24(2):20; Byrne and Soman, *Your True Marcus*, 279; Byron to James McNeill, July 5, 1863, Byron Papers, NC.

15. Mason, *Forty-Second Ohio*, 222; Frank H. Mason and John W. Fry, "Vicksburg Campaign: Col. Kinsman Killed at the Head of His Command, Black River Bridge, Cannons and Small-Arms Captured, the City Invested, Brilliant but Fruitless Charge on the Works," *National Tribune*, October 2, 1884; W. F. Jones, "Grant Coops Up Pemberton," *National Tribune*, February 15, 1900.

16. Bond, *Under the Flag*, 65; A. J. Jacobs, "A Vicksburg Experience," *National Tribune*, May 26, 1898; Enos Pierson to William Rigby, June 21, 1903, 16th Ohio Folder, VNMP; clipping, M. A. Sweetman, "Capture of Vicksburg Desperate Struggle," *Circleville Daily*, and John Pickering to W. P. Gault, May 9, 1903, 114th Ohio Folder, VNMP.

17. Mason, *Forty-Second Ohio*, 223; clipping, M. A. Sweetman, "Capture of Vicksburg Desperate Struggle," *Circleville Daily*, 114th Ohio Folder, VNMP.

18. Frank H. Mason and John W. Fry, "Vicksburg Campaign: Col. Kinsman Killed at the Head of His Command, Black River Bridge, Cannons and Small-Arms Captured, the City Invested, Brilliant but Fruitless Charge on the Works," *National Tribune*, October 2, 1884; Mason, *Forty-Second Ohio*, 223–25.

19. Bond, *Under the Flag*, 65; Frank H. Mason and John W. Fry, "Vicksburg Campaign: Col. Kinsman Killed at the Head of His Command, Black River Bridge, Cannons and

Small-Arms Captured, the City Invested, Brilliant but Fruitless Charge on the Works," *National Tribune*, October 2, 1884.

20. A. J. Jacobs, "A Vicksburg Experience," *National Tribune*, May 26, 1898.

21. "Elias D. Moore Diary" (web page), May 22, 1863; "Michael Sweetman Diary" (web page), May 22, 1863; James Keigwin to William Rigby, March 16, 1903, 49th Indiana Folder, VNMP; E. L. Hawk to Rigby, March 27, 1902, Lindsey's Brigade Folder, VNMP.

22. OR 24(2):354, 361.

23. Diary, May 22, 1863, Roberts Papers, ADAH; *OR* 24(2):354.

24. Fussell, *34th Regiment*, 33; *History of the Forty-Sixth Regiment*, 64; Fulfer, *History of the Trials and Hardships*, 69.

25. Fussell, *34th Regiment*, 33; Frank Swigart, "Vicksburg Campaign: The Gallant but Disastrous Charge of May 22," *National Tribune*, August 9, 1888; unidentified letter fragment from man in Spicely's brigade to brother and sister, June 1, 1863, Civil War Letter, ISL; Whipple, *Diary*, 18.

26. OR 24(1):155.

CHAPTER 9

1. Albert O. Marshall, *Army Life*, 154; Bearss, *Unvexed to the Sea*, 827; Way, *Thirty-Third Regiment Illinois*, 43–44; C. D. Morris, "Vicksburg: A Graphic Description of the Charge," *National Tribune*, October 23, 1884; Charles A. Hobbs diary, May 22, 1863, 99th Illinois Folder, VNMP; Miller Reminiscences, 11, OCHM; I. H. Elliott to A. C. Matthews, May 16, 1902, and to William Rigby, January 21, 1904; and R. B. Fulks to Rigby, January 20, 1904, all in 33rd Illinois Folder, VNMP.

2. Way, *Thirty-Third Regiment Illinois*, 43–44; Albert O. Marshall, *Army Life*, 155; Vance, *Report of the Adjutant General*, 2:652.

3. Way, *Thirty-Third Regiment Illinois*, 44.

4. Erickson, "With Grant at Vicksburg," 478n, 479; Hills, "Failure and Scapegoat," 29–33.

5. Way, *Thirty-Third Regiment Illinois*, 44.

6. C. D. Morris, "Vicksburg: A Graphic Description of the Charge," *National Tribune*, October 23, 1884; Erickson, "With Grant at Vicksburg," 479; Matthews to William Rigby, March 11, 1903, 99th Illinois Folder, VNMP; Bearss, *Unvexed to the Sea*, 827–28.

7. Way, *Thirty-Third Regiment Illinois*, 44.

8. Way, 44.

9. Way, 44.

10. Way, 44; Albert O. Marshall, *Army Life*, 156.

11. Erickson, "With Grant at Vicksburg," 479–80.

12. Erickson, 480–81; Cornelius Du Bois to V. E. Howell, March 9, 1903, 33rd Illinois Folder, VNMP; James B. Black to William Rigby, n.d., and Amos York to Rigby, January 6, 1904, 8th Indiana Folder, VNMP; Miller Reminiscences, 11, OCHM.

13. Way, *Thirty-Third Regiment Illinois*, 44; Erickson, "With Grant at Vicksburg," 480; Cornelius Du Bois to V. E. Howell, March 9, 1903, 33rd Illinois Folder, VNMP.

14. Bigelow, *Abridged History of the Eighth Indiana*, 20; Marshall Diaries, May 22, 1863, MU.

15. C. D. Morris, "Vicksburg: A Graphic Description of the Charge," *National Tribune*, October 23, 1884; James B. Black to William Rigby, n.d., 8th Indiana Folder, VNMP;

W. S. Stott to Rigby, March 9, 1903, and John A. Abbott to Rigby, November 17, 1904, 18th Indiana Folder, VNMP; A. C. Matthews to Rigby, February 27, 1903, 99th Illinois Folder, VNMP; Bearss, *Unvexed to the Sea*, 829; Adams, *Indiana at Vicksburg*, 237.

16. Bearss, *Unvexed to the Sea*, 828; "Come On, You Brave Yank," 198.

17. "Come On, You Brave Yank," 198–99; Higgins to C. A. Hobbs, December 7, 1878, and William Christian to William Rigby, May 28, 1902, 99th Illinois Folder, VNMP; Evans, "Second Texas," 599; Chance, *Second Texas*, 105–6; OR 24(2):613; Ralph J. Smith, *Reminiscences*, 13; Vance, *Report of the Adjutant General*, 5:544.

18. "Come On, You Brave Yank," 200; Matthews to William Rigby, February 27, 1903, and December 27, 1904, 99th Illinois Folder, VNMP.

19. Way, *Thirty-Third Regiment Illinois*, 44; A. C. Matthews to William Rigby, February 27, 1903, 99th Illinois Folder, VNMP.

20. OR 24(2):236; Marshall Diaries, May 22, 1863, MU; [Scott], *67th Regiment*, 36; diary, May 22, 1863, Smith Papers, NC; clipping, Dorothy Murphy, "John W. Paul's View of the Vicksburg Siege," and Joseph Chandler to William Rigby, January 17, 1902, 23rd Wisconsin Folder, VNMP; Bearss, *Unvexed to the Sea*, 829.

21. Bearss, *Unvexed to the Sea*, 829.

22. OR 24(2):33–34; OR 24(1):155; Gerard, *Diary*, 48; William Vilas to William Rigby, December 2, 1901, and Joseph Chandler to Rigby, January 17, 1902, 23rd Wisconsin Folder, VNMP; William H. Willcox to sister, May 26, 1863, 96th Ohio Folder, VNMP; A. C. Matthews to Rigby, December 27, 1904, 99th Illinois Folder, VNMP; John G. Jones to parents, May 29, 1863, Jones Civil War Letters, WHS; Bearss, *Unvexed to the Sea*, 830; SOR, 4(1):393.

23. OR 24(2):34; OR 24(1):181; Theodorus Northrup to "Ira," May 26, 1863, and Joseph Chandler to William Rigby, January 8, 1902, 23rd Wisconsin Folder, VNMP; John G. Jones to parents, May 29, 1863, Jones Correspondence, LC; Marshall Diaries, May 22, 1863, MU; Adams, *Indiana at Vicksburg*, 229.

24. OR 24(2):382, 386, 390; Smith to James M. Loughborough, July 8, 1863, Smith Papers, UTA.

25. OR 24(2):385–86; Evans, "Second Texas," 596.

26. OR 24(2):386.

27. OR 24(2):388.

28. OR 24(2):387; Evans, "Second Texas," 598.

29. Smith to James M. Loughborough, July 8, 1863, Smith Papers, UTA; Evans, "Second Texas," 598; OR 24(2):388.

30. Smith to James M. Loughborough, July 8, 1863, Smith Papers, UTA; Chance, *Second Texas*, 107.

31. OR 24(2):390; C. D. Morris, "The Charge at Vicksburg," *National Tribune*, April 16, 1885; Adams, *Indiana at Vicksburg*, 333; Halsell, "Sixteenth Indiana," 75.

32. Jackson, "Some of the Boys," 97; Marshall Diaries, May 22, 1863, MU; OR 24(2):39.

33. OR 24(3):340.

34. OR 24(2):34; JRSC, "Description of the Storming of the Vicksburg Forts," *Indianapolis Daily Journal*, June 19, 1863.

35. JRSC, "Description of the Storming of the Vicksburg Forts," *Indianapolis Daily Journal*, June 19, 1863.

36. Diary, May 22, 1863, Smith Papers, NC; Bearss, *Unvexed to the Sea*, 830; JRSC, "Description of the Storming of the Vicksburg Forts," *Indianapolis Daily Journal*, June

19, 1863; A. C. Matthews to William Rigby, March 11, 1903, 99th Illinois Folder, VNMP; James B. Black to Rigby, n.d., 8th Indiana Folder, VNMP.

37. *OR* 24(2):34.

38. Ashbel Smith to James M. Loughborough, July 8, 1863, Smith Papers, UTA.

39. *OR* 24(2):388.

40. Smith to James M. Loughborough, July 8, 1863, Smith Papers, UTA.

41. *OR* 24(2):388; Smith to James M. Loughborough, July 8, 1863, Smith Papers, UTA.

42. *OR* 24(2):388; Smith to James M. Loughborough, July 8, 1863, Smith Papers, UTA.

43. Bearss, *Unvexed to the Sea*, 831.

44. Ashbel Smith to James M. Loughborough, July 8, 1863, Smith Papers, UTA; *OR* 24(2):361.

45. *OR* 24(2):34; P. H. White to William Rigby, December 18, 1903, and to Meacham, August 15, 1904, Chicago Mercantile Battery Folder, VNMP; "Within a Few Feet," 188. Charles I. Evans claimed the gun approached the 2nd Texas Lunette sometime after 5:00 P.M. See Evans, "Second Texas," 600.

46. *OR* 24(2):34, 39; "Within a Few Feet," 188–89; [P. H. White] account, Chicago Mercantile Battery Folder, VNMP; James M. Black to William Rigby, November 27, 1903, 18th Indiana Folder, VNMP; clipping, Dorothy Murphy, "John W. Paul's View of the Vicksburg Siege," 23rd Wisconsin Folder, VNMP; Black to Rigby, n.d., 8th Indiana Folder, VNMP; Bod letter, May 24, 1863, *Chicago Daily Tribune*, June 4, 1863; *SOR*, 8(2):463; *OR* 17(1):746.

47. [P. H. White] account, Chicago Mercantile Battery Folder, VNMP; Evans, "Second Texas," 600; "Within a Few Feet," 189.

48. "Within a Few Feet," 189; [P. H. White] account, Chicago Mercantile Battery Folder, VNMP; Joseph Chandler to William Rigby, January 17, 1902, 23rd Wisconsin Folder, VNMP; Matthews to Rigby, March 11, 1903, December 27, 1904, 99th Illinois Folder, VNMP; *OR* 24(1):155.

49. "Within a Few Feet," 188–89; White to Meacham, September 22, 1903, Chicago Mercantile Battery Folder, VNMP; *SOR*, 8(2):463.

CHAPTER 10

1. S. C. Jones, *Reminiscences*, 38; *OR* 24(2):330; *SOR*, 4(1):403; Griffith, "Twenty-Second Iowa," 218; Elmer J. C. Bealer to William Rigby, April 21, 1903, 21st Iowa Folder, VNMP; William J. Landram to W. H. Bentley, July 23, 1885, 77th Illinois Folder, VNMP.

2. Hains, "Incident," 69; *OR* 24(2):181; Stephen D. Lee, "Siege of Vicksburg," 3, folder 33, Claiborne Papers, UNC; Hains, "Vicksburg Campaign," 271; E. W. Pettus to William Rigby, March 14, 1903, 30th Alabama Folder, VNMP.

3. Grabau, *Ninety-Eight Days*, 375; *Report of the Adjutant General*, 1130; Lee, "Siege of Vicksburg," 61; Stephen D. Lee to William Rigby, May 30, 1904, Lee's Brigade Folder, VNMP; Hains, "Vicksburg Campaign," 271; Hains, "Incident," 68; Bearss, *Unvexed to the Sea*, 742.

4. Lee, "Siege of Vicksburg," 61.

5. Hains, "Incident," 68; Barnett, *Twenty-Second Regiment Iowa*, 8.

6. *OR* 24(2):353–55; Pearson to Lee, May 17, June 15, 1902, and to William Rigby, January 19, 1903, 30th Alabama Folder, VNMP.

7. J. P. Benjamin to Governor Lubbock, March 6, 1862, Waul Service Record, NARA;

OR 24(2):357, 359; Waul to William Rigby, September 10, 1902, Waul's Texas Legion Folder, VNMP; Lenert Journal, May 22, 1863, OCHM; Bearss, *Unvexed to the Sea*, 824–25.

8. Bluford Wilson to J. C. Switzer, September 13, 1904, Wilson Letters, ALPL; FJP, "The Twenty-First Iowa at Vicksburg," *National Tribune*, October 18, 1883; Painter, "Bullets, Hardtack and Mud," 152; Bearss, *Unvexed to the Sea*, 824; Landram to W. H. Bentley, July 23, 1885, and Jesse Sawyer to William Rigby, February 14, 1903, 77th Illinois Folder, VNMP.

9. OR 24(1):178; Wilson, *Under the Old Flag*, 1:180; S. C. Jones, *Reminiscences*, 37–39; OR 24(2):242, 244; Holcomb, *Southern Sons*, 65.

10. Crooke, *Twenty-First Regiment*, 83; Harvey Graham to John A. McClernand, September 1, 1862, Graham Letter, GLIAH; OR 24(2):241–42.

11. Wilson to J. C. Switzer, September 13, 1904, Wilson Letters, ALPL.

12. Wilson to Switzer, September 13, 1904.

13. Holcomb, *Southern Sons*, 68; Lewis to friend, May 28, 1863, in newspaper clipping, Lewis and Moulton Family Papers, WHS.

14. Diary, May 22, 1863, Warmoth Papers, UNC; *SOR*, 4(1):393; Pearson to Stephen D. Lee, May 17, 1902, and C. M. Shelley to "General," September 2, 1902, 30th Alabama Folder, VNMP; *Report of the Adjutant General*, 1130.

15. *Report of the Adjutant General*, 1130; S. C. Jones, *Reminiscences*, 38.

16. Lee, "Siege of Vicksburg," 60; Lee, "Gallant Incident," 62–63; Pearson to Lee, May 17, 1902, 30th Alabama Folder, VNMP.

17. "Our Special Correspondent" letter, May 25, 1863, *New-York Daily Tribune*, June 5, 1863; Pearson to Stephen D. Lee, May 17, 1902, and to William Rigby, September 10, 1902, 30th Alabama Folder, VNMP; OR 24(2):242, 344; Griffith, "Twenty-Second Iowa," 218.

18. *Report of the Adjutant General*, 1130; OR 24(2):244.

19. *SOR*, 4(1):393; Stone to McClernand, September 8, 1863, McClernand Collection, ALPL; Harvey Graham to McClernand, September 1, 1863, Graham Letter, GLIAH; *Report of the Adjutant General*, 1130; OR 24(2):140–41; Elmer J. C. Bealer to William Rigby, March 14, 1903, 22nd Iowa Folder, VNMP; Barnett, *Twenty-Second Regiment Iowa*, 9; OR 24(1):180; *SOR*, 4(1):401–2; Holcomb, *Southern Sons*, 69; Silas Hemphill to brother and sister, May 25, 1863, Hemphill Family Papers, SHSI.

20. OR 24(2):242; S. C. Jones, *Reminiscences*, 38–39.

21. OR 24(2):141; Hiram J. Lewis to friend, May 28, 1863, in newspaper clipping, Lewis and Moulton Family Papers, WHS.

22. Crooke, *Twenty-First Regiment*, 84; William Charleton to Hunt, February 25, 1902, 11th Wisconsin Folder, VNMP; J. S. Miller to William Rigby, May 8, 1903, 22nd Iowa Folder, VNMP.

23. Wilson to J. C. Switzer, September 13, 1904, Wilson Letters, ALPL; Hiram J. Lewis to friend, May 28, 1863, in newspaper clipping, Lewis and Moulton Family Papers, WHS; Charles L. Harris to William Rigby, May 12, 1902, 11th Wisconsin Folder, VNMP; Crooke, *Twenty-First Regiment*, 84; OR 24(1):179; S. C. Jones, *Reminiscences*, 39.

24. *SOR*, 4(1):404; Webb letter in Bentley, *77th Illinois*, 151; A. E. Cook to William Rigby, April 12, 1903, 21st Iowa Folder, VNMP; Jesse Sawyer to Rigby, February 14, 1903, and W. H. Bentley to Rigby, January 5, 1903, 77th Illinois Folder, VNMP; Thomas, *Three Years*, 89–90; Grabau, *Ninety-Eight Days*, 378; Bering and Montgomery, *Forty-Eighth Ohio*, 87.

25. *SOR*, 4(1):403–5; A. E. Cook to William Rigby, April 5, [1903], 21st Iowa Folder, VNMP; J. C. Switzer to Rigby, April 23, 1903, 22nd Iowa Folder, VNMP; Webb letter in

Bentley, *77th Illinois*, 152; Vance, *Report of the Adjutant General*, 5:495; John A. Bering to brother, May 28, 1863, and Cyrus Hussey to Bering, January 20, 1903, 48th Ohio Folder, VNMP.

26. A. E. Cook to William Rigby, April 5, [1903], 21st Iowa Folder, VNMP; A. N. Shumard to Rigby, February 21, 1905, 48th Ohio Folder, VNMP; A. N. Shumard, "The Charge at Vicksburg," *National Tribune*, June 18, 1885; *SOR*, 4(1):403, 405; *OR* 24(2):238; unsigned letter to "Friend John," July 9, 1863, Griffen Papers, ALPL; *OR* 24(1):155; "Flag the Rebels Didn't Get," 201.

27. Wilkin, "Vicksburg," 231–32; *OR* 24(1):155; Parker to J. H. Robinson, June 24, 1902, 130th Illinois Folder, VNMP; Mack letter in Bering and Montgomery, *Forty-Eighth Ohio*, 89; Bearrs, *Unvexed to the Sea*, 826.

28. *OR* 24(1):177.

29. Bering and Montgomery, *Forty-Eighth Ohio*, 87–88; "Flag the Rebels Didn't Get," 20.

30. *OR* 24(3):340.

31. *OR* 24(1):181; *OR* 24(3):341.

32. Lee, "Siege of Vicksburg," 61–62; Pearson to Lee, May 17, 1902, and to William Rigby, March 15, 1903, 30th Alabama Folder, VNMP.

33. Pearson to Stephen D. Lee, May 17, 1902, 30th Alabama Folder, VNMP.

34. Griffith, "Twenty-Second Iowa," 218; *SOR*, 4(1):406; *Report of the Adjutant General*, 1130; Hains, "Incident," 69, 71; William M. Stone to John McClernand, September 8, 1863, McClernand Collection, ALPL; Wilson to J. C. Switzer, September 13, 1904, Wilson Letters, ALPL; Graham to McClernand, September 1, 1863, Graham Letter, GLIAH; *OR* 24(2):243. For differing estimates of the number of men who entered Railroad Redoubt, see *SOR*, 4(1):401; *OR* 24(2):244; Lee, "Siege of Vicksburg," 61; and Elmer J. C. Bealer to William Rigby, April 21, 1903, 21st Iowa Folder, VNMP. Messenger later reported that more men would have gone in, but someone ordered them not to do so. See *SOR*, 4(1):406. According to one source, some members of the 77th Illinois also entered the fort. See Lysander R. Webb to McClernand, September 22, 1863, McClernand Collection, ALPL.

35. *OR* 24(1):180; William M. Stone to McClernand, September 8, 1863, McClernand Collection, ALPL; *OR* 24(2):357.

36. William M. Stone to McClernand, September 8, 1863, McClernand Collection, ALPL; Lee, "Siege of Vicksburg," 62.

37. *OR* 24(2):349; *OR* 24(3):907.

38. "The Next Governor of Our State," *Chicago Daily Tribune*, June 20, 1863; Burden, "Into the Breach," 20.

39. "The Next Governor of Our State," *Chicago Daily Tribune*, June 20, 1863; Stone to John McClernand, September 8, 1862, McClernand Collection, ALPL. On May 27, 1863, Stone identified Pvt. Isaac Mickey of Company F, 22nd Iowa, as the man who braved Confederate fire to deliver a message to the main line and then returned to the ditch at the redoubt. See *SOR*, 4(1):408.

40. Stone to John McClernand, September 8, 1862, McClernand Collection, ALPL; *OR* 24(2):241–42.

41. Stone to John McClernand, September 8, 1862, McClernand Collection, ALPL.

42. Graham to John McClernand, September 1, 1863, Graham Letter, GLIAH.

43. *OR* 24(1):178–79; *SOR*, 4(1):406.

44. Burden, "Into the Breach," 31; cards, Oden Service Record, NARA; Shelley to

"General," September 2, 1902, 30th Alabama Folder, VNMP. A historian of the 30th Alabama has asserted that Lt. Col. John Bass Smith initially led the counterattack but was shot immediately, to be replaced by Capt. John C. Francis of Company B. He implies that Oden did not play a leading role in the effort. There is no evidence to support this interpretation. See Stephens, *Bound for Glory*, 132–33.

45. Pearson to Lee, May 17, 1902, 30th Alabama Folder, VNMP; Bearss, *Unvexed to the Sea*, 827; Lee, "Siege of Vicksburg," 62; Kelly, "Thirtieth Alabama," 141.

46. OR 24(2):244; *Report of the Adjutant General*, 1130; Barnett, *Twenty-Second Regiment Iowa*, 9; Elmer J. C. Bealer to William Rigby, April 21, 1903, 21st Iowa Folder, VNMP.

47. Hains, "Incident," 70; Pearson to Stephen D. Lee, May 17, 1902, 30th Alabama Folder, VNMP.

48. Hains, "Incident," 70; Hains, "Vicksburg Campaign," 271. Several postwar sources indicate that Griffith had earlier evacuated the compartment and later reentered it for a second effort and that his capture of Pearson's group occurred when he left the second time. See Stephens, *Bound for Glory*, 131–32; Bearss, *Unvexed to the Sea*, 827; and Burden, "Into the Breach," 30.

49. OR 24(1):154; Hains, "Vicksburg Campaign," 271; Hains, "Incident," 70–71; OR 24(1):180; A. B. Hubbell to William Rigby, June 9, 1904, 22nd Iowa Folder, VNMP; Pearson to Stephen D. Lee, May 17, 1902, 30th Alabama Folder, VNMP; diary, May 22, 1863, Warmoth Papers, UNC.

50. Landram to W. H. Bentley, July 23, 1885, 77th Illinois Folder, VNMP; "Our Special Correspondent" letter, May 25, 1863, *New-York Daily Tribune*, June 5, 1863; SOR, 22(2):797.

51. Adams, *Indiana at Vicksburg*, 203; Bigelow, *Eighth Indiana*, 21; Albert O. Marshall, *Army Life*, 156, 158.

52. Albert O. Marshall, *Army Life*, 158–59, 161.

53. Lee, "Siege of Vicksburg," 62; OR 24(2):360–61; Phillips, *Personal Reminiscences*, 31.

CHAPTER 11

1. OR 24(1):177, 180–81.

2. OR 24(1):180–81; Harvey Graham to McClernand, September 1, 1863, Graham Letter, GLIAH; William M. Stone to McClernand, September 8, 1863, McClernand Collection, ALPL.

3. OR 24(1):181.

4. Warmoth to E. J. McClernand, May 30, 1910, Warmoth Papers, UNC.

5. OR 24(1):181; Hains, "Vicksburg Campaign," 271.

6. OR 24(1):155, 172; OR 24(2):360–61; Phillips, *Personal Reminiscences*, 31.

7. OR 24(1):172.

8. Kiper, *McClernand*, 262; OR 24(1):55; Grabau, *Ninety-Eight Days*, 378.

9. Sherman, *Memoirs*, 1:326–27; Pitzman, "Vicksburg Campaign," 115; OR 24(1):55–56.

10. Pitzman, "Vicksburg Campaign," 115; Sherman, *Memoirs*, 1:327; OR 24(1):163; Ulysses S. Grant, *Memoirs*, 1:355–56. Capt. James H. Greene of the 8th Wisconsin in Brig. Gen. Joseph A. Mower's brigade was close enough to the Grant-Sherman conference to observe that the army commander wore a slouch hat and a "torn blouse, and an eye glass [was] slung over his shoulder." He claimed to have heard Grant remark of McClernand's dispatch "that he did not think it was true—but it might be so." See Greene, *Reminiscences*, 55.

11. *OR* 24(1):55–56, 163; Ballard, *Grant at Vicksburg*, 20.

12. Greene, *Reminiscences*, 56; Pitzman, "Vicksburg Campaign," 115; Bearss, *Unvexed to the Sea*, 837; *OR* 24(1):56.

13. *OR* 24(1):56; editorial note, Simon, *Papers of Ulysses S. Grant*, 8:253n.

14. *OR* 24(1):173.

15. *OR* 24(1):173.

16. *OR* 24(1):56, 155, 173.

17. Kiper, *McClernand*, 262; Bearss, *Unvexed to the Sea*, 833; *OR* 24(3):340.

CHAPTER 12

1. Bearss, *Unvexed to the Sea*, 860.

2. *OR* 24(2):258.

3. Kellogg, *War Experiences*, 41; Bearss, *Unvexed to the Sea*, 818n.

4. Kellogg, *War Experiences*, 42.

5. Ballard, *Vicksburg: The Campaign*, 344; Kellogg, *War Experiences*, 41.

6. *Story of the Fifty-Fifth Regiment*, 243; Kellogg, *War Experiences*, 41.

7. James West Smith, "Confederate Soldier's Diary," 298–99; J. H. Jones, "Rank and File," 21.

8. *OR* 24(2):265; Kirby to William Rigby, February 13, 1903, 8th Missouri Folder, VNMP; Bearss, *Unvexed to the Sea*, 837–38.

9. *OR* 24(2):264; Owen Francis diary, May 22, 1863, 57th Ohio Folder, VNMP; Kellogg, *War Experiences*, 41–43; Bearss, *Unvexed to the Sea*, 838.

10. Russell to mother, May 28, 1863, Russell Brothers Letters, CHM; Werkheiser to brother and sister, August 12, 1863, Werkheiser Papers, NC.

11. *OR* 24(2):300; Charles R. E. Koch to William Rigby, June 10, 1904, and April 30, 1905, 95th Illinois Folder, VNMP; Benjamin W. Underwood to "Mary," May 25, 1863, Underwood Letters, OCHM; Lyman M. Ward to F. H. Magdeburg, February 27, 1903, 14th Wisconsin Folder, VNMP; Bearss, *Unvexed to the Sea*, 795.

12. *OR* 24(2):258, 298, 300; Carrington Diary, May 22, 1863, CHM; Bates to William Rigby, September 16, 1903, and March 7, 1904, Waddell's Alabama Battery Folder, VNMP.

13. Clayton to mother, May 24, 1863, Clayton Papers, MHS; *Minnesota in the Civil and Indian Wars*, 2:369.

14. Carrington Diary, May 22, 1863, CHM; Clayton to mother, May 24, 1863, Clayton Papers, MHS; Wimer Bedford, "Real Life in the Civil War," 46, Bedford Papers, LC.

15. Wood, *Ninety-Fifth Regiment*, 76; Post, *Soldier's Letters*, 213.

16. *OR* 24(2):298; Ward to F. H. Magdeburg, February 27, 1903, 14th Wisconsin Folder, VNMP; Bearss, *Unvexed to the Sea*, 839.

17. *OR* 24(2):258, 298; Clayton to mother, May 24, 1863, Clayton Papers, MHS.

18. Underwood to "Mary," May 25, 1863, Underwood Letters, OCHM; Ransom to McPherson, May 22, 1863, Ransom Letters, GLIAH; *OR* 24(2):298.

19. Benjamin W. Underwood to "Mary," May 25, 1863, Underwood Letters, OCHM; Bod to editor, May 25, 1863, *Chicago Daily Tribune*, June 6, 1863.

20. *OR* 24(2):298.

21. Bearss, *Unvexed to the Sea*, 867–68; *OR* 24(2):300; Byron R. Abernethy, *Private Elisha Stockwell*, 63; Ambrose, *Wisconsin Boy*, 69; Patrick Heffron to friend, May 30, 1863, Willcox Letters, WHS; Clayton to mother, May 24, 1863, Clayton Papers, MHS.

22. Post, *Soldier's Letters*, 213; *OR* 24(2):298, 300; Wood, *Ninety-Fifth Regiment*, 77–78.

23. Underwood to brother and sister, December 8, 1862, and to "Mary," May 25, 1863, Underwood Letters, OCHM; Charles R. E. Koch to William Rigby, January 10, 1904, 95th Illinois Folder, VNMP; Koch to Rigby, January 6, 1904, 72nd Illinois Folder, VNMP.

24. Underwood to "Mary," May 25, 1863, Underwood Letters, OCHM; Charles R. E. Koch to William Rigby, April 30, 1905, 95th Illinois Folder, VNMP; W. M. Mallory diary, May 22, 1863, 72nd Ohio Folder, VNMP.

25. *OR* 24(2):269, 275, 278.

26. *OR* 24(2):275, 281; Oviatt to "Libby," June 14, 1863, Oviatt Papers, NC.

27. Oviatt to "Libby," June 14, 1863, Oviatt Papers, NC; [Griggs], *Opening of the Mississippi*, 135.

28. *OR* 24(2):270.

29. Oviatt to "Libby," June 14, 1863, Oviatt Papers, NC; Grecian, *Eighty-Third*, 30; *OR* 24(2):281; Lacey Diary, May 23, 1863, NL; *OR* 24(2):278.

30. Bryner, *Bugle Echoes*, 85.

31. Bryner, 85–86; Burdette, *Drums of the 47th*, 80; Bearss, *Unvexed to the Sea*, 841; Hubbard, "Minnesota in the Campaigns," 567.

32. McCrory to William Rigby, June 16, 1905, and Ewing to John S. Kountz, May 20, 1902, 30th Ohio Folder, VNMP; Brinkerhoff, *Thirtieth Regiment Ohio*, 75.

33. Farley, *Experience*, 37; Anderson, *Memoirs*, 331; McCall, *Three Years*, 22.

34. Farley Diary, May 22, 1863, KHS; *OR* 24(2):259; Burdette, *Drums of the 47th*, 80; McCall, *Three Years*, 22. Other estimates of the time that Mower started his advance vary. See William C. Porter to G. Moodie White, May 23, 1863, *OR* 24(2):273; and Sherman, *Memoirs*, 1:327.

35. Anderson, *Memoirs*, 331; *OR* 24(2):407.

36. Hubbard, "Minnesota in the Campaigns," 567; "Staff Officer's Pluck," 200–201. Estimates of the number of 11th Missouri men who gained the ditch of Stockade Redan vary. See McCall, *Three Years*, 22; and Anderson, *Memoirs*, 332.

37. Bearss, *Unvexed to the Sea*, 841; Loosley to wife, July 3, 1863, Loosley Papers, SIU; McCall, *Three Years*, 22.

38. Bearss, *Unvexed to the Sea*, 842.

39. Merrilles Diary, May 22, 1863, CHM.

40. Merrilles Diary, May 22, 1863.

41. Merrilles Diary, May 22, 1863; Jefferson Brumbach to "Kate," May 23, 1863, 95th Ohio Folder, VNMP.

42. Bryner, *Bugle Echoes*, 86.

43. Barton, *Autobiography*, 154; [Williams], "*Eagle Regiment*," 61–63.

44. Diary, May 22, 1863, Jacobs Diaries and Lists, LSU; Brinkerhoff, *Thirtieth Regiment Ohio*, 75.

45. Diary, May 22, 1863, Jacobs Diaries and Lists, LSU; Brinkerhoff, *Thirtieth Regiment Ohio*, 75; *OR* 24(2):282; Robert McCrory diary, May 22, 1863, 30th Ohio Folder, VNMP.

46. Diary, May 22, 1863, Jacobs Diaries and Lists, LSU; Saunier, *Forty-Seventh Regiment Ohio*, 148; Ewing to John S. Kountz, May 20, 1902, 30th Ohio Folder, VNMP.

47. Burdette, *Drums of the 47th*, 81–83.

48. Bearss, *Unvexed to the Sea*, 866. Differing estimates of losses in Mower's brigade can be found in Bryner, *Bugle Echoes*, 86; McCall, *Three Years*, 22; [Williams], "*Eagle Regiment*," 17; and [Griggs], *Opening of the Mississippi*, 25.

49. David W. Reed, *Twelfth Regiment*, 123; Bearss, *Unvexed to the Sea*, 866.

50. Buckland to wife, May 26, 1863, Buckland Papers, RBHPC; Estill to "Martha," June 7, 1863, Estill Papers, NC.

51. Lay Diary, May 22, 1863, RBHPC; Bearss, *Unvexed to the Sea*, 866.

52. *OR* 24(2):273.

53. Mitchell, *Badge of Gallantry*, 118; *Story of the Fifty-Fifth Regiment*, 245.

54. *Story of the Fifty-Fifth Regiment*, 245–46.

55. *OR* 24(2):415; Ervin, "Genius and Heroism," 497; Bevier, *First and Second Missouri*, 204.

56. Mitchell, *Badge of Gallantry*, 117–18; "'Forlorn Hope,'" 191; *OR* 24(2):273; Bearss, *Unvexed to the Sea*, 842.

57. Clipping, George Theodore Hyatt account, *Sunday Times-Herald* (Chicago), March 21, 1897, 127th Illinois Folder, VNMP; *Story of the Fifty-Fifth Regiment*, 246; *OR* 24(2):273; J. W. McElroy to J. B. Allen, April 16, 1904, 30th Ohio Folder, VNMP.

58. Bevier, *First and Second Missouri*, 204; Ervin, "Genius and Heroism," 497; *OR* 24(2):415; Bearss, *Unvexed to the Sea*, 842.

59. Mitchell, *Badge of Gallantry*, 118.

CHAPTER 13

1. Bearss, *Unvexed to the Sea*, 818; Ballard, *Vicksburg: The Campaign*, 339.

2. Bearss, *Unvexed to the Sea*, 818n; *OR* 24(2):251; Bennett and Tillery, *Struggle*, 96.

3. *OR* 24(2):394; Baldwin to John G. Devereux, July 10, 1863, Devereux Papers, UNC; Baumgartner, *Blood and Sacrifice*, 78.

4. Ainsworth Diary, May 22, 1863, BHL-UM.

5. Ainsworth Diary, May 22, 1863.

6. Ainsworth Diary, May 22, 1863.

7. Ainsworth Diary, May 22, 1863.

8. Ainsworth Diary, May 22, 1863.

9. Thomas to friend, May 26, 1863, Johns and Thomas Letters, UTK.

10. Thomas to friend, May 26, 1863; S. S. Farwell to J. S. Alexander, April 2, 1903, 31st Iowa Folder, VNMP; Bek, "Civil War Diary," 510; Hess, *German in the Yankee Fatherland*, 99.

11. John W. Niles diary, May 22, 1863, 9th Iowa Folder, VNMP; *OR* 24(2):251–52.

12. Samuel P. Simpson to William Rigby, October 28, 1902, Manter's Brigade Folder, VNMP; W. H. Glick to M. Baumgardner, January 18, 1901, 30th Iowa Folder, VNMP; Henry I. Seaman diary, May 22, 1863, 13th Illinois Folder, VNMP.

13. Bearss, *Unvexed to the Sea*, 842–43; Robert Bruce Hoadley to cousin, May 29, 1863, Hoadley Papers, DU; Alonzo Abernethy to William Rigby, March 3, 7, 1903, 9th Iowa Folder, VNMP.

14. Thomas to friend, May 26, 1863, Johns and Thomas Letters, UTK; Ainsworth Diary, May 22, 1863, BHL-UM.

15. *OR* 24(2):407; Child Diary, May 22, 1863, UI; Guion Log, May 22, 1863, LSU; Bek, "Civil War Diary," 510; Henry Kircher diary, May 22, 1863, Engelmann-Kircher Collection, ALPL.

16. Hoadley to cousin, May 29, 1863, Hoadley Papers, DU.

17. *OR* 24(2):252.

18. Hess, *German in the Yankee Fatherland*, 99–100, 108–9; Hess, "Twelfth Missouri," 154.

19. Hess, *German in the Yankee Fatherland*, 102; Henry Kircher diary, May 22, 1863, Engelmann-Kircher Collection, ALPL.

20. Hess, *German in the Yankee Fatherland*, 100, 109; *SOR*, 4(1):415; W. H. Glick to M. Baumgardner, January 18, 1901, 30th Iowa Folder, VNMP; Alonzo Abernethy to William Rigby, March 7, 1903, 9th Iowa Folder, VNMP.

21. *OR* 24(2):254; Alonzo Abernethy, "Incidents," 415–16; Robert Bruce Hoadley to cousin, May 29, 1863, Hoadley Papers, DU; Otis Crawford, "Color-Guard of the 9th Iowa," *National Tribune*, July 16, 1903.

22. Alonzo Abernethy to William Rigby, March 7, 1903, and John W. Niles diary, May 22, 1863, 9th Iowa Folder, VNMP; Creamer to Rigby, March 14, 1907, 30th Iowa Folder, VNMP; Joseph D. Fegan to Rigby, March 10, 1903, 1st Iowa Battery Folder, VNMP.

23. Hoadley to cousin, May 29, 1863, Hoadley Papers, DU.

24. Ainsworth Diary, May 22, 1863, BHL-UM; Thomas to friend, May 26, 1863, Johns and Thomas Letters, UTK; Henry Kircher diary, May 22, 1863, Engelmann-Kircher Collection, ALPL.

25. Ainsworth Diary, May 22, 1863, BHL-UM; Hess, *German in the Yankee Fatherland*, 100, 102; Robert Bruce Hoadley to cousin, May 29, 1863, Hoadley Papers, DU; Bearss, *Unvexed to the Sea*, 844; diary, May 22, 1863, Seay Papers, UO.

26. Sanders, *Diary in Gray*, 20; *SOR*, 4(1):415–16; Shoup to John G. Devereux, July 8, 1863, Devereux Papers, UNC.

27. Bearss, *Unvexed to the Sea*, 864–65; "Our Special Correspondent" letter, May 25, 1863, *New-York Daily Tribune*, June 5, 1863; Edwin C. Obriham to sister, May 25, 1863, Obriham Letters, Cornell University, Division of Rare and Manuscript Collections, Ithaca, New York; *OR* 24(2):252, 254; Bearss, "Diary of Captain John N. Bell," 211; William H. Nugen to Mary, July 17, 1863, Nugen Letters, DU. For estimates of unit losses in Thayer's brigade, see Hess, *German in the Yankee Fatherland*, 108–9; Alonzo Abernethy, "Incidents," 415; "Our Special Correspondent" letter, May 25, 1863, *New-York Daily Tribune*, June 5, 1863; Child Diary, May 22, 1863, UI; Fowler and Miller, *Thirtieth Iowa*, 28; *SOR*, 4(1):409; and Robert Bruce Hoadley to cousin, May 29, 1863, Hoadley Papers, DU. For estimates of unit losses in Woods's brigade, see Woods Report of Service, 312, NARA; Albert Hiffman reminiscences, Hiffman Family Papers, MHM; "Our Special Correspondent" letter, May 25, 1863, *New-York Daily Tribune*, June 5, 1863; and Diary of Unknown Member, May 22, 1863, Gettysburg College, Special Collections and College Archives, Gettysburg, Pennsylvania.

28. Fowler and Miller, *Thirtieth Iowa*, 28; Bearss, "Diary of Captain John N. Bell," 209; Ainsworth Diary, May 22, 1863, BHL-UM; Bek, "Civil War Diary," 510.

29. William Van Zandt diary, May 22, 1863, Van Zandt Family Papers, ISU.

30. Hess, *German in the Yankee Fatherland*, 100–101; Henry I. Seaman diary, May 23, June 14, 1863, 13th Illinois Folder, VNMP.

31. *OR* 24(2):265, 273; *Story of the Fifty-Fifth Regiment*, 246; Ewing to John S. Kountz, May 20, 1902, 30th Ohio Folder, VNMP; Anderson, *Memoirs*, 332; clipping, George Theodore Hyatt account, *Sunday Times-Herald* (Chicago), March 21, 1897, 127th Illinois Folder, VNMP.

32. *OR* 24(2):273, 280; *Story of the Fifty-Fifth Regiment*, 244.

33. *OR* 52(1):62–64. For other estimates of losses in the Forlorn Hope, see *Story of the Fifty-Fifth Regiment*, 246; and "'Forlorn Hope,'" 194.

34. *OR* 24(2):273–74.

35. *OR* 24(2):282–83; Bearss, *Unvexed to the Sea*, 865–66.

36. *OR* 24(2):415.

37. Creamer to Frank Critz, March 25, 1903, 30th Iowa Folder, VNMP; Hess, *German in the Yankee Fatherland*, 100; Bek, "Civil War Diary," 510; *SOR*, 4(1):415; Anderson, *Memoirs*, 333; Robert Bruce Hoadley to cousin, May 29, 1863, Hoadley Papers, DU; Ainsworth Diary, May 22, 1863, BHL-UM; diary, May 22, 1863, Seay Papers, UO.

38. *OR* 24(3):341–42; Simon, *Papers of Ulysses S. Grant*, 8:255.

39. Bearss, *Unvexed to the Sea*, 844, 866.

CHAPTER 14

1. *OR* 24(2):295; Force, "Personal Recollections," 304–5; Henry O. Dwight to W. P. Gault, September 26, 1901, 20th Ohio Folder, VNMP; M. F. Force to "Loula," May 25, 1862, Force Papers, UW.

2. Bearss, *Unvexed to the Sea*, 846; *OR* 24(2):295.

3. Force to father, May 23, 1863, Force Papers, UW; diary, May 22, 1863, McClure Papers, UCB.

4. Bearss, *Unvexed to the Sea*, 845–46; Ballard, *Vicksburg: The Campaign*, 346; Davis Diary, May 22, 1863, ALPL.

5. Tresilian to J. H. Wilson, August 17, 1863, Comstock Papers, LC.

6. *OR* 24(2):394; *SOR*, 4(1):417.

7. *SOR*, 4(1):417.

8. Bearss, *Unvexed to the Sea*, 867.

9. *OR* 24(1):56, 173; William H. H. Miller to William Rigby, March 14, 1905, Sanborn's Brigade Folder, VNMP.

10. *OR* 24(2):361, 388–89; Chance, *Second Texas*, 106–7; Evans, "Second Texas," 600.

11. *OR* 24(1):180; diary, May 22, 1863, Warmoth Papers, UNC. Warmoth went on sick leave to St. Louis on June 2 to recover from his injury.

12. Bearss, *Unvexed to the Sea*, 846–47; *OR* 24(1):182; [Stone], *George Boardman Boomer*, 272; Trimble, *History of the Ninety-Third Regiment*, 35–36. For another estimate of the time at which Quinby reported to McClernand, see *OR* 24(1):180.

13. Wood to wife, May 25, 1863, Wood Papers, IHS; Sanborn to William Rigby, March 10, 1903, Sanborn's Brigade Folder, VNMP; Bearss, *Unvexed to the Sea*, 847n; Mahan, *Memoirs*, 125.

14. Mahan, *Memoirs*, 125; Wood to wife, May 25, 1863, Wood Papers, IHS.

15. Wood to wife, May 25, 1863, Wood Papers, IHS; Scott, *67th Regiment Indiana*, 38.

16. "Our Special Correspondent" letter, May 25, 1863, *New-York Daily Tribune*, June 5, 1863; Levi Shell to brother, June 23, 1863, Shell Papers, WHS; C. D. Morris, "The Charge at Vicksburg," *National Tribune*, April 16, 1885; *OR* 24(2):236; Gerard, *Diary*, 48; William H. Willcox to sister, May 26, 1863, 96th Ohio Folder, VNMP; Theodorus Northrup to "Ira," May 26, 1863, 23rd Wisconsin Folder, VNMP; Bearss, *Unvexed to the Sea*, 847–48.

17. John B. Sanborn to William Rigby, March 10, 1903, Sanborn's Brigade Folder, VNMP; *OR* 24(2):62; Russ, "Vicksburg Campaign," 268; diary, May 22, 1863, Reeves Papers, MHS; Mahan, *Memoirs*, 125.

18. *OR* 24(2):389, 420; Evans, "Second Texas," 600; Bearss, *Unvexed to the Sea*, 832.

19. Evans, "Second Texas," 600–601; *OR* 24(2):389; Chance, *Second Texas*, 166.

20. *OR* 24(2):389, 420; Bearss, *Unvexed to the Sea*, 848; Evans, "Second Texas," 601.

21. Wood to wife, May 25, 1863, Wood Papers, IHS; Bearss, *Unvexed to the Sea*, 848; diary, May 22, 1863, Reeves Papers, MHS; *OR* 24(2):62; "Our Special Correspondent" letter, May 25, 1863, *New-York Daily Tribune*, June 5, 1863; Levi Shell to brother, June 23, 1863, Shell Papers, WHS; James B. Black to William Rigby, November 27, 1903, 18th Indiana Folder, VNMP; Edwin McCarty to Vicksburg Commission, September 22, 1904, 48th Indiana Folder, VNMP.

22. Diary, May 22, 1863, Reeves Papers, MHS; T. B. Marshall, *Eighty-Third Ohio*, 88; diary, May 22, 1863, Smith Papers, NC.

23. W. A. Bartholomew, "The Charge at Vicksburg," *National Tribune*, November 27, 1884; *OR* 24(2):316; Mahlon Head to William Rigby, April 21, 1903, and E. B. Bascom to Rigby, March 27, 1903, 5th Iowa Folder, VNMP; John A. Spielman to Rigby, December 10, 1901, 17th Iowa Folder, VNMP; [Stone], *George Boardman Boomer*, 282; Ballard, *Vicksburg: The Campaign*, 347.

24. [Stone], *George Boardman Boomer*, 15, 50, 66–67, 117–20, 225, 236, 259.

25. [Stone], 271, 283.

26. JRSC, "Description of the Storming of the Vicksburg Forts," *Indianapolis Daily Journal*, June 19, 1863; H. M. Trimble to William Rigby, March 6, 1903, and Trimble diary, May 22, 1863, 93rd Illinois Folder, VNMP; John A. Spielman to Rigby, December 10, 1901, 17th Iowa Folder, VNMP; Hicks, "Campaign and Capture," 102–3; Dean, *Recollections*, 11.

27. [Stone], *George Boardman Boomer*, 257–58; *OR* 24(2):67, 316; J. Q. A. Campbell diary, May 22, 1863, 5th Iowa Folder, VNMP; E. A. Carr to [Isaac F. Quinby], May 25, 1863, Pride Papers, MHM.

28. Trimble, *History of the Ninety-Third Regiment*, 36.

29. Hicks, "Campaign and Capture," 103; [Stone], *George Boardman Boomer*, 258; H. M. Trimble to William Rigby, March 6, 1903, 93rd Illinois Folder, VNMP; Trimble, *History of the Ninety-Third Regiment*, 36; J. Q. A. Campbell diary, May 22, 1863, 5th Iowa Folder, VNMP; E. A. Carr to [Isaac F. Quinby], May 25, 1863, Pride Papers, MHM; *OR* 24(2):67.

30. Albert O. Marshall, *Army Life*, 159–60.

31. Marshall, 159–60.

32. *SOR*, 13(2):568; H. M. Trimble to William Rigby, March 6, 1903, 93rd Illinois Folder, VNMP; J. Q. A. Campbell to Rigby, October 26, 1901, and E. B. Bascom to Rigby, March 27, 1903, 5th Iowa Folder, VNMP; *OR* 24(2):316.

33. *OR* 24(2):316; E. B. Bascom to William Rigby, March 27, 1903, and J. Q. A. Campbell to Rigby, October 26, 1901, 5th Iowa Folder, VNMP; Dean, *Recollections*, 12; Grabau, *Ninety-Eight Days*, 379; [Stone], *George Boardman Boomer*, 258; Bearss, *Unvexed to the Sea*, 851; W. A. Bartholomew, "The Charge at Vicksburg," *National Tribune*, November 27, 1884.

34. Carr to [Quinby], May 25, 1863, Pride Papers, MHM; *OR* 24(2):68, 316–17; Hicks, "Campaign and Capture," 103; Dean, *Recollections*, 12–13.

35. *OR* 24(2):68, 317; Vance, *Report of the Adjutant General*, 5:385; Bearss, *Unvexed to the Sea*, 868–69.

36. JRSC, "Description of the Storming of the Vicksburg Forts," *Indianapolis Daily Journal*, June 19, 1863; Byers, *With Fire and Sword*, 92.

37. Hicks, "Campaign and Capture," 103.

38. Carr to [Quinby], May 25, 1863, Pride Papers, MHM; JRSC, "Description of the Storming of the Vicksburg Forts," *Indianapolis Daily Journal*, June 19, 1863.

39. Trimble, *Ninety-Third Regiment Illinois*, 37; Hicks, "Campaign and Capture," 104.

40. Kiper, *McClernand*, 263; Samuel Roper to sister, May 27, 1863, Roper Papers, HL; Townsend, *Yankee Warhorse*, 110–11.

41. OR 24(2):232, 234, 240, 312; W. F. Jones, "Grant Coops Up Pemberton," *National Tribune*, February 15, 1900.

42. Whipple, *Diary*, 18.

43. OR 24(2):35; diary, May 22, 1863, Smith Papers, NC.

44. JRSC, "Description of the Storming of the Vicksburg Forts," *Indianapolis Daily Journal*, June 19, 1863; T. B. Marshall, *Eighty-Third Ohio*, 87; Puck, *Sacrifice at Vicksburg*, 63.

45. Ballard, *Grant at Vicksburg*, 21; OR 24(3):339; OR 24(1):182; JRSC, "Description of the Storming of the Vicksburg Forts," *Indianapolis Daily Journal*, June 19, 1863.

46. OR 24(3):339–40; Ballard, *Vicksburg: The Campaign*, 348.

47. Bearss, *Unvexed to the Sea*, 862–64.

48. Bearss, 868–69.

49. OR 24(3):339–40.

CHAPTER 15

1. OR 24(3):907; Stephen D. Lee, "Siege of Vicksburg," 3, folder 33, Claiborne Papers, UNC.

2. Waul to T. A. Hill, June 4, 1891, Connally Papers, AHC; Bearss, *Unvexed to the Sea*, 849.

3. OR 24(2):357–58.

4. OR 24(2):357; Waul to T. A. Hill, June 4, 1891, Connally Papers, AHC; E. W. Pettus to William Rigby, March 14, 1903, 30th Alabama Folder, VNMP.

5. OR 24(2):344, 355, 358; Waul to T. A. Hill, June 4, 1891, Connally Papers, AHC; Bearss, *Unvexed to the Sea*, 825n; Stephen D. Lee, "Siege of Vicksburg," 3–4, folder 33, Claiborne Papers, UNC; Lee, "Siege of Vicksburg," 62; Pettus, "Heroism of Texans," 212; Pettus to William Rigby, March 14, 1903, and William T. Alexander to Rigby, September 18, 1904, 30th Alabama Folder, VNMP.

6. Pettus, "Heroism of Texans," 212.

7. Pettus, 212.

8. Pettus, 212; C. M. Shelley to "General," September 2, 1902, 30th Alabama Folder, VNMP; Kelly, "Thirtieth Alabama," 141–42; Bearss, *Unvexed to the Sea*, 850; SOR, 4(1):407.

9. Pettus, "Heroism of Texans," 212; Lee, "Siege of Vicksburg," 62–63.

10. Pettus, "Heroism of Texans," 212; Lenert Journal, May 22, 1863, OCHM; Lowery Diary, May 22, 1863, ADAH; Lee, "Siege of Vicksburg," 63.

11. "Flag the Rebels Didn't Get," 202; Bering and Montgomery, *Forty-Eighth Ohio*, 88; W. H. Bentley to William Rigby, March 10, 1903, 77th Illinois Folder, VNMP.

12. OR 24(2):351–52.

13. Pettus, "Heroism of Texans," 212; Stephen D. Lee, "Siege of Vicksburg," 4, folder 33, Claiborne Papers, UNC.

14. Pettus, "Heroism of Texans," 212; OR 24(2):349; Lee, "Siege of Vicksburg," 63; Stephen D. Lee, "Siege of Vicksburg," 4, folder 33, Claiborne Papers, UNC.

15. OR 24(2):356, 358; Stamper Diary, May 22, 1863, CPL.

16. Lee, "Siege of Vicksburg," 63; Pettus to William Rigby, March 14, 1903, 30th Alabama

Folder, VNMP; *SOR*, 4(1):406; Sawyer to Rigby, February 14, 1903, 77th Illinois Folder, VNMP.

17. Bering and Montgomery, *Forty-Eighth Ohio*, 88–89; Bentley, *77th Illinois*, 153; A. N. Shumard, "The Charge at Vicksburg," *National Tribune*, June 18, 1885; *OR* 24(2):238; Eddington, "My Civil War Memoirs" (web page).

18. Bentley, *77th Illinois*, 153; Bering and Montgomery, *Forty-Eighth Ohio*, 88; Griffith, "Twenty-Second Iowa," 218; *OR* 24(2):142, 358; *Report of the Adjutant General*, 1130; Harris to William Rigby, May 12, 1902, 11th Wisconsin Folder, VNMP; Sawyer to Rigby, February 14, 1903, 77th Illinois Folder, VNMP; Harwell, "In and around Vicksburg," 334; Pettus to Rigby, March 14, 1903, 30th Alabama Folder, VNMP; Burden, "Into the Breach," 33; *SOR*, 4(1):405.

19. *SOR*, 4(1):407; A. N. Shumard, "The Charge at Vicksburg," *National Tribune*, June 18, 1885; *OR* 24(1):179; Sawyer to William Rigby, February 14, 1903, 77th Illinois Folder, VNMP; Bentley, *77th Illinois*, 153. There is some confusion about exactly which of the two flags belonging to the 77th Illinois wound up in Confederate hands. Capt. Ambrose A. Blount of the 17th Ohio Battery claimed that the national flag rather than the state flag had been "covered with earth in the ditch." See *OR* 24(1):181.

20. *OR* 24(2):350, 358; Waul to T. A. Hill, June 4, 1891, Connally Papers, AHC; Waul to William Rigby, March 10, 1903, Waul's Texas Legion Folder, VNMP; John W. Carroll to Merrick J. Wald and Jahew Buckingham, October 28, 1902; E. J. C. Bealer to J. P. Dolliver, March 24, 1903; and acting secretary of war report, April 13, 1903, all in 77th Illinois Folder, VNMP.

21. Pettus, "Heroism of Texans," 212.

22. S. C. Jones, *Reminiscences*, 39; Griffith, "Twenty-Second Iowa," 219.

23. S. C. Jones, *Reminiscences*, 39.

24. Hiram J. Lewis to friend, May 28, 1863, in newspaper clipping, Lewis and Moulton Family Papers, WHS; Harris to William Rigby, May 12, 1902, 11th Wisconsin Folder, VNMP.

25. Erickson, "With Grant at Vicksburg," 479, 481; Vance, *Report of the Adjutant General*, 2:652, 5:543.

26. Bearss, *Unvexed to the Sea*, 864; *Report of the Adjutant General*, 1130; Burden, "Into the Breach," 33; *OR* 24(2):244; Bentley, *77th Illinois*, 154.

27. Smith to James M. Loughborough, July 8, 1863, Smith Papers, UTA; *OR* 24(2):389.

28. Braudaway, "Civil War Journal," 40; *OR* 24(2):360, 382; John H. Forney to R. W. Memminger, May 22, 1863, "General Maury's Order Book," Confederate States of America Collection, CHM.

29. *OR* 24(2):389.

30. Braudaway, "Civil War Journal," 40; Evans, "Second Texas," 601; Frazier Diary, May 22, 1863, OCHM.

31. Diary, May 22, 1863, Roberts Papers, ADAH.

32. *OR* 24(2):361; Lowery Diary, May 22–23, 1863, ADAH.

CHAPTER 16

1. Pittenger Diary, May 22, 1863, Virginia Polytechnic Institute and State University, Special Collections, Blacksburg, Virginia.

2. Rigby Diary, May 22, 1863, EU.

3. Standifird Civil War Diary, May 22, 1863, SHSM-RCR; Butler to wife, May 22, 1863, Butler Papers, UI.

4. McDonald Civil War Diaries, May 22, 1863, WHS; Boynton Diary, May 22, 1863, SHSI; Lewis Riley to Anna Riley and children, May 27, 1863, Riley Papers, SHSM-RCC; Joseph Crider to brother, May 27, 1863, Crider Letters, SHSM-RCC; Clapp Diary, May 24, 1863, SHSM-RCC; "Our Special Correspondent" letter, May 25, 1863, *New-York Daily Tribune,* June 5, 1863; correspondent letter, May 25, 1863, *Chicago Daily Tribune,* May 28, 1863.

5. George D. Reynolds, "An Enlisted Man's Recollections and Impressions of General U. S. Grant," Reynolds Papers, MHM.

6. Simon, *Papers of Ulysses S. Grant,* 8:255.

7. OR 24(2):360–61, 394; Forney to R. W. Memminger, May 22, 1863, "General Maury's Order Book," Confederate States of America Collection, CHM; *OR* 24(3):907.

8. Ballard, *Vicksburg: The Campaign,* 346; *OR* 24(3):907–9; Maynard, "Vicksburg Diary," 48; Leach Diary, May 22, 1863, SHSM-RCR.

9. *SOR,* 4(1):300; John Cowdry Taylor diary, May 22, 1863, Taylor Family Papers, UVA; John G. Devereux to Vaughn, May 22, 1863, Vaughn Service Record, NARA.

10. *ORN* 25:23–24.

11. *ORN* 25:24, 27.

12. *ORN* 25:21–22; Porter, *Naval History,* 321; Bearss, *Unvexed to the Sea,* 854.

13. *ORN,* May 23, 1863; Porter, *Naval History,* 321–22; Bearss, *Unvexed to the Sea,* 854–55.

14. *ORN* 25:24–29; Mumford Diary, May 22, 1863, OCHM.

15. *ORN* 25:29; *OR* 24(2):337; Bearss, *Unvexed to the Sea,* 855–56.

16. Young, "Vicksburg's Confederate Fort Hill," 19; *OR* 24(1):275; John Cowdry Taylor diary, May 22, 1863, Taylor Family Papers, UVA; *Smith in Service,* 52; Alison Diary, May 22, 1863, UNC; Porter, *Naval History,* 321; Milligan, *From the Fresh-Water Navy,* 180.

17. Diary, May 22, 1863, Connor Family Papers, UGA; Chambers Diaries, May 22, 1863, LSU; *SOR,* 4(1):274.

18. *OR* 24(3):337–38.

19. *OR* 24(3):341.

20. Simon, *Papers of Ulysses S. Grant,* 8:251n; *OR* 24(3):337–38.

21. *ORN* 25:22, 32.

22. Belknap, *Fifteenth Regiment Iowa,* 255–56; Martin, *"Out and Forward,"* 21; *OR* 24(2):301, 308.

23. *OR* 24(2):301–2, 307; Belknap, *Fifteenth Regiment Iowa,* 256; Olynthus B. Clark, *Downing's Civil War Diary,* 117; Sylvester Daniels diary, May 22, 1863, Magaw Papers, HL; Civil War Diaries of Mifflin Jennings (website), May 22, 1863.

24. *OR* 24(3):908.

25. McArthur to H. H. Rood, September 20, 1900, Hall's-Chambers's Brigade Folder, VNMP; Simon, *Papers of Ulysses S. Grant,* 8:256–57.

26. McArthur to H. H. Rood, September 20, 1900, Hall's-Chambers's Brigade Folder, VNMP; *ORN* 25:23.

27. *OR* 24(3):337–38; *ORN* 25:32.

28. Bearss, *Unvexed to the Sea,* 857–58; Ballard, *Vicksburg: The Campaign,* 348; *OR* 24(2):302; Civil War Diaries of Mifflin Jennings (website), May 22, 1863; Belknap, *Fifteenth Regiment Iowa,* 256; *OR* 24(1):155, 181.

29. *OR* 24(3):338; H. H. Rood to William Rigby, January 21, 1901, Ransom's Brigade Folder, VNMP; Bearss, *Unvexed to the Sea,* 867–68.

1. Diary, May 23, 1863, Smith Papers, NC; Molineaux Diaries, May 23, 1863, AC; Marshall Diaries, May 23, 1863, MU; Schmidt to wife, May 24, 1863, Schmidt Family Papers, FHS.

2. *OR* 24(1):87; Force to "Mr. Kebler," May 23, 1863, Force Papers, UW.

3. Diary, May 25, 1863, Leggett Papers, Western Reserve Historical Society, Cleveland, Ohio; *Alexandria Gazette*, May 25, 1863; Grear, "'North-West is Determined,'" 99–100; [Scott], *67th Regiment*, 38; Cox, *Kiss Josey*, 155; Merrilles Diary, May 22, 1863, CHM; "Elias D. Moore Diary" (web page), May 22, 1863; Record Diary, May 22, 1863, LSU; Reese to "Tissee," May 25, June 4, 1863, Reese Papers, SIU; Byers, *With Fire and Sword*, 87; Lacey Diary, May 23, 1863, NL; Orin England to "Dud," May 26, 1863, England Letters, RBHPC; Lay Diary, May 22, 1863, RBHPC; Strong Reminiscences, 13–14, MHM; Post, *Soldiers' Letters*, 222; Silas Hemphill to brother and sister, May 25, 1862, Hemphill Family Papers, SHSI; Halsell, "Sixteenth Indiana," 69–70.

4. *OR* 24(1):37.

5. *OR* 24(3):343.

6. *OR* 24(3):343; McArthur to H. H. Rood, September 20, 1900, Hall's-Chambers's Brigade Folder, VNMP; Sylvester Daniels diary, May 23, 1863, Magaw Papers, HL.

7. Simon, *Papers of Ulysses S. Grant*, 8:258n; *ORN* 25:32.

8. *OR* 24(3):343; *OR* 24(1):37.

9. *OR* 24(3):346, 348–49.

10. *OR* 24(1):56; Ulysses S. Grant, *Memoirs*, 1:357, 359.

11. Erickson, "With Grant at Vicksburg," 479; Walter George Smith, *Life and Letters*, 296; Silas Hemphill to brother and sister, May 25, 1863, Hemphill Family Papers, SHSI; Clayton to mother, May 24, 1863, Clayton Papers, MHS.

12. England to "Dud," May 26, 1863, England Letters, RBHPC; William L. Brown to father, May 25, 1863, Brown Collection, CHM; Albert Chipman to wife, May 23, 1863, Chipman Papers, ALPL; Clapp Diary, May 24, 1863, SHSM-RCC; Clayton to mother, May 24, 1863, Clayton Papers, MHS.

13. William L. Brown to father, May 25, 1863, Brown Collection, CHM; Clayton to mother, May 24, 1863, Clayton Papers, MHS; diary, May 22, 1863, Seay Papers, UO; Clark Wright to "Sallie," May 24, 1863, Wright Papers, NC; Lewis to friend, May 28, 1863, Lewis and Moulton Family Papers, WHS.

14. "Our Special Correspondent" letter, May 25, 1863, *New-York Daily Tribune*, June 5, 1863; *OR* 24(2):39; Bond, *Under the Flag*, 65; Marshall Diaries, May 23, 1863, MU; Albert O. Marshall, *Army Life*, 161; JRSC, "The 16th Regiment at Vicksburg," *Indianapolis Daily Journal*, June 10, 1863.

15. Clark Wright to "Sallie," May 24, 1863, Wright Papers, NC; James Leeper to "Mary," May 23, 1863, Leeper Papers, IHS; Molineaux Diaries, May 22, 1863, AC; C. D. Morris, "Vicksburg: A Graphic Description of the Charge," *National Tribune*, October 23, 1884; Jackson, *"Some of the Boys,"* 102; J. C. Switzer to Bluford Wilson, September 23, 1904, Wilson Letters, ALPL; William L. Brown to father, May 25, 1863, Brown Collection, CHM; Holcomb, *Southern Sons*, 69; *SOR*, 4(1):403; Bod to editor, May 25, 1863, *Chicago Daily Tribune*, June 6, 1863; Howard, "Vicksburg Campaign," 6; James Thomas to "Friend," May 26, 1863, Johns and Thomas Letters, UTK; Hess, *German in the Yankee Fatherland*, 101; Hains, "Vicksburg Campaign," 196; Bek, "Civil War Diary," 510–11; Albert O. Marshall,

Army Life, 154–55, 157; Ira W. Hunt to wife, May 23, 1863, 11th Wisconsin Folder, VNMP; Jefferson Brumbach to "Kate," May 25, 1863, 95th Ohio Folder, VNMP; Benjamin W. Underwood to sister, May 25, 1863, Underwood Letters, OCHM; Miller Reminiscences, 12, OCHM; McDonald, *30th Illinois*, 48; clipping, M. A. Sweetman, "Capture of Vicksburg Desperate Struggle," *Circleville Daily*, 114th Ohio Folder, VNMP.

16. Hess, *German in the Yankee Fatherland*, 98; *OR* 24(2):170, 283; Ephraim C. Dawes to "Folks," June 21, 1863, Dawes Papers, NL; M. F. Force to "Loula," May 25, 1863, Force Papers, UW; Wright to "Sallie," May 24, 1863, Wright Papers, NC; journal, May 22, 1863, Rigby Papers, UI; Ralph P. Buckland to wife, May 26, 1863, Buckland Papers, RBHPC; Elder, *Damned Iowa Greyhound*, 82; William L. Brown to brother, August 11, 1863, Brown Collection, CHM.

17. William H. Willcox to sister, May 26, 1863, 96th Ohio Folder, VNMP; Wood to wife, June 7, 1863, Wood Papers, IHS; Loosley to wife, June 1, 5, 1863, Loosley Papers, SIU; Erickson, "With Grant at Vicksburg," 479; Halsell, "Sixteenth Indiana," 78.

18. Gile to sister, May 24, 1863, Gile Papers, Yale University, Sterling Memorial Library, New Haven, Connecticut; Burdette, *Drums of the 47th*, 79; *OR* 24(2):170; Mahan, *Memoirs*, 126; George D. Reynolds, "An Enlisted Man's Recollections and Impressions of General U. S. Grant," Reynolds Papers, MHM; Carr to C. M. Carr, ca. June 7, 1863, Carr Papers, USAMHI; Hains, "Vicksburg Campaign," 196; Edward H. Ingraham to aunt, May 29, 1863, Ingraham and Ingraham Letters, ALPL; Frank Swigart, "Vicksburg Campaign: The Gallant but Disastrous Charge of May 22," *National Tribune*, August 9, 1888; "Our Special Correspondent" letter, May 25, 1863, *New-York Daily Tribune*, June 5, 1863; Wood, *Ninety-Fifth Regiment*, 80.

19. Simon, *Papers of Ulysses S. Grant*, 8:376.

20. *OR* 24(1):6, 55–56.

21. Badeau, *Military History*, 1:327–28; Ulysses S. Grant, *Memoirs*, 1:355.

22. Simpson and Berlin, *Sherman's Civil War*, 472, 476; Sherman, *Memoirs*, 1:328.

23. *SOR*, 4(1):271; Thomas, *Three Years with Grant*, 92; Dana, *Recollections*, 56; Jenney, "Personal Recollections," 261–62. Col. John B. Sanborn thought after the war that McClernand was responsible for 2,000 Union casualties on May 22. Sanborn, "Campaign against Vicksburg," 134.

24. *OR* 24(1):37, 86–87; Sherman to brother, May 29, 1863, Sherman Papers, LC; Simpson and Berlin, *Sherman's Civil War*, 472.

25. Simon, *Papers of Ulysses S. Grant*, 8:254n–255n.

26. Wilson, *Under the Old Flag*, 1:174–76.

27. Merrilles Diary, May 19, 1863, CHM; Frank Swigart, "Vicksburg Campaign: The Gallant but Disastrous Charge of May 22," *National Tribune*, August 9, 1888; McClernand to Turner, May 27, 31, 1863, Turner Papers, ALPL; *SOR*, 4(1):394, 396; McClernand to Lincoln, May 29, 1863, Lincoln Papers, LC.

28. *OR* 24(1):165–66.

29. *OR* 24(1):103, 159–61.

30. *OR* 24(1):102–3, 162, 164; Jenney, "Personal Recollections," 262; E. J. McClernand to Henry Clay Warmoth, May 27, 1914, Warmoth Papers, UNC.

31. Bearss, *Unvexed to the Sea*, 859; Ballard, *Grant at Vicksburg*, 87–90, 92, 105; Shea and Winschel, *Vicksburg Is the Key*, 152; Wilson, *Under the Old Flag*, 1:186.

32. Kiper, *McClernand*, 261–63, 270, 304.

33. John Cowdry Taylor diary, May 23, 1863, Taylor Family Papers, UVA.

34. *OR* 24(2):362; Guion Log, May 23, 1863, LSU; Tunnard, *Southern Record*, 239; Stamper Diary, May 25, 1863, CPL; *OR* 24(1):276–77; *SOR*, 4(1):301; Fowler Civil War Diary, May 23, 1863, SU; diary, May 23, 1863, Roberts Papers, ADAH.

35. *OR* 24(2):361–62; diary, May 23, 1863, Connor Family Papers, UGA; Ballard, *Pemberton*, 171; Lida Lord Reed, "Woman's Experiences," 923; Wells, *Siege of Vicksburg*, 69.

36. Lee, "Siege of Vicksburg," 60, 64–65; Stephen D. Lee, "Siege of Vicksburg," 3, folder 33, Claiborne Papers, UNC; Synnamon Letter, SHSM-RCR; diary, May 23, 1863, Connor Family Papers, UGA; "The Siege of Vicksburg, by One of the Garrison," *Memphis Daily Appeal*, July 22, 1863; J. H. Jones, "Rank and File," 21.

37. Winter, *Joseph Boyce*, 122; *OR* 24(2):393–94.

38. John Cowdry Taylor diary, May 23, 1863, Taylor Family Papers, UVA; *OR* 24(2):361, 390; Tunnard, *Southern Record*, 239.

39. *OR* 24(2):337–38.

40. Circular, Headquarters, Department of Mississippi and Eastern Louisiana, May 24, 1863, Order Book, VHS.

41. John Cowdry Taylor diary, May 24, 1863, Taylor Family Papers, UVA.

42. *OR* 24(3):916; *OR* 24(1):192–93; McGlothlin Diary, May 22–24, 27, 1863, HL.

43. *OR* 24(1):193; Johnston to Davis, May 23, 1863, Letters Sent, January 28, 1862–July 22, 1863, no. 3, box 4, vol. 4, Johnston Papers, CWM; *OR* 24(3):916–17.

44. David W. Yandill to Johnston, June 17, 1863, Yandill Letter, CHM; *OR* 24(1):190, 192, 194, 220, 222–23; *OR* 24(3):912.

45. *OR* 24(3):916; *OR* 24(1):193.

46. *OR* 24(3):920.

47. *OR* 24(1):194.

CHAPTER 18

1. *OR* 24(2):167; Ballard, *Vicksburg: The Campaign*, 308, 348; Bearss, *Unvexed to the Sea*, 869.

2. *OR* 24(2):260; *OR* 24(1):156; Bearss, *Unvexed to the Sea*, 839, 869; Spencer Diary, May 22, 1863, SHSM-RCR.

3. Merrilles Diary, May 22, 1863, CHM; Griffith Diaries, May 23, 1863, OHS; diary, May 24, 1863, Gordon Papers, USAMHI; Sylvester Bartow to "Helen," May 24, 1863, Bartow Papers, NC; diary, June 2, 1863, Connor Family Papers, UGA; *Memphis Daily Appeal*, July 22, 1863; Abrams, *Full and Detailed*, 35; Lee, "Siege of Vicksburg," 63; Jorantha Semmes to husband, June 3, 1863, Semmes Papers, UNC; Ray, "Civil War Letters," 222.

4. Ballard, *Vicksburg: The Campaign*, 308, 348; Shea and Winschel, *Vicksburg Is the Key*, 151; Hall, *26th Louisiana*, 96–98.

5. *OR* 24(1):276; John G. Devereux to John C. Vaughn, May 24, 1863, Vaughn Service Record, NARA; *OR* 24(3):910, 915; Sanders, *Diary in Gray*, 21; *OR* 24(2):362, 389; Chance, *Second Texas*, 108; Chambers Diaries, May 25, 1863, LSU.

6. *OR* 24(3):910; Cotton, *Pen of a She-Rebel*, 43.

7. Johnson, *Muskets and Medicine*, 102–5; Rice to "Robert," June 5, 1863, Rice Collection, RBHPC; *OR* 24(3):357.

8. "Tabular Statement of the wounded in Hospital 3rd Divis 15th A. C. Collated by Dr. Gill 95th Ohio from the Assault on Vicksburg May 22nd 1863," Hawley Papers, MHM.

9. Walter George Smith, *Life and Letters*, 295–96.

10. Thomas M. Stevenson, *78th Regiment*, 242; Ambrose, *Wisconsin Boy*, 69–70; Kellogg to father, mother, brothers, and sisters, May 25, 1863, 23rd Wisconsin Folder, VNMP; Heffron to friend, May 30, 1863, Willcox Letters, WHS.

11. Harriss to wife, June 13, 1863, Harriss Papers, NC.

12. B. F. Stevenson, *Letters from the Army*, 223–24.

13. Bigelow, *Abridged History*, 22.

14. Diary, May 23, 1863, Smith Papers, NC; Edward J. Lewis diary, May 24, 1863, 33rd Illinois Folder, VNMP; Johnson, *Muskets and Medicine*, 105; Bollet, *Civil War Medicine*, 212.

15. OR 24(3):357; Simon, *Papers of Ulysses S. Grant*, 8:243–45.

16. OR 24(3):915; Crooke, *Twenty-First Regiment*, 85; Silas Hemphill to brothers and sisters, May 25, 1863, Hemphill Family Papers, SHSI.

17. Abrams, *Full and Detailed*, 37; Robert McCrory to J. B. Allen, April 15, 1904, 30th Ohio Folder, VNMP.

18. Diary, May 25, 1863, Jacobs Diaries and Lists, LSU; Butler to wife, May 25, June 2, 1863, Butler Papers, UI.

19. E. M. Joslin to "Dr. Franklin," June 4, 1863, *Chicago Daily Tribune*, June 26, 1863; Phineas T. Underwood to "William," June 12, 1863, Underwood Letters, OCHM; Yeatman to George Partridge, June 9, 1863, *Chicago Daily Tribune*, June 12, 1863.

20. Wood Diary, May 19–21, 25, 27–28, 1863, UCB.

21. Wood Diary, May 28–31, June 2, 1863.

22. Wood Diary, June 8–9, 11–13, 15–16, 20, 1863.

23. Shell to brother, June 23, 1863; to friends, June 10, 1863; and to editor, August 13, 1863, *State Journal*, in undated newspaper clipping, all in Shell Papers, WHS.

24. Kennedy to wife, June 3, 1863; Rose to Jane Kennedy, June 22, 1863; and Mattie I. Morey to Jane Kennedy, June 22, 1863, all in Kennedy Papers, ALPL; *Story of the Fifty-Fifth Regiment*, 246–47.

25. Stephens, *Bound for Glory*, 138; Chambers Diaries, May 23, 1863, LSU.

26. OR 24(3):913.

27. Hall, *26th Louisiana*, 72–73.

28. Hall, 73–74, 86.

29. Foster Letter, UA.

30. Foster Letter, UA.

31. "'Forlorn Hope,'" 194; Higgins to C. A. Hobbs, December 7, 1878, 99th Illinois Folder, VNMP.

32. "'Forlorn Hope,'" 194; Jesse Sawyer to William Rigby, February 14, 1903, 77th Illinois Folder, VNMP.

33. SOR, 13(2):123; Simon, *Papers of Ulysses S. Grant*, 8:243n, 258n; Jesse Sawyer to William Rigby, January 1, February 14, 1903, 77th Illinois Folder, VNMP; M. J. Nald to Rigby, July 12, 1902, 97th Illinois Folder, VNMP; parole issued to Leonidas M. Godley, 22nd Iowa Folder, VNMP; "'Forlorn Hope,'" 194; Milligan, *From the Fresh-Water Navy*, 182.

34. Pearson to Stephen D. Lee, May 17, 1902, 30th Alabama Folder, VNMP.

CHAPTER 19

1. Larkin A. Byron to James McNeill, July 5, 1863, Byron Papers, NC; Robert Bruce Hoadley to cousin, May 29, 1863, Hoadley Papers, DU; diary, May 24, 1863, Kimbell Papers, CHM; Lay Diary, May 22, 1863, RBHPC.

2. Sanders, *Diary in Gray*, 21; Kellogg, *War Experiences*, 47–48.

3. Alonzo Abernethy diary, May 23, 1863, 9th Iowa Folder, VNMP; F. M. Smith to William Rigby, January 28, 1905, 17th Illinois Folder, VNMP; Richards to "Dearly Loved Ones at Home," May 19 and 21, 1863, 17th Ohio Battery Folder, VNMP.

4. Simon, *Papers of Ulysses S. Grant*, 8:254n; Erickson, "With Grant at Vicksburg," 481.

5. Unidentified diary, May 23, 1863, 17th Ohio Battery Folder, VNMP; Simeon R. Martin, "Facts About Co. 'I' of the 46th Mississippi Infantry," 74–75, 46th Mississippi Folder, VNMP.

6. Evans, "Second Texas," 601–2; Anderson, *Memoirs*, 333.

7. Diary, May 22, 1863, Roberts Papers, ADAH; Braudaway, "Civil War Journal," 45; Evans, "Second Texas," 602; Fisher Diary, May 25, 1863, MHM; Dodd, "Recollections," 8; J. H. Jones, "Rank and File," 22; Stamper Diary, May 25, 1863, CPL; Leach Diary, May 24, 1863, SHSM-RCR; Tunnard, *Southern Record*, 240; Willene B. Clark, *Valleys of the Shadow*, 23.

8. Diary, May 25, 1863, Smith Papers, NC; diary, May 25, 1863, Kimbell Papers, CHM; *OR* 24(3):914, 918.

9. *OR* 24(1):276–77.

10. *OR* 24(3):918; Smith to John C. Vaughn, May 25, 1863, Vaughn Service Record, NARA.

11. Trigg, "Fighting around Vicksburg," 120; Merrilles Diary, May 25, 1863, CHM; Davis Diary, May 25, 1863, ALPL; Slack Papers, ISL; Kroff Diary, May 25, 1863, UO; Elliot N. Bush to father and "Mother and All," May 29, 1863, Bush Papers, University of Michigan, William L. Clements Library, Ann Arbor, Michigan; Wells, *Siege of Vicksburg*, 70; Bod to editor, May 25, 1863, *Chicago Daily Tribune*, June 6, 1863; Isaiah Richards to "Dearly Loved Ones at Home," May 19 and 21, 1863, 17th Ohio Battery Folder, VNMP. Reports of the time that the truce flag appeared vary from noon to 6:00 P.M. See Bond, *Under the Flag*, 66; Braudaway, "Civil War Journal," 43; diary, May 25, 1863, Reeves Papers, MHS; Yaggy Diary, May 25, 1863, ALPL; and John Cowdry Taylor diary, May 25, 1863, Taylor Family Papers, UVA.

12. *OR* 24(1):277; *OR* 24(3):348, 918.

13. Abrams, *Full and Detailed*, 37; diary, May 24 [25], 1863, Connor Family Papers, UGA; journal, May 25, 1863, Rigby Papers, UI; *OR* 24(1):89; *SOR*, 4(1):277.

14. *OR* 24(1):276; diary, May 25, 1863, Seay Papers, UO; Carrington Diary, May 25, 1863, CHM; diary, May 26, 1863, Connor Family Papers, UGA; diary, May 25, 1863, Smith Papers, NC; diary, May 25, 1863, Roberts Papers, ADAH; Rigby Diary, May 25, 1863, EU; Marshall Diaries, May 25, 1863, MU; Eddington, "My Civil War Memoirs" (web page); Harvey D. Johnston diary, May 25, 1863, 99th Illinois Folder, VNMP; J. C. Nottingham to William Rigby, December 12, 1901, 8th Indiana Folder, VNMP.

15. *Story of the Fifty-Fifth Regiment*, 247; Johnson, *Muskets and Medicine*, 111; Silas Hemphill to "Fred," May 28, 1863, Hemphill Family Papers, SHSI; Anderson, *Memoirs*, 333; Cantrell, *Sketches*, 62; "History of Company B," 177–78; Henry H. Bush to William Rigby, September 12, 1901, Ransom's Brigade Folder, VNMP; James K. Darby diary, May 25, 1863, 8th Indiana Folder, VNMP.

16. Miller Reminiscences, 12–13, OCHM.

17. *Story of the Fifty-Fifth Regiment*, 247; Abrams, *Full and Detailed*, 37; Foster Letter, UA.

18. T. B. Marshall, *Eighty-Third Ohio*, 86–87; Holcomb, *Southern Sons*, 69; Simpson and Berlin, *Sherman's Civil War*, 472; Bering and Montgomery, *Forty-Eighth Ohio*, 91–92; Lay Diary, May 25, 1863, RBHPC; Lee, "Siege of Vicksburg," 64.

19. *Smith in Service,* 53; R. M. Aiken to William Rigby, April 12, 1903, 33rd Illinois Folder, VNMP.

20. *OR* 24(3):348; diary, May 25, 1863, Smith Papers, NC; Anderson, *Memoirs,* 333; Way, *Thirty-Third Regiment Illinois,* 45; Throne, "Jacob Carroll Switzer," 335–36; Bod to editor, May 25, 1863, *Chicago Daily Tribune,* June 6, 1863; Marshall Diaries, May 26, 1863, MU; Painter, "Bullets, Hardtack and Mud," 156; unidentified diary, May 25, 1863, 17th Ohio Battery Folder, VNMP.

21. Kellogg, *War Experiences,* 48; Erickson, "With Grant at Vicksburg," 482n.

22. John R. Sever to Rachel Beeman Piper, n.d., 99th Illinois Folder, VNMP.

23. *OR* 24(2):390; Marshall Diaries, May 25, 1863, MU; Willene B. Clark, *Valleys of the Shadow,* 23.

24. Slack to "Ann," May 28, 1863, Slack Papers, ISL; Carrington Diary, May 25, 1863, CHM; James West Smith, "Confederate Soldier's Diary," 301; Willett, Pickens Planters Diary, 56, ADAH; diary, May 25, 1863, Rigby Papers, UI; Yaggy Diary, May 25, 1863, ALPL; Richard R. Puffer to sister, May 28, 1863, Puffer Papers, CHM.

25. Cox, *Kiss Josey,* 157; Merrilles Diary, May 25, 1863, CHM; Wells, *Siege of Vicksburg,* 70–71; Hampton Smith, *Brother of Mine,* 130; Fryar Diary, May 26, 1863, Museum of the Confederacy, Richmond, Virginia.

26. Bod to editor, May 25, 1863, *Chicago Daily Tribune,* June 6, 1863; James R. Slack to "Ann," May 28, 1863, Slack Papers, ISL; Farley Diary, May 25, 1863, KHS; Oldroyd, *Soldier's Diary,* 36–37.

27. Abrams, *Full and Detailed,* 37–38; *OR* 24(2):390; Fisher Diary, May 25, 1863, MHM; *SOR,* 4(1):415.

28. Anderson, *Memoirs,* 333–34; Braudaway, "Civil War Journal," 44; Evans, "Second Texas," 602; Theodorus Northrup to "Ira," May 26, 1863, 23rd Wisconsin Folder, VNMP.

29. James West Smith, "Confederate Soldier's Diary," 301; Stamper Diary, May 25, 1863, CPL; Charles Wood diary, May 25, 1863, 29th Wisconsin Folder, VNMP; Henry I. Seaman diary, May 25, 1863, 13th Illinois Folder, VNMP; diary, May 25, 1863, Seay Papers, UO.

30. Oldroyd, *Soldier's Diary,* 37; *OR* 24(1):89.

31. John Reese to "Tissee," May 25, 1863, Reese Papers, SIU; John A. Bowman to friends, May 27, 1863, Bowman Letters, OCHM; Holcomb, *Southern Sons,* 69; Hampton Smith, *Brother of Mine,* 130; diary, May 25, 1863, Schweitzer Papers, HL.

32. Tunnard, *Southern Record,* 240; Ralph J. Smith, *Reminiscences,* 13; Morss, *Helena to Vicksburg,* 89.

33. *Story of the Fifty-Fifth Regiment,* 247; Powell, "Brother Fought against Brother," 463; Anderson, *Memoirs,* 334; Baumgartner, *Blood and Sacrifice,* 78; Knight Diary, May 25, 1863, OCHM.

34. Simon, *Papers of Ulysses S. Grant,* 8:267n.

35. Hickenlooper, "Vicksburg Mine," 540; diary, May 26, 1863, Hickenlooper Collection, CMC.

36. Carrington Diary, May 25, 1863, CHM.

37. Lockett, "Defense of Vicksburg," 489–90.

38. Lockett, 490.

39. Lockett, 490; Samuel Henry Lockett, "The Defence of Vicksburg from an Engineering Point of View," folder 9, Lockett Papers, UNC.

40. Erickson, "With Grant at Vicksburg," 482; M. B. Loop, "In the Trenches before

Vicksburg," *National Tribune*, November 15, 1900; Yaggy Diary, May 25, 1863, ALPL; Wells, *Siege of Vicksburg*, 71.

41. James West Smith, "Confederate Soldier's Diary," 301.

42. Oldroyd, *Soldier's Diary*, 35; Bond, *Under the Flag*, 66; Griffith Diaries, May 25, 1863, OHS; Maynard, "Vicksburg Diary," 48; John Reese to "Tissee," May 25, 1863, Reese Papers, SIU; Marshall Diaries, May 26, 1863, MU.

43. *OR* 24(1):277.

44. Slack to "Ann," May 28, 1863, Slack Papers, ISL; Bod to editor, May 25, 1863, *Chicago Daily Tribune*, June 6, 1863; Sanders, *Diary in Gray*, 21.

45. Ambrose, *Wisconsin Boy*, 72.

46. Diary, May 24 [25], 1863, Connor Family Papers, UGA; Erickson, "With Grant at Vicksburg," 482n; diary, May 25, 1863, Sanders Family Papers, LSU; Osborn, "Tennessean," 359.

47. *OR* 24(2):389–90.

48. Braudaway, "Civil War Journal," 45.

49. Merrilles Diary, May 25, 1863, CHM; Braudaway, "Civil War Journal," 45; Baumgartner, *Blood and Sacrifice*, 78.

50. George P. Clark, "Remenecence of My Army Life," 32; Johnson, *Muskets and Medicine*, 111.

51. Ingraham to aunt, May 29, 1863, Ingraham and Ingraham Letters, ALPL; Albert O. Marshall, *Army Life*, 161; Loosley to wife, July 3, 1863, Loosley Papers, SIU.

52. Knobe Journal, May 25, 1863, ISL; *OR* 24(2):282.

53. [Stone], *George Boardman Boomer*, 259–60, 262.

54. [Stone], 272–73; Eugene A. Carr to [Quinby], May 25, 1863, and T. L. Crawford to "Colonel," June 21, 1863, Pride Papers, MHM.

55. [Stone], *George Boardman Boomer*, 270; Daniel R. Smith to "John," August 4, 1863, Smith Letters, ALPL; General Orders No. 8, Headquarters, Seventeenth Corps, March 18, 1864, Sherman Papers, LC.

CHAPTER 20

1. *OR* 24(2):239.

2. *OR* 24(2):260–61, 273–74, 282; McCarty and McCarty, *Chatfield Story*, 202.

3. Shea and Winschel, *Vicksburg Is the Key*, 147, 149; "'Forlorn Hope,'" 190–97.

4. Simpson and Berlin, *Sherman's Civil War*, 472–73; Fry Certificate, SHSI; Winschel, "First Honor," 18; McAlexander, *Thirteenth Regiment*, 241.

5. Fry Certificate, SHSI; McAlexander, *Thirteenth Regiment*, 241; Shea and Winschel, *Vicksburg Is the Key*, 147.

6. Burden, "Into the Breach," 34; G. W. Crosley diary, May 25, 1863, 3rd Iowa Folder, VNMP; *Report of the Adjutant General*, 1131–32; "The Next Governor of Our State," *Chicago Daily Tribune*, June 20, 1863; Burden, "Into the Breach," 34; Popchock, *Soldier Boy*, 92.

7. Hains, "Incident," 71; Hains, "Vicksburg Campaign," 271; Wilson, *Under the Old Flag*, 1:179; cards and death certificate for Belle Rigg Griffith, Griffith Pension Record, NARA.

8. Declaration for Invalid Pension, October 8, 1868; report, March 12, 1895; Application for Reimbursement, n.d.; Declaration for Widow's Pension, August 15, 1895; and cards, all

in Messenger Pension Record, NARA; Declaration for Pension or for Increase of Pension of Children under Sixteen Years of Age, January 8, 1887; Widow's Declaration for Pension or Increase of Pension, January 19, 1889; and Declaration for Remarried Widow's Pension, January 24, 1922, all in Trine Pension Record, NARA.

9. Pearson to Lee, May 17, June 15, 1902, 30th Alabama Folder, VNMP.

10. Jeremiah N. Sherman to William Rigby, July 1902, Battery A, 1st Illinois, Folder, VNMP; Higgins to Hobbs, December 7, 1878, 99th Illinois Folder, VNMP.

11. J. E. Jayne to William Rigby, February 3, 1903, 47th Indiana Folder, VNMP; *OR* 24(2):282–83; Ralston Service Record, NARA.

12. *OR* 24(2):238–39.

13. Wescott, *Civil War Letters*, not paginated.

14. *SOR*, 3(3):194–95.

15. Circular, Headquarters, Department of Mississippi and Eastern Louisiana, May 23, 1863, Order Book, VHS; *OR* 24(3):909, 913; Foster Letter, UA.

CHAPTER 21

1. McCall, *Three Years*, 22; Oldroyd, *Soldier's Diary*, 32; John N. Moulton to sister, August 5, 1863, Moulton and Lewis Letters, MHM; Alonzo L. Brown, *History of the Fourth Regiment*, 343–44; Heffron to friend, May 30, 1863, Willcox Letters, WHS; Throne, "Civil War Letters," 319; House Diary, May 22, 1863, MHS; Way, *Thirty-Third Regiment Illinois*, 43; *OR* 24(1):156; "Our Special Correspondent" letter, May 25, 1863, *New-York Daily Tribune*, June 5, 1863; "Our Army at Vicksburg," *National Tribune*, May 13, 1882; Logan, *Reminiscences of a Soldier's Wife*, 138; Abraham J. Seay to not stated, August 11, 1863, King Papers, UO; W. F. Jones, "Grant Coops Up Pemberton," *National Tribune*, February 15, 1900; Francis Preston Blair, Jr., to "Judge," June 8, 1863, Blair Family Papers, LC; Strong, "Campaign against Vicksburg," 329; C. D. Morris, "Vicksburg: A Graphic Description of the Charge," *National Tribune*, October 23, 1884.

2. Simpson and Berlin, *Sherman's Civil War*, 482, 489; Charles Ewing to father, June 12, 1863, Ewing Family Papers, LC.

3. Simpson and Berlin, *Sherman's Civil War*, 488–89.

4. Albert O. Marshall, *Army Life*, 173.

5. Waul to Jones, June 28, 1889, Waul Papers, DU.

6. W. H. Bentley, "Ode, To Our Comrades who fell in the Charge at Vicksburg, May 22d 1863," 77th Illinois Folder, VNMP.

7. Hobbs, *Vicksburg*, 5–6, 147–61.

8. McAlexander, *Thirteenth Regiment*, 39–40.

9. Harrison, "Vicksburg in the Round," 54–55.

10. Harrison, 54; *Panorama*, 3–4, HL.

11. Harrison, "Vicksburg in the Round," 54; *Panorama*, 6, HL.

12. Harrison, "Vicksburg in the Round," 53–57.

13. Patricia M. Terrell to "Gentlemen," August 21, 1964, and Albert M. Banton Jr. to Terrell, September 18, 1964, 33rd Illinois folder, VNMP.

14. J. C. Switzer to William Rigby, April 23, June 12, 1903, 22nd Iowa Folder, VNMP.

15. W. H. Bentley to William Rigby, June 1, 1903; E. J. C. Bealer to Jonathan P. Dolliver, March 24, 1903; William Ennis endorsement, April 2, 1903, in Dolliver to Elihu Root,

March 28, 1903; and Chief of Record and Pension Office to Secretary of War, April 9, 1903, all in 77th Illinois Folder, VNMP.

16. "Extracts from Diary," 13, 17–18.

17. "Diary and Letters of Charles A. Hobbs," 99th Illinois Folder, VNMP; Grier to William Rigby, January 20, 1904, 33rd Illinois Folder, VNMP.

18. A. C. Matthews to William Rigby, April 7, 1903, and Albert P. Scheller to Gordon S. Crandall, May 12, 1980, 99th Illinois Folder, VNMP.

19. George H. Hildt to William Rigby, February 8, 1902, and McCrory to Rigby, June 16, 1905, 30th Ohio Folder, VNMP.

20. Jesse Sawyer to Rigby, February 14, 1903, 77th Illinois Folder, VNMP; A. E. Cook to Rigby, April 5, [1903], 21st Iowa Folder, VNMP; James B. Black to Rigby, November 27, 1903, 18th Indiana Folder, VNMP; Cornelius Du Bois to V. E. Howell, March 9, 1903, 33rd Illinois Folder, VNMP; James Keigwin to R. W. McClaughry, March 27, 1903, Keigwin's Brigade Folder, VNMP.

21. Clipping, "Memories of the Siege of Vicksburg," Keigwin's Brigade Folder, VNMP.

22. J. C. Switzer to Stephen D. Lee, October 9, 1903, 22nd Iowa Folder, VNMP.

23. Matthews to Rigby, December 27, 1904, 99th Illinois Folder, VNMP.

CONCLUSION

1. Hess, *German in the Yankee Fatherland*, 101; Simpson and Berlin, *Sherman's Civil War*, 473, 477.

2. McWhiney and Jamieson, *Attack and Die*, 6, 13, 72–73, 82, 103, 121, 144; Hattaway and Jones, *How the North Won*, 93–100, 226–32, 466–72.

3. Hess, *Rifle Musket*, 197–215; Hess, *Civil War Infantry Tactics*, 232–38; Reid, *America's Civil War*, 445–49.

4. Hess, *Civil War Infantry Tactics*, 176–201.

5. Peter J. Osterhaus diary, June 24, 27–28, 1864, Osterhaus Family Papers, MHM.

6. Bearss, *Unvexed to the Sea*, 858.

7. Bearss, 859–60.

8. Bearss, 813–14; Ballard, *Grant at Vicksburg*, 16.

9. Elliott to A. C. Matthews, May 16, 1902, 33rd Illinois Folder, VNMP.

10. Hess, *Union Soldier in Battle*, 82–88.

11. Diary, January 11, 1863, Hammond Papers, FHS.

12. Ballard, *Grant at Vicksburg*, 11.

13. Walker, *Vicksburg*, 165–66.

14. Ballard, *Pemberton*, 181–205; R. H. Chilton to Sherman, October 31, 1872, Sherman Papers, LC; David M. Smith, *Compelled to Appear*, 146–49.

BIBLIOGRAPHY

ARCHIVES

Abraham Lincoln Presidential Library, Springfield, Illinois
    Albert C. Boals Diary
    Albert Chipman Papers
    John P. Davis Diary
    George Ditto Diary
    Engelmann-Kircher Collection
    John Alexander Griffen Papers
    Edward H. Ingraham and Duncan G. Ingraham Letters
    William J. Kennedy Papers
    John McClernand Collection
    Rand Family Papers
    Daniel R. Smith Letters
    Jonathan B. Turner Papers
    Bluford Wilson Letters
    Job H. Yaggy Diary
Alabama Department of Archives and History, Montgomery
    William Lowery Diary
    William Lewis Roberts Papers
    E. D. Willett, Pickens Planters Diary
Atlanta History Center, Atlanta, Georgia
    Emma Calhoun Connally Papers
Augustana College, Special Collections, Rock Island, Illinois
    Gould D. Molineaux Diaries
Chicago History Museum, Chicago, Illinois
    William L. Brown Collection
    George Carrington Diary
    Confederate States of America Collection
    Spencer S. Kimbell Papers
    John Merrilles Diary

Richard R. Puffer Papers
Russell Brothers Letters
David W. Yandill Letter
Cincinnati Museum Center, Cincinnati, Ohio
    Andrew Hickenlooper Collection
Cleveland Public Library, History Branch and
    Archives, Cleveland, Tennessee
    I. J. Stamper Diary
College of William and Mary, Manuscripts and Rare
    Books Department, Williamsburg, Virginia
    Joseph E. Johnston Papers
Cornell University, Division of Rare and Manuscript
    Collections, Ithaca, New York
    Edwin C. Obriham Letters, June and Gilbert Krueger Civil War Letters
Duke University, Rubenstein Rare Book and Manuscript
    Library, Durham, North Carolina
    Sidney S. Champion Papers
    Robert Bruce Hoadley Papers
    William H. Nugen Letters
    John E. Patterson Papers
    Thomas Sewell Papers
    Thomas Neville Waul Papers
Emory University, Manuscript, Archives, and Rare
    Book Library, Atlanta, Georgia
    William H. Brotherton Papers
    Alfred A. Rigby Diary
Filson Historical Society, Louisville, Kentucky
    John Henry Hammond Papers
    Schmidt Family Papers
Gettysburg College, Special Collections and College Archives
    Diary of Unknown Member of the 13th Illinois Infantry
Gilder-Lehrman Institute of American History, New-
    York Historical Society, New York, New York
    Harvey Graham Letter
    Thomas E. G. Ransom Letters
    Sumner Sayles Collection
Huntington Library, San Marino, California
    Jeptha S. Dillon Papers
    Theophilus M. Magaw Papers
    James M. McClintock Papers
    William T. McGlothlin Diary
    Panorama of the Land and Naval Battles of Vicksburg (May 22nd, 1863)
    Samuel Roper Papers
    Edward E. Schweitzer Papers
Indiana Historical Society, Indianapolis
    James Leeper Papers
    Edward Jesup Wood Papers

Indiana State Library, Indianapolis
    Civil War Letter
    Louis Knobe Journal
    James R. Slack Papers
Iowa State University, Special Collections, Ames
    Van Zandt Family Papers
Kentucky Historical Society, Frankfort
    Edwin Farley Diary
Library of Congress, Manuscript Division, Washington, D.C.
    Wimer Bedford Papers
    Blair Family Papers
    C. B. Comstock Papers
    Charles Ewing Family Papers
    John Griffith Jones Correspondence
    Abraham Lincoln Papers
    William T. Sherman Papers
Louisiana State University, Louisiana and Lower Mississippi
      Valley Collection, Special Collections, Baton Rouge
    Rowland Chambers Diaries
    Lewis Guion Log
    Wayne Johnson Jacobs Diaries and Lists
    Alexander R. Miller Diary
    Aaron P. Record Diary
    Jared Young Sanders Family Papers
Miami University, Walter Havighurst Special Collections, Oxford, Ohio
    Thomas B. Marshall Diaries
Minnesota Historical Society, St. Paul
    William Z. Clayton Papers
    Henry A. House Diary
    Richard S. Reeves Papers
Mississippi Department of Archives and History, Jackson
    Claudius Wistar Sears Diary
Missouri History Museum, St. Louis
    Theodore D. Fisher Diary
    Thomas S. Hawley Papers
    Hiffman Family Papers
    John N. Moulton and Thomas N. Lewis Letters, Martin Family Letters
    Osterhaus Family Papers
    David D. Porter Papers
    George Greenwood Pride Papers
    George D. Reynolds Papers
    Joel W. Strong Reminiscences, Alphabetical Files
Museum of the Confederacy, Richmond, Virginia
    John Harvey Fryar Diary
    MC1 Collection
National Archives and Records Administration, Washington, D.C.
    Joseph E. Griffith Pension Record, 22nd Iowa

Nicholas C. Messenger Pension Record, 22nd Iowa

Henry P. Oden Service Record, 30th Alabama

James H. Ralston Service Record, 4th West Virginia

David K. Trine Pension Record, 22nd Iowa

Howell G. Trogden Service Record, 8th Missouri (U.S.)

John C. Vaughn Service Record, M331

Thomas N. Waul Service Record, Waul's Texas Legion

Charles R. Woods, General's Reports of Service, Civil War,
    Vol. 2, Office of the Adjutant General, RG 94

Navarro College, Pearce Civil War Collection, Corsicana, Texas

Sylvester Bartow Papers

Larkin A. Byron Papers

Adnah Eaton Papers

S. Estill Papers

Jordon C. Harriss Papers

Andrew McCormack Papers

Samuel J. Oviatt Papers

Charles F. Smith Papers

Ebenezer Werkheiser Papers

Clark Wright Papers

Newberry Library, Chicago, Illinois

E. C. Dawes Papers, Midwest Manuscript Collection

Curtis P. Lacey Diary

Ohio Historical Society, Columbus

Hugh Boyd Ewing Papers

John W. Griffith Diaries

Old Court House Museum, Vicksburg, Mississippi

John A. Bowman Letters

Alex Frazier Diary

James Darsie Heath Diary

Myron Knight Diary

Albert C. Lenert Journal

Thomas N. McClure Diary

Nicholas Miller Reminiscences

William Taylor Mumford Dairy

Benjamin W. Underwood Letters

Rutherford B. Hayes Presidential Center, Fremont, Ohio

Ralph P. Buckland Papers

Orin England Letters

Harkness Lay Diary

John B. Rice Collection

Southern Illinois University, Special Collections
    Research Center, Carbondale

Edwin A. Loosley Papers

John Reese Papers

Stanford University, Special Collections and University
    Archives, Palo Alto, California

Samuel Fowler Civil War Diary
State Historical Society of Iowa, Iowa City
    Hezekiah Newton Baughman Diary (Iowa City
        Historical Library Manuscripts)
    Henry H. Boynton Diary (Iowa City Historical Library Manuscripts)
    John Fry Certificate (Des Moines Historical Library Manuscripts)
    Hemphill Family Papers (Iowa City Historical Library Manuscripts)
    Silas I. Shearer Correspondence (Des Moines
        Historical Library Manuscripts)
State Historical Society of Missouri, Research Center Columbia
    Fayette Clapp Diary
    Joseph Crider Letters
    Lewis Riley Papers
State Historical Society of Missouri, Research Center Rolla
    John Miller Leach Diary
    William A. Ruyle Letter
    James S. Spencer Diary
    Aquilla Standifird Civil War Diary
    James Synnamon Letter
University of Alabama, Special Collections, Tuscaloosa
    William Lovelace Foster Letter
University of California, Bancroft Library, Berkeley
    William David McClure Papers
University of Colorado, Special Collections, Boulder
    Noble Walter Wood Diary
University of Georgia, Hargrett Rare Book
        and Manuscript Library, Athens
    Wesley O. Connor Family Papers
University of Iowa, Special Collections, Iowa City
    Anson R. Butler Papers
    Joseph Child Diary
    William Titus Rigby Papers
University of Michigan, Bentley Historical Library, Ann Arbor
    Calvin Ainsworth Diary
University of Michigan, William L. Clements Library, Ann Arbor
    Elliot N. and Henry M. Bush Papers, James M.
        Schoff Civil War Collection
University of North Carolina, Southern Historical Collection, Chapel Hill
    Joseph Dill Alison Diary
    J. F. H. Claiborne Papers
    John G. Devereux Papers
    Louis Hébert Papers
    Samuel Henry Lockett Papers
    Benedict Joseph Semmes Papers
    Henry Clay Warmoth Papers
University of Oklahoma, Western History Collections, Norman
    Mrs. A. J. King Papers

Charles Kroff Diary, Sherry Marie Cress Papers
Abraham Jefferson Seay Papers
University of South Carolina, South Caroliniana Library, Columbia
John B. Bannon Papers
University of Tennessee, Special Collections, Knoxville
John T. Johns and James Thomas Letters, Robert T. Jones Papers
C. S. O. Rice Memoir
University of Texas, Dolph Briscoe Center for American History, Austin
Ashbel Smith Papers
University of Virginia, Special Collections, Charlottesville
Taylor Family Papers
University of Washington, Special Collections, Seattle
M. F. Force Papers
U.S. Army Military History Institute, Carlisle, Pennsylvania
Eugene A. Carr Papers
George W. Gordon Papers
Gordon Hickenlooper, ed. "The Reminiscences of General Andrew
Hickenlooper, 1861–1865." *Civil War Times Illustrated* Collection.
William McGlothlin Papers
Vicksburg National Military Park, Vicksburg, Mississippi
30th Alabama Folder
Battery A, 1st Illinois, Folder
8th Illinois Folder
13th Illinois Folder
17th Illinois Folder
33rd Illinois Folder
55th Illinois Folder
72nd Illinois Folder
77th Illinois Folder
81st Illinois Folder
93rd Illinois Folder
95th Illinois Folder
97th Illinois Folder
99th Illinois Folder
116th Illinois Folder
127th Illinois Folder
130th Illinois Folder
8th Indiana Folder
11th Indiana Folder
18th Indiana Folder
47th Indiana Folder
48th Indiana Folder
49th Indiana Folder
59th Indiana Folder
69th Indiana Folder
1st Iowa Battery Folder
3rd Iowa Folder

5th Iowa Folder
9th Iowa Folder
17th Iowa Folder
21st Iowa Folder
22nd Iowa Folder
23rd Iowa Folder
30th Iowa Folder
31st Iowa Folder
27th Louisiana Folder
1st Minnesota Battery Folder
38th Mississippi Folder
46th Mississippi Folder
7th Missouri (U.S.) Folder
8th Missouri (U.S.) Folder
16th Ohio Folder
17th Ohio Battery Folder
20th Ohio Folder
30th Ohio Folder
32nd Ohio Folder
47th Ohio Folder
48th Ohio Folder
57th Ohio Folder
68th Ohio Folder
72nd Ohio Folder
78th Ohio Folder
80th Ohio Folder
95th Ohio Folder
96th Ohio Folder
114th Ohio Folder
120th Ohio Folder
13th U.S. Infantry Folder
6th Wisconsin Battery Folder
11th Wisconsin Folder
14th Wisconsin Folder
18th Wisconsin Folder
23rd Wisconsin Folder
29th Wisconsin Folder
33rd Wisconsin Folder
Botetourt Virginia Artillery Folder
Chicago Mercantile Battery Folder
Hall's-Chambers's Brigade Folder
Keigwin's Brigade Folder
Lee's Brigade Folder
Lindsey's Brigade Folder
Manter's Brigade Folder
Ransom's Brigade Folder
Sanborn's Brigade Folder

Waddell's Alabama Battery Folder
Waul's Texas Legion Folder
Virginia Historical Society, Richmond
Order Book, Department of Eastern Louisiana and Mississippi, 1863
Virginia Polytechnic Institute and State University,
Special Collections, Blacksburg
William J. Pittenger Diary
Western Reserve Historical Society, Cleveland, Ohio
Maria Wells Leggett Papers
Wisconsin Historical Society, Madison
George B. Carter Civil War Letters
Jacob T. Foster Papers
George Hale Diary
John G. Jones Civil War Letters
Alexander McDonald Civil War Diaries
Lewis and Moulton Family Papers
Levi Shell Papers
William W. Willcox Letters
Yale University, Sterling Memorial Library, New Haven, Connecticut
David Herrick Gile Papers, Civil War Manuscripts Collection

NEWSPAPERS

Alexandria (Va.) Gazette
Chicago Daily Tribune
Indianapolis Daily Journal

Memphis Daily Appeal
National Tribune
New-York Daily Tribune

ONLINE SOURCES

The Civil War Diaries of Mifflin Jennings, 11th Iowa Infantry. 1999. http://iagenweb.org
/civilwar/books/mifflinj.htm.
"Elias D. Moore Diary." They Were the 114th Ohio. www.fortunecity.com.
Jordon Carroll Harriss Letters. www.banksgrandretreat.com. No longer available.
"Michael Sweetman Diary." They Were the 114th Ohio. www.fortunecity.com. No longer
available.
W. R. Eddington. "My Civil War Memoirs and Other Reminiscences." http://macoupincty
genealogy.org/war/edding.html. No longer available.
William Robert McCrary Diary. www.geocities.com. No longer available.
William L. Truman, "Memoirs of the Civil War." Cedarcroft. Updated January 10, 2017.
http://www.cedarcroft.com/cw/memoir/index.html.

ARTICLES AND BOOKS

Abbott, John S. C. *The Civil War in America*. 2 vols. Springfield, Mass.: C. A. Nichols,
1883.
Abernethy, Alonzo. "Incidents of an Iowa Soldier's Life, or Four Years in Dixie." *Annals
of Iowa*, 3rd ser., 12, no. 6 (October 1920): 401–28.

Abernethy, Byron R., ed. *Private Elisha Stockwell, Jr. Sees the Civil War.* Norman: University of Oklahoma Press, 1985.

Abrams, A. S. *A Full and Detailed History of the Siege of Vicksburg.* Atlanta: Intelligencer Steam Power, 1863.

Adams, Henry C., Jr., comp. *Indiana at Vicksburg.* Indianapolis: William B. Burford, 1911.

Ambrose, Stephen E., ed. *A Wisconsin Boy in Dixie: Civil War Letters of James K. Newton.* Madison: University of Wisconsin Press, 1989.

Anderson, Ephraim McD. *Memoirs: Historical and Personal; Including the Campaigns of the First Missouri Confederate Brigade.* Dayton, Ohio: Morningside Bookshop, 1972.

Badeau, Adam. *Military History of Ulysses S. Grant.* 2 vols. New York: D. Appleton, 1885.

Balfour, Emma. *Vicksburg, a City under Siege: Diary of Emma Balfour, May 16, 1863–June 2, 1863.* N.p.: Phillip C. Weinberger, 1983.

Ballard, Michael B. *Grant at Vicksburg: The General and the Siege.* Carbondale: Southern Illinois University Press, 2013.

———. *Pemberton: A Biography.* Jackson: University Press of Mississippi, 1991.

———. *Vicksburg: The Campaign That Opened the Mississippi.* Chapel Hill: University of North Carolina Press, 2004.

Barnett, Simeon. *History of the Twenty-Second Regiment Iowa Volunteer Infantry.* Iowa City, Iowa: N. H. Brainerd, 1865.

Barton, Thomas H. *Autobiography.* Charleston: West Virginia Printing, 1890.

Baumgartner, Richard A., ed. *Blood and Sacrifice: The Civil War Journal of a Confederate Soldier.* Huntington, W.Va.: Blue Acorn, 1994.

Bearss, Edwin C., ed. "Diary of Captain John N. Bell of Co. E, 25th Iowa Infantry, at Vicksburg." *Iowa Journal of History* 59, no. 2 (April 1961): 181–221.

———. *Rebel Victory at Vicksburg.* Little Rock, Ark.: Pioneer, 1963.

———. *Unvexed to the Sea: The Campaign for Vicksburg.* Vol. 3. Dayton, Ohio: Morningside, 1986.

Bek, William G., ed. "The Civil War Diary of John T. Buegel, Union Soldier." Pt. 2. *Missouri Historical Review* 40, no. 4 (July 1946): 503–30.

Belknap, William W. *History of the Fifteenth Regiment, Iowa Veteran Volunteer Infantry, from October, 1861, to August, 1865.* Keokuk, Iowa: R. B. Ogden and Son, 1887.

Bennett, Stewart, and Barbara Tillery, eds. *The Struggle for the Life of the Republic: A Civil War Narrative by Brevet Major Charles Dana Miller, 76th Ohio Volunteer Infantry.* Kent, Ohio: Kent State University Press, 2004.

Bentley, W. H. *History of the 77th Illinois Volunteer Infantry, Sept. 2, 1862–July 10, 1865.* Peoria, Ill.: Edward Hine, 1883.

Bering, John A., and Thomas Montgomery. *History of the Forty-Eighth Ohio Vet. Vol. Inf.* Hillsboro, Ohio: Highland News, 1880.

Bevier, R. S. *History of the First and Second Missouri Confederate Brigades, 1861–1865.* St. Louis: Bryan, Brand, 1879.

Beyer, W. F., and O. F. Keydel, eds. *Deeds of Valor: How America's Heroes Won the Medal of Honor.* Detroit: Perrien-Keydel, 1905.

Bigelow, James K. *Abridged History of the Eighth Indiana Volunteer Infantry, from Its Organization, April 21st, 1861, to the Date of Re-enlistment as Veterans, January 1, 1864.* Indianapolis: Ellis, Barnes, 1864.

Bock, H. Riley, ed. "Confederate Col. A. C. Riley: His Reports and Letters." *Missouri Historical Review* 85, no. 3 (April 1991): 264–87.

Bollet, Alfred Jay. *Civil War Medicine: Challenges and Triumphs*. Tucson, Ariz.: Galen, 2002.

Bond, Otto F., ed. *Under the Flag of the Nation: Diaries and Letters of a Yankee Volunteer in the Civil War*. Columbus: Ohio State University Press, 1961.

Braudaway, Douglas Lee, [ed.]. "The Civil War Journal of Major Maurice Kavanaugh Simons, A.C.S., Together with an Account of His Life." Master's thesis, Texas A&M University, 1994.

Brinkerhoff, Henry R. *History of the Thirtieth Regiment Ohio Volunteer Infantry, from Its Organization, to the Fall of Vicksburg, Miss*. Columbus, Ohio: James W. Osgood, 1863.

Brown, Alonzo L. *History of the Fourth Regiment of Minnesota Infantry Volunteers during the Great Rebellion, 1861–1865*. St. Paul, Minn.: Pioneer, 1892.

Brown, George W. "Service in the Mississippi Squadron, and Its Connection with the Siege and Capture of Vicksburg." In *Personal Recollections of the War of the Rebellion: Addresses Delivered before the New York Commandery of the Loyal Legion of the United States, 1883–1891*, 303–13. New York: Commandery, 1891.

Bryner, Cloyd. *Bugle Echoes: The Story of Illinois 47th*. Springfield, Ill.: Phillips Brothers, 1905.

Burden, Jeffry C. "Into the Breach: The 22nd Iowa Infantry at the Railroad Redoubt." *Civil War Regiments* 2, no. 1 (1992): 19–35.

Burdette, Robert J. *The Drums of the 47th*. Indianapolis: Bobbs-Merrill, 1914.

Byers, S. H. M. *With Fire and Sword*. New York: Neale, 1911.

Byrne, Frank L., and Jean Powers Soman, eds. *Your True Marcus: The Civil War Letters of a Jewish Colonel*. Kent, Ohio: Kent State University Press, 1985.

Cable, George W. "A Woman's Diary of the Siege of Vicksburg." *Century Magazine*, September 1885, 767–75.

Camp, Raleigh S. "'What I Know I Know, and I Dare Express It': Major Raleigh S. Camp's History of the 40th Georgia Infantry in the Vicksburg Campaign." *Civil War Regiments* 5, no. 1 (1996): 45–91.

Cantrell, Oscar A. *Sketches of the First Regiment Ga. Vols. Together with the History of the 56th Regiment Georgia Vols., to January 1, 1864*. Atlanta: Intelligencer Steam Power, 1864.

Chance, Joseph E. *The Second Texas Infantry: From Shiloh to Vicksburg*. Austin, Tex.: Eakin, 1984.

Clark, George P., ed. "'Remenecence of My Army Life.'" *Indiana Magazine of History* 101, no. 1 (March 2005): 15–57.

Clark, Olynthus B., ed. *Downing's Civil War Diary*. Des Moines: Historical Department of Iowa, 1916.

Clark, Willene B., ed. *Valleys of the Shadow: The Memoir of Confederate Captain Reuben G. Clark, Company I, 59th Tennessee Mounted Infantry*. Knoxville: University of Tennessee Press, 1994.

"Come On, You Brave Yank." In Beyer and Keydel, *Deeds of Valor*, 198–200.

Cotton, Gordon A., ed. *From the Pen of a She-Rebel: The Civil War Diary of Emilie Riley McKinley*. Columbia: University of South Carolina Press, 2001.

Cox, Florence Marie Ankeny, ed. *Kiss Josey for Me!* Santa Ana, Calif.: Friis-Pioneer, 1974.

Crooke, George. *The Twenty-First Regiment of Iowa Volunteer Infantry*. Milwaukee, Wisc.: King, Fowle, 1891.

Crummer, Wilbur F. *With Grant at Fort Donelson, Shiloh and Vicksburg, and an Appreciation of General U.S. Grant*. Oak Park, Ill.: E. C. Crummer, 1915.

Crumpton, Washington Bryan. *A Book of Memories, 1842–1920*. Montgomery, Ala.: Baptist Mission Board, 1921.

Dana, Charles A. *Recollections of the Civil War with the Leaders at Washington and in the Field in the Sixties*. New York: D. Appleton, 1902.

Dean, Benjamin D. *Recollections of the 26th Missouri Infantry in the War for the Union*. Lamar: Southwest Missourian, 1892.

The Diary of A. Hugh Moss, Coulie Croche, St. Landry Parish, Louisiana. N.p., 1948.

Dodd, W. O. "Recollections of Vicksburg during the Siege." *Southern Bivouac* 1, no. 1 (September 1882): 2–11.

Dudley, Henry Walbridge. *Autobiography*. Menasha, Wisc.: George Banta, [1914].

Elder, Donald C., III, ed. *A Damned Iowa Greyhound: The Civil War Letters of William Henry Harrison Clayton*. Iowa City: University of Iowa Press, 1998.

Erickson, Edgar L., ed. "With Grant at Vicksburg: From the Civil War Diary of Captain Charles E. Wilcox." *Journal of the Illinois State Historical Society* 30, no. 4 (January 1938): 441–503.

Ervin, W. J. "Genius and Heroism of Lieut. K. H. Faulkner." *Confederate Veteran* 14 (1906): 497–98.

Evans, Charles I. "Second Texas Infantry." In *A Comprehensive History of Texas, 1685–1897*, edited by Dudley G. Wooten, 2:575–609. Dallas: William G. Scarff, 1898.

"Extracts from Diary of Chaplain N. M. Baker, 116 Illinois." *Illinois Central Magazine*, October 1915, 9–18.

Farley, Edwin. *Experience of a Soldier, 1861–1865*. Paducah, Ky.: Billings, [1918].

Fike, Claude E., ed. "Diary of James Oliver Hazard Perry Sessions of Rokeby Plantation, on the Yazoo, January 1, 1862–June 1872." *Journal of Mississippi History* 39, no. 3 (August 1977): 239–54.

"A Flag the Rebels Didn't Get." In Beyer and Keydel, *Deeds of Valor*, 201–2.

Force, M. F. "Personal Recollections of the Vicksburg Campaign." In *Sketches of War History, 1861–1865: Papers Read before the Ohio Commandery of the Military Order of the Loyal Legion of the United States, 1883–1886*, 1:293–309. Wilmington, N.C.: Broadfoot, 1991.

"The 'Forlorn Hope' at Vicksburg." In Beyer and Keydel, *Deeds of Valor*, 190–97.

Fowler, James A., and Miles A. Miller. *History of the Thirtieth Iowa Infantry Volunteers*. Mediapolis, Iowa: T. A. Merrill, 1908.

Fulfer, Richard J. *A History of the Trials and Hardships of the Twenty-Fourth Indiana Volunteer Infantry*. [Indianapolis]: Indianapolis Printing, 1913.

Fussell, I. L. *History of the 34th Regiment Indiana Veteran Volunteer Infantry — "Morton Rifles."* [Marion, Ind.: Commercial], n.d.

Gerard, C. W. *A Diary: The Eighty-Third Ohio Vol. Inf. in the War, 1862–1865*. [Cincinnati, Ohio: n.p., 1889].

Gottschalk, Phil. *In Deadly Earnest: The History of the First Missouri Brigade, CSA*. Columbia: Missouri River, 1991.

Grabau, Warren E. *Ninety-Eight Days: A Geographer's View of the Vicksburg Campaign*. Knoxville: University of Tennessee Press, 2000.

Grant, Frederick D. "A Boy's Experience at Vicksburg." In *Personal Recollections of the War of the Rebellion: Addresses Delivered before the Commandery of the State of New York, Military Order of the Loyal Legion of the United States*, 3rd ser., 86–100. Wilmington, N.C.: Broadfoot, 1992.

Grant, Ulysses S. *Personal Memoirs of U. S. Grant*. 2 vols. in 1. New York: Viking, 1990.

Grear, Charles D. "'The North-West is Determined with the Sword': Midwesterners' Reactions to the Vicksburg Assaults." In Woodworth and Grear, *Vicksburg Assaults.*

Grecian, J. *History of the Eighty-Third Regiment, Indiana Volunteer Infantry.* Cincinnati, Ohio: John F. Uhlhorn, 1865.

Greene, J. H. *Reminiscences of the War: Bivouacs, Marches, Skirmishes and Battles.* [Medina, Ohio]: Gazette, 1886.

Griffith, Joseph E. "The Twenty-Second Iowa Infantry at Vicksburg." *Annals of Iowa* 6, no. 3 (July 1868): 215–19.

[Griggs, George W.]. *Opening of the Mississippi: Or Two Year's Campaigning in the South-West.* Madison, Wisc.: William J. Park, 1864.

Hains, Peter C. "An Incident of the Battle of Vicksburg." In *Papers 1–26, March, 1887–April, 1897,* 64–71. Vol. 1 of *Military Order of the Loyal Legion of the United States: Commandery of the District of Columbia.* Wilmington, N.C.: Broadfoot, 1993.

———. "The Vicksburg Campaign." *Military Engineer* 13 (1921): 189–96, 270–72, 288.

Hall, Winchester. *The Story of the 26th Louisiana Infantry, in the Service of the Confederate States.* N.p., n.d.

Halsell, Willie D., ed. "The Sixteenth Indiana Regiment in the Last Vicksburg Campaign." *Indiana Magazine of History* 43, no. 1 (March 1947): 67–82.

Harrison, Noel G. "Vicksburg in the Round." *Civil War Times* 49, no. 3 (June 2010): 52–57.

Harwell, J. D. "In and around Vicksburg." *Confederate Veteran* 30 (1922): 333–34.

Hattaway, Herman, and Archer Jones. *How the North Won: A Military History of the Civil War.* Urbana: University of Illinois, 1983.

Hearn, Chester G. *Admiral David Dixon Porter.* Annapolis, Md.: Naval Institute Press, 1996.

Hess, Earl J. *Civil War Infantry Tactics: Training, Combat, and Small-Unit Effectiveness.* Baton Rouge: Louisiana State University Press, 2015.

———. *The Civil War in the West: Victory and Defeat from the Appalachians to the Mississippi.* Chapel Hill: University of North Carolina Press, 2012.

———, ed. *A German in the Yankee Fatherland: The Civil War Letters of Henry A. Kircher.* Kent, Ohio: Kent State University Press, 1983.

———. *The Rifle Musket in Civil War Combat: Reality and Myth.* Lawrence: University Press of Kansas, 2008.

———. "The Twelfth Missouri Infantry: A Socio-military Profile of a Union Regiment." In *A Rough Business: Fighting the Civil War in Missouri,* edited by William Garrett Piston, 145–65. Columbia: State Historical Society of Missouri, 2012.

———. *The Union Soldier in Battle: Enduring the Ordeal of Combat.* Lawrence: University Press of Kansas, 2007.

Hewitt, Lawrence Lee, Thomas E. Schott, and Marc Kunis, eds. *To Succeed or Perish: The Diaries of Sergeant Edmund Trent Eggleston, 1st Mississippi Light Artillery Regiment, CSA.* Knoxville: University of Tennessee Press, 2015.

Hickenlooper, Andrew. "The Vicksburg Mine." In *Battles and Leaders of the Civil War,* edited by Clarence Clough Buel and Robert Underwood Johnson, 3:539–42. New York: Thomas Yoseloff, 1956.

Hicks, Henry G. "The Campaign and Capture of Vicksburg." In *Glimpses of the Nation's Struggle: Papers Read before the Minnesota Commandery of the Military Order of the Loyal Legion of the United States, January, 1903–1908,* ser. 6, 82–107. Minneapolis, Minn.: Aug. Davis, 1909.

Hills, J. Parker. "Failure and Scapegoat: May 22." In Woodworth and Grear, *Vicksburg Assaults.*

"A History of Company B, 40th Alabama Infantry, C.S.A., from the Diary of J. H. Curry of Pickens County." *Alabama Historical Quarterly* 17, no. 3 (Fall 1955): 159–222.

History of the Fifteenth Regiment, Iowa Veteran Volunteer Infantry, from October, 1861, to August, 1865. Keokuk, Iowa: R. B. Ogden, 1887.

History of the Forty-Sixth Regiment Indiana Volunteer Infantry. Logansport, Ind.: Wilson, Humphreys, 1888.

Hobbs, C. A. *Vicksburg: A Poem.* Chicago: J. Fairbanks, 1880.

Hogane, J. T. "Reminiscences of the Siege of Vicksburg." Pts. 2 and 3. *Southern Historical Society Papers* 11 (1883): 282–97, 484–89.

Holcomb, Julie, ed. *Southern Sons, Northern Soldiers: The Civil War Letters of the Remley Brothers, 22nd Iowa Infantry.* DeKalb: Northern Illinois University Press, 2004.

Howard, R. L. *History of the 124th Regiment Illinois Infantry Volunteers.* Springfield, Ill.: H. W. Rokker, 1880.

———. "The Vicksburg Campaign: A Personal Experience." *Maine Bugle*, campaign 4, call 1 (January 1897): 1–10.

Hubbard, Lucius F. "Minnesota in the Campaigns of Vicksburg, November, 1862, to July, 1863." *Collections of the Minnesota Historical Society* 12 (1908): 554–72.

Jackson, Joseph Orville, ed. *"Some of the Boys . . .": The Civil War Letters of Isaac Jackson, 1862–1865.* Carbondale: Southern Illinois University Press, 1960.

Jenney, William Le Baron. "Personal Recollections of Vicksburg." In *Military Essays and Recollections: Papers Read before the Commandery of the State of Illinois, Military Order of the Loyal Legion of the United States,* 3:246–65. Chicago: Dial, 1899.

———. "With Sherman and Grant from Memphis to Chattanooga—a Reminiscence." In *Military Essays and Recollections: Papers Read before the Commandery of the State of Illinois, Military Order of the Loyal Legion of the United States,* 4:193–214. Chicago: Cozzens and Beaton, 1907.

Johnson, Charles Beneulyn. *Muskets and Medicine, Or Army Life in the Sixties.* Philadelphia: F. A. Davis, 1917.

Jones, J. H. "The Rank and File at Vicksburg." *Publications of the Mississippi Historical Society* 7 (1903): 17–31.

Jones, S. C. *Reminiscences of the Twenty-Second Iowa Volunteer Infantry.* Iowa City, Iowa: n.p., 1907.

Kellogg, J. J. *War Experiences and the Story of the Vicksburg Campaign from "Milliken's Bend" to July 4, 1863.* Washington, Iowa: Evening Journal, 1913.

Kelly, William Milner. "A History of the Thirtieth Alabama Volunteers (Infantry), Confederate States Army." *Alabama Historical Quarterly* 9, no. 1 (Spring 1947): 115–89.

Kiper, Richard L. *Major General John Alexander McClernand: Politician in Uniform.* Kent, Ohio: Kent State University Press, 1999.

Lee, Stephen D. "A Gallant Incident during the Siege of Vicksburg on May 22, 1863." In *Camp Fires of the Confederacy,* edited by Ben La Bree, 61–65. Louisville, Ky.: Courier-Journal, 1899.

———. "The Siege of Vicksburg." *Publications of the Mississippi Historical Society* 3 (1900): 55–71.

Lockett, S. H. "The Defense of Vicksburg." In *Battles and Leaders of the Civil War,* edited by Clarence Clough Buel and Robert Underwood Johnson, 3:482–92. New York: Thomas Yoseloff, 1956.

Logan, Mary S. *Reminiscences of a Soldier's Wife: An Autobiography*. Carbondale: Southern Illinois University Press, 1997.

Mahan, James Curtis. *Memoirs*. Lincoln, Neb.: Franklin, [1919].

Marshall, Albert O. *Army Life: From a Soldier's Journal*. Fayetteville: University of Arkansas Press, 2009.

Marshall, T. B. *History of the Eighty-Third Ohio Volunteer Infantry: The Greyhound Regiment*. Cincinnati, Ohio: Gibson and Perin, 1913.

Martin, William. *"Out and Forward": Or Recollections of the War of 1861 to 1865*. Manhattan, Kans.: Art Craft Printers, 1941.

Mason, Frank H. *The Forty-Second Ohio Infantry*. Cleveland, Ohio: Cobb, Andrews, 1876.

Maynard, Douglas, ed. "Vicksburg Diary: The Journal of Gabriel M. Killgore." *Civil War History* 10, no. 1 (March 1964): 33–53.

McAlexander, U. G. *History of the Thirteenth Regiment United States Infantry*. N.p.: Frank D. Gunn, 1905.

McCall, D. *Three Years in the Service: A Record of the Doings of the 11th Reg. Missouri Vols*. Springfield, Mo.: Baker and Phillips, 1864.

McCarty, Terry M., and Margaret Ann Chatfield McCarty, [eds.]. *The Chatfield Story: Civil War Letters and Diaries of Private Edward L. Chatfield of the 113th Illinois Volunteers*. North Charleston, S.C.: CreateSpace, 2010.

McDonald, Granville B. *A History of the 30th Illinois Volunteer Regiment of Infantry*. Salem, Mass.: Higginson Book, 1998.

McWhiney, Grady, and Perry D. Jamieson. *Attack and Die: Civil War Military Tactics and the Southern Heritage*. Tuscaloosa: University of Alabama Press, 1982.

Milligan, John D., ed. *From the Fresh-Water Navy: 1861–64; The Letters of Acting Master's Mate Henry R. Browne and Acting Ensign Symmes E. Browne*. Annapolis, Md.: United States Naval Institute, 1970.

Minnesota in the Civil and Indian Wars, 1861–1865. 2 Vols. St. Paul, Minn.: Pioneer, 1890–93.

Mitchell, Joseph B. *The Badge of Gallantry: Recollections of Civil War Congressional Medal of Honor Winners*. New York: Macmillan, 1968.

Morris, W. S., L. D. Hartwell, and J. B. Kuykendall. *History 31st Regiment Illinois Volunteers, Organized by John A. Logan*. Carbondale: Southern Illinois Press, 1998.

Morss, Christopher, ed. *From Helena to Vicksburg: A Civil War Odyssey*. Lincoln Center, Mass.: Heritage House, 2000.

Moss, James E., ed. "A Missouri Confederate in the Civil War: The Journal of Henry Martyn Cheavens, 1862–1863." *Missouri Historical Review* 57, no. 1 (October 1962): 16–52.

[Newsome, Edmund]. *Experience in the War of the Great Rebellion*. Carbondale, Ill.: E. Newsome, 1879.

Ninth Reunion of the 37th Regiment O.V.V.I., St. Marys, Ohio, Tuesday and Wednesday, September 10 and 11, 1889. Toledo, Ohio: Montgomery and Vrooman, 1890.

Official Records of the Union and Confederate Navies in the War of the Rebellion. 30 Vols. Washington, D.C.: Government Printing Office, 1894–1922.

Oldroyd, Osborn H. *A Soldier's Story of the Siege of Vicksburg*. Springfield, Ill.: H. W. Rokker, 1885.

Osborn, George C., ed. "A Tennessean at the Siege of Vicksburg: The Diary of Samuel

Alexander Ramsey Swan, May–July, 1863." *Tennessee Historical Quarterly* 14 (1955): 353–72.

Painter, John S., ed. "Bullets, Hardtack and Mud: A Soldier's View of the Vicksburg Campaign." *Journal of the West* 4, no. 2 (April 1965): 129–68.

Payne, James E. "Missouri Troops in the Vicksburg Campaign." *Confederate Veteran* 36 (1928): 377–79.

Pettus, E. W. "Heroism of Texans at Vicksburg." *Confederate Veteran* 15 (1907): 211–12.

Phillips, Brenda D., ed. *Personal Reminiscences of a Confederate Soldier Boy*. Milledgeville, Ga.: Boyd, 1993.

Pitzman, Julius. "Vicksburg Campaign Reminiscences." *Military Engineer* 15, no. 80 (March–April 1923): 112–15.

Popchock, Barry, ed. *Soldier Boy: The Civil War Letters of Charles O. Musser, 29th Iowa.* Iowa City: University of Iowa Press, 1995.

Porter, David Dixon. *The Naval History of the Civil War*. New York: Sherman, 1886.

Post, Lydia Minturn, ed. *Soldiers' Letters from Camp, Battlefield and Prison*. New York: Bunce and Huntington, 1865.

Powell, C. A. "Brother Fought against Brother." *Confederate Veteran* 10 (1902): 463.

Puck, Susan T., ed. *Sacrifice at Vicksburg: Letters from the Front*. Shippensburg, Pa.: Burd Street, 1997.

Ray, Johnette Highsmith, ed. "Civil War Letters from Parsons' Texas Cavalry Brigade." *Southwestern Historical Quarterly* 69, no. 2 (October 1965): 210–23.

Reed, David W. *Campaigns and Battles of the Twelfth Regiment Iowa Veteran Volunteer Infantry from Organization, September, 1861, to Muster-Out, January 20, 1866*. N.p., n.d.

Reed, Lida Lord. "A Woman's Experiences during the Siege of Vicksburg." *Century Magazine*, April 1901, 922–28.

Reid, Brian Holden. *America's Civil War: The Operational Battlefield, 1861–1863*. Amherst, N.Y.: Prometheus Books, 2008.

Report of the Adjutant General and Acting Quartermaster General of the State of Iowa, January 11, 1864, to January 1, 1865. Des Moines, Iowa: F. W. Parker, 1865.

Russ, William A., Jr., ed. "The Vicksburg Campaign as Viewed by an Indiana Soldier." *Journal of Mississippi History* 19, no. 4 (October 1957): 263–69.

Sanborn, John B. "The Campaign against Vicksburg." In *A Series of Papers Read before the Minnesota Commandery of the Military Order of the Loyal Legion of the United States, 1887–1889*, 114–45. Ser. 2 of *Glimpses of the Nation's Struggle*. St. Paul, Minn.: St. Paul Book and Stationery, 1890.

Sanders, Mary Elizabeth, ed. *Diary in Gray: Civil War Letters and Diary of Jared Young Sanders II*. Baton Rouge: Louisiana Genealogical and Historical Society, 1994.

Saunier, Joseph A., ed. *A History of the Forty-Seventh Regiment Ohio Veteran Volunteer Infantry*. Hillsboro, Ohio: Lyle, [1903].

[Scott, R. B.]. *The History of the 67th Regiment Indiana Infantry Volunteers, War of the Rebellion*. Bedford, Ind.: Herald Book and Job, 1892.

Shea, William L., and Terrence J. Winschel. *Vicksburg Is the Key: The Struggle for the Mississippi River*. Lincoln: University of Nebraska Press, 2003.

Sherman, William T. *Memoirs*. 2 Vols. New York: D. Appleton, 1875.

Shoup, Francis A. "Vicksburg: Some New History in the Experience of Gen. Francis A. Shoup." *Confederate Veteran* 2 (1894): 172–74.

Simon, John Y., ed. *The Papers of Ulysses S. Grant*. 28 vols. Carbondale: Southern Illinois University Press, 1967–2005.

Simpson, Brooks D., and Jean V. Berlin, eds. *Sherman's Civil War: Selected Correspondence of William T. Sherman, 1860–1865*. Chapel Hill: University of North Carolina Press, 1999.

Smith, David M., ed. *Compelled to Appear in Print: The Vicksburg Manuscript of General John C. Pemberton*. Cincinnati, Ohio: Ironclad, 1999.

Smith, Hampton, [ed.]. *Brother of Mine: The Civil War Letters of Thomas and William Christie*. St. Paul: Minnesota Historical Society Press, 2011.

Smith, James West. "A Confederate Soldier's Diary: Vicksburg in 1863." *Southwest Review* 28, no. 3 (Spring 1943): 293–327.

Smith, Ralph J. *Reminiscences of the Civil War*. [San Marcos, Tex.: n.p., 1911].

Smith, Timothy B. *Champion Hill: Decisive Battle for Vicksburg*. El Dorado Hills, Calif.: Savas Beatie, 2011.

———. *The Decision Was Always My Own: Ulysses S. Grant and the Vicksburg Campaign*. Carbondale: Southern Illinois University Press, 2018.

———. *The Union Assaults at Vicksburg: Grant Attacks Pemberton, May 17–22, 1863*. Lawrence: University Press of Kansas, 2020.

Smith, Walter George. *Life and Letters of Thomas Kilby Smith, Brevet Major-General United States Volunteers, 1820–1887*. New York: G. P. Putnam's Sons, 1898.

A Smith in Service: Diaries of Calvin Morgan Smith, 1847–1864. Rogersville, Tenn.: Hawkins County Genealogical and Historical Society, 2000.

"A Staff Officer's Pluck." In Beyer and Keydel, *Deeds of Valor*, 200–201.

Stephens, Larry D. *Bound for Glory: A History of the 30th Alabama Infantry Regiment, C.S.A.* Ann Arbor, Mich.: Sheridan Books, 2005.

Stevenson, B. F. *Letters from the Army, 1862–1864*. Cincinnati, Ohio: W. E. Dibble, 1884.

Stevenson, Thomas M. *History of the 78th Regiment O.V.V.I., from Its "Muster-In" to Its "Muster-Out."* Zanesville, Ohio: Hugh Dunne, 1865.

[Stone, M. Amelia]. *Memoir of George Boardman Boomer*. Boston: George C. Rand and Avery, 1864.

The Story of the Fifty-Fifth Regiment Illinois Volunteer Infantry in the Civil War, 1861–1865. Clinton, Mass.: W. J. Coulter, 1887.

Strong, William E. "Campaign against Vicksburg." In *Military Essays and Recollections: Papers Read Before the Commandery of the State of Illinois, Military Order of the Loyal Legion of the United States*, 2:313–54. Chicago: A. C. McClurg, 1894.

Supplement to the Official Records of the Union and Confederate Armies. 100 Vols. Wilmington, N.C.: Broadfoot, 1995–99.

Temple, Wayne C., ed. *The Civil War Letters of Henry C. Bear: A Soldier in the 116th Illinois Volunteer Infantry*. Harrogate, Tenn.: Lincoln Memorial University Press, 1961.

Thomas, Benjamin P., ed. *Three Years with Grant: As Recalled by War Correspondent Sylvanus Cadwallader*. New York: Alfred A. Knopf, 1955.

Throne, Mildred, ed. "Civil War Letters of Abner Dunham, 12th Iowa Infantry." *Iowa Journal of History* 53, no. 4 (October 1955): 303–40.

———. "Reminiscences of Jacob Carroll Switzer of the 22nd Iowa." *Iowa Journal of History* 55, no. 4 (October 1957): 319–50.

Townsend, Mary Bobbitt. *Yankee Warhorse: A Biography of Major General Peter Osterhaus*. Columbia: University of Missouri Press, 2010.

Trigg, S. C. "Fighting around Vicksburg." *Confederate Veteran* 12 (1904): 120.

Trimble, Harvey M., ed. *History of the Ninety-Third Regiment Illinois Volunteer Infantry from Organization to Muster Out.* Chicago: Blakely, 1898.

Tunnard, W. H. *A Southern Record: The History of the Third Regiment Louisiana Infantry.* Dayton, Ohio: Morningside Bookshop, 1970.

Vance, J. W., ed. *Report of the Adjutant General of the State of Illinois.* 8 vols. Springfield, Ill.: H. W. Rokker, 1886.

Walker, Peter. *Vicksburg: A People at War, 1860–1865.* Chapel Hill: University of North Carolina Press, 1960.

"War Diary of Thaddeus H. Capron, 1861–1865." *Journal of the Illinois State Historical Society* 12, no. 3 (October 1919): 330–406.

The War of the Rebellion: A Compilation of the Official Records of the Union and Confederate Armies. 70 vols. in 128. Washington, D.C.: Government Printing Office, 1880–1901.

Way, Virgil G., comp. *History of the Thirty-Third Regiment Illinois Veteran Volunteer Infantry.* Gibson City, Ill.: Gibson Courier, 1902.

Wells, Seth J. *The Siege of Vicksburg.* Detroit: William H. Rowe, 1915.

Wescott, M. Ebenezer. *Civil War Letters, 1861 to 1865, Written by a Boy in Blue to his Mother.* [Mora, Minn.]: n.p., 1909.

Whipple, Henry P. *The Diary of a Private Soldier.* Waterloo, Wisc.: n.p., 1906.

Wilkin, Jacob W. "Vicksburg." In *Military Essays and Recollections: Papers Read before the Commandery of the State of Illinois, Military Order of the Loyal Legion of the United States,* 4:214–37. Chicago: Cozzens and Beaton, 1907.

Willett, Elbert Decatur. *History of Company B (Originally Pickens Planters) 40th Alabama Regiment, Confederate States Army, 1862 to 1865.* [Anniston, Ala.: Norwood, 1902].

[Williams, John Melvin]. *"The Eagle Regiment," 8th Wis. Inf'ty Vols.* Belleville, Wisc.: Recorder, 1890.

Wilson, James Harrison. *Under the Old Flag.* 2 Vols. New York: D. Appleton, 1912.

Winschel, Terrence J. "The First Honor at Vicksburg: The 1st Battalion, 13th U.S. Infantry." *Civil War Regiments* 2, no. 1 (1992): 1–18.

———. *Triumph and Defeat: The Vicksburg Campaign.* Mason City, Iowa: Savas, 1999.

Winter, William C., ed. *Captain Joseph Boyce and the 1st Missouri Infantry, C.S.A.* St. Louis: Missouri History Museum, 2011.

"Within a Few Feet of the Enemy." In Beyer and Keydel *Deeds of Valor,* 188–90.

Wood, Wales W. *A History of the Ninety-Fifth Regiment Illinois Infantry Volunteers.* Chicago: Tribune, 1865.

Woodworth, Steven E. *Nothing but Victory: The Army of the Tennessee, 1861–1865.* New York: Alfred A. Knopf, 2005.

Woodworth, Steven E., and Charles D. Grear, eds. *The Vicksburg Assaults, May 19–22, 1863.* Carbondale: Southern Illinois University Press, 2019.

Young, Rogers W. "Vicksburg's Confederate Fort Hill, 1862–1863." *Journal of Mississippi History* 6, no. 1 (January 1944): 3–29.

INDEX

Conklin, Ketchum S., 118
Connor, Wesley O., 25
Cotton, R. N., 55
Countryman Road, 23
Cowan, Luther H., 113
Cox, Robert M., 107
Cradlebaugh, John, 129
Crawford, Otis, 198
Creamer, Robert D., 199, 203
Crescent City (boat), 80
Crooke, George, 155, 254
Crooker, Lucien B., 48
Crow, William C., 34
Crummer, Wilbur F., 113
Cumming, Alfred, 164
Curtis, David R., 164
Curtiss, Frank S., 182

Dale, James W., 45
Dallas, battle of, 45
Dallmer, Benjamin, 197
Dana, Charles A., 237, 242–43, 264
Darby, James K., 265
Davis, Jefferson, 4, 12, 62, 238, 247–49
Davis, John P., 110
Davis's Bridge, battle of, 290
Dawson, N. H. R., 221
Dayton, James H., 277
Dean, Benjamin D., 213–15
De Soto Point, 9, 76, 80–82, 229, 234, 259
Dhelo, Charles, 106
Dillon, Henry, 55
Dillon, Jeptha S., 58, 126
Dockery, Thomas P., 211
Dollins, James J., 116–17
Dowdell, J. F., 141
Dudley, Henry Walbridge, 79, 84
Dunlap, Cornelius W., 153, 161
Dunn, Frank, 156
Durden's Ridge, 56–57
Dwight, William, 81

Ector, Matthew D., 86
Edwards, Martha, 46
Eggleston, Edmund Trent, 10
Eldridge, Hamilton N., 35, 96
Elliott, Isaac H., 133–35, 292

England, Orin, 240
Ervin, W. J., 190
Estill, Samuel, 189
Evans, Charles I., 10, 138–39, 141–42, 146, 207,
    211, 226, 262, 328n45
Evans, Nathan, 86
Ewing, Charles, 22, 38–40, 45, 49, 67, 274
Ewing, Hugh, 22, 41–42, 45, 67, 77, 94, 96–110,
    114, 183–85, 187–91, 202–4, 241, 272, 274,
    277, 292

Farley, Edwin, 89, 185
Farragut, David G., 29
Faulkner, King Hiram, 190–91
Ferguson House, 74
Finley, John H., 126
Fisher, Cyrus W., 35–37
Fisher, Theodore D., 263
Fleitas, J. B., 150
Flies, 255–56, 258
Florence, Louis, 48
Fly, George W. L., 226
Fonda, John G., 126
Force, Manning F., 55, 118, 205, 238
USS *Forest Rose*, 29, 84
Forney, John H., 5–6, 11, 19, 32, 61, 63, 67, 69,
    74–76, 124, 145, 206, 219, 227, 230, 251, 263
Fort Beauregard, 114, 148, 154
Fort Donelson campaign, 290
Fort Hill, 17–18, 24, 32, 61, 71, 110
Fort Hill Ridge, 17, 23–24, 27–28, 36, 41–42,
    46–47, 192, 195, 197–99, 202
Fort Pemberton, 148, 285
Fort Pettus, 148
Foster, William Lovelace, 63, 258, 278
Fowler, Samuel, 74
Francis, John C., 331n44
Frost, George H., 21, 24
Frazier, Alex, 226
Fry, John W., 128
Fryar, John Harvey, 267
Fulgham, Tom E., 281–82
Fussell, I. L., 91

Gamble, Hamilton, 213
Gardner, Franklin, 62
Gardner, Thomas, 282

Index

Schmidt, Henry, 98, 104, 237
Schweitzer, Edward E., 102
Seaman, Henry I., 201
Sears, Claudius Wistar, 24, 48
Seay, Abraham Jefferson, 47, 74
Sebastopol, Siege of, 242
2nd Texas Lunette, xiii, 17–18, 61, 72, 122–24, 130–47, 157, 165, 167, 207–12, 217, 219, 226, 246, 256, 264–65, 271, 283, 285–86, 292, 293, 328n45
Sergent, Lucien, 282
Senteney, Pembroke S., 42
Sessions, James Oliver Hazard Perry, 30
Sewell, Thomas, 22, 44–45, 68
Shea, William L., xii–xiii, 244
Shell, Levi, 256
Shelley, Charles M., 162, 220
Sherman, Ellen, 274
Sherman, William T., 2, 13, 21–25, 72–73, 86, 88–89, 265, 269, 274, 279–80, 289, 291; attack of May 19, 32, 36, 44, 48–49; attack of May 22, 94, 97–99, 108, 131, 229, 233, 242–44; renewal of attack on May 22, 170–71, 174–75, 183, 185, 188, 192, 201–2, 204, 331n10
Sherman, Willie, 280
Shiloh, battle of, 160, 279, 291
Shirley, James, and family, 55, 110–13, 118
Shoup, Francis A., 5, 8, 19–23, 27–28, 41, 48–49, 75, 185, 193, 200
Shunk, David, 133, 136, 143–44, 147, 164, 214, 225
USS *Signal*, 82, 232
Simons, Maurice Kavanaugh, 62–63, 74, 124, 271
Simons, William A., 193–94
Sitton, William B., 139
Skinner, Henry C., 254
Slack, James R., 73, 79, 266, 270
Sloan, Thomas J., 112
Smiley, John, 90
Smith, Andrew J., 25, 56, 71, 123, 131, 143, 151, 167, 215, 292
Smith, Ashbel, 61, 141–42, 144, 207, 210, 226, 246, 251, 272
Smith, Charles F., 30, 65, 140, 211, 216, 264
Smith, Giles A., 22, 33, 36–40, 66, 94, 119, 174–77, 182–83, 202, 268
Smith, James West, 53, 63, 75, 270

Smith, Joe, 96
Smith, John Bass, 331n44
Smith, John E., 55, 110–12, 118, 178, 206
Smith, Martin L., 5, 9, 19, 61, 64, 67, 75, 206, 230, 251, 263, 277
Smith, Milo, 198
Smith, Thomas Kilby, 22, 32–33, 35–37, 42–44, 66–67, 87, 94, 105–6, 174–75, 177, 182–83, 185, 202–3, 240, 253, 282
Smith, Thomas S., 265
Smith, Timothy B., xii–xiii
Snyder's Bluff, 5–6, 22, 29, 81, 83–85, 291
Southern Railroad of Mississippi, 2, 18, 122–23, 136, 139, 148, 287
South Fort, 18, 23, 65, 82, 231, 233–36
Spence, William T., 145
Spicely, William T., 125, 129, 157, 169, 172, 251
Spiegel, Marcus M., 58–60, 71, 127
Spooner, Benjamin J., 35, 39, 66
Springfield, Illinois, 139, 229
Square Fort, 16–17, 58–60, 124, 126–27, 129, 131, 150
Standifird, Aquilla, 78–79, 229
Stanton, Edwin M., 242–43
Starring, Frederick A., 180–81, 282
State Historical Society of Iowa, 285
Steele, Frederick, 13, 21, 23, 28, 32, 41–42, 46–48, 64, 66, 70, 89, 94, 174, 191–92, 195, 197, 201–3, 233, 251
Steele, Lindsay, 118
Steele, O., 150
Steinauer, Nicholas, 163–64
Sterling, Jim, 225
Stevenson, Benjamin Franklin, 253
Stevenson, Carter L., 4, 6–7, 19, 23, 61–63, 67, 76, 150, 159, 165, 222–24, 234, 247, 263
Stevenson, James, 143
Stevenson, John D., 110, 114–18
Steward, J. A., 145
Stockade Redan, 17, 19–20, 22, 31–33, 35–39, 41, 44, 51, 66–67, 70, 87, 92–109, 169, 177, 183–90, 202–4, 229, 241, 254, 263, 268–69, 273–74, 286, 290, 292–93, 333n36
Stockton, Joseph, 180
Stone, George A., 193
Stone, William M., 90, 151–53, 155–58, 160–61, 330n39

Printed in the USA
CPSIA information can be obtained
at www.ICGtesting.com
CBHW021522151024
15903CB00002B/37